CompTIA®
Cloud+®
Study Guide
Second Edition
Exam CV0-002

Todd Montgomery

Stephen Olson

SYBEX®
A Wiley Brand

Senior Acquisitions Editor: Kenyon Brown
Development Editor: David Clark
Technical Editor: Kunal Mittal
Production Manager: Kathleen Wisor
Copy Editor: Kim Wimpsett
Editorial Manager: Pete Gaughan
Executive Editor: Jim Minatel
Book Designer: Judy Fung and Bill Gibson
Proofreader: Nancy Carrasco
Indexer: Johnna VanHoose Dinse
Project Coordinator, Cover: Brent Savage
Cover Designer: Wiley
Cover Image: @Jeremy Woodhouse/Getty Images, Inc.

Copyright © 2018 by John Wiley & Sons, Inc., Indianapolis, Indiana

Published simultaneously in Canada

ISBN: 978-1-119-44305-6
ISBN: 978-1-119-44306-3 (ebk.)
ISBN: 978-1-119-44296-7 (ebk.)

Manufactured in the United States of America

For general information on our other products and services or to obtain technical support, please contact our Customer Care Department within the U.S. at (877) 762-2974, outside the U.S. at (317) 572-3993 or fax (317) 572-4002.

Wiley publishes in a variety of print and electronic formats and by print-on-demand. Some material included with standard print versions of this book may not be included in e-books or in print-on-demand. If this book refers to media such as a CD or DVD that is not included in the version you purchased, you may download this material at http://booksupport.wiley.com. For more information about Wiley products, visit www.wiley.com.

Library of Congress Control Number: 2018933560

10 9 8 7 6 5 4 3 2 1

To my awesome son, William, and incredible daughter, Allison: This book is dedicated to both of you.
—Todd Montgomery

To my amazing wife, Melissa, and children, Cole and Kate: I am humbled by your patience and love as I write and work long hours. Thank you for keeping me grounded.
—Stephen Olson

About the Authors

Todd Montgomery   has been in the networking industry for more than 35 years and holds many certifications from CompTIA, Cisco, Juniper, VMware, and other companies. He is CompTIA Cloud+, Network+, and Security+ certified.

Todd has spent most of his career out in the field working on-site in data centers throughout North America and around the world. He has worked for equipment manufacturers, systems integrators, and end users of data center equipment in the public, service provider, and government sectors. He is currently working as a writer and technical editor and is involved in cloud projects.

Todd lives in Austin, Texas, and in his free time enjoys auto racing, general aviation, and Austin's live music venues. He can be reached at toddmont@thegateway.net.

Stephen Olson   has been in the networking industry for almost 15 years and holds many certifications including Cisco's CCIE #21910, the Cisco CCNA, and CCNP, among others. Steve has spent the majority of his career working in large enterprises as well as consulting for service providers around the world in the cloud, WAN, and data center segments. He is currently working on SDN projects in the WAN and data center spaces as well as cloud networking. He resides in Austin, Texas, and enjoys music and guitar in his free time. Steve can be reached at stephenjolson@gmail.com.

Acknowledgments

There are many people who work to put a book together, and although as authors we dedicate an enormous amount of time to writing the book, it would never be published without the dedicated, hard work of the whole team at Wiley. They are truly a fantastic group to work with, and without the Wiley team this book would have never been possible.

First, we'd like to thank Kenyon Brown, our senior acquisitions editor, who offered us support and guidance through the writing process. Ken was always there to answer questions and point us in the right direction. Without Ken as a mentor, we could never have pulled this one off.

We also can never thank our development editor, David Clark, too many times; David is a true professional who stayed on top of the schedule and professionally reminded us of the next upcoming deadline we were working to meet. Without David's help, putting this book together would have been much more difficult. David has the ability to take the raw text from the authors, who are primarily engineers, and manage to turn it into presentable copy. Thanks again, David!

Kunal Mittal offered excellent input as our technical editor. He gave us invaluable feedback on how to make the technical concepts more understandable to the readers and pointed out where we needed to modify our technical content for accuracy. It was great that Kunal was able to be on this project with us.

A big thank you to Katie Wisor, the production editor on this project. Kim Wimpsett worked the markup magic in the background as the copyeditor. The authors are both amazed at how Katie and Kim along with their team of professionals could take our work and transform it into such a presentable book. We're sure there is a whole staff at Wiley lurking in the background, and we will never know how much they helped, but to everyone at Wiley, a big thank-you! You made the late nights and long weekends of writing and putting this book together all worthwhile.

Contents

Introduction   *xvii*

Cloud+ Assessment Test   *xl*

**Chapter   1   An Introduction to Cloud Computing
                Configurations and Deployments   1**

Introducing Cloud Computing   3
   Cloud Service Models   7
   Cloud Reference Designs and Delivery Models   11
   Introducing Cloud Components   13
   Connecting the Cloud to the Outside World   14
   Initial Documentation   14
   Selecting Cloud Compute Resources   14
   Validating and Preparing for the Move to the Cloud   15
   What Is the Architecture?   15
   Choosing Elements and Objects in the Cloud   16
Creating and Validating a Cloud Deployment   16
   The Cloud Shared Resource Pooling Model   16
   Organizational Uses of the Cloud   19
   Scaling and Architecting Cloud Systems
     Based on Requirements   20
   Understanding Cloud Performance   21
   Delivering High Availability Operations   21
   Connecting Your Organization to the Remote
     Cloud Data Center   22
   What Are the Tools Used for Remote Management?   22
   Cloud Testing   25
Verifying System Requirements   26
   Correct Scaling for Your Requirements   26
   Making Sure the Cloud Is Always Available   27
   Understanding Direct and Virtual Cloud Connections   28
   Keeping Your Data Safe (A Word About Data Integrity)   32
   Making Sure Your Cloud Deployment Is
     Functioning as Expected   32
   Writing It All Down (Documentation)   33
   Creating a Known Reference Point (Baselines)   33
   What Is the Responsibility of the Cloud
     Service Provider?   33
   Variations in the Cloud: Performance Metrics   34
Summary   34
Exam Essentials   35
Written Lab   37
Review Questions   38

Chapter	**2**	**Cloud Deployments**	**43**
		Executing a Cloud Deployment	48
		Understanding Deployment and Change Management	48
		Cloud Deployment Models	54
		Network Deployment Considerations	56
		Comparing Benchmarks	62
		Matching Physical Resources to the Virtualized World of the Cloud	62
		What Are Available and Proposed Hardware Resources?	63
		Physical Resource High Availability	65
		Introducing Disaster Recovery	65
		Physical Hardware Performance Benchmarks	66
		Costs Savings When Using the Cloud	66
		Energy Savings in the Cloud	66
		Shared vs. Dedicated Hardware Resources in a Cloud Data Center	67
		Configuring and Deploying Storage	67
		Identifying Storage Configurations	67
		Storage Provisioning	70
		Storage Priorities: Understanding Storage Tiers	72
		Managing and Protecting Your Stored Data	73
		Storage Security Considerations	78
		Accessing Your Storage in the Cloud	81
		Managing Cloud Storage	82
		Performing a Server Migration	82
		Different Types of Server Migrations	83
		Understanding the Virtualization Formats Needed When Migrating	85
		Addressing Application Portability	86
		Workload Migration Common Procedures	86
		Examining Infrastructure Capable of Supporting a Migration	86
		Managing User Identities and Roles	88
		RBAC: Identifying Users and What Their Roles Are	88
		Identity Applications in the Public Cloud	89
		What Happens When You Authenticate?	89
		Giving Authorization to Access Specific Cloud Services	89
		Understanding Federations	89
		Single Sign-on Systems	90
		Understanding Infrastructure Services	90
		Summary	93
		Exam Essentials	94
		Written Lab	95
		Review Questions	97

Chapter	**3**	**Security in the Cloud**	**101**
		Cloud Security Compliance and Configurations	103
		Establishing Your Company's Security Policies	104
		Selecting and Applying the Security Policies to Your Cloud Operations	105
		Some Common Regulatory Requirements	105
		Encrypting Your Data	108
		Security Certificates and Keys	111
		Remote Access Security	113
		Automating Cloud Security	114
		Security Templates for Compute Platforms	114
		Access Control	116
		Accessing Cloud-Based Objects	116
		Cloud Service Models and Security	118
		Cloud Deployment Models and Security	119
		Applying Access Controls	120
		Summary	122
		Exam Essentials	123
		Written Lab	124
		Review Questions	125
Chapter	**4**	**Implementing Cloud Security**	**129**
		Implementing Security in the Cloud	131
		Data Classification	131
		Segmenting Your Deployment	132
		Implementing Encryption	134
		Applying Multifactor Authentication	135
		Regulatory and Compliance Issues During Implementation	136
		Automating Cloud Security	137
		Automation Tools	137
		Techniques for Implementing Cloud Security	140
		Security Services	141
		Summary	144
		Exam Essentials	145
		Written Lab	146
		Review Questions	148
Chapter	**5**	**Maintaining Cloud Operations**	**153**
		Applying Security Patches	155
		Cloud Element Security	155
		Patching Methodologies	157
		Patching Order of Operations and Dependencies	161

Updating Cloud Elements	161
Understanding the Different Types of Updates	161
Workflow Automation	163
Virtualization Automation Tools and Activities	164
Storage Operations	166
Types of Backups	167
Backup Targets	169
Backup and Restore Operations	171
Summary	173
Exam Essentials	173
Written Lab	174
Review Questions	176

Chapter	**6**	**Disaster Recovery, Business Continuity, and Ongoing Maintenance**	**181**

Implementing a Disaster Recovery and Business Continuity Plan	183
Service Provider Responsibilities and Capabilities	184
Disaster Recovery Models and Techniques	186
Business Continuity	192
Establishing a Business Continuity Plan	193
Establishing Service Level Agreements	195
Cloud Maintenance	196
Establishing Maintenance Windows	196
Maintenance Interruptions to Operations	197
Maintenance Automation Impact and Scope	197
Common Maintenance Automation Tasks	197
Summary	202
Exam Essentials	203
Written Lab	203
Review Questions	205

Chapter	**7**	**Cloud Management**	**211**

Introduction to Cloud Management	214
Cloud Metrics	215
Monitoring Your Deployment	216
Cloud Support Agreements	221
Standard Cloud Maintenance Responsibilities	222
Configuration Management Applications and Tools	222
Change Management Processes	222
Adding and Removing Cloud Resources	224
Determining Usage Patterns	224
Bursting	224
Migrating Between Cloud Providers	224

Scaling Resources to Meet Requirements   225
Extending the Scope of the Cloud   228
Understanding Application Life Cycles   228
Corporate Changes   229
Managing Account Provisioning   230
Account Identification   231
Authentication   231
Authorization   232
Managing the Account Life Cycle   232
Account Automation and Orchestration   233
Summary   234
Exam Essentials   235
Written Lab   236
Review Questions   238

Chapter   8   Cloud Management Baselines, Performance, and SLAs   243

Measuring Your Deployment
  Against the Baseline   245
    Object Tracking for Baseline Validation   246
    Applying Changes to the Cloud to Meet
      Baseline Requirements   249
    Changing Operations to Meet Expected
      Performance/Capacity Requirements   253
    Cloud Accounting, Chargeback, and Reporting 255
Summary   257
Exam Essentials   258
Written Lab   259
Review Questions   260

Chapter   9   Troubleshooting   265

Examining Common Cloud Issues   267
  Automation   267
  Cloud Interoperability   268
  Interconnections   269
  Language Support   269
  Licensing   269
  Networking   270
  Resource Contention and Starvation   271
  Service Outages   271
  Templates   272
  Time Synchronization   272
  Workflow   272

Troubleshooting Cloud Capacity Issues   272
   Capacity Boundaries in the Cloud   273
   Exceeding Your Baseline Measurements   275
   Expecting the Unexpected, Unplanned Expansions   276
Troubleshooting Automation
   and Orchestration   276
   Process and Workflow Issues   276
Summary   280
Exam Essentials   281
Written Lab   282
Review Questions   283

**Chapter 10   Troubleshooting Networking and Security
               Issues and Understanding Methodologies   287**

Troubleshooting Cloud Networking Issues   290
   Identifying the Common Networking Issues in
      the Cloud   291
   Network Troubleshooting and Connectivity Tools   298
   Remote Access Tools   307
Troubleshooting Security Issues   310
   Account Privilege Escalation   310
   Sign-On Issues   311
   Authentication   311
   Authorization   311
   Confederations   312
   Certificate Configuration Issues   312
   Device-Hardening Settings   312
   External Attacks   313
   Identifying Weak or Obsolete Security Technologies   313
   Internal Attacks   313
   Maintain Sufficient Security Controls and Processes   313
   Network Access Tunneling and Encryption   314
   Physical Access, Infrastructure, and Availability   314
   Unencrypted Communications and Data   315
Troubleshooting Methodology   315
   Corporate Policies, Procedures, and the Impact
      of Implementing Changes   317
   Steps to Identify the Problem   318
Summary   320
Exam Essentials   320
Written Lab   322
Review Questions   323

Appendix   A   Answers to Review Questions   329

Chapter 1: An Introduction to Cloud Computing
   Configurations and Deployments   330
Chapter 2: Cloud Deployments   331
Chapter 3: Security in the Cloud   332
Chapter 4: Implementing Cloud Security   334
Chapter 5: Maintaining Cloud Operations   335
Chapter 6: Disaster Recovery, Business Continuity, and
   Ongoing Maintenance   337
Chapter 7: Cloud Management   338
Chapter 8: Cloud Management Baselines, Performance,
   and SLAs   340
Chapter 9: Troubleshooting   341
Chapter 10: Troubleshooting Networking and Security
   Issues and Understanding Methodologies   342

Appendix   B   Answers to Written Labs   345

Chapter 1: An Introduction to Cloud Computing
   Configurations and Deployments   346
Chapter 2: Cloud Deployments   346
Chapter 3: Security in the Cloud   346
Chapter 4: Implementing Cloud Security   347
Chapter 5: Maintaining Cloud Operations   347
Chapter 6: Disaster Recovery, Business Continuity,
   and Ongoing Maintenance   348
Chapter 7: Cloud Management   348
Chapter 8: Cloud Management Baselines, Performance,
   and SLAs   349
Chapter 9: Troubleshooting   349
Chapter 10: Troubleshooting Networking and Security
   Issues and Understanding Methodologies   350

Index   *351*

CompTIA.

CompTIA Cloud+

Becoming a CompTIA Certified IT Professional is Easy

It's also the best way to reach greater professional opportunities and rewards.

Why Get CompTIA Certified?

Growing Demand

Labor estimates predict some technology fields will experience growth of over 20% by the year 2020.* CompTIA certification qualifies the skills required to join this workforce.

Higher Salaries

IT professionals with certifications on their resume command better jobs, earn higher salaries and have more doors open to new multi-industry opportunities.

Verified Strengths

91% of hiring managers indicate CompTIA certifications are valuable in validating IT expertise, making certification the best way to demonstrate your competency and knowledge to employers.**

Universal Skills

CompTIA certifications are vendor neutral—which means that certified professionals can proficiently work with an extensive variety of hardware and software found in most organizations.

 Learn 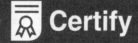 Certify  Work

Learn more about what the exam covers by reviewing the following:

- Exam objectives for key study points.

- Sample questions for a general overview of what to expect on the exam and examples of question format.

- Visit online forums, like LinkedIn, to see what other IT professionals say about CompTIA exams.

Purchase a voucher at a Pearson VUE testing center or at CompTIAstore.com.

- Register for your exam at a Pearson VUE testing center:

- Visit pearsonvue.com/CompTIA to find the closest testing center to you.

- Schedule the exam online. You will be required to enter your voucher number or provide payment information at registration.

- Take your certification exam.

Congratulations on your CompTIA certification!

- Make sure to add your certification to your resume.

- Check out the CompTIA Certification Roadmap to plan your next career move.

Learn more: Certification.CompTIA.org/certifications/cloud

* Source: CompTIA 9th Annual Information Security Trends study: 500 U.S. IT and Business Executives Responsible for Security
** Source: CompTIA Employer Perceptions of IT Training and Certification

Introduction

Welcome to the exciting world of cloud computing and CompTIA certifications! If you picked up this book because you want to improve yourself with a secure and rewarding job in the new and fast-growing cloud computing space, you have come to the right place. Whether you are striving to enter the thriving, dynamic IT sector or seeking to enhance your skills in the emerging cloud computing field, being CompTIA Cloud+ certified can seriously stack the odds of success in your favor.

CompTIA certifications are powerful instruments of success that will most certainly improve your knowledge of cloud computing. As you progress through this book, you'll gain a broad and deep understanding of cloud computing operations that offers unprecedented exposure to this dynamic field. The knowledge and expertise you will gain are essential for your success in all areas of the cloud computing field.

By deciding to become Cloud+ certified, you're proudly announcing to the world that you want to become an unrivaled cloud computing expert, a goal that this book with get you well on your way to achieving. Congratulations in advance on the beginning of your brilliant future!

> For up-to-the-minute updates covering additions or modifications to the CompTIA certification exams, as well as additional study tools, videos, practice questions, and bonus material, be sure to visit the Sybex website and forum at www.sybex.com.

Why Should You Become Certified in Cloud Technologies?

CompTIA has created the world's leading vendor-neutral family of certifications in the technology industry. CompTIA's certifications are recognized and respected worldwide for their quality and rigorous standards. They offer a broad range of certifications on a wide variety of technology topics. When you become Cloud+ certified, you have validated your skills and expertise in the implementation and ongoing support of cloud-based services. Becoming a CompTIA Cloud+ certified professional validates that you have the knowledge to be a successful cloud engineer.

The Cloud+ certification is recognized as one of the premier cloud certifications in the market today. Studying for and passing the Cloud+ exam gives engineers a set of skills to succeed in the fast-growing field of cloud computing.

Rest assured that when you pass the CompTIA Cloud+ exam, you're headed down a path to certain success!

What Does This Book Cover?

This book follows the most recent version of the CompTIA Cloud+ exam, CV0-002. The exam blueprint is divided into five sections consisting of ten chapters that cover all the major topic areas. Each section is explained in sufficient detail to help you become a Cloud+ certified professional.

Chapter 1: An Introduction to Cloud Computing Configurations and Deployments   The book starts out investigating the most common cloud components such as applications, compute, storage, and networking. Then how to determine the correct size and scale of the systems is discussed. You will get a basic understanding of configurations found in the cloud and learn about production, quality assurance, and development cloud systems.

Chapter 2: Cloud Deployments   In this chapter you'll learn about deploying services in the cloud and how to execute a deployment plan; the most common service models; and the various ways that clouds are delivered such as public, private, and community. Common cloud terminology and storage are explained.

Next, the technical background is presented on how to determine the needs and design an effective cloud deployment. This includes what virtualization is, its benefits, and why it is a central technology in cloud computing. You'll learn about hypervisors, virtual machines, and how to migrate from your existing operations to the cloud.

Chapter 3: Security in the Cloud   Chapter 3 covers cloud security starting with security polices, laws and standards. You will then learn about specific security technologies, applications, and services.

Chapter 4: Implementing Cloud Security   Chapter 4 builds on your security knowledge by explaining how to implement secure storage, networks, and compute systems. Security tools, intrusion systems, encryption, tools, techniques, and services are introduced.

Chapter 5: Maintaining Cloud Operations   This chapter focuses on keeping your cloud deployment current with the latest updates and discusses the processes to follow. Automation is introduced, and you will learn about the importance of cloud automation and orchestration systems. The chapter concludes with a discussion on backing up your data in the cloud.

Chapter 6: Disaster Recovery, Business Continuity, and Ongoing Maintenance   We'll take a step back in this chapter and cover how to go about developing a disaster recovery plan and the common models available. You will learn the importance of business survivability during a severe outage and understand the issues concerning recovery. The chapter ends with describing how to perform ongoing maintenance in your cloud environment.

Chapter 7: Cloud Management   You'll now delve deep into the operations aspects of cloud computing. Chapter 7 begins with a discussion of monitoring the cloud and then moves on to look at the allocation and provisioning of resources. Then you will learn about business requirements, application life cycles, and the impact they have on managing your cloud deployment. The chapter concludes with discussion on security of your cloud operations with accounts, automation, authentication and automation models.

Chapter 8: Cloud Management Baselines, Performance, and SLAs   Chapter 8 explains how to determine what is considered normal cloud operations by creating and maintaining baseline measurements. Based on these measurements, we go on to discuss how to monitor your cloud fleet for deviations from the baseline and the steps to take when this occurs. Service level agreements and chargeback models are also explained in this chapter.

Chapter 9: Troubleshooting   Chapter 9 goes deep into the technical aspects identifying and correct cloud technical issues. We cover troubleshooting of new and existing deployments. You will learn about common problems found in the cloud that you will need to resolve. We will teach you how to identify and resolve deviations from your baselines and what to do when breakdowns in the workflow occur. Be sure to pay close attention to this chapter!

Chapter 10: Troubleshooting Networking and Security Issues and Understanding Methodologies   The final chapter continues investigating troubleshooting with a focus on tools and techniques. We will present common troubleshooting utilities found in Linux and Windows systems and how to perform a structured troubleshooting approach.

Appendix A: Answers to Review Questions   This appendix contains the answers to the book's review questions.

Appendix B: Answers to Written Labs   This appendix contains the answers to the book's written labs.

Interactive Online Learning Environment and Test Bank

We've put together some great online tools to help you pass the Cloud+ exam. The interactive online learning environment that accompanies the Cloud+ exam certification guide provides a test bank and study tools to help you prepare for the exam. By using these tools, you can dramatically increase your chances of passing the exam on your first try.

Sample Tests   Many sample tests are provided throughout this book and online, including the assessment test at the end of this Introduction and the review questions at the end of each chapter. In addition, there are two *exclusive* online practice exams with 50 questions each. Use these questions to test your knowledge of the study guide material. The online test bank runs on multiple devices.

Flashcards   The online text banks include 100 flashcards specifically written to hit you hard, so don't get discouraged if you don't ace your way through them at first! They're there to ensure that you're ready for the exam. Armed with the review questions, practice exams, and flashcards, you'll be more than prepared when exam day comes. Questions are provided in digital flashcard format (a question followed by a single correct answer). You can use the flashcards to reinforce your learning and provide last-minute test prep before the exam.

Other Study Tools   A glossary of key terms from this book and their definitions is available as a fully searchable PDF.

Go to http://www.wiley.com/go/sybextestprep to register and gain access to this interactive online learning environment and test bank with study tools.

How to Use This Book

If you want a solid foundation for the serious effort of preparing for the CompTIA CV0-002 Cloud+ exam, then look no further. We've spent hundreds of hours putting together this book with the sole intention of helping you to pass the exam as well as learn about the exciting field of cloud computing! The book is completely updated and refreshed from the original to match the new version of the CompTIA Cloud+ exam, CV0-002.

This book is loaded with valuable information, and you will get the most out of your study time if you understand why the book is organized the way it is.

To maximize your benefit from this book, we recommend the following study method:

1. Take the assessment test that's provided at the end of this Introduction. (The answers are at the end of the test.) It's OK if you don't know any of the answers; that's why you bought this book! Carefully read over the explanations for any question you get wrong and note the chapters in which the material relevant to them is covered. This information should help you plan your study strategy.

2. Study each chapter carefully, making sure you fully understand the information and the test objectives listed at the beginning of each one. Pay extra-close attention to any chapter that includes material covered in questions you missed.

3. Complete all written exams in each chapter, referring to the text of the chapter so that you understand the reason for each answer.

4. Answer all the review questions related to each chapter. Many of the questions are presented in a scenario format to emulate real-world tasks that you may encounter. (The answers appear in Appendix A.) Note the questions that confuse you, and study the topics they cover again until the concepts are crystal clear. Again, do not just skim these questions! Make sure you fully comprehend the reason for each correct answer. Remember that these will not be the exact questions you will find on the exam, but they're written to help you understand the chapter material and ultimately pass the exam.

5. Each chapter also concludes with a fill-in-the-blank type of written exam that is designed to improve your memory and comprehension of key items that were presented in the chapter. These are great for test preparation. We suggest going over these questions until you are able to consistently answer them error free. (The answers appear in Appendix B.)

6. Try your hand at the practice questions that are exclusive to this book. The questions can be found at http://www.wiley.com/go/sybextestprep.

7. Test yourself using all the flashcards, which are also found at http://www.wiley.com/go/sybextestprep. These are new flashcards to help you prepare for the Cloud+ exam.

To learn every bit of the material covered in this book, you'll have to apply yourself regularly and with discipline. Try to set aside the same time period every day to study, and select a comfortable and quiet place to do so. We're confident that if you work hard, you'll be surprised at how quickly you learn this material.

If you follow these steps and study in addition to using the review questions, the practice exams, and the electronic flashcards, it would actually be hard to fail the Cloud+ exam. But understand that studying for the CompTIA exams is a lot like getting in shape—if you do not go to the gym every day, it's not going to happen!

According to the CompTIA website, the Cloud+ exam details are as follows:

- **Exam code:** CV0-002
- **Exam description:** CompTIA Cloud+ covers competency in cloud models, virtualization, infrastructure, security, resource management and business continuity.
- **Number of questions:** 100
- **Type of questions:** Multiple choice
- **Length of test:** 90 minutes
- **Passing score:** 750 (on a scale of 100–900)
- **Language:** English
- **Recommended experience:**
  - At least 24–36 months of work experience in IT networking, network storage or data center administration
  - Familiarity with any major hypervisor technologies for server virtualization, though vendor-specific certifications in virtualization are not required
  - CompTIA Network+ and/or CompTIA Server+, though CompTIA certifications are not required
  - Knowledge of cloud service model (IaaS, PaaS, SaaS) definitions
  - Knowledge of common cloud deployment model (Private, Public, Hybrid) definitions
  - Hands-on experience with at least one public cloud IaaS platform

How Do You Go About Taking the Exam?

When the time comes to schedule your exam, you will need to create an account at www.comptia.org and register for your exam.

You can purchase the exam voucher on the CompTIA website at https://certification .comptia.org/testing/buy-voucher. The voucher is proof of purchase and is a code number that you will use to actually schedule the exam at https://certification.comptia.org/ testing/schedule-exam.

CompTIA testing is provided by its global testing partner Pearson VUE. You can locate your closest testing center at https://wsr.pearsonvue.com/testtaker/registration/ SelectTestCenterProximity/COMPTIA/292833; you can schedule at any of the listed testing centers worldwide.

When you have a voucher and have selected a testing center, you can go ahead and schedule the Cloud+ CV0-002 exam by visiting www.pearsonvue.com/comptia. There you can also locate a testing center or purchase vouchers if you have not already done so.

When you have registered for the Cloud+ certification exam, you will receive a confirmation e-mail that supplies you with all the information you will need to take the exam. Remember to take a printout of this e-mail and two forms of ID (one with a photograph) with you to the testing center.

Certification Exam Policies

This section explains CompTIA's exam policies and was taken from the CompTIA website. We recommend that you visit `https://certification.comptia.org/testing/test-policies` to become familiar with CompTIA's policies.

Candidate Agreement   Explains the rules and regulations regarding certification, including the retake policy, the candidate conduct policy, and the candidate appeals process

Candidate Testing Policies   Includes accommodations during an exam, exam scoring, exam content, and out-of-country testing policies

CompTIA Voucher Terms & Conditions   Details the terms and conditions governing CompTIA vouchers

Candidate ID Policy   Details the acceptable forms of identification candidates may bring to an exam

Certification Retake Policy   Details the circumstances in which a candidate can retake a certification exam

Exam Delivery Policies   Includes testing center suspensions, delivery exclusions, and beta testing policies

Continuing Education Policies   Covers certification renewal, candidate code of ethics, and audit findings as related to the Continuing Education Program

Exam Development   Explains the exam development process

Sharing Your Exam Results   Explains the exam results sharing policy

Unauthorized Training Materials   Defines unauthorized training materials and the consequences for using them

Candidate Appeals Process   Describes the process for candidates to appeal sanctions imposed due to exam security or policy violations

CompTIA Exam Security Hotline   Can be used to report security breaches, candidate misconduct, IP infringement, use of unauthorized training materials, and other exam security-related concerns

Tips for Taking Your Cloud+ Exam

The CompTIA Cloud+ exam contains 100 multiple-choice questions and must be completed in 90 minutes or less. This information may change over time, and we advise you to check `www.comptia.org` for the latest updates.

Many questions on the exam offer answer choices that at first glance look identical, especially the syntax questions. Remember to read through the choices carefully because close just doesn't cut it. If you get information in the wrong order or forget one measly character, you may get the question wrong. Many of the questions will be presented in a scenario format that can be a long, involved statement that is designed to confuse or misdirect you. Read these questions carefully and make sure you completely understand what is being asked. It is important to filter out irrelevant statements in scenario questions and focus on what they are asking you to identify as the correct answer. So, to practice, do the practice exams and hands-on exercises from this book's chapters over and over again until they feel natural to you. Do the online sample test until you can consistently answer all the questions correctly. Relax, read the question over and over until you are 100 percent clear on what it is asking, and then you can usually eliminate a few of the obviously wrong answers.

Here are some general tips for exam success:

- Arrive early at the exam center so you can relax and review your study materials.

- Read the questions *carefully*. Don't jump to conclusions. Make sure you're clear about *exactly* what each question asks. "Read twice, answer once!" Scenario questions can be long and contain information that is not relevant to the answer. Take your time and understand what they are *really* asking you.

- Ask for a piece of paper and pencil if it is offered to take quick notes and make sketches during the exam.

- When answering multiple-choice questions that you're not sure about, use the process of elimination to get rid of the obviously incorrect answers first. Doing this greatly improves your odds if you need to make an educated guess.

After you complete an exam, you'll get immediate, online notification of your pass or fail status, a printed examination score report that indicates your pass or fail status, and your exam results by section. (The test administrator will give you the printed score report.) Test scores are automatically forwarded to CompTIA after you take the test, so you don't need to send your score to them. If you pass the exam, you'll receive confirmation from CompTIA and a package in the mail with a nice document suitable for framing showing that you are now a Cloud+ certified professional!

Cloud+ Exam Renewal

The Cloud+ certification is good for three years from the date of the exam. You can keep your certification up-to-date by following CompTIA's continuing education program outlined at https://certification.comptia.org/continuing-education.

CompTIA Cloud+ Study Guide: Exam CV0-002 Objective Map

The following objective map will assist you with finding where each exam objective is covered in the chapters in this book.

1.0 Configuration and Deployment

Exam Objective	Chapter
1.1 Given a scenario, analyze system requirements to ensure successful system deployment.	1

- Appropriate commands, structure, tools, and automation/orchestration as needed
- Platforms and applications
- Interaction of cloud components and services
  - Network components
  - Application components
  - Storage components
  - Compute components
  - Security components
- Interaction of non-cloud components and services
- Baselines
- Target hosts
- Existing systems
- Cloud architecture
- Cloud elements/target objects

1.2 Given a scenario, execute a provided deployment plan.	2

- Apply the Change Management Process
  - Approvals
  - Scheduling
- Refer to documentation and follow standard operating procedures
- Execute workflow
- Configure automation and orchestration, where appropriate, for the system being deployed
- Use commands and tools as needed
- Document results

Exam Objective	Chapter
1.3 Given a scenario, analyze system requirements to determine if a given testing plan is appropriate.	1

- Underlying environment considerations included in the testing plan
  - Shared components
    - Storage
    - Compute
    - Network
  - Production vs. development vs. QA
  - Sizing
  - Performance
  - High availability
  - Connectivity
  - Data integrity
  - Proper function
  - Replication
  - Load balancing
  - Automation/orchestration
- Testing techniques
  - Vulnerability testing
  - Penetration testing
  - Load testing

1.4 Given a scenario, analyze testing results to determine if the testing was successful in relation to given system requirements.	1

- Consider success factor indicators of the testing environment
  - Sizing
  - Performance
  - Availability
  - Connectivity
  - Data integrity
  - Proper functionality
- Document results
- Baseline comparisons
- SLA comparisons
- Cloud performance fluctuation variables

Exam Objective	Chapter
1.5 Given a scenario, analyze sizing, subnetting, and basic routing for a provided deployment of the virtual network.	2

- Cloud deployment models
  - Public
  - Private
  - Hybrid
  - Community
- Network components
- Applicable port and protocol considerations when extending to the cloud
- Determine configuration for the applicable platform as it applies to the network
  - VPN
  - IDS/IPS
  - DMZ
  - VXLAN
  - Address space required
  - Network segmentation and micro-segmentation
- Determine if cloud resources are consistent with the SLA and/or change management requirements

| 1.6 Given a scenario, analyze CPU and memory sizing for a provided deployment. | 2 |

- Available vs. proposed resources
  - CPU
  - RAM
- Memory technologies
  - Bursting and ballooning
  - Overcommitment ratio
- CPU technologies
  - Hyperthreading
  - VT-x
  - Overcommitment ratio
- Effect to HA/DR
- Performance considerations
- Cost considerations
- Energy savings
- Dedicated compute environment vs. shared compute environment

Exam Objective	Chapter
1.7 Given a scenario, analyze the appropriate storage type and protection capability for a provided deployment.	2

- Requested IOPS and read/write throughput
- Protection capabilities
  - High availability
    - Failover zones
  - Storage replication
    - Regional
    - Multiregional
    - Synchronous and asynchronous
  - Storage mirroring
  - Cloning
  - Redundancy level/factor
- Storage types
  - NAS
  - DAS
  - SAN
  - Object storage
- Access protocols
- Management differences
- Provisioning model
  - Thick provisioned
  - Thin provisioned
  - Encryption requirements
  - Tokenization
- Storage technologies
  - Deduplication technologies
  - Compression technologies
- Storage tiers
- Overcommitting storage
- Security configurations for applicable platforms
  - ACLs
  - Obfuscation
  - Zoning
  - User/host authentication and authorization

Exam Objective	Chapter
1.8 Given a scenario, analyze characteristics of the workload (storage, network, compute) to ensure a successful migration.	2

- Migration types
  - P2V
  - V2V
  - V2P
  - P2P
  - Storage migrations
  - Online vs. offline migrations
- Source and destination format of the workload
  - Virtualization format
  - Application and data portability
- Network connections and data transfer methodologies
- Standard operating procedures for the workload migration
- Environmental constraints
  - Bandwidth
  - Working hour restrictions
  - Downtime impact
  - Peak timeframes
  - Legal restrictions
  - Follow-the-sun constraints/time zones

	Chapter
1.9 Given a scenario, apply elements required to extend the infrastructure into a given cloud solution.	2

- Identity management elements
  - Identification
  - Authentication
  - Authorization
    - Approvals
    - Access policy
- Federation
  - Single sign-on
- Appropriate protocols given requirements
- Element considerations to deploy infrastructure services such as:
  - DNS
  - DHCP
  - Certificate services
  - Local agents
  - Antivirus
  - Load balancer
  - Multifactor authentication
  - Firewall
  - IPS/IDS

2.0 Security

Exam Objective	Chapter
2.1 Given a scenario, apply security configurations and compliance controls to meet given cloud infrastructure requirements.	3

- Company security policies
- Apply security standards for the selected platform
- Compliance and audit requirements governing the environment
  - Laws and regulations as they apply to the data
- Encryption technologies
  - IPSec
  - SSL/TLS
  - Other ciphers
- Key and certificate management
  - PKI
- Tunneling protocols
  - L2TP
  - PPTP
  - GRE
- Implement automation and orchestration processes as applicable
- Appropriate configuration for the applicable platform as it applies to compute
  - Disabling unneeded ports and services
  - Account management policies
  - Host-based/software firewalls
  - Antivirus/anti-malware software
  - Patching
  - Deactivating default accounts

2.2 Given a scenario, apply the appropriate ACL to the target objects to meet access requirements according to a security template.	3

- Authorization to objects in the cloud
  - Processes
  - Resources
    - Users
    - Groups
    - System
      - Compute
      - Networks
      - Storage
  - Services

Exam Objective	Chapter

- Effect of cloud service models on security implementations
- Effect of cloud deployment models on security implementations
- Access control methods
  - Role-based administration
  - Mandatory access controls
  - Discretionary access controls
  - Nondiscretionary access controls
  - Multifactor authentication
  - Single sign-on

2.3 Given a cloud service model, implement defined security technologies to meet given security requirements.   4

- Data classification
- Concepts of segmentation and micro-segmentation
  - Network
  - Storage
  - Compute
- Use encryption as defined
- Use multifactor authentication as defined
- Apply defined audit/compliance requirements

2.4 Given a cloud service model, apply the appropriate security automation technique to the target system.   4

- Tools
  - APIs
  - Vendor applications
  - CLI
  - Web GUI
  - Cloud portal
- Techniques
  - Orchestration
  - Scripting
  - Custom programming
- Security services
  - Firewall
  - Antivirus/anti-malware
  - IPS/IDS
  - HIPS
- Impact of security tools to systems and services
  - Scope of impact
- Impact of security automation techniques as they relate to the criticality of systems
  - Scope of impact

3.0 Maintenance

Exam Objective	Chapter
3.1 Given a cloud service model, determine the appropriate methodology to apply given patches.	5

- Scope of cloud elements to be patched
  - Hypervisors
  - Virtual machines
  - Virtual appliances
  - Networking components
  - Applications
  - Storage components
  - Clusters
- Patching methodologies and standard operating procedures
  - Production vs. development vs. QA
  - Rolling update
  - Blue-green deployment
  - Failover cluster
- Use order of operations as it pertains to elements that will be patched
- Dependency considerations

3.2 Given a scenario, apply the appropriate automation tools to update cloud elements.	5

- Types of updates
  - Hotfix
  - Patch
  - Version update
  - Rollback
- Automation workflow
  - Runbook management
    - Single node
  - Orchestration
    - Multiple nodes
    - Multiple runbooks
- Activities to be performed by automation tools
  - Snapshot
  - Cloning
  - Patching
  - Restarting
  - Shut down
  - Maintenance mode
  - Enable/disable alerts

Exam Objective	Chapter
3.3 Given a scenario, apply an appropriate back up or restore method.	5

- Backup types
    - Snapshot/redirect-on-write
    - Clone
    - Full
    - Differential
    - Incremental
    - Change block/delta tracking
- Backup targets
    - Replicas
    - Local
    - Remote
- Other considerations
    - SLAs
    - Backup schedule
    - Configurations
    - Objects
    - Dependencies
    - Online/offline

3.4 Given a cloud-based scenario, apply appropriate disaster recovery methods.	6

- DR capabilities of a cloud service provider
- Other considerations
    - SLAs for DR
    - RPO
    - RTO
    - Corporate guidelines
    - Cloud service provider guidelines
    - Bandwidth or ISP limitations
- Techniques
    - Site mirroring
    - Replication
    - File transfer
    - Archiving
    - Third-party sites

Exam Objective	Chapter
3.5 Given a cloud-based scenario, apply the appropriate steps to ensure business continuity.	6

- Business continuity plan
    - Alternate sites
    - Continuity of operations
    - Connectivity
    - Edge sites
    - Equipment
    - Availability
    - Partners/third parties
- SLAs for BCP and HA

Exam Objective	Chapter
3.6 Given a scenario, apply the appropriate maintenance automation technique to the target objects.	6

- Maintenance schedules
- Impact and scope of maintenance tasks
- Impact and scope of maintenance automation techniques
- Include orchestration as appropriate
- Maintenance automation tasks
    - Clearing logs
    - Archiving logs
    - Compressing drives
    - Removing inactive accounts
    - Removing stale DNS entries
    - Removing orphaned resources
    - Removing outdated rules from firewall
    - Removing outdated rules from security
    - Resource reclamation
    - Maintain ACLs for the target object

4.0 Management

Exam Objective	Chapter
4.1 Given a scenario, analyze defined metrics to determine the presence of an abnormality and/or forecast future needed cloud resources.	7

- Monitoring
    - Target object baselines
    - Target object anomalies

Exam Objective	Chapter

- Common alert methods/messaging
- Alerting based on deviation from baseline
- Event collection
- Event correlation
- Forecasting resource capacity
  - Upsize/increase
  - Downsize/decrease
- Policies in support of event collection
- Policies to communicate alerts appropriately

4.2 Given a scenario, determine the appropriate allocation of cloud resources.   7

- Resources needed based on cloud deployment models
  - Hybrid
  - Community
  - Public
  - Private
- Capacity/elasticity of cloud environment
- Support agreements
  - Cloud service model maintenance responsibility
- Configuration management tool
- Resource balancing techniques
- Change management
  - Advisory board
  - Approval process
  - Document actions taken
    - CMDB
    - Spreadsheet

4.3 Given a scenario, determine when to provision/deprovision cloud resources.   7

- Usage patterns
- Cloud bursting
  - Auto-scaling technology
- Cloud provider migrations
- Extending cloud scope
- Application life cycle
  - Application deployment
  - Application upgrade
  - Application retirement
  - Application replacement
  - Application migration

Exam Objective	Chapter

- Application feature use
    - Increase/decrease
- Business need change
    - Mergers/acquisitions/divestitures
    - Cloud service requirement changes
    - Impact of regulation and law changes

4.4 Given a scenario, implement account provisioning techniques in a cloud   7
environment to meet security and policy requirements.

- Identification
- Authentication methods
    - Federation
        - Single sign-on
- Authorization methods
    - ACLs
    - Permissions
- Account life cycle
- Account management policy
    - Lockout
    - Password complexity rules
- Automation and orchestration activities
    - User account creation
    - Permission settings
    - Resource access
    - User account removal
    - User account disablement

4.5 Given a scenario, analyze deployment results to confirm they meet the   8
baseline.

- Procedures to confirm results
    - CPU usage
    - RAM usage
    - Storage utilization
    - Patch versions
    - Network utilization
    - Application version
    - Auditing enable
    - Management tool compliance

Exam Objective	Chapter
4.6 Given a specific environment and related data (e.g., performance, capacity, trends), apply appropriate changes to meet expected criteria.	8

- Analyze performance trends
- Refer to baselines
- Refer to SLAs
- Tuning of cloud target objects
  - Compute
  - Network
  - Storage
  - Service/application resources
- Recommend changes to meet expected performance/capacity
  - Scale up/down (vertically)
  - Scale in/out (horizontally)

4.7 Given SLA requirements, determine the appropriate metrics to report.	8

- Chargeback/showback models
  - Reporting based on company policies
  - Reporting based on SLAs
- Dashboard and reporting
  - Elasticity usage
  - Connectivity
  - Latency
  - Capacity
  - Overall utilization
  - Cost
  - Incidents
  - Health
  - System availability
    - Uptime
    - Downtime

5.0 Troubleshooting

Exam Objective	Chapter
5.1 Given a scenario, troubleshoot a deployment issue.	9

- Common issues in the deployments
  - Breakdowns in the workflow
  - Integration issues related to different cloud platforms
  - Resource contention
  - Connectivity issues
  - Cloud service provider outage
  - Licensing issues
  - Template misconfiguration
  - Time synchronization issues
  - Language support
  - Automation issues

5.2 Given a scenario, troubleshoot common capacity issues.	9

- Exceeded cloud capacity boundaries
  - Compute
  - Storage
  - Networking
    - IP address limitations
    - Bandwidth limitations
  - Licensing
  - Variance in number of users
  - API request limit
  - Batch job scheduling issues
- Deviation from original baseline
- Unplanned expansions

5.3 Given a scenario, troubleshoot automation/orchestration issues.	9

- Breakdowns in the workflow
  - Account mismatch issues
  - Change management failure
  - Server name changes
  - IP address changes
  - Location changes
  - Version/feature mismatch
  - Automation tool incompatibility
  - Job validation issue

Exam Objective	Chapter
5.4 Given a scenario, troubleshoot connectivity issues.	10

- Common networking issues
    - Incorrect subnet
    - Incorrect IP address
    - Incorrect gateway
    - Incorrect routing
    - DNS errors
    - QoS issues
    - Misconfigured VLAN or VXLAN
    - Misconfigured firewall rule
    - Insufficient bandwidth
    - Latency
    - Misconfigured MTU/MSS
    - Misconfigured proxy
- Network tool outputs
- Network connectivity tools
    - ping
    - tracert/traceroute
    - telnet
    - netstat
    - nslookup/dig
    - ipconfig/ifconfig
    - route
    - arp
    - ssh
    - tcpdump
- Remote access tools for troubleshooting

| 5.5 Given a scenario, troubleshoot security issues. | 10 |

- Authentication issues
    - Account lockout/expiration
- Authorization issues
- Federation and single sign-on issues
- Certificate expiration
- Certification misconfiguration
- External attacks
- Internal attacks
- Privilege escalation
- Internal role change

Exam Objective	Chapter

- External role change
- Security device failure
- Incorrect hardening settings
- Unencrypted communication
- Unauthorized physical access
- Unencrypted data
- Weak or obsolete security technologies
- Insufficient security controls and processes
- Tunneling or encryption issues

5.6 Given a scenario, explain the troubleshooting methodology.   10

- Always consider corporate policies, procedures and impacts before implementing changes

  Identify the problem

  - Question the user and identify user changes to the computer and perform backups before making changes

  Establish a theory of probable cause (question the obvious)

  - If necessary, conduct internal or external research based on symptoms

  Test the theory to determine cause

  - Once the theory is confirmed, determine the next steps to resolve the problem
  - If the theory is not confirmed, reestablish a new theory or escalate

  Establish a plan of action to resolve the problem and implement the solution

  Verify full system functionality and, if applicable, implement preventive measures

  Document findings, actions, and outcomes

Cloud+ Assessment Test

1. Bob is accessing a self-service portal in the cloud to instantly create additional servers, storage, and database instances for his firms DevOps group. Which of the options offered best describes this operation?

    A. Bursting

    B. Pay-as-you-grow

    C. Multitenancy

    D. On-demand

2. Jillian is working on a project to interconnect her company's private data center to a cloud company that offers e-mail services and another that can provide burstable compute capacity. What type of cloud delivery model is she creating?

    A. Public

    B. Hybrid

    C. Community

    D. Private

3. Carl is learning about how cloud service providers allocate physical resources into a group. These resources are then dynamically associated with cloud services as demand requires. What virtualization technology is this?

    A. On-demand virtualization

    B. Dynamic scaling

    C. Resource pooling

    D. Elasticity

4. Liza is a new Cloud+ architect for BigCo Inc. She is investigating cloud services that provide server hardware, but the operating system is not included. What cloud service is she using?

    A. IaaS

    B. PaaS

    C. SaaS

    D. CaaS

5. Harold is investigating his options to migrate his company's time and attendance application to the cloud. He only wants to be responsible for the application and would prefer that the public cloud company manage all underlying infrastructure and servers that are required to support his application. Harold calls you and asks for assistance in selecting a cloud service model that would meet his requirements. What would you suggest he implement?

    A. IaaS

    B. PaaS

    C. SaaS

    D. CaaS

6. Jane is a Cloud+ architect working on a physical-to-virtual migration to the public cloud. She has matched VM performance levels to her established baselines. She knows that her organization may need to adjust hardware resources in the future. What cloud characteristics can she use to match cloud capacity with future growth? (Choose three.)

A. Elasticity

B. On-demand computing

C. Availability zones

D. Resiliency virtualization

E. Pay-as-you grow

F. Resource pooling

7. Peter is creating a change management document to redeploy applications for a private to public cloud for his employer. When moving to the public cloud, what technologies can he take advantage of to enable cloud operations? (Choose two.)

A. Load balancing

B. Automation

C. Auto-scaling groups

D. Virtualization

8. Dawn is investigating the various cloud service models; she is interested in selecting a community cloud provider that offers a specialized financial reporting application. You are brought in to assist. What type of cloud model would you recommend Dawn investigate to meet her requirements?

A. IaaS

B. PaaS

C. SaaS

D. CaaS

9. Carol is a cloud customer that your consulting company is assisting with their migration. She is asking you about the demarcation point of operations for her public PaaS service. What model defines what you are responsible for and the responsibility of the provider?

A. Availability zones

B. Community

C. Shared responsibility

D. Baselines

10. Jonathan is architecting his client's global public cloud presence for an upcoming e-commerce deployment. You have been brought on to help design the network; he asks about providing local connections in Singapore and Malaysia. What would you suggest he investigate?

A. Regions

B. Auto-scaling groups

C. Availability zones

D. Global DNS affinity

11. Zale is working on a collaborative project that requires the implementation of a large-scale NoSQL database that will access three petabytes of historical data. He needs durable block storage in remote flash arrays. You have been tasked to design the storage connectivity from the database to the stored data. What type of network connection would you recommend for NoSQL read/write access to the arrays?

   A. Block access

   B. Zoning

   C. VMFS

   D. SAN

12. Physical resources are virtualized and presented as resources to virtual machines running on hypervisors. What common resources does the hypervisor consume? (Choose three.)

   A. Bare-metal cores

   B. Virtual RAM

   C. SaaS

   D. Virtual CPUs

   E. RAID

   F. Virtual Storage

13. As a new Cloud+ professional you have been hired by a company that operates its own data center; however, the company is calling it a cloud. What delivery model are you working with?

   A. Hybrid

   B. Public

   C. Private

   D. Community

14. Tim just logged into his cloud management dashboard to check the health monitors of his server fleet. What is the process he completed at login?

   A. Authorization

   B. Accounting

   C. Authentication

   D. Federation

   E. Identity access

15. Martha is studying SAN technologies that use the Fibre Channel protocol and is asking about disk configuration in the remote storage array. She asks you which type of storage she can use on her Linux servers. What storage type can she deploy? (Choose the best answer.)

   A. Meta

   B. Object

C. Block

D. File

16. Patesh is becoming familiar with the interfaces available for his operations team to use to access his hybrid cloud deployment. You have been asked to explain the common types of user-based interfaces available to manage cloud objects. What are the common interfaces you would explain to Patesh? (Choose three.)

   A. Web console

   B. SNMP

   C. API

   D. PaaS

   E. CLI

17. Sabil works for a company that offers cloud services to the railroad industry. All railroads have a similar set of requirements and access the same applications. BigWest Rail has contacted you about becoming a customer and is asking what applications are shared with other rail operators; they also ask what type of cloud model your company offers. What type of cloud is this?

   A. Hybrid

   B. Public

   C. Private

   D. Community

18. Kevin is exploring a durable block storage option that offers high utilization rates. It also needs to support striping that allows a parity bit to be used to reconstruct a volume if a single magnetic disk fails in his array. Which storage type stripes file data and performs a parity check of data over multiple disks that can recover from a single hard disk failure?

   A. RAID 0

   B. RAID 1

   C. RAID 3

   D. RAID 5

19. You are involved in a large-scale migration project that requires moving a Windows OS running on a dual-slot, eight-core server with no hypervisor in a data center to a VMware-based server in the public cloud. What type of migration is this?

   A. vMotion

   B. P2V

   C. Private to public

   D. V2V

   E. Synchronous replication

20. You have been asked by a new customer what type of authentication systems require something you have and also something you know. What type of authentication technology would you recommend?

    A. Single sign-on

    B. Confederations

    C. Active Directory/LDAP

    D. Multifactor

21. Beatriz stops at her bank's ATM on her way home from work. She inserts her card into the ATM and then enters her PIN on the keypad. What type of authentication is she using?

    A. SSO

    B. Two-factor

    C. LDAP

    D. User-based

22. Roman is the cloud administrator for a company that stores object-based data in a hybrid cloud. Because of the sensitivity of the data and various regulatory restrictions on allowing users access to sensitive security data, what type of access control would meet his security policies?

    A. Mandatory access control

    B. Nondiscretionary

    C. Roles

    D. Multifactor

23. William is implementing an access control rollout for a cluster of Windows SQL database servers in a hybrid cloud environment. He has defined the required tasks and then puts users, groups, and servers into this task-based implementation. What type of access control should William deploy?

    A. Mandatory access control

    B. Nondiscretionary

    C. Roles

    D. Multifactor

24. Quentin is a defense contractor investigating server compliance requirements needed to be certified to meet the U.S. Department of Defense security requirements for contractors. What requirement would you recommend he focus on?

    A. FedRAMP

    B. DIACAP

    C. FISMA

    D. Section 405.13 for DoD rule A286

25. Leanna wants to deploy a public cloud service that allows her to retain responsibility only for her applications and require the cloud provider to maintain the underlying operating system and virtualized hardware. Which service model would you recommend she implement?

A. IaaS

B. PaaS

C. SaaS

D. CaaS

26. Robert is configuring a new cloud interconnect to access his locally hosted Active Directory services. He wants to prevent his user base from having fragmented rights and no unified authorization services. You are brought in as a service consultant to assist in optimizing and controlling user access by implementing a technology that will give access to all allowed systems at the time of user authentication. He is implementing the LDAP protocol to enable this service. What type of system are you deploying?

A. Token-based 2FA

B. SSO

C. RSA

D. Nondiscretionary

27. Cathy is preparing her company's migration plan from a private to a hybrid cloud. She wants to outline firewall and DDoS requirements. What document should she create?

A. DIACAP

B. Security policy

C. Service level agreement

D. SOC-2

28. Perry is investigating options for interconnecting a private cloud to a new public cloud region that supports analysis of customer-streamed IoT data. She is planning on implementing a tunnel across the Internet to interconnect the two locations to avoid the high costs of a dedicated interconnection. What transport protocol would you suggest that can offer a secure connection across the unsecure Internet?

A. AES

B. SOC-3

C. IPSec

D. RC5

29. Jarleen is a consultant tasked with migrating Heath Med Records Inc. customer records to a cloud-based service offering a long-term archival system. Which U.S. compliance mandate must her company align with?

A. SOC 3

B. HIPAA

C. MPAA

D. ISA 2701

30. Fluentes is a security consultant for a day trading company that must implement strong encryption of data at rest for their cloud storage tiers. What is the best option that meets most security regulations for the encryption of stored data?

    A. 3DES

    B. RSA

    C. AES-256

    D. Rivest Cipher 5

31. Randy is developing a new application that will be deployed in an IaaS-based public cloud. He builds a test image and deploys a test VM in his private cloud's development zone. When he restarts one of the Linux-based servers, he notices that his storage volume data is missing. What type of storage did he implement? (Choose all that apply.)

    A. Durable

    B. RAID

    C. Ephemeral

    D. Nondurable

    E. Block

    F. Object

32. Matts has finished running some security automation scripts on three newly deployed Linux servers. After applying intrusion detection, virus, and malware protection on the Linux images, he notices an increase in which VM metric on his server management dashboard?

    A. DMA

    B. BIOS

    C. CPU

    D. IPsec

    E. I/O

33. Jillian works in the operations center and is tasked with monitoring security operations. What cloud-based GUI can she use for a real-time overview of security operations?

    A. Puppet automation

    B. Gemalto system

    C. Dashboard

    D. Vendor-based security appliance

34. Larken is reviewing the SLA and statement of responsibility with their community cloud provider PaaS. Who does the responsibility for stored data integrity in the cloud belong to?

    A. Cloud provider

    B. Compliance agency

    C. Cloud customer

    D. Shared responsibility

35. Mindy has been tasked to develop a new QA test logging application but is concerned that the application must pull data from many different cloud locations and devices. What is a good interface for her to use to meet her requirements?

A. Python

B. XML

C. API

D. SNMP

E. TLS

36. What technology was instrumental in the growth of cloud services?

A. XML

B. Python

C. Automation

D. Authentication

E. Scripting

F. Workflow services

G. Encryption

37. Vicky is investigating multiple hacking attempts on her cloud-based e-commerce web servers. She wants to add a front-end security system that can actively deploy countermeasures that shuts down the hacking attempts. What application would you suggest that Vicky deploy?

A. DMZ

B. IDS

C. IPS

D. RAID

E. HIDS

38. What options can you offer your user base for MFA tokens? (Choose two.)

A. Python app

B. Smartphone app

C. Automation systems

D. Key fob

E. Cloud vendor management dashboard

39. Linda works in the IT security group of her firm and has been tasked to investigate options that will allow customers to securely access their personal records stored on the cloud deployment accessed via tablets. What is the most common in-flight e-commerce security posture on the market?

A. MD5

B. SSL/TLS

C. IPsec

D. VPN

40. Your company has purchased a specialized intrusion prevention system that is virtualized and designed for cloud-based network micro-segmentation deployments. When reading the documentation, Siri notices a link to download a Java-based application to monitor and configure the IPS application. What kind of automation system is this?

    A. CLI

    B. GIU

    C. Vendor-based

    D. API

    E. RESTful

41. Name the type of software update that is designed to address a known bug and to bring a system up-to-date with previously released fixes?

    A. Hotfix

    B. Patch

    C. Version update

    D. Rollout

42. Your employer has developed a mission-critical application for the medical industry, and there can be no downtime during maintenance. You have designed a web architecture to take this into account and that allows you to have an exact copy of your production fleet that can be brought online to replace your existing deployment for patching and mainte-nance. What type of model did you implement?

    A. Cluster

    B. DevOps

    C. Blue-green

    D. Rolling

43. Jill is performing a Tuesday night backup of a Tier 2 storage volume that she has already completed a full backup of on Sunday night. She only wants to back up files based on changes of the source data since the last backup. What type of backup is she performing?

    A. Full

    B. Differential

    C. Incremental

    D. Online

44. What virtual machine backup method creates a file-based image of the current state of a VM including the complete operating system and all applications that are stored on it?

    A. Full backup

    B. Snapshot

    C. Clone

    D. Replicate

45. Ronald is a Cloud+ student studying systems that abstract and hide much of the complexity of modern cloud systems. What is he learning about?

    A. Runbooks

    B. Workflow

    C. Orchestration

    D. REST/API

46. Cloud services depend on highly automated operations. What are common automation systems that are used for patch management? (Choose three.)

    A. Chef

    B. Cloud-patch

    C. Ansible

    D. DevOps

    E. Puppet

    F. Cloud Deploy

47. Marlene is updating her horizontally scaled Internet-facing web servers to remediate a critical bug. Her manager has agreed to operate under reduced computing capacity during the process but stipulates that there can be no downtime during the process. What upgrade approach should Marlene perform to meet these requirements?

    A. Orchestration

    B. Rolling

    C. Hotfix

    D. Blue-green

48. What VM backup method can be used to create a master image to be used as a template to create additional systems?

    A. Full backup

    B. Snapshot

    C. Clone

    D. Replicate

49. A new application patch is being validated prior to release to the public. The developers have a release candidate, and the DevOps manager is requesting a report that shows the pass/fail data to verify that the fix does, in fact, resolve the problem. What process is he verifying?

    A. Rollout

    B. Orchestration

    C. Automation

    D. QA

50. Jane has found a table merge issue in her SQL database hosted in a private cloud. While reviewing the log files, the vendor requested she install a software change that is designed for rapid deployment that corrects a specific and critical issue. What are they referring to?

A. Hotfix

B. Patch

C. Version update

D. Rollout

51. To meet regulatory requirements, a medical records company is required to store customer transaction records for seven years. The records will most likely never be accessed after the second year and can be stored offline to reduce expenses. What type of storage should they implement to achieve her goal?

A. File transfer

B. Archive

C. Replication

D. Data store

52. Mark is creating a disaster recovery plan based on directives from his company's executive management team. His company's business is an e-commerce website that sells children's apparel with 85 percent of its revenue received during the holiday season. If there was a severe disruption in operations, the loss of business could put the company's ability to continue as a financially viable operation in peril. Mark is creating a plan that will restore operations in the shortest amount of time possible if there was an outage. What DR model is he implementing?

A. Hot site

B. Active/active

C. Warm site

D. Active/passive

E. Cold site

F. Rollover

53. Ahmed is a cloud+ professional researching data replication options for his MySQL database. For redundancy reasons, he decided to create a backup replica in a different availability zone that could become master should the primary zone go offline. For performance reasons, he has decided to update the replica in near real time after the initial write operation on the primary database. What type of solution is this?

A. Synchronous

B. Asynchronous

C. Volume sync

D. Remote mirroring

E. RAID 5

54. Pierre is deploying a solution that allows data for his e-commerce operations hosted in a public cloud to be reached at remote locations worldwide with local points of presence. He wants to reduce the load on his web servers and reduce the network latency of geographically distant customers. What are these facilities called?

A. Region

B. Edge location

C. Availability zone

D. Replication

55. Melinda is updating her firm's disaster recovery plans, and after receiving direction for his company's board of directors, she has been instructed to create a plan that restores operations within 48 hours of a disaster. What part of the plan should she update with the new requirements?

A. RSO

B. RPO

C. RTO

D. DBO

56. Jillian is a Cloud+ consultant for an auto parts company based in central Michigan. She is putting together a disaster recovery plan that includes a remote backup site that has a SQL server instance running at that location with a synchronously refreshed data replica. Her plan calls for activating all other services in the event of a hurricane causing an outage at her primary data center. What model is Jillian going to deploy to meet the requirements?

A. Hot site

B. Warm site

C. Cold site

D. Active/passive

57. Pete has been busy updating the disaster recovery procedures for his client's business continuity plan. The DR facility will need to be ready with floor space, power, and cooling and have loading docks to unload server and equipment racks to restore service. What type of DR implementation is Pete planning on deploying?

A. Hot site

B. Active/active

C. Warm site

D. Active/passive

E. Cold site

F. Rollover

58. Connie has been directed by her employer's finance department that they cannot afford to lose any more than 30 minutes of data in the case of a database failure or other catastrophic event. Connie has updated her corporate business continuity and disaster recovery plans. What metric did she change?

    A. RSO

    B. RPO

    C. RTO

    D. DBO

59. Will is testing his backup DR site and using his DNS configuration to load balance the primary and backup sites. He wants to verify that the database in the DR facility is updated in real time and remains current with the production replica in the primary data center. What type of updates should he define in his primary data center servers prior to enabling the DNS load balancing?

    A. Synchronous replication

    B. Asynchronous replication

    C. Volume sync

    D. Mirroring

    E. RAID 5

60. Leonard is creating disaster recovery documents for his company's online operations. He is documenting metrics for a measurable SLA that outlines when you can expect operations to be back online and how much data loss can be tolerated when recovering from an outage. Which metrics is he documenting? (Choose all that apply.)

    A. RSO

    B. RTO

    C. RPO

    D. DR

    E. VxRestore

61. The ability to dynamically add additional resources on demand such as storage, CPUs, memory, and even servers is referred to as what?

    A. Bursting

    B. Pooling

    C. Elasticity

    D. Orchestration

62. Margo is reviewing the maintenance responsibilities between her company and its public cloud service provider. She notices that the cloud provider takes responsibility for the operating system, and her company assumes responsibility for all applications and services running on the operating system. What type of service model is she operating under?

    A. IaaS

    B. PaaS

C. SaaS

D. XaaS

63. Akari is developing a cross-cloud provider migration plan as part of her company's business continuity plan. As she assesses the feasibility of migrating applications from one public cloud provider to another, what does she find is the service model that has the most lock-ins and is the most complex to migrate?

   A. IaaS

   B. PaaS

   C. SaaS

   D. XaaS

64. Joe is in the planning stages to make sure that an upcoming company promotion during a major sporting event will not overwhelm his company's cloud-based e-commerce site. He needs to determine his options to add capacity to the web server farm so it can process the anticipated additional workload. You are brought in to consult with him on his options. What do you recommend as possible solutions? (Choose three.)

   A. Vertical scaling

   B. Horizontal scaling

   C. Edge cache

   D. Cloud bursting

   E. Core elasticity

65. Janice manages the MySQL database back end that runs on a multi-CPU instance that has reached 100 percent utilization. The database can run on only a single server. What options does she have to support the requirements of this database?

   A. Horizontal scaling

   B. Vertical scaling

   C. Pooling

   D. Bursting

66. A popular e-commerce site is hosting its public-facing front-end web server fleet in a public cloud. You have been tasked with determining what the normal day-to-day web hit count is so that capacity plans for the upcoming holiday selling season can be assessed. You want to track incoming web requests and graph them against delayed and missed connection counts. What type of data set are you producing?

   A. Metric

   B. Variance

   C. Baseline

   D. Smoothing

67. Eva is the network architect for her company's large cloud deployment; she has interconnected her private cloud to a community cloud in another province. She is investigating using the community cloud to supplement her private cloud workload during end-of-month processing. What operation is she going to perform?

   A. Elasticity

   B. Bursting

   C. Vertical scaling

   D. Auto-scaling

68. A cloud customer web server dashboard shows that CPU utilization on a database server has been consistently at more than 80 percent utilization. The baselines show that 57 percent utilization is normal. What is this called?

   A. Deviation

   B. Variance

   C. Triggers

   D. Baseline imbalance

69. Harold will modify an NACL to modify remote access to a cloud-based HR application. He will be submitting a detailed plan that outlines all details of the planned change. What process is he following?

   A. Cloud automation

   B. Change advisory

   C. Change management

   D. Rollout

70. To increase TipoftheHat.com's security posture, Alice is reviewing user accounts that access the community cloud resources. Alice notices that the summer interns have left to go back to school, but their accounts are still active. She knows they will return over the winter break. What would you suggest Alice do with these accounts?

   A. Do nothing

   B. Delete the accounts

   C. Disable the accounts

   D. Change the resource access definitions

   E. Modify the confederation settings

   F. Change the access control

71. Object tracking can be helpful in identifying which of the following? (Choose three.)

   A. Resiliency

   B. Trends

   C. Metrics

   D. ACLs

   E. Peak usage

   F. Anomalies

72. Capacity and utilization reporting often contains data on which of the following objects? (Choose three.)

   A. CPU

   B. OS version

   C. Volume tier

   D. RAM

   E. Network

73. What does a cloud management system monitor to collect performance metrics?

   A. Database

   B. Server

   C. Hypervisor

   D. Objects

74. Object tracking should be aligned with which of the following?

   A. VPC

   B. SLA

   C. RDP

   D. JSON

75. What is a visual representation of current cloud operations?

   A. Operational matrix

   B. Management console

   C. Dashboard

76. Hana is monitoring performance metrics on a video server; she sees that the server is utilizing 100 percent of the available network bandwidth. What action should she take that will most likely address the problem?

   A. Implement 802.1Q tagging.

   B. Install a second network adapter.

   C. Update the network adapter's firmware.

   D. Install a network coprocessor ASIC.

77. What type of scaling includes adding servers to a pool?

   A. Horizontal

   B. Round robin

   C. Elasticity

   D. Auto-scale

   E. Vertical

78. What type of scaling involves replacing an existing server with another that has more capabilities?

   A. Horizontal

   B. Round robin

   C. Elasticity

   D. Auto-scale

   E. Vertical

79. Ichika is preparing a change management plan to increase the processing abilities of one of her middleware servers. What components can she upgrade to increase server performance? (Choose three.)

   A. CPU

   B. SLA

   C. RAM

   D. Network I/O

   E. ACL

   F. DNS

80. Niko is generating baseline reports for her quarterly review meeting. She is interested in a public cloud application server's memory utilization. Where does she generate these reports?

   A. Hypervisor

   B. Databases

   C. Logging servers

   D. Cloud management and monitoring application

81. SaaS orchestration systems are whose responsibility in the public cloud?

   A. Customer

   B. Provider

   C. Automation vendor

   D. DevOps

82. What type of application commonly uses batch processing?

   A. DNS

   B. NTP

   C. Databases

   D. Middleware

83. Giulia posted a new software update to her company's popular smartphone application. After announcing the release, she has been monitoring her dashboard information and has noticed a large spike in activity. What cloud resource should she focus on?

- **A.** CPU
- **B.** Network bandwidth
- **C.** RAM
- **D.** API
- **E.** Storage

84. Cloud capacity can be measured by comparing current usage to what?

- **A.** Orchestration
- **B.** Automation
- **C.** NTP
- **D.** Baseline
- **E.** APIs

85. Emma is modifying a publicly accessible IP subnet on her company's e-commerce site hosted in a hybrid cloud. After performing address changes for all of his public-facing web servers, she validated the change by connecting from a bastion host located offshore. She was unable to connect to the web servers. What does she need to modify to allow the remote site to connect to the web server?

- **A.** NTP
- **B.** STP
- **C.** DNS
- **D.** API

86. Maria has noticed an increase in the response time of the NoSQL application she runs in her IaaS cloud deployment. When comparing current results against her baseline measurements that she recorded when the database was originally deployed, she verified that there has been a steady increase in the number of read requests. You have been asked to evaluate the baseline variances. Where should you focus your troubleshooting efforts?

- **A.** Memory
- **B.** CPU
- **C.** Storage
- **D.** Networking

87. Derek is monitoring storage volume utilization and is preparing a company change request to add storage capacity. He has decided to automate the volume allocation size. What cloud feature can he take advantage of?

- **A.** SaaS
- **B.** API
- **C.** Elasticity
- **D.** OpenStack

88. What application tracks a process from start to finish?

   A. API

   B. NTP

   C. Workflow

   D. Orchestration

89. Common cloud resources in your deployment that may saturate over time include which of the following? (Choose three.)

   A. RAM

   B. Power

   C. CPU

   D. Storage

   E. Monitoring

   F. IaaS

90. Homer designed an application tier for his company's new e-commerce site. He decided on an IP subnet that uses the /28 IPv4 subnet. He is planning for a maximum of 14 servers. You are brought in as a cloud architect to validate his design. What other devices may be on this subnet other than the servers that would also require IP address assignments? (Choose three.)

   A. SLA

   B. Default gateway

   C. DNS

   D. NTP

   E. API

   F. SNMP

91. Elena manages user accounts for her company's cloud presence. She has a trouble ticket open with Jill to assist her in accessing an SSD storage volume in the San Paulo region of the public cloud. What kind of user issue is she investigating?

   A. Authentication

   B. Authorization

   C. Federation

   D. SSO

92. Emma is unable to reach her Linux-based web server hosted in the Singapore zone of the cloud. She is located in Austin, Texas. What utility can she use to verify the connection path?

   A. traceroute

   B. ipconfig

   C. arp

D. netstat

E. ping

F. tcpdump

G. route print

93. After deploying a new public website, your validation steps ask you to check the domain name to IP address mappings. What utility can you use for validation? (Choose two.)

A. RDP

B. dig

C. SSH

D. nslookup

E. IPsec

F. IPS

94. Nicola is deploying a new fleet of IIS web servers on her IaaS e-commerce site. The company has elected to use a hybrid approach and desires graphical connections to the Windows bastion hosts. What traffic must he permit through the external-facing firewall to the host?

A. SSH

B. RDP

C. DNS

D. IPS

95. Martina is troubleshooting a networking problem and needs to capture network frames being sent and received from the server's network adapter. What utility would she use to collect the traces?

A. dig

B. netstat

C. tcpdump

D. nslookup

96. The remote disaster recovery location follows the warm site model. To configure the network switches, routers, and firewalls remotely, Joyce will need serial port access from her company's operations center. She has 14 serial ports currently available but needs to be prepared for any unplanned expansion requirements during a disaster recover cutover. What device would you recommend she install at the warm site?

A. RDP

B. Telnet

C. IPsec

D. SSH

E. Terminal server

97. The cloud data center is in a large industrial park with no company signage, extensive video cameras in the parking lot, high security fences, and biometrics at the guard shack. What type of security is the provider implementing?

    A. Building

    B. Device

    C. Infrastructure

    D. Tunneling

98. Mergie is documenting different methods that her remote operations center can use to access the Perth fleet of servers operating in a community cloud. Which of the following are not viable methods? (Choose two.)

    A. RDP

    B. Telnet

    C. IDS/IPS

    D. Terminal server

    E. DNS

    F. HTTP

99. Vasile is working a support ticket that shows the connection between the Ames field office and the Kansas City cloud edge location has dropped. She confirms it is a secure Internet-based access solution. What type of connection is this?

    A. Direct peering

    B. IDS

    C. VPN

    D. AES-256

    E. RDP

100. Company users are complaining that they cannot log in to a cloud-based collaboration system. The operations center has been investigating and has, so far, verified that the MFA applications are operational. What user system are they troubleshooting?

    A. Authentication

    B. Authorization

    C. Federation

    D. Kerberos

Answers to Assessment Test

1. D. On-demand cloud computing allows the consumer to dynamically add and change resources with the use of an online portal.

2. B. The interconnection of multiple cloud models is referred to as a hybrid cloud.

3. C. Resource pooling is the allocation of compute resources into a group, or pool, and then these pools are made available to a multitenant cloud environment.

4. A. Infrastructure as a Service offers computing hardware, storage, and networking but not the operating systems or applications.

5. B. Platform as a Service offers computing hardware, storage, networking, and the operating systems but not the applications.

6. A, B, E. Elasticity, on-demand computing, and pay-as-you-grow are all examples of being able to expand cloud compute resources as your needs require.

7. B, D. One of the prime advantages of cloud-based computing and the automation and virtualization it offers in the background is the ability to leverage the rapid provisioning of virtual resources to allow for on-demand computing.

8. C. Software as a Service offers cloud-managed applications as well as the underlying platform and infrastructure support.

9. C. The shared responsibility model outlines what services and portions of the cloud operations the cloud consumer and provider are responsible for.

10. A. Cloud operators segment their operations into regions for customer proximity, regulatory compliance, resiliency, and survivability.

11. D. A storage area network (SAN) is a high-speed network dedicated to storage transfers across a shared network. Block access is not a networking technology. Zoning is for restricting LUNs in a SAN, and VMFS is a VMware filesystem.

12. B, C, E. A hypervisor will virtualize RAM, compute, and storage; the VMs operating on the hypervisor will access these pools.

13. C. A private cloud is used exclusively by a single organization.

14. C. Authentication is the term used to describe the process of determining the identity of a user or device.

15. C. Storage area networks support block-based storage.

16. A, C, E. Application programmable interfaces, command-line interfaces, and GUI-based interfaces are all commonly used tools to migrate, monitor, manage, and troubleshoot cloud-based resources.

17. D. A community cloud is used by companies with similar needs such as railroad companies.

18. D. RAID 5 uses parity information that is striped across multiple drives that allows the drive array to be rebuilt if a single drive in the array fails. The other options do not have parity data.

19. B. When migrating a server that is running on bare metal to a hypervisor-based system, you would be performing a physical-to-virtual migration.

20. D. Multifactor authentication systems use a token generator as something that you have and a PIN/password as something you know.

21. B. Two-factor authentication includes something that you have and something that you know.

22. A. The mandatory access control approach is implemented in high-security environments where access to sensitive data needs to be highly controlled. Using the mandatory access control approach, a user will authenticate, or log into, a system. Based on the user's identity and security levels of the individual, access rights will be determined by comparing that data against the security properties of the system being accessed.

23. C. The question outlines the function of a role-based access control approach.

24. B. The Department of Defense Information Assurance Certification and Accreditation Process (DIACAP) is the process for computer systems' IT security. DIACAP compliance is required to be certified to meet the U.S. Department of Defense security requirements for contractors.

25. B. The Platform as a Service model offers operating system maintenance to be provided by the service provider.

26. B. Single sign-on allows a user to log in one time and be granted access to multiple systems without having to authenticate to each one individually.

27. B. The security policy outlines all aspects of your cloud security posture.

28. C. IPsec implementations are found in routers and firewalls with VPN services to provide a secure connection over an insecure network such as the Internet.

29. B. The Health Insurance Portability and Accountability Act defines the standards for protecting medical data.

30. C. Advanced Encryption Standard is a symmetrical block cipher that has options to use three lengths, including 128, 192, and 256 bits. AES 256 is a very secure standard, and it would take an extremely long time and a lot of processing power to even come close to breaking the code.

31. C, D. Temporary storage volumes that are only in existence when the VM is deployed are referred to as ephemeral or nondurable storage.

32. C. Applying security applications on a virtual server will cause an increase in CPU usage.

33. C. A dashboard is a graphical portal that provides updates and an overview of operations.

34. C. Ultimately the responsibility for data in the cloud belongs to the organization that owns the data.

35. C. An application programming interface (API) offers programmatic access, control, and configuration of a device between different and discrete software components.

36. C. Automation of cloud deployments was instrumental in the growth of cloud-based services.

37. C. Intrusion prevention systems will monitor for malicious activity and actively take countermeasures to eliminate or reduce the effects of the intrusion.

38. B, D. One-time numerical tokens are generated on key fob hardware devices or smartphone soft-token applications.

39. B. SSL/TLS security is the most common remote access encryption technology and is commonly used in browsers and smartphone applications. MD5 is a hash algorithm, and IPsec is a security framework; they do not apply to the question. VPNs are not as common as SSL/TLS for the scenario given.

40. C. Based on the information given, the description is for a vendor-based management application.

41. B. A patch is a piece of software that is intended to update an application, operating system, or any other software-based system to fix or improve its operations.

42. C. Blue-green is a software deployment methodology that uses two configurations for production that are identical to each other. These deployments can alternate between each other, with one being active and the other being inactive.

43. C. Incremental backups are operations based on changes of the source data since the last incremental backup was performed.

44. B. A snapshot is a file-based image of the current state of a VM including the complete operating systems and all applications that are stored on them. The snapshot will record the data on the disk, its current state, and the VM's configuration at that instant in time.

45. C. Orchestration systems enable large-scale cloud deployments by automating operations.

46. A, C, E. Common patch management offerings are Chef, Puppet, and Ansible.

47. B. A rolling configuration will sequentially upgrade the web servers without causing a complete outage and would meet the requirements outlined in the question.

48. C. Cloning takes the master image and clones it to be used as another separate and independent VM. Important components of a server are changed to prevent address conflicts; these include the UUID and MAC addresses of the cloned server.

49. D. The manager is requesting data on the results of the quality assurance testing on the release.

50. A. A hotfix is a software update type that is intended to fix an immediate and specific problem.

51. B. Inactive data moved to a separate storage facility for long-term storage is referred to as archiving.

52. A. The hot site model is the most viable option given the requirements. A hot site is a fully functional backup site that can assume operations immediately should the primary location fail or go offline.

53. B. Asynchronous replication is when data is written to the primary first, and then later a copy is written to the remote site on a scheduled arrangement or in near real time.

54. B. Edge locations are not complete cloud data centers. There are cloud connection points located in major cities and offer local caching of data for reduced response times.

55. C. The recovery time objective is the amount of time a system can be offline during a disaster; it is the amount of time it takes to get a service online and available after a failure.

56. B. A warm site approach to recovering from a primary data center outage is when the remote backup of the site is offline except for critical data storage, which is usually a database.

57. E. A cold site is a backup data center provisioned to take over operations in the event of a primary data center failure, but the servers and infrastructure are not deployed or operational until needed.

58. B. The restore point objective is the point in time that data can be recovered.

59. A. Synchronous replication offerings write data to both the primary storage system and the replica simultaneously to ensure that the remote data is current with local replicas.

60. B, C. The restore point and restore time objectives are the measurements for the amount of data lost and the time needed to get back online after an outage.

61. C. Cloud automation systems offer the ability to dynamically add and remove resources as needed; this is referred to as elasticity.

62. B. With the PaaS model, the cloud provider will maintain the operating system and all supporting infrastructure.

63. C. The higher up the services stack you go, from IaaS to PaaS to SaaS, the more difficult it will be to migrate. With IaaS, most of the cloud operations are under your direct control, which gives you the most flexibility to migrate. However, if the cloud provider controls the application, you may not have many migration options.

64. A, B, D. Cloud computing operates with a utility business model that charges you only for the resources you consume. This model enables you to scale your cloud fleet to meet its current workload and be able to add and remove capacity as needed. There are many options to use elasticity to scale cloud operations including vertical and horizontal scaling and bursting.

65. B. Scaling up, or vertical scaling, will add resources such as CPU instances or more RAM. When you scale up, you are increasing your compute, network, or storage capabilities.

66. C. The establishment of average usage over time is the data that gets collected for a baseline report.

67. B. Cloud bursting allows for adding capacity from another cloud service during times when additional resources are needed.

68. B. The measurement of the difference between a current reading and the baseline value is referred to as the variance.

69. C. Change management includes recording the change, planning for the change, testing the documentation, getting approvals, evaluating and validating, writing instructions for backing out the change if needed, and doing post-change review if desired.

70. C. The ability to disable an account can be helpful in situations where the account will need to be re-activated at a future date and does not need to be deleted.

71. B, E, F. Trends, usage, and deficiencies are all management report outputs that can be identified using object tracking.

72. A, D, E. CPU, RAM, and network utilization are all important objects to manage for capacity and utilization tracking. Storage volume tiers and OS versions do not apply to this scenario.

73. D. Objects are queried to gather metric data.

74. B. Tracking object performance data should match with the guaranteed levels outlined in the service level agreement.

75. C. A dashboard is a configurable graphical representation of current operational data.

76. B. If a server is using all of its network bandwidth, then the most logical solution is to increase the network adapters' bandwidth or add a second adapter and create a teaming configuration.

77. A. Horizontal scaling is the process of adding servers to a pool for increased capacity. Round robin is a load-balancing metric and does not apply. Elasticity is the ability to add and remove resources, auto-scaling is the automated process of adding and removing capacity, and vertical scaling is expanding a server.

78. E. Vertical scaling is the process of upgrading or replacing a server with one that has greater capabilities.

79. A, C, D. Server performance can be increased by adding CPU processing, memory, and network capacity. SLA, ACL, and DNS are not related to increasing server capacity.

80. D. Cloud reports are formatted collections of data contained in the management or monitoring applications.

81. B. The cloud service provider owns its automation and orchestration systems, and they cannot be directly accessed by the customer.

82. C. It is common for batch processing to be performed on database applications.

83. B. A large number of users downloading a new application would cause an increase in network bandwidth usage.

84. D. A baseline measurement is used as a reference to determine cloud capacity increases and decreases.

85. C. The Domain Name System records need to be changed to reflect the new IP address mapped to the domain name.

86. C. Databases read and write requests utilize storage I/O and should be the focus for troubleshooting.

87. C. Elasticity allows for cloud services to expand and contract based on actual usage and would be applicable to increasing storage capacity.

88. C. Workflow applications track a process from start to finish and sequence the applications that are required to complete the process.

89. A, C, D. Resources such as the amount of RAM needed, CPU cycles, and storage capacity are common systems that may become saturated as your cloud compute requirements grow.

90. B, C, D. In addition to the web servers, IP addresses may be required for the NTP and DNS services and the default gateway.

91. B. The question is asking about being able to access a specific cloud service. This would concern Jill having authorization to access the storage volume. Authentication and SSO are login systems and not rights to services. A federation links user databases.

92. A. The tracert and traceroute utilities are useful for network path troubleshooting. This utility shows the routed path a packet of data takes from source to destination. You can use it to determine whether routing is working as expected or whether there is a route failure in the path. The other options are all incorrect because they do not provide network path data.

93. B, D. The Windows command-line utility nslookup resolves domain names to IP addressing. The Linux equivalent is the dig utility. The other answers offered are not valid for the solution required in the question.

94. B. The Windows Remote Desktop Protocol allows for remote connections to a Windows graphical user desktop.

95. C. The tcpdump utility allows a Linux system to capture live network traffic and is useful in monitoring and troubleshooting. Think of tcpdump as a command-line network analyzer. dig and nslookup show DNS resolution but do not display the actual packets going across the wire. netstat shows connection information and is not DNS related.

96. E. In a data center, terminal servers are deployed and have several serial ports, each cabled to a console port on a device that is being managed. This allows you to make an SSH or a Telnet connection to the terminal server and then use the serial interfaces to access the console ports on the devices you want to connect to. The other options given do not provide serial port connections.

97. C. Infrastructure security is the hardening of the facility and includes the steps outlined in the question including nondescript facilities, video surveillance, and biometric access.

98. C, E. Common remote access tools include RDP, SSH, and terminal servers. IDSs/IPSs are for intrusion detection, and DNS is for domain name to IP address mappings and is not a utility for remote access.

99. C. A secure Internet-based connection would be a VPN.

100. A. Logging into systems is referred to as authentication. Also, the question references multifactor authentication (MFA) as part of the system.

Chapter

1

An Introduction to Cloud Computing Configurations and Deployments

THE FOLLOWING COMPTIA CLOUD+ EXAM OBJECTIVES ARE COVERED IN THIS CHAPTER:

✓ **1.1 Given a scenario, analyze system requirements to ensure successful system deployment.**

- Appropriate commands, structure, tools, and automation/orchestration as needed
- Platforms and applications
- Interaction of cloud components and services
  - Network components
  - Application components
  - Storage components
  - Compute components
  - Security components
- Interaction of non-cloud components and services
- Baselines
- Target hosts
- Existing systems
- Cloud architecture
- Cloud elements/target objects

✓ **1.3 Given a scenario, analyze system requirements to determine if a given testing plan is appropriate.**

- Underlying environment considerations included in the testing plan

- Shared components
  - Storage
  - Compute
  - Network
- Production vs. development vs. QA
- Sizing
- Performance
- High availability
- Connectivity
- Data integrity
- Proper function
- Replication
- Load balancing
- Automation/orchestration
- Testing techniques
  - Vulnerability testing
  - Penetration testing
  - Load testing

✓ **1.4 Given a scenario, analyze testing results to determine if the testing was successful in relation to given system requirements.**

- Consider success factor indicators of the testing environment
  - Sizing
  - Performance
  - Availability
  - Connectivity
  - Data integrity
  - Proper functionality
- Document results
- Baseline comparisons
- SLA comparisons
- Cloud performance fluctuation variables

Introducing Cloud Computing

You will begin your Cloud+ journey with a general overview of cloud computing. With a strong understanding of cloud terminology and architectures, you will have a good base to understand the details of the cloud, which in turn means you'll be better prepared for the Cloud+ exam and be effective when deploying and supporting cloud deployments.

Cloud computing is essentially outsourcing *data center* operations, applications, or a section of operations to a provider of computing resources often called a *cloud company* or cloud *service provider.* The *consumer* of the cloud services pays either monthly or by the amount of service used. You will explore many models and types of cloud computing in this chapter and throughout this study guide.

This book will be referencing the National Institute of Standards (*NIST*) SP 800-145 as the main source of cloud computing definitions. NIST defines cloud computing as follows: CLOUD COMPUTING DEFINITION:

> ...a model for enabling convenient, on-demand network access to a shared pool of configurable computing resources (e.g., networks, servers, storage, applications, and services) that can be rapidly provisioned and released with minimal management effort or service provider interaction. This cloud model is composed of five essential characteristics, three service models, and four deployment models.

In this study guide, you will take a close look at all aspects of cloud computing as you progress on your journey to obtaining the Cloud+ certification. As an analogy to cloud computing, think of the services you get in your home through *utilities* such as the electricity and water service. You probably are not involved in the details of how these services are created and delivered; you just want the final product and to pay for what you use. Traditionally, computing did not follow this model. Instead, a company or individual would purchase all the hardware and software necessary to meet their needs. Organizations had to purchase the most up-to-date systems because the investment was high, and they couldn't always afford newer models. For large companies, this would be an even bigger capital investment because they needed to maintain a staff of specialized engineers to operate and maintain the systems. Also, the solution needed to have the added capacity to grow and to handle peak processing loads even if not being used often. Special rooms were needed to host the equipment and to power and cool the data center servers. Security of the data and access to the facilities had to be stringently enforced and constantly upgraded to guard against the constantly changing security threats to data and systems.

Cloud computing follows the utilities model where a provider sells computing resources using an as-needed or as-consumed model. This allows companies and individuals to pay for only what they use and has many additional advantages that you will explore throughout this book.

The market and adoption of the cloud computing business has exploded worldwide; it has been adopted by mainstream companies by moving from early adopters to general acceptance in the marketplace today. While there are many statistics and measurements of the size of the cloud services market, they tend to vary widely; however, it is generally agreed upon that the market has been growing between 15 and 30 percent annually worldwide. There are many estimates saying the total cloud market worldwide will be more than $300 billion by the year 2020.

What is clear is that the economics and business advantages of cloud computing are compelling companies to move more and more applications to the cloud, fueling additional growth well into the future.

There are many advantages to moving to the cloud, but three stand out as compelling business and operations alternatives to hosting computing resources internally in a privately owned data center.

- In the past when computing resources were initially needed, there was often a long delay of procuring, installing, and configuring all of the pieces needed to host an application. With a cloud solution, the equipment is already running in a cloud provider's data center, and you can begin using the service in record time, often as short as a few minutes.

- From a financial perspective, a company's expenditures can be reduced as cloud computing avoids the large up-front costs of purchasing the needed computing equipment and ongoing support expenses associated with maintaining your own computing environment. Cloud computing, with its pay-as-you-go billing model, frees up a company's cash flow to be used for other needs within a company.

- As capacity is reached, a cloud computing model can expand almost immediately as compared to a corporate data center, where long delays are often experienced because of the need to procure, install, and configure the new equipment.

In-house computing requires a data center full of the needed computing gear to support the company's operations. Engineers are needed to tend to the operating systems, applications, storage, and networks. As illustrated in Figure 1.1, all computing is owned and operated by a single corporate entity.

FIGURE 1.1 In-house computing

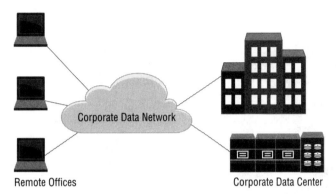

When moving to the cloud, the data center operations are no longer owned by the company and are outsourced to a cloud service provider that can reach economies of scale by sharing resources with many companies, as shown in Figure 1.2.

FIGURE 1.2 Cloud computing model

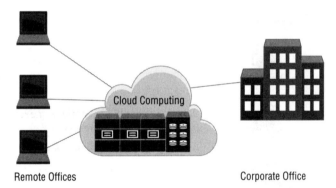

In the past, computing was the realm of large *mainframe computers* with a staff of highly specialized engineers and teams of programmers and administrators to manage and run the operations. Figure 1.3 shows a typical mainframe architecture. Mainframe computing was a highly capital-intensive operation that was needed to supply computing resources to a corporation. As we evolved, the client-server architecture shown in Figure 1.4 became prevalent, and we saw the rise in departmental computing that was distributed throughout a company's operations.

FIGURE 1.3   Mainframe computing

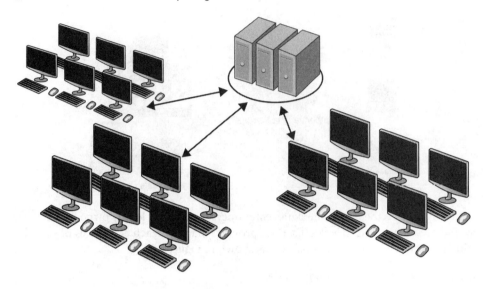

FIGURE 1.4   Client-server computing

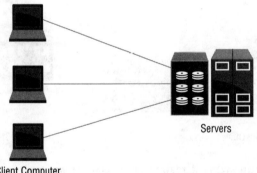

Servers

Client Computer

Today the *virtualization* of hardware resources has exploded to fully utilize the processing capabilities of a server and reduce power consumption, cooling, and the footprint in data centers. This is illustrated in Figure 1.5, where many virtual software machines are sharing common hardware platforms. Also, many companies are now hosting their servers in rented data center space owned and managed by companies specializing in *co-location* facilities.

FIGURE 1.5   Virtualized computing

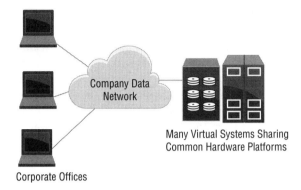

Corporate Offices

Many Virtual Systems Sharing
Common Hardware Platforms

As current trends are showing, the future rests with cloud computing and the computing as a utility-like service model (see Figure 1.6). The cloud will continue to grow and mature, as you will see as you pursue your Cloud+ certification. The cloud is instrumental in supporting many new applications and devices such as smartphones, tablets, and other portable electronics. The cloud supports instant access in an always-on environment.

FIGURE 1.6   Cloud computing

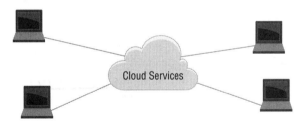

Multiple Customers Accessing Cloud Computing Services

Cloud Service Models

Cloud service models are characterized by the term *as a service* and are accessed by many types of devices, including web browsers, thin clients, and mobile devices. There are three primary service types, with many others being created all the time. Software as a Service (*SaaS*), Infrastructure as a Service (*IaaS*), and Platform as a Service (*PaaS*) are the core service offerings. Many cloud service providers offer more descriptive terms in their marketing and sales offerings, including Communications as a Service (*CaaS*), Anything as a Service (*XaaS*), Desktop as a Service (*DaaS*), and Business Process as a Service (*BPaaS*), to name a few. However, all of these newer names fit into either SaaS, IaaS, or PaaS.

Software as a Service

NIST offers standard definitions of cloud computing terms and describes Software as a Service as follows:

> The capability provided to the consumer is to use the provider's applications running on a cloud infrastructure. The applications are accessible from various client devices through a thin client interface such as a Web browser (e.g., Web-based e-mail), or a program interface. The consumer does not manage or control the underlying cloud infrastructure including network, servers, operating systems, storage, or even individual application capabilities, with the possible exception of limited user-specific application configuration settings.

The Software as a Service model is where the customer of the service accesses the application software that is owned and controlled by the cloud company, which has complete responsibility for the management and support of the application, as shown in Figure 1.7. All networking, processing, storage, and applications are offered as a service in this model. Business applications are good examples of SaaS and can include customer relationship management, enterprise resource planning, human resources, payroll, and software development applications. Hosted applications such as e-mail or calendars that are accessible from a browser are examples of SaaS.

FIGURE 1.7   SaaS

Infrastructure as a Service

Infrastructure as a Service is described by NIST as follows:

> The capability provided to the consumer is to provision processing, storage, networks, and other fundamental computing resources where the consumer is able to deploy and run arbitrary software, which can include operating systems and applications. The consumer does not manage or

control the underlying cloud infrastructure but has control over operating systems, storage, deployed applications; and possibly limited control of select networking components (e.g., host firewalls).

Infrastructure a Service offers the customer the most flexibility of any of the e-service models. IaaS offers complete control over the base offerings, such as storage and networking and, more importantly, software and applications. The cloud consumer purchases a basic computing hardware platform and can build their solutions on top of that. IaaS (shown in Figure 1.8) allows the company's data center equipment to be replaced by the cloud equivalent but retains the ability to build software infrastructure on top of the hardware as can be done in a private data center.

FIGURE 1.8   IaaS

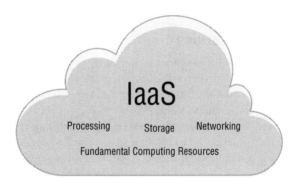

Platform as a Service

Using NIST as the standard reference for cloud definitions, you will learn that Platform as a Service is:

> The capability provided to the consumer is to deploy onto the cloud infrastructure consumer-created or -acquired applications created using programming languages and tools supported by the provider. The consumer does not manage or control the underlying cloud infrastructure including network, servers, operating systems, or storage, but has control over the deployed applications and possibly application hosting environment configurations.

Platform as a Service offers the compute and operating systems as a service and allows customers to install their applications on the cloud platform, as shown in Figure 1.9. The cloud provider takes responsibility up to the operating system level, including all hardware and OS software. The consumer can deploy their applications quickly without having to purchase and install their own servers and associated equipment. This allows for the rapid deployment of applications.

FIGURE 1.9   PaaS

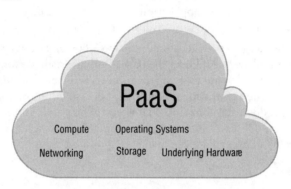

Communications as a Service

Communications as a Service includes hosted voice, video conferencing, instant messaging, e-mail, collaboration, and all other communication services that are hosted in the cloud. These outsourced corporate communication services can support on-premise or mobile users accessing the applications hosted in the cloud.

The service allows even small to medium-sized businesses to implement advanced technologies at a reasonable metered cost. New features can be quickly implemented, and there is no need for a staff to manage these communication services since the CaaS cloud provider takes responsibility. Another common term for this service is Unified Communications as a Service (*UCaaS*).

Anything as a Service

Anything as a Service (XaaS) could best be described as offering complete IT services as a package. Anything as a Service is the combination of the services described in this section. It is a broad term that is a catchall of the various service offerings.

Desktop as a Service

Desktop as a Service supports a virtual desktop that is hosted in the cloud and accessed by desktop computers, laptops, tablets, and phones as well as any thin client solution. This solution is sometimes called virtual desktop infrastructure (*VDI*). All desktop applications are hosted in the cloud and can consist of any type of application such as spreadsheets, word processing, and any other common application. The DaaS provider manages all maintenance and configurations as well as licensing and version updates. DaaS virtualizes a Windows interface, for example, and delivers it over the Internet from a hosted DaaS cloud provider.

Business Process as a Service

Business Process as a Service is a specialized area that outsources many of a company's day-to-day operations such as inventory, shipping, supply chain, finance, and many other services to the cloud. BPaaS is similar to SaaS except it focuses specifically on applications that support a company's business operations. This allows for small and medium-sized businesses to access sometimes very expensive applications from a BPaaS service provider that pools its resources and allows for economies of scale in providing these services.

Cloud Reference Designs and Delivery Models

To establish a good baseline to help people understand how cloud computing is structured, the industry has created what is commonly called *reference designs* and *delivery models*. These models help to differentiate between cloud offerings in the marketplace. By understanding the types of models, you can get the big-picture overview of the overall scope of cloud computing.

This section will introduce the cloud models, and then in Chapter 2, I will expand on each one. These are the four primary cloud delivery models.

- Public — INTERNET
- Private — INTRANET
- Community — XTRX NET - FIREWALL PORTION OF NETWORK; SELECTIVE BUSINESS HAS ACCESS
- Hybrid — 2 OR MORE OF ABOVE

The primary focus of the Cloud+ certification is the public cloud, which is the most common delivery model deployed. The public cloud is defined as infrastructure designed for use by public consumers. This is the utility-based pay-as-you-go service where the customer uses external, or public, compute resources. Figure 1.10 illustrates a basic public cloud deployment.

FIGURE 1.10 Public cloud

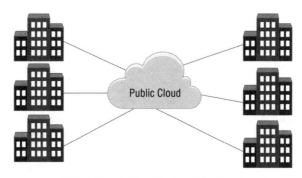

Multiple Organizations Sharing a Cloud Service

A *private cloud* can be thought of as the traditional corporate data center with a new name applied to it to keep up with modern times. It is for the exclusive use of a single organization but may be used by many units or entities inside a company. Figure 1.11 illustrates a basic private cloud deployment.

FIGURE 1.11   Private cloud

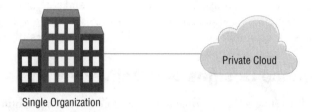

Single Organization

Community clouds are offered for a specific community of interest and shared by companies with similar requirements for regulatory compliance, security, or policy. Examples may be community cloud sites deployed for medical, financial, or e-commerce sites that all share common use case architectures. Figure 1.12 shows an example of a common community cloud deployments.

FIGURE 1.12   Community cloud

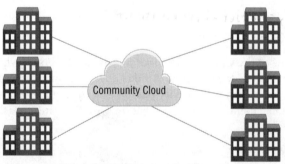

Healthcare, Banking, E-Commerce, Nonprofits,
or Any Other Organizations with Similar Requirements

As you will learn in your cloud studies, there are often many gray or in-between areas to contend with. This is the case with delivery models where many clouds are interconnected by companies to meet their requirements. For example, a corporation may use a public cloud to augment its internal or private cloud operations. A dentist's office may use the public cloud for its compute requirements and also connect to a community cloud shared by other dentists to access a specific dental application. Figure 1.13 shows examples of hybrid computing.

Finally, to be complete, I'll explain the differences between on-premise and off-premise hosting. *On-premise* hosting describes creating and managing your own cloud service in-house in a private enterprise data center. This type of approach can be found in large enterprise environments where control of the operations and data is required to be within corporate data centers.

Off-premise is a hosting service that is located remotely from a company's data center and is usually in a cloud service company's data center.

FIGURE 1.13　Hybrid cloud

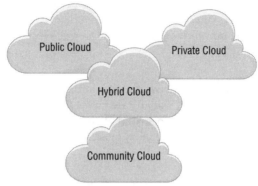

Combination of Cloud Services

BURSTING = LOAD BALANCING WITHIN PUBLIC, PRIVATE, COMMUNITY, HYBRID

Introducing Cloud Components

The cloud can be viewed as any other modern data center with the primary differentiator being that cloud deployments make heavy use of on-demand self-service provisioning, broad network access, resource pooling, rapid elasticity, virtualization, and a measured or pay-as-you-go pricing model. In this section, we will discuss some common cloud components.

Applications

The term *application* is broad but in this context is used to signify user applications, including databases, web servers, e-mail, big data, and other common business software applications.

Automation

Automation plays a critical role in modern cloud services. Automation software systems operate in a cloud provider's data center that automates the deployment and monitoring of cloud offerings.

Everything from network, storage, and compute can be virtualized and automated. This makes rapid deployment possible and enables users to have control over their cloud usage.

Computing

The compute resources are the actual central processing of data and applications on either a physical or virtualized server running a variety of operating systems.

Networking

Network cloud services include traditional switching and routing as well as services such as load balancing, DNS, DHCP, and virtual private networks.

Security

Just as security is a critical component in private and corporate data centers, so is it in the cloud. Cloud service providers offer many security services including firewalls, access control, intrusion detection and prevention systems, and encryption services.

Storage

Large storage arrays and storage area networks exist in the cloud for use by cloud service consumers. Common storage media are solid-state drives (SSDs) and magnetic physical drives. Storage systems include object, block, and file-based systems. Some storage is optimized for high availability and durability, and others are less expensive and offer long-term, or archival, storage.

Virtualization

Virtualization is the ability to take physical data center resources such as RAM, CPU, storage, and networking and create a software representation of those resources in large-scale cloud offerings. These virtualized resources are consumed by a hypervisor for allocation to virtualized computers, or virtual machines as they are commonly called, for the dynamic elasticity of modern cloud offerings.

Connecting the Cloud to the Outside World

Ubiquitous access refers to the ability to access cloud resources from anywhere in the network from a variety of devices such as laptops, tables, smartphones, and thin or thick clients. Access can be over a corporate network sitting behind a firewall or public over the Internet.

Initial Documentation

For a successful migration to the cloud to take place, there is a large amount of up-front data collection and documentation that must take place. In other words, to move to the cloud, you must have a very clear and detailed understanding of what it is that you are actually moving. This means that your documentation must be updated (or created) to reflect all aspects of your operations. To perform a migration, you must know exactly which applications you are running, their dependencies, storage, network, operating system, processing, memory, and any other relevant requirements. The more detailed assessment of your current operations, the greater success you will have when moving your operations to a cloud-based model.

Selecting Cloud Compute Resources

In an previous section, I discussed the physical or hardware resources that are installed onto the actual hardware or *bare-metal* server. At the hypervisor level, these resources are pooled together and shared by the virtual machines (VMs) running on the server. In this section, you will take a closer look at what all of this means and go into some detail on how a virtual machine will use these pooled resources.

Guest virtual machines need to be designed based on their intended role. For example, if the VM is going to be used to host a database, care should be given to make sure that there is ample I/O and low latency for storage access and that there is enough processing and memory allocated to ensure the proper level of performance expected. If the virtual machine is to support a web server, then an adequate amount of LAN capacity needs to be taken into consideration.

Validating and Preparing for the Move to the Cloud

To perform a successful migration to the cloud, your company must undertake a lot of background data gathering, testing, validation, and much more. It is important to bring together all of the interested parties and stakeholders when preparing for a move to the cloud. The traditional IT groups such as development, operations, OSs, storage, networking, and security will be integral parts of the migration teams. Others, such as finance, will need to be involved as cloud computing can significantly change the cost and accounting models of a company.

If the company does not have the in-house expertise with cloud migrations, it may be advised to enlist the skills of companies specializing in assisting companies moving to the cloud. Also, especially with larger projects, a project manager should be assigned to track and manage the undertaking.

Once your needs have been defined, you should have an understanding of what your cloud requirements will be. Your needs may fit the community, public, private, or hybrid models. Do you need software as a service where the cloud provider assumes responsibility, or is your company taking responsibility with either the IaaS or PaaS model? With this information, you can evaluate the many different cloud company's service offerings in the marketplace.

A common practice is to determine what less critical or low-risk applications could be good candidates to move to the cloud. These applications can be used as a validation or proof-of-concept project for your company.

As part of the preparation, keep the finance group involved from the start of the project. IT expenses and budgeting often are a significant expense for any company, from the smallest local mom-and-pop shop to multibillion conglomerates. The cloud computing pay-as-you-go utility cost models shift the expenses away from the large up-front capital expenditures of equipment, services, and software. Cloud computing requires little, if any, up-front capital costs, and costs are operational based on usage.

What Is the Architecture?

When the initial assessments are completed on your existing operations, you should have a clear insight into your operations and documentation of what you are starting your project with. In Chapter 2, we will go into detail on migrations, but in this introductory chapter it is important that you understand the big picture of cloud computing and operations.

Based on your criteria, your project team must determine the models that best fit your organization's needs. These include, as we just discussed, the cloud service models and architectures.

Choosing Elements and Objects in the Cloud

Identify what services and capabilities are available in the cloud that fit your needs and requirements as part of the migration planning process. As service providers have expanded their offerings and capabilities, understanding all of your options has become almost overwhelming. Some of the largest public cloud companies have more than 1,000 objects and services to choose from, with more being announced and added every week.

Cloud elements and objects include the basics such as which operating systems to use. Because of the architecture and scaling of the virtual servers, you can choose from an extensive list of options including CPU, memory, storage, storage I/O, co-processing and video processing options, and network I/O. There are network options to choose from including load balancing, Domain Name System (DNS) services, routing, subnetting, network address translation (NAT), and many others. Most cloud companies have storage options that will meet every requirement you may have, including regulatory and corporate mandates.

Applications offered include managed database services, messaging, programming, and development applications. I could write a whole book on all of the objects available in service offerings and could still not be able to keep up with the rapid innovation and product rollouts.

Creating and Validating a Cloud Deployment

In this section, I will go deeper into the technology architectures and processes that you will find in the world of cloud computing. It is important to see how much of an effect virtualization has had in the creation of cloud computing and to understand the process of taking physical hardware resources, virtualizing them, and then assigning these resources to systems and services running in the virtualized data center.

The Cloud Shared Resource Pooling Model

In this section, you will be introduced to resource pooling and learn what this means in the virtualized world of the cloud.

Resource pooling is when the cloud service provider allocates resources into a group, or pool, and then these pools are made available to a multitenant cloud environment. The resources are then dynamically allocated and reallocated as the demand requires. Resource pooling hides the physical hardware from the virtual machines and allows for many tenants to share resources such as storage, processors, RAM, and networks to allow for the economies of cloud computing.

The hypervisor will pool the resources and make them available to the VMs for consumption; Figure 1.14 shows this relationship between the virtual machines and the hardware resources.

FIGURE 1.14   Shared resource pooling

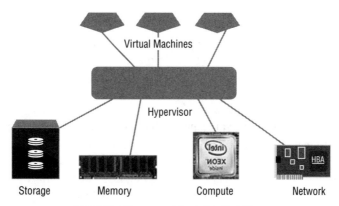

Virtual Machines

Hypervisor

Storage   Memory   Compute   Network

Virtual Host Resources Allocated to the VMs

When resources are placed into pools, these pools can be used by cloud consumers to dynamically allocate and consume resources on an as-needed basis. This is an advantage over using physical servers where there is a finite number of resources available.

The pools will contain resources as we have discussed throughout this chapter and provide rapid deployment or elasticity as required by the virtual machines. Changes to levels of service can be rapidly implemented as required to meet business needs by using the resources available in the pools on each server.

Compute Pools

Just as a physical server running an operating system uses the processing power of the CPU installed on its motherboard, so too does a VM need to consume processing power. The difference is that the hypervisor will virtualize the physical CPU into *compute pools*, or, more commonly, *virtual CPUs*, and the VMs running on the hypervisor will use these virtual CPUs for processing. The concept of a virtualized CPU allows for VMs to be assigned or allocated CPUs for use that are not physical. The virtualization function is the role of the hypervisor. Pools of CPUs are created using administrative controls, and these pools are used, or consumed, by the virtual machines. Generally, when a VM is created, the resources will be defined that will determine how much CPU, RAM, storage, and LAN capacity it will consume. These allocations can be dynamically expanded up to the hard quota limits based on the cloud provider's offerings.

CPU *affinity* is the ability to assign a processing thread to a core instead of having the hypervisor dynamically allocate it. A VM can have CPU affinity enabled, and when a processing thread is received by the hypervisor, it will be assigned to the CPU it originally ran on. CPU affinity can sometimes increase performance if remnants of the previous process are still in the CPU that will allow for efficiencies in cache hits.

However, affinity can and often does result in suboptimal allocation of compute resources. A particular CPU assigned to a VM can have a very high utilization rate while another CPU might be sitting idle; affinity will override the hypervisor's CPU selection algorithms and be forced to use the saturated CPU instead of the underutilized one. It is often recommended by hypervisor companies to disable this feature and allow the hypervisor to assign processing threads based on its knowledge of physical CPU utilization rates.

Memory Pools

Memory virtualization and its allocations to the virtual machines use the same concepts that I discussed earlier with virtualizing CPUs. There is a total and finite amount of RAM installed in the bare-metal or physical server. This RAM is then virtualized by the hypervisor software into *memory pools* and allocated to virtual machines. It is the same concept as when I discussed allocation with processing resources; you can assign a base amount to RAM per virtual machine and dynamically increase the memory available to the VM based on the cloud provider's offerings. When the VM's operating system consumes all the memory available, it will begin to utilize storage for its operations. This *swap file*, as it is called, will be used in place of RAM for its operation.

When configuring a VM, it is important to consider that storage space must be allocated for the swap file and that the storage latency of the swap file will have a negative impact on the performance of the server.

Network Pools

Network resources and services also become virtualized and allocated as pooled resources. A typical server in the cloud data center will be connected to an external LAN switch with multiple Ethernet LAN interfaces. These interfaces are grouped together or aggregated into channel groups for additional throughput and fault tolerance. The LAN interfaces in the server are connected to a *virtual switch* running as a software application on the hypervisor. Each VM will have one or more connections to this virtual switch using its *virtual network interface card (vNIC)*. The LAN bandwidth and capacity are then allocated to each VM as was done with the processing, memory, and storage discussed earlier. By using multiple physical NIC connections to multiple external switches, the network can be designed to offer a highly fault-tolerant operation. However, since the available amount of LAN bandwidth is a finite resource just like the other resources on the server, quotas must be allocated to each virtual machine, as you will learn about in the next section.

Storage Pools

In a cloud or enterprise computing environment, the storage systems are external from the servers themselves. Each server will usually not have a large array of hard or solid-state drives installed on it for use by the VMs running on that server; in fact, many servers will contain no hard drives at all.

Instead, large storage systems are external to the servers and connected over a storage area network. These storage resources can be grouped together into *storage pools* and allocated to VMs as locally attached storage. The design of the SAN and storage arrays is critical for server and application performance. If there is high read and write latency on the drives or contention over the storage network, then performance will suffer. To alleviate the performance issues, it is critical that the cloud provider use enterprise-grade storage systems with high disk RPM rates, fast I/O interconnections, ample bandwidth to the storage controller, and SAN interfaces that are fast enough to handle the anticipated storage traffic load across the network.

Storage resources are also allocated based on the requirements of the guest operating systems.

When storage is remote from the virtual machines they support, you can move the VMs from one hypervisor to another both inside a cloud data center or even between data centers. The VM will move and continue to access its storage over the storage network. This can even be accomplished with stateful moves where an application on a VM will continue to operate even as it is being moved between physical servers. Centralized storage is an enabler of this technology and is useful for maintenance, cloud bursting, fault tolerance, and disaster recovery purposes.

Organizational Uses of the Cloud

While there are an almost limitless number of uses for cloud-based computing, many are readily apparent, and with the rapid pace of innovation, new applications and uses for cloud computing are constantly being introduced. The innovation is so fast and relentless that it is often called "drinking water from the firehose"! However, you can take a step back and look at the bigger picture of the development and operations of cloud-based operations. One effective way is to look at the life cycle of deployed applications and services from the initial development to the rollout "go live" process to the ongoing maintenance of your operations.

It is common practice and strongly encouraged to separate these operations into isolated sections of the cloud to prevent interference between development, operations, and quality assurance networks. These life cycles can be broken down into the categories of development, production, and quality assurance.

Development Networks

The *development network* is used in the creation and testing of new cloud-based services and is primarily used by software programmers and DevOps groups in the creation of new applications and services.

Production Networks

Production networks are the live and in-use applications that are usually public-facing in the cloud.

Quality Assurance Networks = Audits or Compliance

Quality assurance networks are for the ongoing offline maintenance networks used for the testing of your company's applications and software systems.

Scaling and Architecting Cloud Systems Based on Requirements

One of the prime advantages of cloud-based computing and the automation and virtualization that is operating in the background is the ability to leverage the rapid provisioning of virtual resources to allow for *on-demand computing*. This allows you to deploy and pay for the computing capacity that you are actually using and not have to absorb the costs of servers sitting on standby to address any bursts or cyclical higher compute requirements such as end-of-month processing or holiday sales loads if, for example, you are a retailer.

Clouds are often designed with a feature that enables the automatic scaling of pooled resources based on demand and then, when the demand is diminished, scales back down to the required compute resources to match your current load requirements. This pay-as-you-go or pay-for-what-you-use model creates fantastic economics and leverages the on-demand capabilities of the cloud.

For example, let's look at a small sporting goods retailer that uses a public cloud provider to host its e-commerce website. During normal operations, it deploys and pays for three web servers from its public cloud service provider. This works well because the retailer can match the load on the website with the needed amount of computing, memory, storage, and other backend resources in the cloud. This pay-as-you-go model is cost efficient because it does not have to expend money to purchase the hardware for any peak loads or future growth; it will just provision more capacity when needed from the cloud provider. With automation and rapid provisioning, adding capacity can be as simple as a few clicks in a console, and the resources are immediately deployed!

Taking this a step further, you can use the automation capabilities offered to have resources added and removed as needed based on current load. Getting back to our friends at the sporting goods retailer, they may decide to run a TV commercial on a Saturday afternoon televised game. When the viewers watch the commercial on television, the company notices a huge spike of users on their website and a heavy increase of online orders. In a static e-commerce web platform, the web servers and other associated backend applications and database servers could not be expanded as they are affixed assets and may, in a worst-case scenario, slow down or crash. With cloud automation, you can define ahead of time autoscaling groups that will see the increase in load and incrementally add servers as needed. The management applications will also notice when the workload drops and automatically remove the servers to reduce cloud compute capacity to match the lower workload. The beauty of this is that the company only has to pay for the additional computing resources during the time of peak usage, and then they are no longer being billed when the usage drops back down to its normal workload.

Understanding Cloud Performance Metrics

Cloud performance encompasses all of the individual capabilities of the various components as well as how they interoperate. The performance you are able to achieve with your deployment is a combination of the capabilities and architecture of the cloud service provider and how you design and implement your operations.

A well-architected framework includes many different components, including but not limited to the following:

- Application performance
- Bandwidth
- Caching · waiting your turn
- Database performance
- Filesystem performance
- Inter-availability zone performance
- Network latency
- Scalability
- Storage I/O operations per second
- Storage read/write performance
- Swap file utilization

Ongoing network monitoring and management allow you to measure and view an almost unlimited number of cloud objects. If any parameter extends beyond your predefined boundaries, alarms can be generated to alert operations and even to run automated scripts to remedy the issue.

Delivering High Availability Operations

By implementing a well-architected network using best design practices and by selecting a capable cloud service provider, you can achieve high availability operations.

There is a shared responsibility between the cloud provider and the consumer to achieve high availability in the consumer's operations. The cloud regions and availability zones must be taken into account when deploying the consumer's cloud solution to eliminate any single point of failure; load balancing and autoscaling are used as well as database and storage replications.

The cloud provider must engineer its data centers for redundant power, cooling, and network systems and create an architecture for rapid failover if a data center goes offline for whatever reason.

It is the responsibility of you, the cloud customer, to engineer and deploy your applications with the appropriate levels of availability based on your requirements and budgetary constraints.

Connecting Your Organization to the Remote Cloud Data Center

By definition, the cloud data center will be remote from your base of operations. This raises the question of how to connect to the remote cloud data center in a way that is both reliable and secure. You will look at this question in this chapter. Finally, you will learn about firewalls, a mainstay of network security, and you will see the role of a firewall in cloud management deployments.

What Are the Tools Used for Remote Management?

In this section, I will discuss several protocols and technologies that are commonly used in remote management.

VPN Access

A virtual private network (*VPN*) allows for secure and usually encrypted connections over a public network, as shown in Figure 1.15. Usually a VPN connection is set up between the network management location or customer managing their cloud deployment and the cloud services being monitored and managed. Numerous types of VPN offerings are available on the market and are beyond the scope of this certification exam. However, a cloud provider will offer network connections for management or monitoring using a direct dedicated connection or a VPN connection either from the enterprise cloud customer's management operations center or from a managed service provider.

FIGURE 1.15   Remote VPN access to a data center

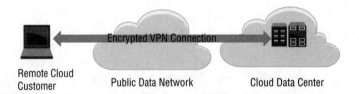

Remote Cloud Customer   Public Data Network   Cloud Data Center

A VPN is not a management protocol but rather a means to connect to the cloud management network to access your hosted applications in the cloud data center.

Is My Data Safe? (Replication and Synchronization)

Replication is the transfer and synchronization of data between multiple data centers, as illustrated in Figure 1.16. For disaster recovery purposes and data security, your data must be transferred, or replicated, between data centers. Remote copies of data have traditionally been implemented with storage backup applications. However, with the virtualization of servers in the cloud, you can now replicate complete VM instances, which allows you to replicate complete server instances, with all of the applications, service packs, and content, to a remote facility.

FIGURE 1.16   Site-to-site replication of data

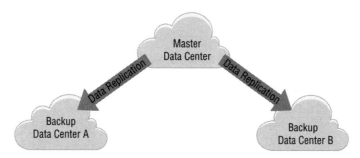

Applications such as databases have replication processes built-in that can be utilized based on your requirements. Also, many cloud service offerings can include data replication as an included feature or as a chargeable option.

Synchronous replication is the process of replicating data in real time from the primary storage system to a remote facility, as shown in Figure 1.17. Synchronous replications allow you to store current data at a remote location from the primary data center that can be brought online with a short recovery time and limited loss of data.

FIGURE 1.17   Synchronous replication

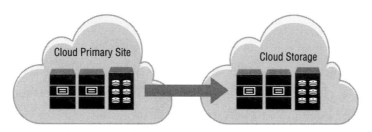

Real-Time Data Replication

Asynchronous replication works off a store-and-forward model and is a cost-effective protection and backup solution.

With asynchronous replication, the data is first written to the primary storage system in the primary storage facility or cloud location. After the data is stored, it is then copied to remote replicas on a scheduled basis or in nearly real time, as shown in Figure 1.18. Many asynchronous backup offerings can be implemented in the storage controller—as an application such as backup software running on a server; as a cloud service offering; or even in the hypervisor itself, which means complete virtual machines can be replicated to a remote site to allow for a failover in the event that the primary location experiences a failure.

FIGURE 1.18   Asynchronous replication

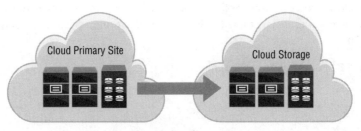

Delayed or Scheduled Data Replication

Asynchronous replication is much more cost effective than implementing a synchronous replication offering. Since asynchronous replication is not in real time, it works well over slower wider area network links, where a certain amount of network delay is to be expected.

Understanding Load Balancers

Load balancing addresses the issues found when cloud workloads and connections increase to the point where a single server can no longer handle the workload or performance requirements of web, DNS, or FTP servers; firewalls; and other network services. Load balancer functions include offloading applications and tasks from the application server, such as the processing for SSL, compression, and TCP handshakes. With load balancing, you can configure the cloud for many servers working together and sharing the load. Therefore, redundancy and scalability can be achieved, as shown in Figure 1.19.

FIGURE 1.19   Load balancing web servers

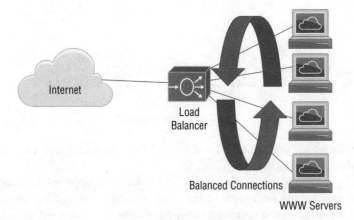

A load balancer is commonly found in front of web servers. The website's IP address is advertised on the network via DNS. This IP address is not of the real web server but instead is an interface on the load balancer. The load balancer allocates the traffic by distributing the connections to one of many servers connected to it. Load balancing allows a website to scale by allocating many servers in the cloud to handle the workload. Also, a load balancer can check the health of each server and remove a server from the network if there is a hardware, network, or application issue.

Introducing Automation and Orchestration

Orchestration platforms automate the provisioning of cloud services and often include a self-service dashboard that allows the consumer to manage and deploy cloud services with a web browser. The automation used by cloud providers allows for fast deployment of new services and applications.

Cloud Testing

As you progress through this book, I will include information on the testing and validations that are required to make sure that changes and ongoing operations are valid and working as expected. In this chapter, you will be introduced to three validations. The vulnerability and penetration tests are security related and will be expanded on in throughout this book and you will be introduced to load testing to ensure that your application works as expected when it is deployed into a heavily used production network.

Vulnerability Scanning WEAKNESS

Vulnerability scanning is used to find objects in your cloud deployment that can be exploited or are potential security threats. The vulnerability scanner is an application that has a database of known exploits and runs them against your deployment to see whether your cloud deployment may be susceptible or have security holes that need to be remediated. The scanner will detect and report on weaknesses in your cloud deployment.

Penetration Testing

Penetration testing is the process of testing your cloud access to determine whether there is any vulnerability that an attacker could exploit. Pen testing is usually performed from outside your cloud deployment to assess the ability to access systems into your cloud from, for example, the Internet.

Loading

Load testing puts a demand or load on your application or compute system and measures the response. By performing load testing, you can determine how your applications and cloud deployment can be expected to perform in times of heavy production usage. Load testing is performed to determine a system's behavior under both normal and anticipated peak load conditions. All systems will fail at some point when under heavy loads, and by performing tests, you can identify and rectify any issues on your design.

Verifying System Requirements

After you have completed your assessments and needs analysis, you will have then defined your requirements and which cloud service and deployment models best meet them. The next step is to select a pilot or trial application to migrate to the cloud from your existing data center.

Prior to performing the migration, the engineering team should sit down and review the complete design, from the application, configuration, hardware, and networking to the storage and security. As part of this verification, it is helpful to stage the system in the cloud as a proof-of-concept design. This allows everyone to test the systems and configuration in a cloud environment prior to going live.

Correct Scaling for Your Requirements

The ability to automatically and dynamically add resources such as storage, CPUs, memory, and even servers is referred to as *elasticity*. This is done "on the fly" as needed and is different from provisioning servers with added resources that may be required in the future. This allows for cloud consumers to automatically scale up as their workload increases and then have the cloud remove the services after the workload subsides. With elastic computing, there is no longer any need to deploy servers and storage systems designed to handle peak loads—servers and systems that may otherwise sit idle during normal operations. Now you can scale the cloud infrastructure to the normal load and automatically expand as needed when the occasion arises.

On-demand cloud services allow the cloud customer to access a self-service portal and instantly create additional servers, storage, processing power, or any other services as required. If the computing workload increases, then additional cloud resources can be created and applied as needed. On-demand allows customers to consume cloud services only as needed and scale back when they are no longer required. For example, if a website is expecting an increased load for a short period of time, on-demand services can increase the resources of the website only during the time they are required and then return to normal after the workload goes back to normal. This is also referred to as a *just-in-time* service because it allows cloud services to be added as they are required and removed after the workload subsides.

Pay as you grow (PAYG) is like a basic utility such as power or water where you pay for only what you use. This is very cost effective as there are no up-front costs and the costs track your actual consumption of the service. No resources are wasted since there is no overprovisioning for future growth.

With a normal data center operation, the computing must be overprovisioned to take into account peak usage or future requirements that may never be needed. The pay-as-you-grow model avoids this need. Many cloud providers allow you to select your CPU, memory, storage, and application needs, and the charges are based on what you actually use.

Making Sure the Cloud Is Always Available

In this section, you will become familiar with common deployment architectures used by many of the leading cloud providers to address availability, survivability, and resilience in their services offerings.

Regions

Large cloud operations will actually partition operations into *regions* for fault tolerance and to offer localized performance advantages. A region is not a monolithic data center but rather a geographical area of presence. For example, a cloud company may offer regions throughout the world, as shown in Figure 1.20. They may have regions in Sydney and Tokyo in the Asia Pacific region, and in Europe there may be regions called London and Oslo. In North America there could be regions in Boston, Ottawa, Austin, and San Jose.

FIGURE 1.20   Cloud regions

All of the regions are interconnected to each other and the Internet with high-speed optical networks but are isolated from each other, so if there is an outage in one region, it should not affect the operations of other regions.

When you deploy your cloud operations, you will be given a choice of what region you want to use. Also, for a global presence and to reduce network delays, the cloud customer can choose to replicate operations in multiple regions around the world.

Also, understanding regions are important for many regulatory and compliance issues that require data to be stored in its country of origin.

Availability Zones

You just learned that a region is not an actual data center but defines a geographical area of presence. The actual data centers in each region are referred to as *availability zones (AZs)*. Each region will usually have two or more availability zones for fault tolerance. The AZs are isolated locations within the cloud data center regions that the public cloud services providers originate and operate. Each availability zone is a physically separate data center with its own redundant power and telecommunication connections. If they are in a geologically sensitive area, such as along a fault line or in a coastal area that may be subject to hurricanes or typhoons, they will be located a greater distance apart to minimize a natural disaster affecting more than one availability zone. Figure 1.21 illustrates the concept of availability zones.

FIGURE 1.21   Availability zones

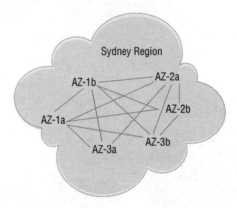

Understanding Direct and Virtual Cloud Connections

In this section, you will learn about remote access techniques and look at what tools are available to manage the servers themselves. For maintenance, management, and monitoring of the day-to-day operations of the servers running in the cloud data center, there is a need to connect to them as if you were local to the server. If you can connect to and administer the servers remotely, there is less need to rely on the support staff in the cloud, and data center issues can be resolved quickly. Also, the servers are most certainly in a secure data center, and access to the physical server is restricted; remote access is usually your only option for managing your servers.

Let's explore the options you can use to accomplish this task.

Remote Hypervisor Access   Almost every hypervisor product on the market has a management application that can be installed on a workstation and can be used to fully configure and manage the hypervisor, as Figure 1.22 illustrates. With the management application installed on your local workstation or laptop, you can connect to the hypervisors from almost any location over either the Internet or a VPN depending on the security configurations. These applications can control all hypervisors in a group and the movement of VMs from one hypervisor to another, and they offer full monitoring capabilities and resource allocations. User access controls are implemented to allow for viewing only all the way up to full control of the environment. The ability to control these functions will depend on the type of cloud services purchased as the cloud provider will generally restrict access to any portion of the service they control. However, in environments such as IaaS, this is a viable option. If you are using PaaS or SaaS from the cloud, then you would not be responsible for the maintenance of the VMs and usually would not be allowed to access the hypervisor.

FIGURE 1.22   Local computer running the hypervisor management application

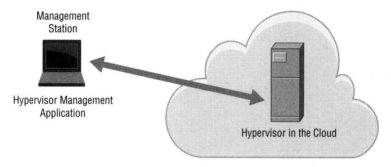

Management
Station

Hypervisor Management
Application

Hypervisor in the Cloud

The remote application is usually a graphical interface that communicates over specific TCP ports, so it is important to ensure that all firewalls between your location and the cloud data center allow the application to communicate. Figure 1.23 shows an example of a common graphical hypervisor management interface.

RDP   Remote Desktop Protocol (RDP) is a proprietary protocol developed by Microsoft to allow remote access to Windows devices, as illustrated in Figure 1.24. Microsoft calls the application Remote Desktop Services, formerly Terminal Services. It is a client-server application, which means RDP has to be installed and running on both the server and the local workstation you are using to access the cloud server. The remote desktop application comes preinstalled on most versions of Windows. You need to open the TCP and UDP port 3389 in your firewalls, and you will be ready to connect.

The graphical client will request the name of the remote server in the cloud, and once it's connected, you will be presented with a standard Windows interface to log in. Then you will see the standard Windows desktop of the remote server on your local workstation.

RDP is invaluable for managing remote Windows virtual machines since it allows you to work remotely as if you were locally connected to the server.

FIGURE 1.23   Remote hypervisor management application

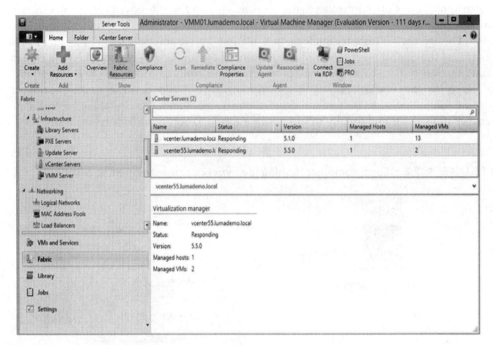

FIGURE 1.24   Local computer running Remote Desktop Services to remotely access a Windows server graphical interface in the cloud

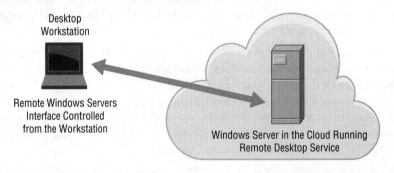

SSH   The Secure Shell (SSH) protocol has largely replaced Telnet as a remote access method. SSH supports encryption, whereas Telnet does not, making Telnet insecure. To use SSH, the SSH service must be supported on the server in the cloud data center and enabled. This is pretty much standard on any Linux distribution and can also be installed on Windows devices.

Many SSH clients are available on the market as both commercial software and free of charge in the public domain. The SSH client connects over the network using TCP port 22 via an encrypted connection, as shown in Figure 1.25. Once you are connected, you have a command-line interface to manage your cloud services. SSH is a common remote connection method used to configure network devices such as switches and routers.

FIGURE 1.25   Secure Shell encrypted remote access

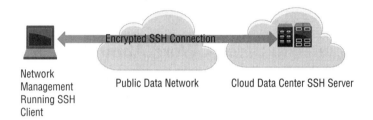

Network
Management   Public Data Network   Cloud Data Center SSH Server
Running SSH
Client

Console Port   Console ports are common in the networking environment to configure switches and routers from a command-line interface. Linux servers also use the console or serial ports for CLI access. In a data center, devices called *terminal servers* are deployed that have many serial ports, each cabled to a console port on a device that is being managed, as shown in Figure 1.26. This allows you to make an SSH or Telnet connection to the terminal server and then use the serial interfaces on it to access the console ports on the devices you want to connect to. Also, a VM can use port redirections to connect to a physical serial port on the server for console connections.

FIGURE 1.26   Console port access

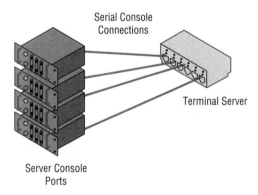

Serial Console
Connections

Terminal Server

Server Console
Ports

HTTP   Probably the most common and easiest way of managing remote devices is to use a standard browser and access the remote device's web interface. Most devices are now supporting web access with the secure version of HTTPS, which is the most common for security reasons. When connected and authenticated, the web-based applications provide a graphical interface that can be used to monitor and configure the device.

There has been a trend to move away from client applications that need to be installed on the local workstation, as is the case with the remote hypervisor management applications discussed earlier, and move everything to a web interface for ease of use. It is also common to use a web browser to connect to a hypervisor, virtual machine, or network device and then download and install the management application.

HTTPS uses TCP port 443 and is the suggested remote access protocol for web-based access because it is secure. The insecure HTTP port 80 is rarely supported because of its lack of security.

Keeping Your Data Safe (A Word About Data Integrity)

Proper protection of your data is a critical concern for any organization, and there is often a lot of apprehension when migrating your data to a shared resource such as the cloud. Cloud providers are aware of this and offer a wide variety of encryption services that can be implemented with your storage solution.

Data can be encrypted at rest and in transit using strong encryption algorithms such as AES-256. The encryption keys can be managed by the cloud providers, or you can elect to manage your own keys if that is your company's security policy. I will expand on this topic throughout this book as security is an important topic on the Cloud+ exam.

Making Sure Your Cloud Deployment Is Functioning as Expected

Just because you have created an operational cloud deployment doesn't mean your work is over! You must continually monitor performance and also make sure there are no interruptions to services. Fortunately, this function has largely been automated. As you will learn in later chapters, events can be collected and analyzed with monitoring applications. Trends and acceptable performance metrics can be defined. Should these be exceeded, events can be generated by the management systems to run scripts for a large number of desired responses to the event. Also, alerts such as text messages, e-mails, or calls to other applicators can be defined and deployed.

The use of variances also assists in the *automation* of the cloud. For example, you can use the CPU utilization example discussed earlier to alert the cloud automation servers to add additional virtual CPUs to a VM if utilization has, for example, exceeded 98 percent for more than 10 minutes. This of course can be applied to storage, networking, and all server and applications that are automated. These automated responses to events make cloud operations more efficient, responsive, and resilient than traditional data centers.

The cloud customer can set predefined thresholds with the cloud provider. When these thresholds are exceeded, the cloud provider can use automation applications to add capacity that has been agreed upon and contracted for.

Another example may be a company that is hosting its corporate e-commerce website on the cloud. If the company were to run a very successful advertising campaign for its products, the traffic and load on the web services may spike. With this known variance from the baseline, the cloud provider's automation systems may automatically add web compute resources dynamically to handle the additional workload.

Writing It All Down (Documentation)

Documentation should be created by the many different teams involved in the cloud deployment, such as the server, virtualization, storage, networking, developer, security, and management teams, as well as the cloud provider.

Once the document is complete, it should be readily accessible, and the procedures to maintain consistency should be clear. A corporate compliance group may be formed to monitor and maintain adherence to the standardization process. Also, since the operations and deployment are constantly evolving and changing, the documentation will need to be constantly modified and updated.

Creating a Known Reference Point (Baselines)

Baselines collect data and provide trend analysis and capacity utilization information measured over time to determine average or expected metrics of a service in normal operation. Establishing baselines is helpful when you need to determine the size of the virtual machines required when migrating servers to the cloud. Baselines also are used to determine what is out of normal operations. You can use your baseline statistics as a reference, and if a counter has a variance above or below that value, it will be considered a serious issue. You can set these values as a threshold to notify the management station.

To set a baseline sample of computing resources you are using, you will set a sampling interval that is not too short as to monopolize bandwidth, storage, and other resources but also not too long of a sampling time window where the information becomes inaccurate.

When you have your baseline established, you can then determine what deviations from this are considered normal and what would require an investigation or a support call.

For example, if CPU utilization on a database server is expected to run in the 70 percent range when averaged over a 10-minute interval, you can configure the application to send out SMS or e-mail alerts if it is now averaging 95 percent CPU utilization. These values can be tailored to the requirements of your organization.

You use the monitoring and alerting functions of the application to determine the baseline and then use the baseline as your reference point to determine what is to be considered out of range. This is referred to as the *variance*.

What Is the Responsibility of the Cloud Service Provider?

Cloud operations are the responsibility of both your organization and the cloud service provider. The models are usually referred to as the shared responsibility model that defines what you are responsible for and what the provider is responsible for. The model will vary depending on what you are contracting to use and the offerings of the service provider.

For example, if you are using Infrastructure as a Service, then the cloud company would usually take responsibility for all cloud connections and networking up to the hypervisor level, and the cloud consumer would have responsibility for the operating system and application. Platform as a Service would be defined as the cloud provider taking responsibility up to the operating system level and you, the customer, being responsible for the applications you choose to run on the operating system. If, for example, you chose the Software as a Service model, then the cloud provider would assume full responsibility up to the operating system and the application running on it.

Variations in the Cloud: Performance Metrics

The assessments and benchmark testing are intended to allow you to collect statistics and measurements of your operations at various states. For example, what is the CPU utilization under low, normal, and heavy workloads? How many storage I/O operations are occurring during the day compared to overnight? By constantly monitoring and measuring your operations, you can assign alarms when a metric exceeds the thresholds you define.

There are an almost infinite number of measurement points in the cloud it seems. You can select the measurements that are important to you and define the metrics of normal and abnormal operations. Based on these triggers, the alarms can be created to alert users via text or e-mail or, more commonly, another application that will run a script to take action on the alarm.

Summary

In this introductory chapter, you explored the big picture of cloud computing. You investigated the many types of service models offered in the marketplace today. The core models include Infrastructure as a Service, which is defined as the networking, storage, and computing offered by the cloud provider, with the customer taking the responsibility of loading and managing the operating systems and applications. Platform as a Service extends this by including the server operating systems and leaves the responsibility of application software to the consumer. The next level is Software as a Service, which allows the consumer to access application software from the cloud.

Cloud delivery models are important to understand for the exam. You looked at the various types of models, including private, public hybrid, and community clouds, and what the general use cases and differences are for each type of delivery model.

You then moved on to some of the characteristics found in cloud computing by exploring concepts such as elasticity, on-demand, pay-as-you-grow, chargeback, and access models. The chapter discussed resource pooling and virtualization of resources such as storage, CPU, memory, storage, and networking into pools that can be dynamically allocated to virtual systems.

The chapter also covered how to prepare to migrate your operations to the cloud and how it's important to test systems in the cloud, including sizing, performance, availability, connectivity, data integrity, and others, and that you must document the results.

It cannot be said too many times: The concepts covered in this chapter are important to keep in mind, as they provide a structure that you will build on as you progress on your journey to become Cloud+ certified.

Exam Essentials

Know that cloud computing is similar in operation to a utility.   Cloud computing follows the utilities model where a provider will sell computing resources using an as-needed or as-consumed model. This allows a company or individual to pay for only what they use.

Know what cloud computing is.   Cloud computing is a model for enabling convenient, on-demand network access to a shared pool of configurable computing resources (e.g., networks, servers, storage, applications, and services) that can be rapidly provisioned and released with minimal management effort or service provider interaction. This cloud model is composed of five essential characteristics, three service models, and four deployment models.

Understand the different cloud service models and how to differentiate between them.   Cloud service models are characterized by the phrase *as a service* and are accessed by many types of devices, including web browsers, thin clients, and mobile devices. There are three primary service types. Software as a Service, Infrastructure as a Service, and Platform as a Service are the core service offerings. Many cloud service providers offer more descriptive terms in their marketing and sales offerings, including Communications as a Service, Anything as a Service, Desktop as a Service, and Business Process as a Service. However, all of these newer terms fit into either the SaaS, IaaS, or PaaS service model. The basic terms and concepts are important to know for the exam. Study the service models and know the differences between IaaS, PaaS, and SaaS as well as the other service models.

Know the primary cloud delivery models.   The four primary cloud delivery models are public, private, community, and hybrid clouds. Know what each one is and its function. It is critical that you understand the way cloud services are delivered in the market today and what they offer.

Be able to identify and explain cloud components.   Common cloud components include applications, automation, computing, networking, security, and virtualization.

Know the cloud shared resource pooling model and how it is used.   Understand that resource pooling is when the cloud service provider allocates resources into a group, or pool, and then these pools are made available to a multitenant cloud environment. The resources are then dynamically allocated and reallocated as the demand requires. Resource pooling hides the physical hardware from the virtual machines and allows for many tenants to share resources such as storage, processors, RAM, and networks to allow for the economies of cloud computing.

Know the basic cloud concepts covered in this chapter.   Cloud characteristics will certainly be on the exam, and the concepts of elasticity, on-demand, pay-as-you-grow, and others covered in this chapter must be understood not only for the exam but to provide a good background of information for you to build on as you progress through your preparation to be a Cloud+ certified professional.

Understand cloud performance components.   Cloud performance encompasses all of the individual capabilities of the various components as well as how they interoperate. The performance you are able to achieve with your deployment is a combination of the capabilities and architecture of the cloud service provider and how you design and implement your operations.

A well-architected framework includes many different components, including but not limited to application performance, bandwidth, caching, database performance, filesystem performance, inter-availability zone performance, network latency, scalability, storage I/O operations per second, storage read/write performance, and swap file utilization.

Know what replication and synchronization are.   Know that replication is the transfer and synchronization of data between multiple data centers. For disaster recovery purposes and data security, your data must be transferred, or replicated, between data centers. Remote copies of data have traditionally been implemented with storage backup applications. However, with the virtualization of servers in the cloud, you can now replicate complete VM instances, which allows you to replicate complete server instances, with all of the applications, service packs, and content, to a remote facility.

Understand automation and orchestration concepts.   Orchestration platforms automate the provisioning of cloud services and often include a self-service dashboard that allows the consumer to manage and deploy cloud services with a web browser. The automation used by cloud providers allows for fast deployment of new services and applications.

Know the cloud scaling requirements.   The ability to automatically and dynamically add additional resources such as storage, CPUs, memory, and even servers is referred to as *elasticity*. This is done "on the fly" as needed and is different from provisioning servers with added resources that may be required in the future. This allows for cloud consumers to automatically scale up as their workload increases and then have the cloud remove the services after the workload subsides. On-demand cloud services allow the cloud customer to access a self-service portal and instantly create additional servers, storage, processing power, or any other services as required. If the computing workload increases, then additional cloud resources can be created and applied as needed. On-demand allows customers to consume cloud services only as needed and scale back when they are no longer required. Pay as you grow (PAYG) is like a basic utility such as power or water where you pay for only what you use.

Know what regions and availability zones are.   Large cloud operations partition operations into geographical regions for fault tolerance and to offer localized performance advantages. A region is not a monolithic data center but rather a geographical area of presence. The actual data centers in each region are availability zones. Each region will usually have two or more availability zones for fault tolerance. The AZs are isolated locations within cloud data center regions that public cloud providers originate and operate. Each availability zone is a physically separate data center with its own redundant power and telecommunication connections.

Know how to prepare for a cloud deployment. Creating complete documentation, creating baselines, and preparing for a migration to the cloud will be fair game for questions on the exam.

Written Lab

Fill in the blanks for the questions provided in the written lab. You can find the answers to the written labs in Appendix B.

1. With the _____ as a Service model, the cloud provider owns and manages all levels of the computing environment.

2. With the _____ as a Service model, the cloud provider owns and manages the computing hardware but not the operating systems or the applications.

3. With the _____ as a Service model, the cloud provider owns and manages the hardware and operating system but not the application software.

4. _____ _____ refers to the ability to access the cloud resources from anywhere in the network from a variety of devices such as laptops, tables, smartphones, and thin or thick clients.

5. _____ is the ability to take physical data center resources such as RAM, CPU, storage, and networking and create a software representation of those resources that enables large-scale cloud offerings.

6. Network interconnectivity between your corporate data center and your cloud operations is accomplished using either _____ _____ or a _____.

7. _____ is the transfer and synchronization of data between multiple data centers.

8. _____ _____ addresses the issues found when cloud workloads and connections increase to the point where a single server can no longer handle the workload by spreading the workload across multiple cloud computing resources.

9. Common remote access protocols used to manage servers in the cloud include _____ and _____.

10. _____ collect data and provide trend analysis and capacity utilization information measured over time to determine the average or expected metric of a service in normal operation.

Review Questions

The following questions are designed to test your understanding of this chapter's material. For more information on how to obtain additional questions, please see this book's Introduction. You can find the answers in Appendix A.

1. What cloud model delivers server hardware with no operating system?

    A. IaaS

    B. PaaS

    C. SaaS

    D. CaaS

2. A cloud service provider allocates resources into a group. These resources are then dynamically allocated and reallocated as the demand requires. What is this referred to as?

    A. On-demand virtualization

    B. Dynamic scaling

    C. Resource pooling

    D. Elasticity

3. What are three examples of cloud elements? (Choose three.)

    A. CPU

    B. Resource groups

    C. Memory

    D. Storage

    E. Scalability

    F. SSH

4. Which of the following is not a valid pooled resource?

    A. Memory

    B. Storage

    C. Security

    D. Networking

    E. CPU

5. What technologies are used to enable on-demand computing? (Choose two.)

    A. Load balancing

    B. Automation

    C. Autoscaling groups

    D. Virtualization

6. When you migrate your operations to the cloud and you decide to match computing resources with your current requirements, what can you take advantage of to expand your compute capacity in the future? (Choose three.)

   A. Elasticity

   B. On-demand computing

   C. Availability zones

   D. Resiliency virtualization

   E. Pay-as-you grow

   F. Resource pooling

7. Your company has decided to interconnect its cloud services with three different service providers. What type of cloud delivery model is it creating?

   A. Public

   B. Hybrid

   C. Community

   D. Private

8. Server interfaces are grouped together or aggregated into channel groups for additional throughput and fault tolerance. The LAN interfaces in the server are connected to what device in a hypervisor?

   A. Virtual NIC

   B. Region

   C. Virtual switch

   D. LAN

9. Which cloud characteristic allows you to pay for only the services used?

   A. Bursting

   B. Pay-as-you-grow

   C. Chargeback

   D. Metering

10. What are three organizational uses commonly found in the cloud? (Choose three.)

   A. Development networks

   B. Public

   C. Production networks

   D. Converged networks

   E. Community

   F. XaaS

   G. Quality assurance

   H. Hybrid

11. Which cloud characteristic allows you to access a self-service portal to instantly create additional servers, storage, or other services?

   A. Bursting

   B. Pay-as-you-grow

   C. Multitenancy

   D. On-demand

12. What cloud model delivers all services, including the application?

   A. IaaS

   B. PaaS

   C. SaaS

   D. CaaS

13. A well-architected framework includes which of the following cloud performance components? (Choose four.)

   A. Network latency

   B. Stateful firewall

   C. Encryption

   D. Inter-availability zone latency

   E. Storage I/O operations per second

   F. IaaS

   G. Swap file utilization

   H. Memory pools

   I. Scalability

14. Cloud service providers will often segment their operations to allow for resiliency, survivability, and geographic proximity. What are these geographical segmentations referred to as?

   A. Regions

   B. Autoscaling groups

   C. Availability zones

   D. Global DNS affinity

15. What are critical steps to take prior to performing a migration to the cloud? (Choose three.)

   A. Baselines

   B. Capacity requirements

   C. Variance measurements

   D. Documentation

   E. Automation rollout

16. Cloud operations are the responsibility of both your organization and the cloud service provider. What model defines what you are responsible for and the responsibility of the provider?

   A. Availability zones

   B. Community

   C. Shared responsibility

   D. Baselines

17. What is the process of testing your cloud access to determine whether there is any vulnerability that an attacker could exploit?

   A. Elasticity

   B. On-demand

   C. Penetration testing

   D. Load testing

18. A medical records company wants to take advantage of a complex application but wants to realize the cost savings by accessing a shared instance of the application hosted in the cloud. Because of regulatory requirements, what type of cloud delivery model would you recommend they use?

   A. Public

   B. Hybrid

   C. Community

   D. Private

19. What systems do cloud providers implement for rapid deployment of customer-requested services?

   A. RDMS

   B. Orchestration

   C. On-demand provisions

   D. Service catalogs

20. What cloud model delivers all services except the application?

   A. IaaS

   B. PaaS

   C. SaaS

   D. CaaS

Chapter

2

Cloud Deployments

THE FOLLOWING COMPTIA CLOUD+ EXAM OBJECTIVES ARE COVERED IN THIS CHAPTER:

✓ **1.2 Given a scenario, execute a provided deployment plan.**

  - Apply the Change Management Process
    - Approvals
    - Scheduling
  - Refer to documentation and follow standard operating procedures
  - Execute workflow
  - Configure automation and orchestration, where appropriate, for the system being deployed
  - Use commands and tools as needed
  - Document results

✓ **1.5 Given a scenario, analyze sizing, subnetting, and basic routing for a provided deployment of the virtual network.**

  - Cloud deployment models
    - Public
    - Private
    - Hybrid
    - Community
  - Network components
  - Applicable port and protocol considerations when extending to the cloud
  - Determine configuration for the applicable platform as it applies to the network
    - VPN
    - IDS/IPS

- DMZ
- VXLAN
- Address space required
- Network segmentation and micro-segmentation
- Determine if cloud resources are consistent with the SLA and/or change management requirements

✓ **1.6   Given a scenario, analyze CPU and memory sizing for a provided deployment.**

- Available vs. proposed resources
  - CPU
  - RAM
- Memory technologies
  - Bursting and ballooning
  - Overcommitment ratio
- CPU technologies
  - Hyper-threading
  - VT-x
  - Overcommitment ratio
- Effect to HA/DR
- Performance considerations
- Cost considerations
- Energy savings
- Dedicated compute environment vs. shared compute environment

✓ **1.7   Given a scenario, analyze the appropriate storage type and protection capability for a provided deployment.**

- Requested IOPS and read/write throughput
- Protection capabilities
  - High availability
    - Failover zones

- Storage replication
  - Regional
  - Multiregional
  - Synchronous and asynchronous
- Storage mirroring
- Cloning
- Redundancy level/factor
- Storage types
  - NAS
  - DAS
  - SAN
  - Object storage
- Access protocols
- Management differences
- Provisioning model
  - Thick provisioned
  - Thin provisioned
  - Encryption requirements
  - Tokenization
- Storage technologies
  - Deduplication technologies
  - Compression technologies
- Storage tiers
- Overcommitting storage
  - Security configurations for applicable platforms
  - ACLs
  - Obfuscation
  - Zoning
  - User/host authentication and authorization

✓ **1.8 Given a scenario, analyze characteristics of the workload (storage, network, compute) to ensure a successful migration.**

- Migration types
  - P2V
  - V2V
  - V2P
  - P2P
  - Storage migrations
  - Online vs. offline migrations
- Source and destination format of the workload
  - Virtualization format
  - Application and data portability
- Network connections and data transfer methodologies
- Standard operating procedures for the workload migration
- Environmental constraints
  - Bandwidth
  - Working hour restrictions
  - Downtime impact
  - Peak timeframes
  - Legal restrictions
  - Follow-the-sun constraints/time zones

✓ **1.9 Given a scenario, apply elements required to extend the infrastructure into a given cloud solution.**

- Identity management elements
  - Identification
  - Authentication
  - Authorization
    - Approvals
    - Access policy
  - Federation
    - Single sign-on

- Appropriate protocols given requirements
- Element considerations to deploy infrastructure services such as:
  - DNS
  - DHCP
  - Certificate services
  - Local agents
  - Antivirus
  - Load balancer
  - Multifactor authentication
  - Firewall
  - IPS/IDS

In Chapter 1 you learned about cloud computing and were introduced to the basic terminology and concepts used. The various components and architectures were explored, and you began to learn about how these components and subsystems come together to make a fully functioning deployment of your operations in the cloud.

In this chapter, the focus will be on deploying your computing resources in the cloud. The chapter will begin by discussing many of the business and nontechnical aspects including project-based issues and the various cloud deployment models that must be considered. The second part of this chapter will discuss the technical issues that must be understood for a successful migration including the compute, data format conversions, recovery, storage, security, and networking functions.

This is an important chapter that covers many of the core concepts on the Cloud+ exam. It also creates a foundation that you can build on in future chapters.

Executing a Cloud Deployment

For a successful migration to cloud-based computing from the legacy data center approach, you must understand how to prepare and execute the migration process. This section covers the Cloud+ objectives for planning, meeting your business needs, knowing what to document, and the workflows used during the process.

Understanding Deployment and Change Management

In this section, you will learn about the process of planning to deploy your operations into the cloud. The various steps required will be discussed.

Change Management

Change management is the process of managing all aspects of ongoing upgrades, repairs, and reconfigurations of your cloud services. The end goal is to minimize any disruptions of service.

During the change management process, you create a standardized process to follow, including recording the change, planning for the change, testing the documentation, getting approvals, evaluating and validating the change, creating instructions for backing out the change if needed, and conducting any post-change reviews if desired. Change management is a standard process in the operations of the cloud or enterprise data center.

It uses well-known and established processes when implementing changes to the existing operations.

With the need to gather baseline information and to ensure that your cloud architecture meets your immediate and future needs, the marketing hype of how easy it is to move to the cloud can sometimes be overstated. The need to manage the migration and ongoing changes is critical to a successful cloud operation and is often far from a trivial undertaking. That's why you should consider implementing a change management process for a successful project implementation and to limit disruptions to ongoing operations.

The process of managing technical configuration and customization changes can be detailed in large data center or cloud operations. A change management procedure usually includes the name of the requester, what the change is going to be, and the reason or justification for making the change. Other areas include a description of the expected result of making the change and what risks are involved. You must also outline what resources will be needed and coordinate the activities of the various groups involved in the change. A list of individuals responsible for the various aspects of the change including the design, configuration, deployment, and validation steps must be prepared. There also needs to be an investigation into other changes that are taking place to make sure no conflicts exist between those changes and yours. Also, if one change requires another change to take place before it can be implemented, the change sequences will have to be coordinated.

Obtaining Buy-In from All Involved Parties

As part of the migration plan, it is important to keep all interested parties up-to-date on the plans and progress. This will include all timelines and any changes that have the potential to impact existing operations within your organization. This will include many groups that are outside of IT operations such as finance, production, human resources, and any others that may need ongoing updates on the migration projects.

In most medium to large organizations, a formal change review group meets to manage and approve all pending changes. This committee often consists of managers, architects, and representatives of all the project stakeholders.

The change review group's responsibility is to manage risk and to ensure that no conflicting changes are scheduled for the same maintenance window. Subjects that must be addressed include the following: What is the reason you are implementing this change? What do you expect to gain from making the change? What are the risks involved when implementing or not implementing the change? What functional departments are going to be involved in implementing the change? How long will it take to implement the change and to validate that the change is performing as expected? How long will it take to back out the change if necessary? The change review process will investigate the impact the change may have on your ongoing operations, service level agreements you have with your customers, and the monetary cost if the change causes an outage. The verification and back-out plan will need to be investigated in detail so as to reduce the risk of the change implementation.

Each change request will be approved, denied, or returned for further investigation by the change review team.

Setting a Realistic Migration Timeline

As part of the planning and implementation process, timelines must be established for the migration. Most migrations will be better served if performed incrementally to reduce the risk of an outage or having to back out the migration because of unforeseen issues. The migration will take place during a *maintenance window,* which is a scheduled time that maintenance can be performed and outages are planned for ongoing support of operations.

Following the "start small and deploy over time" field of thought, it is best to begin your migrations with small, easy-to-implement, noncritical systems as candidates to migrate to the cloud. This will give you experience in the migration process and allow you to better determine what realistic time frames will need to be arranged for migrations.

Assuming that the migration project team has done ample planning, the actual time window is determined by allocating time for all of the processes that need to occur sequentially during the migration. There must be time for testing and validation after the migration where all stakeholders can test and verify that the systems are working as planned after the migration. Time must be allocated in the event that a back-out is required and that the original site or installation must come back online.

As you can see, all of this must be condensed into your downtime window, and it is a good idea to extend the amount of time allocated per phase as a buffer in case of unforeseen issues.

Documenting and Following Procedures

Complete documentation is a critical component of a successful migration. You must know exactly what you are starting with, so the current documentation should be reviewed and updated as required. All systems should be accurately diagrammed, and configurations should be saved in a file separate from the systems being migrated.

The project management team is primarily responsible for creating and maintaining complete and accurate documentation. Sources for collecting information to create documents include network monitoring and management systems, downloads of device configurations, and vendor support documents.

In addition, proper documentation is critical for the ongoing support of the cloud deployment, or any other network implementation. This process includes creating detailed documentation on IP numbering plans, the routing and security protocols to be used on all the interconnections, VLANs, redundancy, and management interconnections. The documentation should show what security devices will be used and where they are to be placed in the network. Because of the nature of a constantly evolving cloud operation, network diagrams and documentation will need to be updated on a regular basis to make sure all information is current and matches the configuration of your cloud network.

Network planning and documentation should start early in the cloud rollout process and be performed in collaboration with the cloud service provider. This collaboration will allow for the correct selection and procurement of all needed networking hardware and software that may not be included by the cloud provider. In addition, this process includes ordering data circuits for the service provider to interconnect locations.

The network core should have detailed explanations and drawings of the network showing the numbering of all interfaces and their associated IP subnets and VLANs. A section detailing redundancy and configuration scripts will be invaluable when performing the initial installation and for ongoing maintenance and troubleshooting. As you can imagine, it can be very time-consuming and frustrating when troubleshooting a network if there is no map to show what the big picture looks like and how the small details are implemented. Much critical time can be spent troubleshooting a critical issue by gathering background information instead of restoring a service without proper and detailed network diagrams and documentation.

The network documentation should also include sections on the access and distribution networks in the cloud. The documents and drawings will show all redundancy protocols, layer 2 implementation information, and overlay networks such as Spanning Tree, VLANs, FabricPath, TRILL, and Virtual Extensible LAN (VXLAN). The diagrams should show where in the cloud network each server is connected and what VLANs they are connected to. The access network diagrams will show all wide area networking connections, including VPN links, routing tables, access control lists, the connection to the cloud provider's network, and links to the corporate office and all data centers. Include a network management section that provides a map for the network operations center and illustrates how the network management systems are connected to the network and what devices they are monitoring.

There is a good possibility that if you are purchasing the networking services for the cloud provider, the network will be their responsibility, and detailed network information may not be made available to you.

A services section in the documentation will detail all network services information such as caching systems, Domain Name Systems, logging, load balancers, network optimization servers, IDS/IPS information, and any network analyzers that are connected to the services network.

Some cloud-based companies offer applications that can automate the network discovery after the network has been deployed into a production environment. Network mapping applications can provide detailed diagrams and configuration documents, they constantly monitor and record changes in the network and automatically update the drawings. Off-the-shelf applications are also available.

A detailed network diagram and IP addressing plan should always be created in the design phase of your cloud deployment. It is critical to identify any potential issues and provide remediation before they occur, and accurate documentation can help you meet that goal. The documentation benefits both the cloud provider and the consumer by detailing how all the associated networks are interconnected and interoperate. During the implementation phase, detailed documentation acts as a road map, and during ongoing operations of the cloud deployment, the networking document is an invaluable troubleshooting tool. When performing capacity planning for network growth, network diagrams can serve as a starting place to plan additions and expansions in your cloud deployment.

What Is a Cloud Workflow?

Cloud service offerings include workflow architectures that manage the state of a project. Today's applications often require multiple steps in a process that can, and often do, include the interoperation of many different components and applications in the cloud. A *workflow* is defined as a series of steps or activities that are required to complete a task.

For example, if your site includes an e-commerce offering, there will be many steps that are required to complete the online transaction. This would include the shopping cart, checkout, financial transaction, warehousing, and shipping functions to name just a few. Each step has a specific set of requirements before and after its process where usually an outside event occurs to start the process. A cloud workflow service will manage the steps to complete a process that could include human processes, parallel steps, and sequential steps. Think of workflow as a state tracking and coordination system in the cloud.

This same analytical processing can be used when undertaking the cloud migration process, with the project management team designing and implementing a workflow-based approach to the migration.

Setting Up Your Cloud for Automation

Cloud automation is a fundamental characteristic of the virtualized data center. Automation in the public cloud infrastructure is provided by the cloud service provider and offered to the customers as a web dashboard, API, or command-line interface. Global cloud management systems are offered by a variety of vendors and service providers that allow hybrid cloud deployments to be centrally managed with automation systems that connect to multiple clouds simultaneously.

As you can imagine, automation is a complex and detailed topic with details beyond the scope of the Cloud+ exam. However, I will be giving examples of automation systems used in the cloud deployment models.

What Are Cloud Tools and Management Systems?

Managing and monitoring the entire deployment is a critical part of successfully implementing and operating your cloud environment. Once the applications are deployed and fully operational, ongoing monitoring will ensure that all components of the cloud deployment are operating within defined ranges and that all the performance metrics are being met.

The area of cloud management is constantly and rapidly evolving as new services and management techniques are being introduced to the market from cloud service providers, third-party support organizations, and internal management systems used to accommodate cloud computing.

To make sure that your cloud deployment is optimized for your applications, meets performance agreements, is secure, has no faults or alarms, is configured correctly, and collects all accounting data, a method of monitoring and managing the cloud is of upmost importance.

Many components and services all come together under the umbrella of cloud management. Traditional network management tools have been extended for cloud-based services, and at the same time, many new products and services have been introduced that specifically address this new and fast-growing market. In addition to the traditional information technology management providers, a lot of investments have been made in startup companies developing products and services for this market.

The term *network management* is very broad, so let's drill down and look at the components that encompass a complete network management solution. The basic architecture consists of one or more network management operations centers housing systems that monitor and collect information from the devices hosted in a private or public data center, as shown in Figure 2.1.

FIGURE 2.1   Managing your cloud deployment

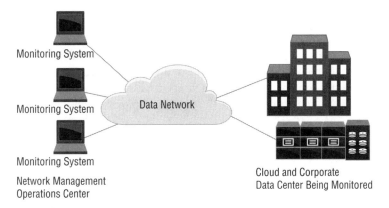

The acronym FCAPS is commonly used to cover the main areas under the management umbrella. It is broken down into the following areas: fault, configuration, accounting, performance, and security, as illustrated in Figure 2.2.

FIGURE 2.2   The FCAPS management umbrella

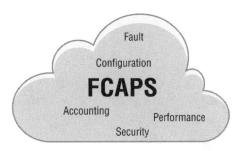

There are many data points in a cloud deployment that can be monitored and managed to ensure complete coverage of the hosted applications. This can include the CPU, memory, and disk usage on servers; network interface statistics; temperature readings; and application logging. There are thousands of objects that can be monitored, and you should take care to make sure you are monitoring what is important to your ongoing operations.

The basic architecture of a managed service operation consists of servers running specialized monitoring applications that poll or request metrics and measurements from the endpoint devices. Management systems collect logs from servers, network equipment, storage systems, and many other devices such as load balancers, VPN concentrators, and firewalls.

There are many applications, tools, services, and approaches to managing your data center to meet compliance requirements, protect your data, and deal with ongoing maintenance and problem resolution. However, the nature of a cloud service being remote from your operations center and hosted in a shared cloud environment can greatly add to the complexity of cloud management.

Cloud Deployment Models

In this section, you will take a look at the various models used to deliver cloud services. As you'll see, the cloud computing market is rapidly evolving, and undoubtedly new models will develop over time. Also, as you've seen with the service models earlier, it can be common to find combinations of the various deployment models offered to the market.

Public

A *public cloud* delivery model is infrastructure designed for use by the public consumers. Public clouds can be offered by private corporations, government organizations, and academia. A public delivery model hosts the service on the premise of the organization providing the service and uses shared hardware, as shown in Figure 2.3.

FIGURE 2.3   Public cloud

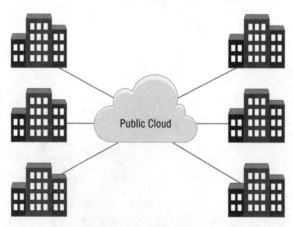

Multiple Organizations Sharing a Cloud Service

Private

A *private cloud* model is for use by a single organization, as shown in Figure 2.4, but it may be used by many units of a company. It can be wholly owned by the organization, a third-party provider, or a combination. It can also be hosted either on-site or off-premise at a hosting facility and is usually identified as using dedicated hardware rather than a shared hardware design.

FIGURE 2.4   Private cloud

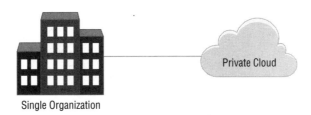

Single Organization

Hybrid

A *hybrid cloud* is a combination of two or more delivery models such as private, community, or public. Examples of a hybrid model include cloud bursting to handle peak processing loads or balancing the load between delivery models, as shown in Figure 2.5.

FIGURE 2.5   Hybrid cloud

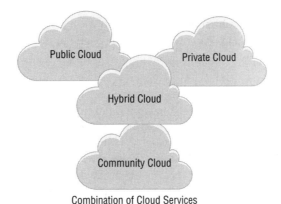

Combination of Cloud Services

Community - BUSINESS TO BUSINESS

Community clouds are designed for a specific community of interest and shared by companies with similar requirements for business needs, regulatory compliance, security, or policy. Community clouds can be owned and operated by a group of companies, a specialized cloud provider, or other interested parties, as illustrated in Figure 2.6. They can exist in or outside of a company's data center or hosting facility.

FIGURE 2.6   Community cloud

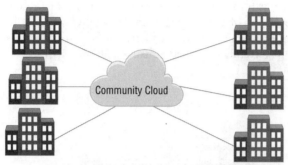

Healthcare, Banking, E-Commerce, Nonprofits,
or Any Other Organizations with Similar Requirements

Network Deployment Considerations

Networking is a whole study area in itself, so we will cover the topic broadly enough to give you a fundamental understanding of the concepts. This will help you when deploying networks in the cloud, and it will also serve as knowledge to build upon.

In this section, you will be introduced to the common network ports that are used, some basic configurations, and virtual private networks. Then you will look at common network addressing, some services such as intrusion detection and prevention, and the concept of the demilitarized zone in the cloud.

You will look at network addressing, the network types, how applications are identified and used, network protocols to send information between the cloud, and the customers network.

Network Protocols

On any network based on TCP/IP (which is pretty much everything now), there are thousands of protocols and applications being sent and received. However, there are many that are common to sending files or e-mail, accessing a web server, and doing background tasks such as performing a DNS name query. We will describe a few here so you are familiar with not only well-known port numbers but also the applications they represent.

HTTP   *HTTP* refers to the Hypertext Transfer Protocol and uses port 80. HTTP is a common application and is used primarily on web browsers to access World Wide Web servers in the cloud.

FTP   *FTP*, or the File Transfer Protocol, dates back to the earliest days of IP networking and is used to send and receive files between systems on a network. FTP has a standard command set to achieve this and uses both ports 20 and 21.

HTTPS   *HTTPS* is the Hypertext Transfer Protocol Secure and uses port 443, as I discussed earlier. HTTPS provides an encrypted connection from the client to the server to protect the interception of critical information such as e-commerce or banking websites.

FTPS   As you learned, there are often a nonsecure version and a secure version for each IP application. For example, the World Wide Web uses HTTP for unencrypted traffic and HTTPS for encrypted traffic. *FTPS*, or File Transfer Protocol Secure, is the encrypted version of the FTP and uses ports 989 and 990. FTPS uses the TLS/SSL encryption processes.

SFTP   *SFTP* is closely related to FTPS and uses port number 22 for secure file transfers.

SSH   Secure Shell, or *SSH*, is the encrypted version of the Telnet protocol and is used to access remote devices using a command-line interface. SSH uses port 22 with other security protocols.

DNS   To resolve a name to an IP address that the IP protocols uses to connect to a remote device, the server or workstation will perform a *DNS* or domain name service server. The DNS server will have the domain name to IP address mapping and reply with the correct IP address for any given domain name. DNS uses well-known port 53.

DHCP   The Dynamic Host Configuration Protocol, or *DHCP*, allows for automatic assignment of IP addressing information to devices on a network. This eliminates the need to statically configure addressing information when you connect to a network. DHCP listens on port number 68.   67=Server   68=Client

SMTP   The Simple Mail Transfer Protocol (*SMTP*) is used to send e-mail messages between mail servers and uses port 25. OUTBOUND MAIL

Network Ports

In the TCP/IP specification, there are many applications that are assigned their own unique port number and are often referred to as *well-known port numbers*. When an application needs to access a service on the remote end, a field inside of the TCP header will contain the well-known port number in its destination port. When that IP frame arrives at the remote server, the server will look at the destination port and, based on its value, forward the data to the correct application for processing.

For example, if you enter into your browser www.comptia.org, the browser will see that the www section is for web traffic and will use the HTTP protocol. HTTP has the well-known port number of port 80. The TCP/IP header will have a destination port number of 80 inserted into it and then transmitted to the remote web server. When this frame arrives at the remote web server in the CompTIA cloud, the server will look at the destination port number and see that port 80 is HTTP and forward the data internally to the web server application.

There are thousands of well-known ports reserved, but here are a few of the most common found in the cloud:

Port 80   Port 80 is reserved for HTTP, which is used for World Wide Web traffic.

Port 21   Port 21 is reserved for FTP applications, and the FTP server listens on port 21 for incoming client connection requests.

Port 22   The SSH command-line interface, Secure Copy (SCP), and SFTP use port 22 for communications. Notice that several applicators are sharing the same port number, which is acceptable.

Port 25   The protocol that routes mail between e-mail servers is SMTP. This protocol is assigned port 25.

Port 53   DNS and the domain name lookup use TCP port 53.

Port 443   When you type https in your web browser, you are requesting a secure World Wide Web connection. HTTPS uses port 443 to set up an encrypted connection from the browser to a secure web server in the cloud using the SSL/TLS protocols.

Port 68   Many devices on a TCP/IP network do not have statically defined IP configurations and instead rely on the DHCP or bootstrap protocol to automatically download its network configurations when it connects to the network. These two applicators use well-known port number 68 for this function.

Network Configurations

The cloud service provider will own the network inside its data centers. However, most deployments will allow you to configure your own virtual private clouds inside of the provider's networks. This is usually done with dashboard controls using a web browser, via APIs, or via a command-line interface. Network configurations consist of network services such as maintaining the routing tables, access control and security groups, and any firewall rules that control traffic into and out of as well as inside your cloud operations. Other network services that can be configured include load balancers, content delivery, caching systems, and DNS services.

Virtual Private Networks

Virtual private networks (VPNs) allow for a secure encrypted connection over an insecure network such as the Internet, as shown in Figure 2.7. VPNs are commonly used for encrypted access to cloud services from a remote location. VPNs are also used to create business-to-business connections that use a public network and save the expense of a private dedicated circuit.

FIGURE 2.7   A VPN creates a secure tunnel over an insecure network such as the Internet.

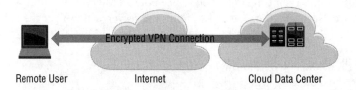

Remote User   Internet   Cloud Data Center

There are many types of VPN implementations, ranging from software running on a client computer to VPN services on a firewall or router to standalone dedicated VPN concentrators. The configuration of a VPN solution can be quite complex and involves a bewildering array of options that are beyond the scope of the Cloud+ exam.

Watching Out for the Bad Guys: Understanding IDSs/IPSs

Intrusion detection systems (IDSs) and *intrusion prevention systems* (IPSs) are similar in that they are used to monitor network traffic looking for suspicious activity. Both solutions can detect, in real time, suspicious activity on a network. Intrusion systems passively monitor traffic looking for signatures of network activity that indicates an intrusion based on predefined rule sets that are kept up-to-date by the IDS/IPS vendors. The intrusion detection system will alert a management system or can be configured to send out e-mails or text notifications if an attack is discovered, as shown in Figure 2.8. However, the intrusion detection system will not take action to remedy the situation—it only monitors and reports.

FIGURE 2.8 Intrusion detection systems monitor incoming network traffic for suspicious activity and generate alerts.

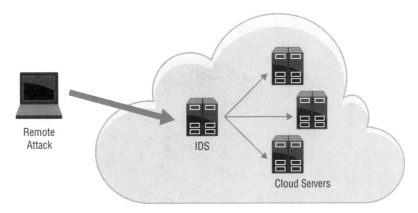

The intrusion prevention system, shown in Figure 2.9, takes the IDS concept a step further and can actively take measures to mitigate the attack with configuration scripts and methods to stop the attack that is underway. The IPS communicates with network devices such as routers and firewalls to apply rules to block the effects of the attack.

FIGURE 2.9 Intrusion prevention systems monitor activity and prevent network attacks.

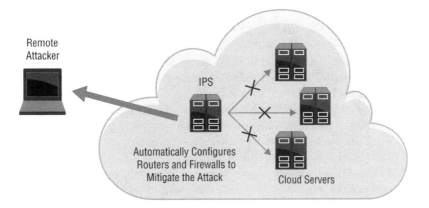

Demilitarized Zone

A *demilitarized zone* (DMZ) is a section of the network that often hosts systems and servers that need to be accessed by the outside world via the Internet as well as internally (see Figure 2.10). The DMZ is a special network security zone that exposes a cloud's computers to the Internet. A DMZ will be created and configured on a firewall as a network hosting applications, such as mail, DNS, FTP, or web servers that should not be placed on the internal network but also should not be exposed directly to the Internet without security protection.

FIGURE 2.10 DMZ servers are accessed by the outside world via the Internet and also internally.

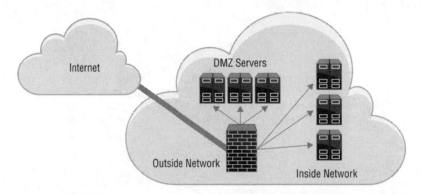

The DMZ area will have specific firewall rules to protect the internal network from unauthorized access if the servers on the DMZ are compromised. Also, there will be extensive policies configured on the firewall to limit access to the DMZ servers for only their intended purpose.

VxLAN Deployments

A virtual extensible LAN (VxLAN) was created to overcome the limitations of traditional VLANs.

Traditional VLANs support only a maximum of 4,094 total VLANs. In addition, some vendors reserve VLANs for specific internal purposes. You may not be able to use all 4,094. Even if the number were 4,000, imagine the cloud provider scale of hundreds of thousands of customers. If a provider of cloud services used traditional VLANs, how would their network be scoped? They may very well have more than the 4,000 customers that traditional VLANs can support.

VLANs that are scoped locally have no mobility outside of their area. This would simply mean that subnets stay attached to certain physical hardware in certain physical areas that can never move. This wouldn't work for most cloud customers.

VxLAN changes the way VLANs transit a network. VxLAN is an encapsulation method. It takes an Ethernet frame and encapsulates it in an IP packet using UDP as its transport. Another name for this is MAC-in-IP encapsulation because the layer 2 frame is untouched and wrapped in a normal IP/UDP packet.

The VXLAN header is 8 bytes or 64 bits. The VxLAN Network Identifier (VNI) uses 24 bits of that header. The VNI is synonymous with the traditional 802.1q VLAN identifier. In the VxLAN case, however, the VNI scales to more than 16 million segments. Now that's some serious scalability over the previous 4,094 limitation!

So, how do you scale and move these subnets around? VxLAN introduces a concept of a VxLAN tunnel endpoint (VTEP). A VTEP is any device that can process VxLAN packets. This includes encapsulating them for routing or bridging or removing the encapsulation to natively route or bridge. When a VTEP receives a packet that is destined to a local host, it removes all the fancy encapsulation, and the original frame is left. The VTEP then switches this normally. From a host or network perspective, the original frame is simply standard Ethernet again.

Addressing the Network

Network addressing concerns the segmentation of TCP/IP networks based on current and future requirements. When performing a cloud migration, a carefully designed network addressing plan must be devised. The cloud service providers will own a block of publically accessible IP addresses that are reachable from the Internet. Also, a limited number of public IP addresses will be assigned to your Internet-facing devices for reachability from the outside world.

Looking deeper into your cloud operations, it will be common to use IP address blocks from the private, or non-Internet routable, address blocks set aside in RFC 1918, as shown in Table 2.1.

TABLE 2.1   Private IP address blocks

RFC1918 name	IP address range	Number of addresses
24-bit block	10.0.0.0 to 10.255.255.255	16,777,216
20-bit block	172.16.0.0 to 172.31.255.255	1,048,576
16-bit block	192.168.0.0 to 192.168.255.255	65,536

Using private addressing preserves the public IP addresses and is useful for addressing devices that are not connected to the Internet. Based on a cloud provider's policies, you may be able to select an address block of your choosing, or the cloud provider may assign address blocks for you to use.

Using Many Smaller Networks or One Large Block

It is common for the cloud provider to assign one large block of IP addresses for your operations and then leave it up to you to segment them into smaller subnetworks. It is advantageous to create as many subnets as you require and to group applications or network segments into each subnet. By creating multiple subnets, you can use network security resources such as access control listings, security groups, and firewalls to control the flow of traffic into and out of each subnet.

Comparing Benchmarks

Benchmarking is taking sample performance metrics that need to be collected as part of the documentation process. Benchmarks include documenting object usage such as CPU and memory utilization, storage consumption, database I/O performance, and network bandwidth consumed. The number of objects that can be measured is almost endless, and you should decide which metrics are most important for your operations.

Once the baseline measurements have been obtained, you have established a reference point that can be used to measure performance and identify potential issues when performing post-migration validations. When the migration is complete, it is advantageous to perform another round of benchmark testing and compare the post-migration values to those taken in the original, pre-migration state. If there are any issues, the benchmark comparison may disclose where to troubleshoot.

Service Level Agreements   *LEGALLY BINDING, ACCEPTABLE AMOUNT OF PERFORMANCE*

The cloud service provider can provide management solutions as part of its offerings and will outline these offerings in detail in the *service level agreement*. The service level agreement is a document that outlines specific metrics and the minimum performance or availability level and outlines the penalties for failing to meet the metrics. The SLA will outline who owns the data and who owns the rights and responsibilities. Most SLAs have a severability clause that outlines penalties, up to and including the termination of the cloud contract.

However, you must understand that, as the cloud consumer, you must accept the primary responsibility for the overall management of your network and applications. Most companies will ultimately end up with a shared management model where the cloud company provides a basic level of management in the data center that is enhanced and expanded upon by the company using the cloud service.

Matching Physical Resources to the Virtualized World of the Cloud

When migrating to the cloud from a nonvirtualized data center, an assessment will need to be performed that will ensure that the virtualized servers have access and are scaled properly to meet their anticipated requirements. This will require performing an inventory of what the hardware requirements are for each operating system and application and scaling the VM instance in the cloud to meet those requirements. In this section, you will be introduced to the required process to evaluate and scale the cloud compute resources properly.

What Are Available and Proposed Hardware Resources?

Cloud service providers will offer a wide range of VM configurations that are designed for different requirements such as general compute, graphics processing, and heavy I/O needs such as a database application; there are also options for CPU and memory-centric configurations. These are generally referred to as *instances* and are offered prepackaged by the cloud providers. Instances will be defined with the number of CPUs, RAM, network I/O performance, and many other parameters that vary by cloud service provider. In the following sections, you will learn about the virtualization of the hardware resources and how they are allocated to the VMs running on the cloud servers.

Physical and Virtual Processors

With advancements made in chip fabrication capabilities, CPU densities and capabilities have dramatically increased with the introduction of multicore processors. The physical server will supply the processing power to the VMs, and as such, there must be ample processing capabilities on the physical server to support a large number of VMs running on top of it. Just as with the process of determining the amount of RAM required, the CPU requirements of all of the VMs hosted in the server must be calculated and then the server configured to meet their total requirements. The servers' motherboards will contain multiple slots for the insertion of CPUs, and each CPU may contain many processing cores. A single-server platform can be scaled to meet the processing needs of hundreds of VMs running on it.

Physical and Virtual Memory

Virtual machines will consume *RAM* on the host server. The amount of memory required will depend on the number of virtual machines and how they are individually configured. The memory will reside on the motherboard of the server as physical circuit cards. Care must be taken by the cloud provider when implementing the servers that adequate memory is installed on the server for the VMs that are being hosted. Additional memory should also be installed to accommodate for future growth and also for what is needed for the hypervisor. Modern server designs can accommodate ever-increasing memory density. In addition to memory sizes, other parameters considered are access speeds and error correction capabilities.

Bursting and Ballooning, How Memory Is Handled

Memory ballooning is a hypervisor function that allows the hypervisor to reclaim unused memory from a VM running on top of the hypervisor and to allocate that memory for other uses. By being able to reuse unused memory on the VMs, the hypervisor can optimize the RAM installed on the system.

Keep in mind that the hypervisor sits between the VMs and the physical hardware. Also, the operating systems on the virtual machines think they are talking to the actual hardware in the chassis and not a piece of hypervisor software. The hypervisor can take advantage of this by restricting what hardware resources each VM can access and balance those resources between the virtual machines running on top of the hypervisor.

For example, while a VM may have 4GB of memory allocated to it by the hypervisor, the VM sees that as real memory on a server. The hypervisor can use the ballooning process to reclaim 2GB of memory from this VM for use elsewhere, and the VM may need to start using its pagefile process as it now has less RAM available to it. The ballooning driver is the hypervisor process that reclaims and reallocates physical RAM to virtual servers.

Overcommitting Your Memory Resources

The hypervisors used in cloud server virtualization have a feature called *overcommitting* that enables a virtual machine running on that hypervisor to use more memory than is physically installed on the server's motherboard. As an example, the server's physical RAM installed on the motherboard may be 64GB, and the 32 VMs running on that server are all configured for 4GB of RAM each; this would be a 2:1 overcommitment with 128GB allocated and with 64GB physically available.

The concept of overcommitting is based on the assumption that not all servers will use the memory assigned to them. This unused memory is dynamically allocated to the other VMs that require additional RAM for operations.

Understanding Hyper-Threading in a CPU

Hyper-threading allows a single microprocessor core to act as if it were two separate CPUs to the operating system. Hyper-threading uses simultaneous multithreading processes developed by Intel Corporation.

Each logical or virtual processor can be started, stopped, and controlled independently from the other. The technology shares the same silicon resources on the CPU chip for command executions.

Hyper-threading is transparent to the operating system or hypervisor accessing the CPU, and the virtual machines see two cores when there is only one that is simulating two. The hypervisor or operating system must support symmetrical multiprocessing to take advantage of hyper-threading.

Hypervisor CPU Optimization with AMD-V and VT-x

When hypervisor and server virtualization technologies were introduced into the marketplace, emulation software was used to enhance the capabilities and functionality of the CPUs supporting the hypervisor's virtualized servers. VM performance suffered with the software emulation approach, and both Intel and AMD moved this functionality to silicon and added microcode specifically to support virtualization. With this support, hypervisor and VM performance was greatly increased.

AMD-Virtualization (AMD-V) is the microcode and silicon extensions to support virtualization and is now a common feature on AMD's CPU releases.

Intel's answer to enhanced hardware virtualization support in its CPU products is called Intel Virtualization Technology (Intel-VT).

With any virtualized system, it is important that this feature be enabled in the system BIOS to increase the performance of the servers.

CPU Overcommitment Ratios

As you have learned, the cloud server hypervisors overcommit RAM resources; the same is true for CPU resources. The CPU overcommitment ratio is also called the virtual CPU (vCPU) to physical CPU (pCPU) ratio. Overcommitments are largely determined by the applications running on the virtual machines. If they are CPU intensive, then a low ratio may be required. However, if the applications are not CPU bound and present a light load on the physical CPUs, then a higher overcommitment ratio can be implemented.

By overcommitting physical resources to the virtual services, the allocation and usage of the physical resources can be maximized, resulting in a lower cost of operations.

Overcommitting is based on the assumption that not all servers will use the CPU resources allocated to them and those cycles can be dynamically reassigned to VMs that require the allocated compute resources.

CPU wait time is the time that a process or thread has to wait to access a CPU for processing. With a hypervisor supporting many virtual machines running on it, the VMs may, at times, have to wait for the finite physical CPU resources to become available. The hypervisors will present each VM with a configurable amount of virtual CPU resources and control access to the actual physical resources. When there is contention, the VM may be paused from accessing the CPU to allow other virtual machines equitable access to the CPU. Hypervisor and monitoring tools can collect and display CPU wait statistics for performance tuning and capacity planning of processing requirements.

Physical Resource High Availability

Data centers implement high availability using redundant systems configured in active/active or active/standby configurations, where one or more systems are active and another may be on standby with a current configuration ready for immediate promotion to the master should there be a failure. Critical systems can benefit from high availability to prevent a single point of failure from causing a large-scale outage. It is important for the cloud service provider to design and implement highly available systems to meet service level agreement commitments and to keep customer satisfaction high.

I will discuss high availability, redundancy, and survivability throughout this book.

Introducing Disaster Recovery

There are many disaster recovery failover models, technologies, and designs that the cloud can offer, both externally and internally, to back up a corporate data center in the event of a disaster. Hot sites, warm sites, and cold sites are common disaster recovery architectures used in the enterprise world and have been migrated to the cloud as cost-effective backup resources.

Most cloud service providers architect their networks with fault tolerance and disaster recovery built in using regions and availability zones.

You will explore disaster recovery options and techniques later in this book.

Physical Hardware Performance Benchmarks

Earlier in this chapter the concept of benchmarks was introduced and used as an example of how to document your current deployment and compare them with your new cloud deployment as part of the migration validation process. This includes collecting hardware performance benchmarks to establish baselines.

All operating systems log metrics such as I/O operations and LAN statistics such as throughput, link utilization, and errors. Statistics can be collected for RAM and storage as well.

It is important to collect and document these benchmarks to have a reference and, from that reference point, track deviations. Benchmarks can also alert you to the need to add capacity for CPU, memory, storage, and networking, for example, as you now have the data to perform trending analysis. It should be noted that most cloud management and monitoring tools can collect and analyze this data as part of the cloud provider's service offerings.

Costs Savings When Using the Cloud

Cloud economics can be compelling to a company's finance and budget groups. The primary advantage is that cloud computing offers the pay-as-you-grow model discussed in Chapter 1. There are no up-front capital expenses for servers, storage, networking, and so on. With the requirements for massive capital expenses removed from a company for computing and data center operations, that money can be better allocated elsewhere in the organization. Also, there is no requirement to purchase capacity for peak usage; with cloud computing and with resiliency and scaling, adding any needed additional capacity can be enabled in the cloud in a short time frame that is often measured in minutes.

While the cost savings in cloud computing over owning and managing a private data center can be significant, care must be taken to manage your resources effectively. Many cloud billing models are based on hours of usage. If you turn up hundreds of servers and forget to shut them down or have automation scale up and then fail to scale back down when the workload subsides, you may get a very large bill from your cloud company for many CPU instances that were running but unused. Let's all be careful out there!

Energy Savings in the Cloud

Many cloud data centers were constructed in the past 10 or so years and implement up-to-date energy-saving technologies and procedures. Also, these data centers are placed in geographical areas that offer benefits such as green power or near cold water sources for cooling the data centers. The more energy efficient a cloud data center is, the lower the cost of operations. This offers increased operating margins and lower service costs to their customers.

Energy savings can also be realized with the higher utilization ratios found in cloud computing as compared to enterprise data centers that do not benefit from the shared service model and often have servers sitting idle or with low utilization that are still powered up and consuming energy. Modern management systems can power off servers, storage, and other systems that are not being used and can reenable them as needed.

Shared vs. Dedicated Hardware Resources in a Cloud Data Center

The primary economic cost advantages of cloud computing are based on shared virtualized resources. Virtualized storage, networking, and, of course, compute compose the vast majority of a cloud data center's operations. However, there may be times where a dedicated server is your only option. This usually is because of security regulations or application restrictions and special hardware requirements that limit you to a bare-metal server dedicated to one customer.

While the shared model is the most common and most cost effective, most cloud service providers offer dedicated servers at a much higher cost because of the need to allocate a complete server to one customer.

Configuring and Deploying Storage

In a cloud or enterprise computing environment, the storage systems are external from the servers. Each server will usually not have a large array of hard or solid-state drives installed locally inside for use by the VMs running on that specific server. In fact, many servers may not contain any hard drives at all.

Instead, large storage systems that are external to the servers and interconnected over a storage area network are implemented. The design of the SAN and storage arrays is critical for server and application performance. If there is a high read and write latency on the drives or contention over the storage network, performance will suffer. To alleviate the performance issues, the cloud provider may implement enterprise-grade storage systems with solid-state drives or high RPM rates on mechanical disks, fast I/O interconnections, ample bandwidth to the storage controller, and SAN interfaces that are fast enough to handle the anticipated storage traffic load across the network.

When storage is remote from the virtual machines that access them, the ability to move VMs from one hypervisor to another server inside a cloud data center or even between data centers is greatly enhanced. The VM will move and continue to access its storage over the storage network. This can even be accomplished with stateful moves, where an application on a VM will continue to operate even as it is being moved between physical servers. Centralized storage is an enabler of this technology and is useful for maintenance, cloud bursting, fault tolerance, and disaster recovery purposes.

Identifying Storage Configurations

Storage is a core infrastructure component found in any cloud data center. To get started, let's investigate common storage systems and how they attach and are accessed both in the cloud and locally. After reviewing the basics of storage, you'll learn about storage area networking as you look at SANs and the technologies that make up storage area networks that are found in every large data center.

Network-Attached Storage

Network-attached storage (NAS) is file-level access to data across a network. For example, a file server sitting on an Ethernet-based LAN and hosting shared directories is a type of NAS. In a NAS configuration, files are sent over the network rather than blocks of data as in storage area networks. The data is not stored on a local computer, as with direct-attached storage, but over a LAN (see Figure 2.11).

FIGURE 2.11   Network-attached storage

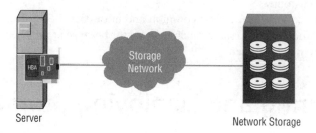

Server

Network Storage

Direct-Attached Storage

In home and small business environments, direct-attached storage (DAS) is common and the easiest method to implement. Just as the name implies, a computer, laptop, or other computing device that has its own storage directly connected is considered to be direct-attached storage, as shown in Figure 2.12. These devices can be hard drives, flash drives, or any other type of storage that is connected to the computer and not over a network. The connection used is commonly an ATA, SATA, or SCSI interface connecting the storage media to the motherboard of the computer.

FIGURE 2.12   Direct-attached storage

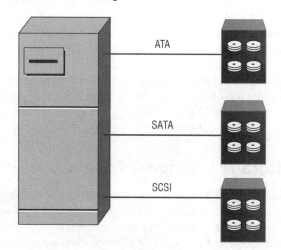

Storage Area Networks

In large computing environments, storage systems are disaggregated from the servers and are enclosed in their own racks in a data center. These storage arrays are connected to networks dedicated to storage traffic and are separate from the Ethernet LANs you are familiar with. A *storage area network* (SAN) is high-speed, highly redundant, and completely dedicated to interconnecting storage devices as illustrated in Figure 2.13. When a server accesses storage over a SAN network, the SAN must be completely lossless and highly available. The most common dedicated store networking technology is Fibre Channel. Typically you configure a SAN_A network and a SAN_B network for redundancy, and the two networks operate in parallel to each other but are not interconnected. This architecture offers two paths from the server to the storage arrays, with a primary network and a standby ready to take over should the primary fail.

SSD= FAST COST MORE
IDE = COST LESS

FIGURE 2.13   Storage area network

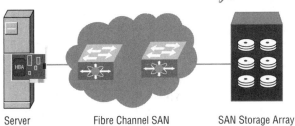

Server   Fibre Channel SAN   SAN Storage Array

Object-Based Storage

Cloud object storage is commonly found in cloud storage deployments and is different from the common file storage technologies such as file and block modes. Data (such as a common file) is paired with metadata and combined to create a storage object. Instead of the hierarchical structures found in traditional block and file storage systems, objects are stored as a flat file in the storage system. With the pool of objects, they are addressed by their object IDs, which is analogous to a filename.

An *object ID* is a pointer to a stored piece of data and is a globally unique identifier for the stored data. Object storage does not use a traditional system such as block- or file-based storage. The object ID is used to locate the data or metadata in the filesystem of the cloud storage arrays.

Metadata is part of a file or sector header in a storage system that is used to identify the content of the data. It is used in big data applications to index and search for data inside the file. Metadata can consist of many different types of information, such as the type of data or application and the security level. Object storage allows the administrators to define any type of information in metadata and associate it with a file.

Extended metadata includes a long list of data that can be attached to a data file. Examples include the author, authentication type, username, password, certificates, encoding, or any other type of user-defined attribute. User-defined information about the files, its access, and its usage enables the creation of specific and sophisticated index schemes.

Storage Provisioning

When creating a cloud presence, the storage systems are as important as managing the compute resources. In this section, you will be introduced to the creation, or *provisioning*, of storage resources in the cloud. Storage provisioning consists of creating and assigning storage, usually as volumes that are mounted or accessed from a server or remote user. In the enterprise data center, storage provisioning is a complex process that requires a dedicated team of storage engineers to implement, monitor, and manage. Storage area networks must be installed and configured, LUNs and VSANs must be created, and all the security and everything that entails must be applied. These new storage volumes must be mounted on the VMs using host bus adapters. These are just the high-level topics with storage because there are many ongoing operational tasks required for storage redundancy, security, and backup operations, for example.

Cloud operations have automated this process and greatly simplified the provisioning of storage for cloud consumers. It is often as simple as accessing the cloud management console with a web browser and clicking the options you desire for storage such as replications, backups, volume size, storage type, encryption, service levels or tiers, and security parameters. Once the desired options are selected, provisioning storage is as simple as clicking the Create button and in several minutes the storage system has been created and deployed.

Thick Provisioning

When deploying a new storage system in the cloud, the automation systems can either allocate all the storage capacity at the time of the volume creation or start with a smaller volume size and add storage capacity as needed.

Thick provisioning is the allocation of all of the requested virtual storage capacity at the time the disk is created. For example, when creating a virtual disk in the cloud, you request a capacity of 100GB for your volume. With thick provisioning, all 100GB will be pre-allocated when the disk is created.

Thin Provisioning

Thin provisioning refers to storage capacity that is allocated on an as-needed basis. This prevents wasting storage capacity if it is unused. When the volume is created, it will not allocate all the capacity requested. Instead, a smaller amount is provisioned, and then additional capacity is added, up to the maximum volume size as required.

Because of the need of a thin-provisioned volume to occasionally add capacity, there will at times be greater latency in accessing your storage resources than compared to thick provisioning, which has all of the storage capacity allocated and ready for use.

In the example given earlier for thick provisioning, you learned that when you request a capacity of 100GB for your volume, all 100GB is allocated. Thin provisioning does not do this as there is a possibility that this space will go unused and is an inefficient allocation of storage capacity. Thin provisioning may only allocate 10GB, for example, and then expand to the maximum requested volume size of 100GB as storage needs require. If the additional space is never needed, then the additional capacity never gets allocated to the disk volume.

With thick provisioning, all 100GB will be pre-allocated when the disk is created.

Storage Overcommitment

Over committing storage resources allows you to allocate more storage space that is physically available to increase operational efficiency. When overcommitting storage, you configure disk capacity to be larger than the actual available disk capacity. You will also need to configure the storage volumes to be thin provisioned, the actual disk allocation for each VM starts small and expands are required. By overcommitting disk resources, the VMs that actually need the additional storage are allowed to access the storage up to its maximum configured value. Overcommitting storage allows for more efficient use of your storage pools since storage is only allocated to virtual resources if they are required.

Since you are allocating more storage to VMs than is actually available, you will need to closely manage your storage to avoid resource starvation such as storage write failures due to lack of disk space.

Physical to Physical

Many applications that need to be migrated are running directly on server hardware in the legacy data center. You may find some of these applications that are not able to be virtualized and require that the cloud provider offer actual physical machines to accommodate this need. While this is not very common and conflicts with the virtualization model of the cloud, many cloud providers offer actual physical servers to accommodate this requirement. It can be very expensive since it requires dedicated server hardware and, often, custom monitoring to be configured. To migrate from your source physical server to the target physical server, you must either do a complete new installation of the operating system and the application or perform a migration. The physical to physical migration will move the application and operating system to the cloud and take into consideration device drivers and differences in the hardware platforms. A P2P migration requires conversation utilities to be run to perform the migration; these are often provided by the cloud provider or by third party software companies.

Encrypting Your Data at Rest

When storing data securely, it is advantageous to encrypt the data on the actual drive as it is stored. *Data at rest* is stored data as compared to data that is passing over a network or being transferred from a storage array to a remote destination for processing.

Encrypting data at rest is as it sounds: The data gets encrypted in the storage volume. Encryption keys are used to encrypt and decrypt the files, and these keys can be managed by either the cloud service provider or the end user depending on feature offerings.

Often encrypting data at rest is required to meet regulatory or corporate compliance issues. When the storage volumes are configured properly, the actual encryption process is hidden, or transparent from the systems accessing the data. It is important to make sure that your encrypted storage implementation takes into account the need to also encrypt the replicated, mirrored, and backed-up data as well.

Token Models

A method of securing access to storage resources is to use tokens. Think of a token as a key to the door; you can use it to unlock it and gain access. The same concept applies to the use of security tokens that are generated and stored in the storage system and remote devices that need access to the stored data.

For example, a web browser may have a storage security token downloaded from the website and use it when requesting access to files stored on a web server's volume. If the key matches, the browser is allowed access.

A storage token is a cryptographic key that is used to gain access to secure files on a storage system. Tokens are electronic keys used to unlock access to stored data. If the user attempting to gain access to the data possesses a valid cryptographic token, they are able to prove that they are who they claim to be since the token was issued by the originating site they are attempting to gain access to.

Tokens are also used in cloud operations to authenticate APIs or command-line access to cloud servers, storage, and other services.

Storage Priorities: Understanding Storage Tiers

Since the data stored in the cloud or data center may have different storage requirements, we will discuss the concept of tiered storage. Data can have different requirements, such as how critical it is, how often it needs to be accessed, geographical placement or encryption, and security requirements. Certain applications may need high read or write speeds for better performance, other data may need to be accessed frequently, and other data can be stored and seldom accessed by an application. Different storage tiers can be defined and assigned to best meet the levels of storage the cloud customer may require.

Tier 1 storage is used for the most critical or frequently accessed data and is generally stored on the fastest, most redundant, or highest quality media available. We will cover storage arrays later in this chapter, but for now, know that with Tier 1, it is important to use a storage configuration that will allow one or more disks to fail with no data being lost and access still available. Tier 1 storage arrays have the greatest manageability and monitoring capabilities and the highest I/O performance and are designed to have the most reliable reliability and durability ratings.

Tier 2 is a notch below and is generally used for data that does not have fast read or write performance requirements or that is accessed infrequently. Tier 2 data can use less expensive storage devices and can even be accessed over a remote storage network. Some examples of Tier 2 data are e-mail storage, file sharing, or web servers where performance is important but less expensive solutions can be used.

Data that is often at rest and rarely accessed, or backups of Tier 1 and Tier 2 data, can be stored at the Tier 3 level. Examples of Tier 3 media are DVD, tape, or other less expensive media types. Tier 3 offers low cost for large amounts of capacity. The trade-off is that it may take hours to access the stored data for retrieval.

There can be many different tiers in a storage design in the cloud. More than three tiers can be implemented based on the complexity and the requirements of the storage system's performance. With the use of automation and scripting, data can be migrated from one tier to the other over time to meet your data retention policies.

The higher the tier, the more critical the data is considered to be and the more the design focuses on faster performance, redundancy, and availability. For example, a Tier 1 data set would generally offer better performance than a Tier 2, which in turn would have higher performance than Tier 3. This is by design; for example, a Tier 3 or higher may be accessed only infrequently and have no need to offer the performance of a Tier 1 data set. By properly classifying the data needs in a multitiered cloud storage system, you can realize significant cost savings by not paying for more than what you require in your cloud design.

A company can establish storage policies and assign data requirements to the needs of the organization, thereby assigning data to be stored in the proper tier. This can allow for cost savings because the organization will pay only for what is required during the data storage life cycle. For example, for regulatory purposes some data may need to be retained well after it has been in use in an organization. Current e-mail may be stored and accessed as Tier 1 or 2 data and then moved to Tier 3 as it ages and becomes less frequently accessed. If the company is required to retain the e-mail files for long periods of time, the data may be stored offline since it will be classified as a higher tier than the online requirements.

Managing and Protecting Your Stored Data

In this section, you will be introduced to methods and technologies to protect data in the cloud. I will expand on this in later chapters as it is a critical topic for the Cloud+ exam.

The shared responsibility model states that both the cloud service provider and the cloud customer share responsibility for cloud operations and security.

In the case of managing and protecting the data stored in the cloud, the cloud provider will perform operations in the background to protect and manage the data and also offer different options that the cloud customer can select from to extend their capabilities for data management. You will learn about these in this section with more detail to be discussed in later chapters.

High Availability and Failover

High availability is the ability of a resource to remain available after a failure of a system. There may be downtime involved during which the resource is recovered and restored. However, the system was designed to recover and remain available.

Fault tolerance refers to a system that will remain operational even after there has been a degradation of its systems. A fault-tolerant system can maintain functionality because of its highly resilient design that takes into account the possibility of system failures and works to mitigate or work around any failures to maintain operations. *CERTAIN LEVEL OF PERFORMANCE*

Replication In and Outside of a Region

Data replication is the process of placing copies of stored data on more than one system for disaster recovery and resiliency purposes. If all of your data is contained in one availability zone and that zone is lost, you will be down until the cloud provider has restored operations. Obviously, this is not a good arrangement! So, it is common to replicate, or place copies of your storage data in more than one availability zone or even across cloud regions for a broader geographical disbursement.

Cloud providers may offer replication services as part of their standard storage offerings. For example, a block storage volume purchased from the provider may include automatically copying the data to more than one availability zone or even regions.

Replication offerings are not only for storage volumes but are also common for managed database services.

Replication Types: Understanding Synchronous and Asynchronous Replications

Since replication uses more than one copy of the data, an issue arises as to how fresh the data is between the primary systems and the backup locations. This may or may not be important depending on the application and your storage objectives. However, if you are operating an active database system and storing replicas of the data at various cloud data centers, the freshness of the data may become a big concern.

There are two primary types of replications, synchronous and asynchronous.

Synchronous replication copies the data to the primary storage system and simultaneously over the network to remote sites and ensures that all replicas are up-to-date and in sync with each other. Synchronous replication is used to support high-end transactional databases that need consistent data and instantaneous failover capabilities. By using synchronous replications, you can achieve a very fast recovery time objective in the event of a failover since the data is in sync with the central depository. Synchronous replication works by writing the data to the primary and secondary storage systems at the same time and acknowledging to the host a successful operation only after both sites have completed the transaction. This approach ensures that both copies are always synchronized.

Asynchronous replication writes the data to the primary storage location and then later will send copies to the remote replicas. With asynchronous replication, there will be a delay as the data is copied to the backup site and provides eventual consistency as it uses a store-and-forward design. The backup storage array is normally several transactions behind the primary.

Using Mirrors in Cloud-Based Storage Systems

Site *mirrors* in the cloud refer to a site that is updated constantly with data files and server information. In case of a primary site failure, the mirror can assume processing and availability. Also with the use of mirroring, multiple sites can be active at the same time for availability, geographical proximity, and capacity management and high-demand purposes. With the frequent updates, the contents of the original site are sent to the mirror site.

Cloning Your Stored Data

Cloud service providers may offer the ability to clone your storage data. This can be automated with scripts, performed on a scheduled basis, or performed manually. The storage volume can be cloned and replicated to other regions for creating new application instances, or the cloned volume can be stored as a backup or a snapshot for disaster recovery purposes.

Using RAID for Redundancy

It is rare to see a single storage drive attached to a server in cloud data centers. What is commonly done is to group sets of drives together to achieve performance gains, achieve storage redundancy, and large storage densities.

The term *RAID* has several definitions and is often referred to as a Redundant Array of Independent Disks. By combining physical disks, you can achieve redundancy without having to sacrifice performance. The groupings of many disks can be used to create very large volumes. When a storage logical unit spans multiple hard drives, increases in performance, speed, and volume size can be achieved.

Disks can be configured in various ways using RAID arrays. These are referred to as *RAID levels*, and you will explore them to see where they are best used and discover the differences between the various levels.

The configuration and operation of RAID arrays can take place either in software running on the operating system or by hardware cards called *RAID controllers*. In the cloud and in data centers, hardware RAID is almost exclusively used because of the performance gains over the software approach. The hardware RAID controller relieves the CPU of cycles that are required with a software-based array.

RAID 0

RAID 0 (pronounced "RAID zero") is where you take a block of data to be stored and spread it across two or more disks. This process is called *striping*—the file is stored across more than one hard drive. You break a file into blocks of data and then stripe the blocks across disks in the system.

Although RAID 0 is simple, it provides no redundancy or error detection, so if one of the drives in a RAID 0 array fails, all data in lost. However, since RAID 0 allows for parallel read and write operations, it is very fast and is often found in storage-intense environments such as many database applications where storage speed can often be a bottleneck.

Figure 2.14 shows striping across multiple disks in RAID 0.

FIGURE 2.14   RAID level 0

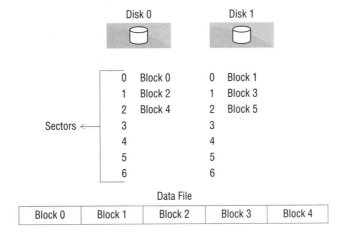

RAID 1

With *RAID 1* you get into the variations that are actually redundant, and in the case of a drive failure, there will be no data loss. RAID 1 is pretty basic in that a complete file is stored on a single disk, and then a second disk is used to contain an exact copy of the same file. By storing the same file on two or more separate disks, complete data redundancy is achieved. Another advantage of RAID 1 is that the data can be read off two or more disks at the same time, which allows for an improvement of read times over reading off a single disk because the data can be read in parallel. However, write performance suffers since the file needs to be written out twice.

RAID 1 is the most expensive RAID implementation since 50 percent of the storage space is for redundancy and not usable. This is because of the requirement of a backup drive, as explained earlier and illustrated in Figure 2.15.

FIGURE 2.15 RAID level 1

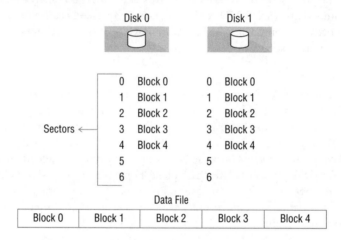

RAID 1+0

RAID levels can be combined in various ways. One common method is to create two separate RAID 1 arrays and then use RAID 0 to mirror them. This is often referred to as RAID 1+0 (see Figure 2.16). With *RAID 1+0* the data is mirrored, and then the mirrors are striped. This configuration offers higher performance than RAID 1; the trade-off is a higher cost.

FIGURE 2.16 RAID level 1+0

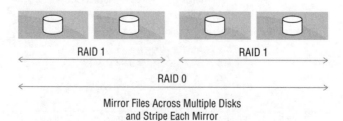

RAID 0+1

Just when you thought this could not get any more confusing, along comes *RAID 0+1*. Actually the two types are very close to being identical. The difference involves the order of operations. With RAID 0+1, the stripe is created first, and then the stripe is written to the mirror, as shown in Figure 2.17.

FIGURE 2.17   RAID level 0+1

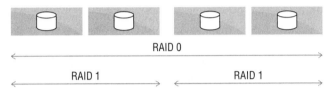

RAID 0

RAID 1   RAID 1

Stripe Files Across Multiple Disks
and Mirror Each Stripe

RAID 5

With *RAID 5*, stripes of file data and check parity data are stored over all the disks; there is no longer a single parity check disk or write bottleneck, as shown in Figure 2.18. RAID 5 dramatically improves the performance of multiple writes since they are now done in parallel. With disk reads, there is a slight improvement since one more disk is used for reading. If any disk in a RAID 5 array fails, the parity information stored across the remaining drive can be used to re-create the data and rebuild the drive array.

FIGURE 2.18   RAID level 5

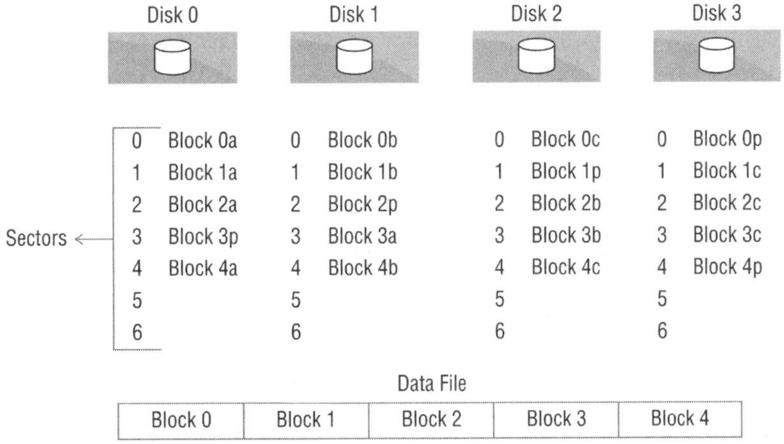

	Disk 0	Disk 1	Disk 2	Disk 3
	0 Block 0a	0 Block 0b	0 Block 0c	0 Block 0p
	1 Block 1a	1 Block 1b	1 Block 1p	1 Block 1c
	2 Block 2a	2 Block 2p	2 Block 2b	2 Block 2c
Sectors ←	3 Block 3p	3 Block 3a	3 Block 3b	3 Block 3c
	4 Block 4a	4 Block 4b	4 Block 4c	4 Block 4p
	5	5	5	5
	6	6	6	6

Data File

Block 0	Block 1	Block 2	Block 3	Block 4

The minimum number of disks in a RAID 5 array is three, but I suggest you use at least five or more disks to realize higher performance.

RAID 5 has read and write performance close to that of RAID 1. However, RAID 5 requires much less disk space compared to other RAID levels and is a popular drive redundancy implementation found in cloud data centers.

The drawback of using RAID 5 arrays is that they may be a poor choice for use in write-intensive applications because of the performance slowdown with writing parity information. Also, when a single disk in a RAID 5 array fails, it can take a long time to rebuild a RAID 5 array. Also, during a disk rebuild, performance is degraded.

RAID 6

RAID 6 is an extension of the capabilities of RAID 5. The added capability offered in the RAID 6 configuration is that a second parity setting is distributed across all the drives in the array, as shown in Figure 2.19. The advantage of adding the second parity arrangement is that RAID 6 can suffer two simultaneous hard drive failures and not lose any data. However, there is a performance penalty with this configuration: The disk write performance is slower than with RAID 5 because of the need to write the second parity stripe.

FIGURE 2.19   RAID level 6

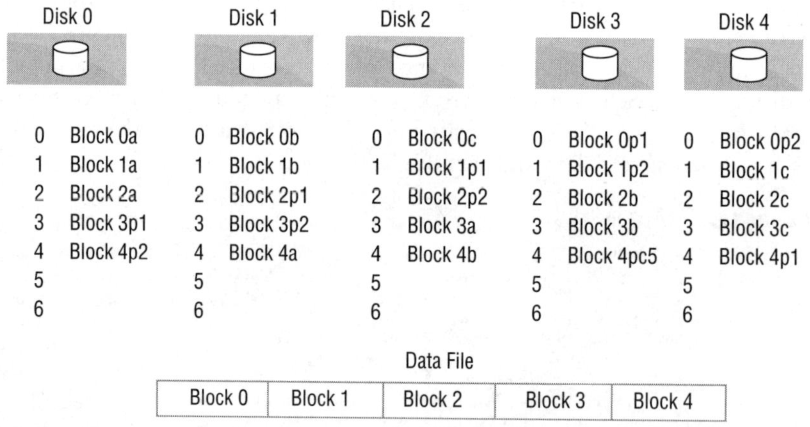

Storage Security Considerations

This section takes a look at security as it applies to storage. Securing your data in the cloud is a primary concern of companies considering migrating their critical data. This is a valid concern and one that should be fully investigated and understood. Also, there are many regulatory statutes concerning privacy of data that may apply. For example, there may be local specific laws that require data be stored in its country of origin or that it must be encrypted while in transit and at rest on the storage device.

Each cloud provider will offer a variety of storage security options that will include the options in the following sections.

Access Control for Your Cloud-Based Storage

A storage access control list (ACL) is a security mechanism that consists of an ordered list of permit and deny statements. ACLs are used to secure access to storage resources in the cloud by explicitly either permitting or denying access to storage resources. Controlling access to storage with the use of ACLs is similar to the use of ACLs for Ethernet switches, routers, and firewalls that you learned about in the previous section. You can selectively permit or deny access to storage objects. Each storage object can have an ACL that defines which remote devices can access it and what rights are granted. For example, a specific user group can be allowed only read access to a storage bucket in the cloud storage system, whereas another group can perform both read and write operations on the same bucket. A customer who has authenticated on your website may then become a member of the authenticated users group and be allowed to access storage resources on a specific volume based on the configuration of that volume's ACL. Groups can be defined as everyone, authenticated users, anonymous users, administrators, or whatever your organization requires. These groups are then filtered using an ACL to allow read, write, and full control to storage system objects.

Understanding Obfuscation

One of the more unusual terms in the cloud computing world, *obfuscation* is defined as a means to complicate, confuse, or bewilder. So, obfuscating is used to hide information in stored data in the cloud.

Obfuscation is a technique used to increase the security of storage data by making it difficult to read legitimate data stored in files. Using obfuscation processes on storage systems makes it difficult for hackers or hijackers to make sense of the stored data because the data is so deeply buried (obfuscated) with random data that it is hard to determine what is actual data and what is not.

To prevent hackers from disassembling data, one of the processes used is obfuscation, which is data scrambling. Data is purposely scrambled, which renders it unreadable until the obfuscation process is reversed.

Storage Area Networking, Zoning, and LUN Masking

By default, Ethernet switches and routers can communicate with each other, and any restrictions on what will or won't be allowed are imposed by configuring and applying access control lists. Fibre Channel switches take a completely different approach; by default, the SAN ports are not allowed to communicate with each other until you configure zoning on the SAN network fabric switches. Zoning is a SAN network security process that restricts storage access between initiators and targets. For example, when configuring zoning on a SAN network, you define what storage volumes each individual server can access. In a cloud data center, storage is usually centralized in large storage arrays and accessed by a large number of virtual machines over a SAN. The process of zoning allows you to define what storage volumes each individual virtual machine can access, as shown in Figure 2.20.

FIGURE 2.20   Zoning filters access to storage resources on the SAN switching fabric.

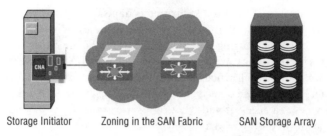

Storage Initiator   Zoning in the SAN Fabric   SAN Storage Array

Each zone is defined by groups of ports (called *hard zoning*) or worldwide names (called *soft zoning*) that are allowed to communicate with each other. You can group multiple zones into zone sets on a SAN fabric switch and activate the complete group. Zoning is performed in the storage network in the Fibre Channel switch, and not on the endpoint devices. Zoning defines what storage resources a server can access on the remote storage array. A practical application is to only allow Windows servers to access Windows block storage LUNs and for Linux to only be allowed to access Linux logical units. Problems would arise if, for example, a Linux system attempted to access a Windows filesystem; this would lead to the filesystems becoming corrupted and unusable. Also, another practical example of zoning is for each virtual machine to boot from a SAN and not use any local storage on the service it resides on. By implementing zoning, you can ensure that each VM mounts its correct storage volumes.

LUN masking is similar to zoning, but instead of being defined at the SAN switch level, LUN masking is configured at the storage controller level. LUN masking defines the access rights between the LUNs and individual VMs or bare-metal servers. LUN masking is access control for the initiators on the SAN to the targets. Since LUN masking takes place on the storage controller, as shown in Figure 2.21, and not on the SAN switching fabric, a much more granular configuration can be achieved.

FIGURE 2.21   LUN masking filters initiator access to storage volumes on the storage controller.

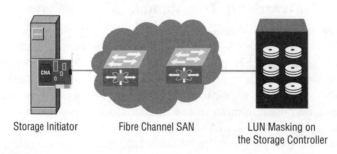

Storage Initiator   Fibre Channel SAN   LUN Masking on
                                                       the Storage Controller

In the cloud data center, a storage array will host a large number of LUNs. It is not secure or desirable to have these LUNs accessible to all servers on the network. With LUN masking, you can restrict the storage resources to the specific servers that require access to them. There are many configuration options, which can include a single server accessing a LUN or a group of servers in a cluster all accessing the same storage resources. The configuration options are important when a server needs to boot off the storage area network and requires exclusive access to a LUN. Another instance is when an application (such as VMware's VMotion) that moves VMs between bare-metal servers needs a less restrictive configuration to allow a number of VMs to access a central storage area.

Setting Up Access to Your Storage Data

The following section will discuss how to access your stored data in the cloud and the steps that should be taken when migrating to the cloud to ensure that your data access is properly configured.

User and Host Access

Storage information can be accessed by a user requesting data stored on a volume hosted in the cloud or by a machine or application such as a web server or a database. While these different systems may access the same stored data in some cases, the methods used may be different, as you will learn in this section.

Authentication and Authorization

Authentication is the process of determining the identity of a client usually by a login process. By authenticating the user, you learn the identity of that user and can authorize or grant permissions to cloud resources by either allowing or denying access to specific resources. User authentication usually consists of a username and password combination or some variation of that, such as a token or biometric access method. Cookies can be used for web access to identify and authenticate a user connecting to your website. For example, a visitor to your e-commerce site may be prompted initially for a username and password through their browser. Once authentication is completed, a cookie is stored in the local computer with an identity token that will grant authorization to their account. Servers such as virtual machines and the applications hosted on the servers may also be required to authenticate with other applications. They use a service account and can authenticate using APIs, a form of application-to-application communications based on standard programmable interfaces such as XML or JSON.

Accessing Your Storage in the Cloud

For hosting services in the cloud that utilize virtual machines, there will be storage volumes created in the cloud, and these volumes will be mounted locally as disks on the VMs.

Cloud vendors offer remote access to your cloud-based storage that uses special client software that synchronizes files stored on your local device to the cloud and then replicates the files to other devices connected to the same account using services such as Google Drive, Dropbox, and OneDrive. Other offerings such as Amazon S3 use a standard browser.

Other common storage access methods include software API calls and CLI access and are specific to the various cloud storage offerings.

Managing Cloud Storage

Storage is managed using the common shared responsibility model of cloud vendors. The cloud provider will manage all of the physical hardware, storage networking, configuration, and ongoing support of the storage infrastructure.

The customer accessing the storage offerings will usually be given a web-based dashboard, CLI, or API interface to manage their cloud storage. Customer storage management usually includes creating new volumes, backing up and replicating data, and configuring security and encryption requirements. Other options may include defining policies for the storage tiers desired for lifecycle management and creating roles and polices for access.

Performing a Server Migration

With the cloud being a predominantly virtualized environment, you should understand how to take your existing servers and applications running directly on their own hardware and migrate them to the virtualized world of hypervisors and VMs. In this section, you will learn about this process. We will start by showing you how to gather background information. Then you will learn about creating the virtual images and address the issues of storage and how you will migrate the data for the application.

Careful and detailed planning is critical to a successful migration of operating systems off a physical server and onto a hypervisor as a virtual server. To establish what will be required as a virtual server, you must collect information such as CPU, memory, storage, and I/O needs from the existing server. You can do so by establishing a baseline of the server to be migrated. The monitoring and data collection process will vary as to what types of applications the servers are running and the time-of-day CPU, disk, or I/O workload increases that may need to be taken into consideration. Once the baseline requirements have been collected, you can use that valuable information to scale and configure the new virtual server's hardware profile.

When you are migrating from a physical to a virtual server environment, some downtime may be required. You can schedule standard data center maintenance windows for the changes to be implemented. Other changes such as IP addressing, VLAN, and VSAN configurations and Domain Name System (DNS) server settings may need to be changed at the same time that the server is being migrated from a physical to a virtual server. It is common to create an implementation document that covers all the required steps to be taken during the change and how to back those changes out if the change goes bad and needs to be restored before the maintenance window closes. The implementation document should also cover in detail all the steps to be taken to validate that the migration is working as expected.

When undertaking a physical-to-virtual migration project, the implementation team will take into consideration any existing server performance issues and work to mitigate them on the new virtualized cloud computing platform. Performance issues can be identified from the collected baseline information and include such areas as CPU, storage, memory, or network contention. Based on this data, changes can be made during the migration to mitigate issues. When the migration is complete, a prepared testing plan should be followed to validate that the changes made are operating as expected. It can be a detailed and time-consuming process to test and verify all the various components in the new VM. After the migration of a server from a hardware physical machine to a virtual machine running on a hypervisor, another baseline should be performed. The baseline data can be compared with the original information to see whether the new server is performing as expected.

Different Types of Server Migrations

Migrating servers to the cloud will require some planning and preparation for the move. It will be the case the majority of the time that the cloud operations will be virtualized. It will be necessary to convert your server deployments into a format that is compatible with your cloud service provider. Most cloud operations offer the ability to install the operating systems directly on the bare-metal server for specialized use cases where the application does not support virtualization.

The terminology and concepts of server migrations are straightforward to understand, and the process has matured over the years and has become a straightforward process to complete.

Physical to Virtual

When undertaking a migration, you have several options. A *physical-to-virtual (P2V)* migration means taking a server that is running an operating system and applications and then migrating it to a VM running on top of a hypervisor (see Figure 2.22). A P2V migration may require reinstalling the operating system, application, and data files onto a new VM from scratch. Many companies offer software utilities, such as VMware vCenter Converter and Microsoft's Virtual Machine Manager, that can perform the conversion. Several third-party software companies and cloud providers offer fully automated P2V utilities.

FIGURE 2.22   Physical-to-virtual migration

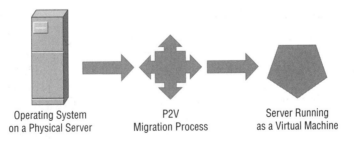

Operating System   P2V   Server Running
on a Physical Server   Migration Process   as a Virtual Machine

Virtual to Virtual

Virtual-to-virtual (V2V) migrations are much more straightforward than a P2V migration. Generally, a V2V migration involves cloning the existing VM and installing that image at the cloud provider's hosting center, as shown in Figure 2.23.

FIGURE 2.23   Virtual-to-virtual migration

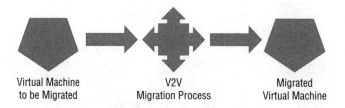

Virtual Machine
to be Migrated

V2V
Migration Process

Migrated
Virtual Machine

Virtual to Physical

While not as common, there is an option of converting from a virtual server to a physical server known as *virtual-to-physical (V2P)*, as shown in Figure 2.24. A use case for this type of migration would be if more processing power is needed and can be provided if the server is hosted on its own server hardware. Virtual-to-physical conversions have lots of details that must be sorted through based on the hardware and virtualization software being used. It may be that a fresh installation of the operating system and application will be required. This type of migration would need to be researched and options explored based on each migration's unique requirements.

FIGURE 2.24   Virtual-to-physical migration

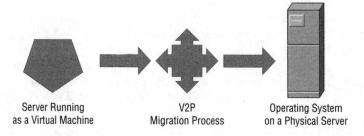

Server Running
as a Virtual Machine

V2P
Migration Process

Operating System
on a Physical Server

Migrating Your Storage Data

A server's data storage volumes can be migrated separately from or as part of a server migration. Storage can be moved from a Fibre Channel SAN to other environments, such as network-attached or direct-attached storage models. Data transferred between storage devices also allows for disaster recovery scenarios. The cloud service provider will work with you to make the transition to the cloud. This will vary based on the cloud provider's storage offerings and infrastructure (see Figure 2.25).

When planning the storage migration, take into account the amount of bandwidth and how long it will take to upload the storage data from your internal data center to the cloud. For example, if you are accessing the cloud over the Internet with a relatively slow connection, determine how long it will take to transmit the storage data or whether other options are available to transfer the data.

FIGURE 2.25   Storage migration

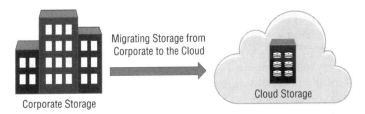

Migrating Storage from
Corporate to the Cloud

Corporate Storage

Cloud Storage

With the large amount of storage data residing in corporate data centers, it may not be feasible to upload the storage data to your new cloud-based storage solution. With petabyte-scale storage arrays, it could literally take years to transfer the data over a network. Many workarounds have been developed including appliances that can be shipped to the private data center and directly connected to the storage network for a local transfer of stored data. Then the appliance can be shipped to the cloud service provider and the data directly transferred to the cloud storage arrays. There are options to use these appliances as local data stores in the private data center with them performing the upload to the cloud as a background process. Each provider has unique offerings to mitigate the delays encountered when transferring such large amounts of data including shipping-container-sized storage systems that are pulled by large semi-tractors between the remote storage sites and the cloud data centers.

Online or Offline

When you are considering the migration of servers to the cloud, *online migrations* are often preferable to offline migrations because they are performed in a much shorter period of time. One restriction of an online migration is the amount of networking bandwidth that is available between the data center, where the existing server resides, and the cloud data center, where the new virtual machine will be migrated to. If there is insufficient bandwidth to perform the migration in a reasonable amount of time, then offline should be your backup choice. In an *offline migration*, the virtual server is stored on storage media and shipped to the cloud provider to be installed. This requires a delay in the migration because of the transport times of the files. In addition, experienced staff will be required at the remote location to complete the process at the cloud provider's data center.

Understanding the Virtualization Formats Needed When Migrating

Each hypervisor model and cloud service provider may have unique VM file formats that need to be considered when migrating to the cloud. The disk file formats for the VM that is being imported must be supported by the cloud provider.

Common formats include VDI from Oracle, which is VirtualBox's disk image, VMDK from VMware, VHD from Microsoft, and Amazon's AMI images.

Addressing Application Portability

Application portability is the ability to move applications from one cloud provider to another without a requirement for a major format conversion. Application portability enables the customer to migrate their applications from one provider to another and avoid a situation where they are locked into a cloud vendor because of proprietary extensions that make application migrations difficult or impossible. It is important to consider portability as part of your migration plans to enable you to move operations to another provider if there is a breach in the service level agreement; extended outages; or geographical, regulatory, or pricing issues that arise. Portability of VMs and applications will require that the template formats match between the source and destination cloud providers. This favors cloud providers that support open standards or offer conversion utilities that will modify the formats to match what is required at the destination.

Portability is a general term that encompasses any type of migration such as private to public, public to private, community to public, and other combinations.

Workload Migration Common Procedures

Workload migrations require extensive planning and preparation prior to the move. Applications that are selected as candidates to run in a cloud-based infrastructure should be tested and evaluated for interoperability. It is desirable to set up a test environment to validate that the application is working as expected prior to moving the application into production mode. When performing validations, it is important to check for performance, service levels/uptime, serviceability, compliance, and security, and to evaluate any trade-offs from hosting internally in your private data center or in the cloud.

Migrations should be performed under the guidance of a project manager and as a collaborative effort of all interested groups in your organization. Current best practices should be followed to ensure a smooth transition.

Examining Infrastructure Capable of Supporting a Migration

In this section, you will learn about the underlying infrastructure and potential issues that should be examined and mitigated prior to the migration. For example, it is important to investigate the delays of transferring data, the downtime needed, any regulatory or legal concerns that may need to be addressed, and when is a good time to schedule the migration.

Available Network Capacity

As you learned earlier in the chapter when I discussed whether to perform your migration offline or online, the amount of network bandwidth may be a limiting factor. If you have a large amount to data to transfer and limited network capacity to the cloud, there may be an excessive time window required to perform the migration. This may require you to add Internet bandwidth prior to the migration or consider an offline migration.

As part of the planning process for your migration, the project team must determine the amount of data that needs to be transferred to the cloud and calculate the time needed when using an online migration with existing network capacity.

Downtime During the Migration

Downtime will need to be calculated by the project management team and is the sum of all the steps needed to perform the migration process. It is usually a given that there will be a certain amount of downtime to perform a migration. However, with cloud computing, staging the application in the cloud is rather straightforward. This allows a prototype to be installed and configured in the cloud. Using this as a development deployment, it can be tested offline and validated that it is ready for production. Once the development deployment is ready, it can be moved to production status and the workload transferred to the new cloud deployment with a minimal amount of downtime.

It is important to plan for the unexpected and to allocate additional downtime as a buffer in case the migration does not go as expected. Plan for the time required to roll back to the original pre-migration state in case the cutover is not successful.

When to Migrate (Peak Timeframes and Working Hour Restrictions)

Selecting a time window to migrate workloads will be dependent on your organization's local policies and requirements. It is logical that the migration window should be performed during times that there is an anticipated light workload where downtime would have a limited impact on your operations.

Legal Questions About Migrating to the Cloud

Any legal issues such as legal compliance requirements must be fully investigated prior to the migration taking place. In fact, this should be an integral part of the project management team's pre-migration planning process. Any legal or compliance requirements must be included in the initial design phase of the project to ensure that the cloud architecture meets all legal restrictions.

Local time zones and follow the sun migration constraints

Care should be taken when performing migrations across multiple time zones to prevent any additional downtime impact than is necessary. Take into account the local times of the data centers you are migrating servers into and make sure that the migration takes place during periods of low usage in those local times. If you are working in Europe performing migrations in Asia, make sure that you are not impacting Asian operations in the middle of their production hours. All time zone constraints should be identified and managed as part of your migration plan.

A common support model for not only cloud computing, but also all information technology disciplines is the follow the sun support model. This is where a support operation is active in the part of the world that is traditionally open for business. For example, a global operation will have multiple world wide support centers that open and cloud based on the time of day. A site in one time zone closes and hands off operations at the end of the work shift to the next site to the west that picks up operations.

Managing User Identities and Roles

In this section, you will learn about user access control, or the ability to identify users in your cloud environment and, after authenticating the users, to determine who they are. You can then apply access rights to define what they are allowed to do on the network. You will learn about granting rights based on an administrative user's role on the network. Then you will learn about the differences between mandatory and discretionary access controls. To add security, you must use several steps to log into a network; this is referred to as *multifactor authentication*, which will be covered. Finally, the concept of federations will be introduced and explained.

RBAC: Identifying Users and What Their Roles Are

Role-based access control (RBAC) is a method in which access rights are granted to, or restricted from, users based on which roles they perform in an organization. RBAC uses different defined permission levels to assign routine activities and allows and restricts access to cloud resources based on these roles. The roles are defined based on the task, and users are then assigned to the roles. Based on the permissions of the roles, the users will inherit those rights. What exactly is a role? It can be almost anything you decide to define it as. Many common roles are defined in applications, operating systems, and networking equipment. Some examples are shown in Table 2.2; these are just examples, and you may have a long list of roles based on your organization's needs.

TABLE 2.2   Role-based access control

Organizational Role	Role Description
Administrator	The superuser/root account that has full system control
Guest	Usually given limited rights such as read-only access
Auditor	Rights granted for auditing purposes such as resources consumed, license usage, or access to corporate compliance data
Sustaining/patch management	Rights are granted to allow members of this group to access the systems for the purpose of upgrades and software patch management.
Storage administrator	Group rights are assigned here for the storage management role in monitoring and maintaining the cloud-based storage systems.

The scope of role-based administration should be broad enough to cover all systems the user must access to perform their assigned tasks but not too broad as to grant access to systems that the users in the role may not need access to. The scope can be defined in a role for such responsibilities as remote offices, network infrastructure, Linux-based servers, and database operations. When users are assigned to the role, the scope will determine which systems the role grants access to.

Identity Applications in the Public Cloud

Most cloud service providers will offer their own identity applications to manage access to cloud objects such as VMs, load balancers, databases, and storage. Users can be created and assigned to groups that have rights to access cloud resources. Also, roles can be defined for servers to simplify management cloud. For example, all web servers could be placed into a role called WWW that limits access to the load balancers on specific ports.

When using identity applications, once the device or use has been successfully identified, then the lists of operations they are authorized to perform can be assigned.

What Happens When You Authenticate?

Authentication is the process of determining the identity of a client usually by a login process. By authenticating the user, you learn the identity of that user and can authorize or grant permissions to cloud resources by either allowing or denying access to specific resources.

User authentication usually consists of a username and password combination or some variation of that, such as a token or biometric access method. Cookies can be used for web access to identify and authenticate a user connecting to your website. For example, a visitor to your e-commerce site may be prompted initially for a username and password through their browser. Once authentication is completed, a cookie is stored in the local computer with an identity token that will grant authorization to their account. Servers such as virtual machines and the applications hosted on the servers may also be required to authenticate with other applications. They use a service account and can authenticate using APIs, a form of application-to-application communications based on standard programmable interfaces such as XML and JSON.

Giving Authorization to Access Specific Cloud Services

When a device or user has been identified through authentication systems, then they can be given authorization to perform their specific duties.

Access control systems will assign specific roles and duties to users or groups of users. For example, database administrators can be given full access to manage a database application but be restricted from performing VM or storage operations.

Understanding Federations

Identity systems using *federations* allow multiple organizations to use the same data for identification when accessing the networks or resources of everyone in the group.

In cloud-based solutions, where multiple organizations are sharing the same application, the federated identity management approach allows all participants to consolidate resources. Users share a common set of policies and access rights across multiple organizations.

While a federation may sound like it is identical to the SSO approach, the difference is that SSO is concerned with just authentication and is used by one organization instead of the multi-organization scope in a federation implementation.

The federated approach is based on industry standards that allow for the needed interoperability between different organizations' systems. The approach is common in cloud-based e-commerce sites. You log into the site with your web browser, and the cloud application may be in a federation with banks and payment systems. Using the federated approach, you will not be required to log into each system to shop, check out, arrange shipping, and purchase warranties since all these elements are integrated.

The federated approach can be used for machine-to-machine or application-to-application communications between organizations in addition to the user example given here.

Single Sign-on Systems

Single sign-on (SSO) is an approach that reduces the need to sign into multiple systems for access. SSO allows a user to log in just one time and be granted access rights to multiple systems. Using SSO, you can centralize authentication of multiple systems into just one area, easing user administration significantly.

For example, a web server administrator may need to manage multiple web servers in the cloud simultaneously. Since all of these web servers are under the administrator's control, you can create an SSO group called "web administrators," and when they log into the servers, they are granted access to all servers in the group without having to log into each one individually.

Directory servers using the Lightweight Directory Access Protocol (LDAP) are an example of SSO systems. You log into the directory services one time, and based on your rights, you are allowed to access systems on the network without any additional login requirements.

Single sign-on eliminates the need to remember multiple username and password combinations and saves the time of having to enter your authentication information over and over as you log into different systems.

SSO is also effective when terminating a session. When you log off, the directory services will log out, or disconnect you from the multiple systems you had accessed.

Understanding Infrastructure Services

Networking services are applications that are considered to fall under the realm of networking and include the management of IP addressing, load balancing, network security devices such as firewalls, intrusion and prevention systems, security services, and domain name services.

Domain Name Service

To resolve a name to an IP address that the IP protocol uses to connect to a remote device, the server or workstation will perform a DNS server lookup. The DNS server will have the domain name to IP address mapping and reply with the correct IP address for any given domain name. Think of this as a phonebook where you know the name of a business but not the number; the phone book provides the name-to-number lookup function. DNS works the same way but references domain names to the IP address that is needed to route to that location. DNS uses well-known port 53.

Dynamic Host Configuration Protocol

The *Dynamic Host Configuration Protocol (DHCP)* allows for automatic assignment of IP addressing information to devices on a network. This eliminates the need to statically configure addressing information when you connect to a network. DHCP listens on port 68.

Certificate Services

Most cloud providers offer their customers the ability to outsource the creation, management, and deployment of digital security certificates. For example, SSL, public/private, and many other token-based certificates can be managed by the cloud service provider. Certificate management offerings that may be available are services that will rotate the keys, update the servers, and load balancers with current keys, and ensure the private keys are securely stored.

Load Balancing

Load balancing addresses the issues found when cloud workloads and connections increase to the point where a single server can no longer handle the workload or performance requirements of web, DNS, and FTP servers; firewalls; and other network services. Load balancer functions include offloading applications and tasks from the application server, such as the processing for SSL, compression, and TCP handshakes. With load balancing, you can configure the cloud for many servers working together and sharing the load. Therefore, redundancy and scalability can be achieved, as shown in Figure 2.26.

FIGURE 2.26   Load balancing web servers

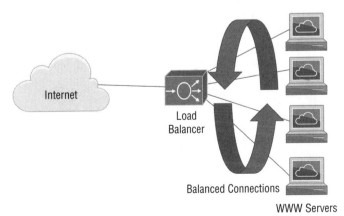

A load balancer is commonly found in front of web servers. The website's IP address is advertised on the network via DNS. This IP address is not of the real web server but instead is an interface on the load balancer. The load balancer allocates the traffic by distributing the connections to one of many servers connected to it. Load balancing allows a website to scale by allocating many servers in the cloud to handle the workload. Also, a load balancer can check the health of each server and remove a server from the network if there is a hardware, network, or application issue and can terminate secure connections such as SSL to offload security processing from the web servers.

Multilayer User Authentication Services

Multifactor or multilayer authentication adds an additional layer of authentication by adding token-based systems in addition to the traditional username and password authentication model.

Common multilayer authentication follows the "something you have and something you know" model. For example, when you go to the bank down the street to use the ATM machine, to authenticate you will need to possess the ATM card (something you have) and enter a PIN (something you know) to withdraw money.

Multifactor authentication systems use one-time token generation systems that will generate a random number that is usually four or more characters. This number has a short life span and must be entered into your regular login as you authenticate. The token generators can be hardware based and are commonly attached to a keychain or software that runs on a smartphone or laptop.

Firewall Security

Firewalls are generally deployed between the cloud network and the cloud consumer for protection of unauthorized access into the networks. A firewall is either hardware based or a virtualized device that inspects network traffic and compares the traffic to a defined rules' list to determine whether that traffic is allowed. If it is not permitted, the firewall will block the traffic from entering the network. Hence, firewalls provide a secure barrier in and out of a network. Many firewalls can also provide the VPN services discussed earlier to interconnect the network management center to the cloud data center of a secure encrypted connection. A firewall will inspect all traffic passing through it and determine whether to permit or deny the packets. Generally such objects as source and destination IP addresses, protocol number, and port or application type are used in the rules' sets to make these decisions. Also, since firewalls can sit at the edge of a network, they provide valuable logging of network and security information for analysis. Standard firewall deployments are shown in Figure 2.27 and Figure 2.28.

FIGURE 2.27   Network firewall for security

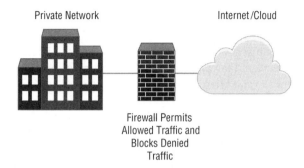

Private Network

Internet/Cloud

Firewall Permits
Allowed Traffic and
Blocks Denied
Traffic

FIGURE 2.28   Firewalls define what traffic is allowed in and out the network.

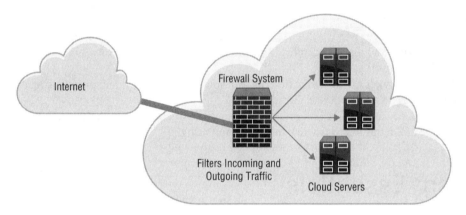

Internet

Firewall System

Filters Incoming and
Outgoing Traffic

Cloud Servers

Summary

In this chapter, you learned about the concepts, practices, and technologies involved in deploying and migrating to the cloud. The chapter covered a lot of topics, including how to analyze and prepare for a migration and then how to execute the deployment plan.

To prepare for the migration, it is important that you fully understand the basic cloud models of community, hybrid, private, and public. These are key concepts in cloud computing.

Other core migration topics include understanding the cloud networking infrastructure including ports and protocols, virtual private networks, intrusion detection and prevention, VxLAN overlay topologies, the concept of a DMZ, basic IP addressing using public and private IP, and segmenting a network.

The chapter also introduced you to the network services you will need to understand for the exam. These include services such as DNS, DHCP, certificate servers, and agents, as well as antivirus systems, load balancers, firewalls, and IDS/IPS systems.

The chapter described how to size the virtualized resources such as CPU and memory for your VM servers with discussions of bursting, ballooning, and overcommitments. You learned about CPU designs and how hyper-threading and multithreading is implemented in the virtualized cloud servers. High availability was discussed and will be explored in greater detail later in this book.

Storage is a key component in the cloud, and you learned about many storage different topics such as availability, replications, mirroring, and cloning. The chapter then discussed storage tiers and redundancy levels including the RAID types. I detailed the primary storage types that include network-attached, direct-attached, and storage area networks. Then you learned that there are two types of storage provisioning used in the cloud, thick and thin. Storage security was also covered.

To perform a migration, you must prepare your servers by doing any necessary migration conversions. The common migration processes of physical to virtual, virtual to virtual, and virtual to physical were discussed and detailed. Next I talked about virtualization formats, application and data portability, and the potential issues of performing a migration either online or offline.

The different types of authentication and authorization included federations, single sign-on, multifactor, and directory services.

Finally, we covered deploying networking services, which is important to understand not only for the exam but for your work in cloud computing.

Exam Essentials

Know the key concepts of creating and executing a cloud deployment.   Cloud migrations are a key exam topic and the primary focus of this chapter. It is critical that you understand all of the project topics concerning the preparation and deployment process. I suggest you read this chapter multiple times until you fully understand the migration process.

Differentiate between the cloud service models.   The cloud deployment models are used constantly in the day of a cloud professional; these help apply structure to the more detailed concepts that will be introduced later in this study guide. For the exam and your day-to-day work, know what community, hybrid, private, and public clouds are. By combining your knowledge of the deployment models and the service models introduced in Chapter 1, you will have a good foundation to do well on the exam.

Understand and differentiate the technical concepts of performing a migration.   Know the CPU and memory sizing topics. Memory topics such as bursting, ballooning, and overcommitments are all fair game for exam questions. CPU topics that you must know are threading, virtualization extensions in the CPU silicon, performance, and dedicated vs. shared computing.

Explain the storage technologies used in cloud computing.   This chapter provided extensive details on storage theory and practical implementation. Storage plays a key role in running your operations in the cloud, and you learned about the various types of storage, redundancy, provisioning models, security, availability, and redundancy. Storage is a key exam topic.

Identify and be able to describe how to perform workload migrations.   To migrate your workloads to the cloud, migrations will most likely need to be performed. This is a key topic in the compute section of the exam. Know what V2V, P2V, and V2P migrations are and when you may need to perform each one. Understand the issues involved with storage migrations as well as how to determine whether an online or offline migration will be required.

Explain the different types of user and machine authentication and authorization techniques.   Be able to identify and explain what the different types of authentication are. These include local, federated, directory servers, single sign-on, and multifactor. The exam may give you a scenario where you will need to identify the best authentication for the given requirements.

Explain what network servers are and be able to both identify them and explain their use in cloud computing.   Core network services in the cloud include domain name servers, Dynamic Host Control Protocol, security certificates, agents, antivirus systems, load balancers, firewalls, and intrusion detection and prevention systems. These are all critical components for any cloud deployment model and application. Read this section over multiple times until you fully understand the basics of each technology and be able to identify when, where, and why each is used in the cloud network.

Written Lab

Fill in the blanks for the questions provided in the written lab. You can find the answers to the written labs in Appendix B.

1. A hypervisor function that allows the hypervisor to reclaim unused memory from a VM running on top of the hypervisor and to allocate that memory for other uses is referred to as _____ _____.

2. A _____ _____ _____ is very high-speed, highly redundant, and completely dedicated to interconnecting storage devices.

3. _____ _____ refers to a system that will remain operational even after there has been a degradation of its systems. These systems can maintain functionality because of its highly resilient design that takes into account the possibility of system failures and works to mitigate or work around any failures to maintain operations.

4. _____ _____ copies the data to the primary storage system and simultaneously over the network to remote sites and ensures that all replicas are up-to-date and in sync with each other.

5. If your cloud provider is running a different type of hypervisor, you may need to perform a _____ migration prior to moving the VMs to the new cloud service provider.

6. _____ _____ is the ability to move applications from one cloud provider to another without a requirement for a major format conversion.

7. _____ allow multiple organizations to use the same data for identification when accessing the networks or resources of everyone in the group.

8. A _____ _____ offers performance enhancements, scalability, and encryption termination services for public web servers.

9. Taking sample performance metrics that need to be collected as part of the documentation process is referred to as creating a _____.

10. The _____ _____ _____ monitors network traffic for malicious activity and actively attempts to prevent the attack.

Review Questions

The following questions are designed to test your understanding of this chapter's material. For more information on how to obtain additional questions, please see this book's Introduction. You can find the answers in Appendix A.

1. Carl is documenting his employers cloud deployments and needs to label the cloud delivery model is used by his single organization. As a Cloud+ consultant, what would you suggest he name his internal cloud?

    A. Hybrid

    B. Public

    C. Private

    D. Community

2. A national tax preparation firm is accessing industry-specific productivity applications in the cloud; many other tax preparation companies are also subscribing to the same service. What model of cloud are they accessing?

    A. Hybrid

    B. Public

    C. Private

    D. Community

3. Mary is a Cloud+ certified security consultant for her company. She is researching enhanced security access systems. What could she suggest that requires something you have and something you know?

    A. Single sign-on

    B. Confederations

    C. Active Directory/LDAP

    D. Multifactor

4. Pete is concerned about stored data that is replicated to a standby zone but not immediately. The delay means there is going to be a short period of time where the data is not consistent. What storage replication service ensures eventual consistency?

    A. Synchronous

    B. Asynchronous

    C. Block

    D. Tier 1

    E. File-based

    F. RAID 6

5. Scott is planning his company's upload of stored data to the cloud. What are two common storage migration types? (Choose two.)

   A. Physical to virtual

   B. Block to object

   C. Online

   D. Offline

   E. Synchronous

   F. Asynchronous

6. Judy is migrating a Linux OS from running on a dual-slot, eight-core server in a private cloud to a VMware-based server in the public cloud, what type of migration would she perform?

   A. vMotion

   B. P2V

   C. Private to public

   D. V2V

   E. Synchronous replication

7. Christina has been asked by the firewall administration group to identify secure network protocols that can be used to prevent network analyzers from being able to read data in flight. Which of the following are considered secure network protocols that she recommend using? (Choose three.)

   A. SHHTP

   B. DHCP

   C. HTTPS

   D. DNS

   E. SSH

   F. SMTP

   G. FTPS

8. What is the process of complicating the ability to read stored data?

   A. PKI

   B. Obfuscation

   C. Cipher

   D. Symmetrical

9. Jerry is learning about cloud storage systems, she is interested in learning about high-speed network storage solutions, What would you recommend she focus her research on?

   A. Block access

   B. Zoning

   C. VMFS

   D. SAN

10. What is the process of determining the identity of a client usually by a login process?

   A. Authorization

   B. Accounting

   C. Authentication

   D. Federation

   E. Identity access

11. What are common management interfaces that are used to migrate and manage cloud-based resources? (Choose three.)

   A. Web console

   B. SNMP

   C. API

   D. PaaS

   E. CLI

12. VMs running on a hypervisor consume which of the following resources? (Choose three.)

   A. Bare-metal cores

   B. Virtual RAM

   C. SaaS

   D. Virtual CPUs

   E. RAID

   F. Memory pools

13. What system was developed to address the different types of storage needs a cloud consumer may require for availability, response times, backups, and economics?

   A. RAID

   B. Multipathing

   C. Tiering

   D. Policies

14. Terri is planning on implementing physical disk redudenacy on her SQL database in the public cloud. She is creating specifications for her virtual machine image that will become the template for the database servers. What time of disk redundancy options could she implement to meet the needs of a SQL deployment?

   A. Multipathing

   B. RAID

   C. Masking

   D. Tiering

15. Which storage type stripes file data and performs a parity check of data over multiple disks that can recover from a hard disk failure?

   A. RAID 0

   B. RAID 1

   C. RAID 1+0

   D. RAID 5

16. Jill is reviewing a document form her secondary community cloud provider, what is the document that outlines specific metrics and the minimum performance that is offered by the cloud provider?

   A. SSL

   B. SLA

   C. Benchmark

   D. Baseline

17. Storage area networks support which type of storage? (Choose the best answer.)

   A. Meta

   B. Object

   C. Block

   D. File

18. What identity system gives multiple discrete organizations access to your NoSQL community cloud database via your cloud-based application server?

   A. Single sign-on

   B. Federations

   C. LDAP

   D. Authorization manager

19. When performing a migration from your on-site private cloud to a new community cloud data center, which of the following are project management pre-migrations action items? (Choose two.)

   A. RAID array durability rating

   B. VM file format

   C. Benchmark compatibility

   D. Online migration bandwidth

20. What systems monitor the network and report security issues?

   A. CloudShield

   B. Intrusion prevention system

   C. Firewall

   D. Intrusion detection system

Chapter

3

Security in the Cloud

THE FOLLOWING COMPTIA CLOUD+ EXAM OBJECTIVES ARE COVERED IN THIS CHAPTER:

✓ **2.1 Given a scenario, apply security configurations and compliance controls to meet given cloud infrastructure requirements.**

- Company security policies
- Apply security standards for the selected platform
- Compliance and audit requirements governing the environment
  - Laws and regulations as they apply to the data
- Encryption technologies
  - IPSec
  - SSL/TLS
  - Other ciphers
- Key and certificate management
  - PKI
- Tunneling protocols
  - L2TP
  - PPTP
  - GRE
- Implement automation and orchestration processes as applicable
- Appropriate configuration for the applicable platform as it applies to compute
  - Disabling unneeded ports and services
  - Account management policies
  - Host-based/software firewalls

- Antivirus/anti-malware software

- Patching

- Deactivating default accounts

✓ **2.2 Given a scenario, apply the appropriate ACL to the target objects to meet access requirements according to a security template.**

- Authorization to objects in the cloud

  - Processes

  - Resources

    - Users

    - Groups

    - System

      - Compute

      - Networks

      - Storage

    - Services

- Effect of cloud service models on security implementations

- Effect of cloud deployment models on security implementations

- Access control methods

  - Role-based administration

  - Mandatory access controls

  - Discretionary access controls

  - Non-discretionary access controls

  - Multifactor authentication

  - Single sign-on

In this chapter, you will learn about cloud providers' security efforts in obtaining and maintaining compliance with many government and industry compliance initiatives. Also, you will learn about many of the security components, concepts, and configurations that are implemented by the cloud provider and the customer.

Security topics such as compliance, encryption technologies, and security configuration systems and methods will be covered; this chapter will also discuss protecting resources and access.

Cloud Security Compliance and Configurations

Security compliance by the cloud service provider is implemented to meet industry and government regulatory guidelines. Meeting various security requirements allows a cloud service provider to offer solutions specific to industries such as finance and healthcare and to meet the regulatory constraints placed on companies wanting to do business in most jurisdictions around the world.

To be able to contract and do business with many regulated entities, the cloud provider must be able to obtain and maintain many different regulatory compliance accreditations. Without meeting these regulatory requirements, the cloud provider would not be able to host or do business with regulated companies that can only host compute resources with companies that are able to prove that they meet any of the industry or governmental regulations they are required to meet.

The cloud service providers may elect to obtain certifications to win additional business. For example, if they want to host healthcare processing in the United States, they would need to show that they are HIPPA compliant.

For example, if your company plans on offering financial transactions such as processing credit cards, it must meet PCI-level compliance to provide for data security and integrity. If the cloud infrastructure does not meet PCI standards, it will not be able to participate in that marketplace. Another example is HIPPA compliance for the processing of medical records in the United States. The cloud provider must meet HIPPA compliance to be able to host applications and store records that fall under the HIPPA regulations.

To meet governance and regulatory compliance in the public cloud, extensive records must be retained and extensive documentation created. *Logging* is the detailed transaction records generated by all elements in the cloud for transactions and interactions of a device or system. For example, anytime a user logs into a system or accesses a storage system, a log can be generated and stored for later evaluation; in addition, changes made to the system must be recorded, and all the required steps to maintain compliance must be retained. It is important to protect your log data by placing the files in a highly secure and backed-up storage service that offers encryption and versioning. Each regulatory requirement will specify a detailed listing of what logs are required to be collected to meet compliance standards. Often there is a compliance audit process to validate that your deployment meets all requirements prior to being permitted to go live with your service offering.

Cloud companies offer many utilities and tools to aid in meeting these security requirements. The provider offerings can make it easy to collect and download performance metrics and logs to other services offered internally or through specialized service providers.

For example, a cloud provider can store log files and offer log analysis applications to search across hundreds of thousands, or even millions, of files. Data can be converted into a graphical format to be presented in a web browser using dashboard applications for a constantly updated real-time visual display of your operations. This information can also be stored in a database, and specialized applications can monitor and report compliance metrics.

Another security service offering is saving and archiving configuration changes made on your systems with user and date timestamps that record specifically what configuration changes were made to each element in your fleet of devices. These systems record what was changed and how it was changed, for example, if it was a command line or API change that was made and from what device. Both successful and failed attempts are recorded.

There are many third-party tools and offerings on the market to enhance and outsource your security and regulatory compliance requirements.

Establishing Your Company's Security Policies

Even though your cloud provider will have extensive security policies and procedures in place, ultimately you are responsible for your data. As you go through this chapter, keep in mind that you own and are ultimately responsible for your data and cloud operations. Your company must develop a comprehensive security plan with operational polices.

A *security policy* is a document that defines your company's cloud controls, organizational policies, responsibilities, and underlying technologies to secure your cloud deployment.

Establishing security polices can be a long and detailed process that should include many different groups in your company. The security policy must be drafted and followed to prevent any breaches, and it must outline the steps to take if there is a security violation and how to recover.

Security policies can encompass topics such as account credentials, authentication, and authorization policies. For data, a security policy will outline the need to encrypt the data in flight and at rest and defines the type and strength of encryption. Replications and storage diversity are security concerns, as well as securing the data in transit across a network.

Once the company security policies are completed, they must be approved by the top management of the company as this document will outline the level of risk and exposure the company is willing to accept as there is always a trade-off between security, ease of use, and cost.

Selecting and Applying the Security Policies to Your Cloud Operations

After the security policy has been approved by your company, it's time to adopt the requirements outlined in the policy. All polices must be converted to actual configurations and applied to the devices and services running on your cloud fleet. For example, when addressing identity requirements, it is possible that the corporate security policy may require strong passwords over a certain length, use special characters, and be changed on a regular schedule. The change request process will be followed to implement and test these types of changes. This will be ongoing and encompass a large number of devices including firewalls, security groups, network and storage access control lists, encryption policies for your data, software patching, and virus scan policies. The complete list will depend on each organization's needs and requirements.

It is important to keep your security documents and maintenance schedules constantly up-to-date and to make changes to your operations as needed depending on the security threat landscape and its changes over time.

Some Common Regulatory Requirements

Cloud companies often go to great efforts to become compliant with a large number of industry and governmental compliance requirements, certifications, and recommendations to be able to solicit business from companies and government agencies that must meet one or more of these requirements. While they are extensive and vary by jurisdiction around the world, here you will see an overview of some of the most common in the U.S. marketplace. If you are in a different market, you can check with your local regulatory requirements, which may be similar. This is not intended to be a complete list but, rather, an example of some of the many governmental and industry regulatory requirements.

- A Service Organization Controls 1 report (*SOC 1* report), also known as SSAE 16 and ISAE 3402, outlines the internal controls of financial reporting operations. For example, a cloud provider would meet the requirements if it has outlined in detail its operational financial reporting procedures and that they are in compliance with the steps outlined in SOC 1. Customers such as medical claim companies, payroll processing or loan servicing companies may require SOC 1 compliance from their service providers.

- The *SOC 2* report concerns a business's nonfinancial reporting controls for the availability, confidentiality, privacy, processing integrity, and security of a system. With the history of IT security breaches, SOC 2 fills the need for information on the security controls behind financial transactions.

- The *SOC 3* report is for the public disclosure of financial controls and security reporting. Since the SOC 2 report can contain sensitive and technical information, the SOC 3 report was created to offer a diluted, marketing-oriented, or nontechnical summary of the SOC 2 report.

- *FISMA* is the Federal Information Security Management Act. It is a U.S. federal law that outlines the framework to protect federal government information, operations, and facilities. FISMA is a comprehensive outline for data security and is offered by cloud companies hosting U.S. government processing in their data centers.

- *FedRAMP* is the Federal Risk and Authorization Management Program, which is a U.S. federal program that outlines the standards for security assessments, authorization, and continuous monitoring for cloud products and services. For a cloud provider to host federal government systems, they will need to be FedRAMP compliant.

- *DIACAP* is the Department of Defense Information Assurance Certification and Accreditation Process, which is the process for computer systems' IT compliance. DIACAP compliance is required to be certified to meet the U.S. Department of Defense security requirements for contractors. DoD outsources commercial interconnections to the DoD and other systems. Cloud providers doing business with or connecting to the U.S. Department of Defense need to comply with the DIACAP requirements.

- *PCI-DSS* is the Payment Card Industry Data Security Standard, which sets the requirements to guarantee that companies that process, store, or transmit credit card information offer secure processing and handling of credit card data. PCI requirements are important for companies that store, process, and transmit credit card information or connect to third-party credit-processing companies. Cloud companies may be PCI-DSS compliant, but you as the cloud customer must also meet the requirements in addition to the cloud provider, and you will have to undergo a PCI audit for compliance.

- *ISO 27001* is the International Organization for Standardization (ISO) standards for quality that ensure the cloud provider meets all regulatory and statutory requirements for its product and service offerings. ISO 27001 includes the seven quality management principles that the ISO 9001 certification is based on. This standard is an extension of a cloud provider's existing quality management certifications from the ISO and demonstrates confidence, credibility, satisfaction, and trust between the cloud company and its customers, providers, stakeholders, and the general community.

- *ITAR* is the International Traffic in Arms Regulations, which is a U.S. government regulation that affects the technology industry. ITAR restricts information from being disseminated to certain foreign entities that could assist in the import or export of arms. ITAR has a list of data security requirements that cloud companies can certify as being compliant to meet this U.S. requirement.

- *FIPS 140-2* is a National Institute of Standards and Technology (NIST) publication that coordinates the requirements and standards for cryptography modules. Cryptographic systems can be either hardware or software created in the public sector and are registered in FIPS-140-2 as approved for U.S. government use.

- The *Motion Picture Society of America (MPAA)* has published a set of best practices for storing, processing, and delivering protected media and content securely over the Internet. MPAA is not a certification but provides guidance and recommendations on best practices to assess risk and security of its content and infrastructure. Cloud providers can align their offerings to the MPAA guidance for the processing of MPAA-protected media.

- *HIPAA* is the *Health Insurance Portability and Accountability Act*. HIPAA defines the standard for protecting medical patient data. Companies that work with protected health information must ensure that all the required physical, network, and process security measures are in place and followed to meet HIPAA compliance requirements.

Protecting Your Data

Your data is your responsibility, meaning your company must take the steps necessary to protect it in your private data center as well as in your cloud deployments.

Cloud companies offer an extensive array of offerings to protect your data, which includes replication of your files to other remote data centers and elaborate storage array technologies that offer impressive durability and availability specifications. Data in the cloud can be stored in different tiers that offer different levels of protection at different cost levels.

Most cloud providers offer the option of encrypting your data both in flight and at rest. You may have the option of using their encryption key management offerings or you can use your own if desired or required for compliance purposes.

There are offerings to back up your private cloud data in the public cloud and to store replicas of your data with great geographical distances between data centers as needed for your corporate and regulatory needs.

Performing Compliance Audits

I cannot stress this enough: You own your data and your operations. You are renting infrastructure, storage, and compute services from the cloud provider. However, ultimately, they are not responsible for what happens to your data. You are. They can offer the most secure platform in the world, but if you spin up public-facing servers with connections to sensitive data stores and do not implement any, or implement incorrect, security configurations, you will probably get hacked. You must secure your cloud operations on top of what the cloud provider is already doing for you. They will let you know what they have secured and where your responsibility lies. Many providers even offer security audits of your configurations and will offer suggestions on your security configurations.

A cloud company may become certified in many areas that allow you to host your operations in its data centers with the knowledge that the provider has been verified to meet certain requirements that you must adhere to. However, this does not mean you are automatically approved for operations.

For example, a company that processes medical records may decide to move its operations to the public cloud. After a vendor selection and migration process, the company has its applications and data running at a HIPPA-approved public cloud company. This does not mean, however, that the company is HIPPA-complaint just because its cloud provider is. The company must still undergo the compliance validation and approval process. Remember, it is your operations and data.

This example applies to many other industries and government edicts from around the world. It is important that you understand and comply with all regulatory needs for your business, which may require complying with audits or proving you meet the law.

Encrypting Your Data

Encryption technologies, their frameworks, and how they are implemented and supported are complex topics. Encryption technologies in the security realm and a deep dive on this topic are beyond the scope of the Cloud+ certification exam.

Here you will get a brief introduction to common technologies and then see how to encrypt the data while it is in transit over a network and at rest in a storage system.

IP Security

IP Security (IPsec) is a framework, or architecture, that uses many different protocols to provide integrity, confidentiality, and authentication of data on a TCP/IP network. Since IPsec is not a protocol but a framework that implements many different security and encryption protocols under one umbrella, it can be challenging to understand all the details and to correctly implement and troubleshoot it.

Most IPsec implementations are found in the VPNs, application security, and network security technologies that are commonly implemented in operating systems, routers, and firewalls.

There are two primary modes of operation with IPsec: transport mode and tunnel mode. The main difference lies in where the IPsec functions take place.

With *transport mode*, the source and destination hosts will perform the cryptographic functions. The encrypted data is sent through an encrypted session to the remote host. The data, which is called the *ciphertext*, is created by the source host and retrieved by the destination host. Transport mode allows for end-to-end security.

When you use *tunnel mode*, it is common for either a router or a firewall to perform all the IPsec functions, and all the traffic passing over the link is encrypted and decrypted by the network or security device, as shown in Figure 3.1. This arrangement off-loads security and processing from the host machines and enables a central point of control. The trade-off is that complete end-to-end security is not provided since the hops from the router or firewall terminating the encrypted tunnel to the endpoint will not be secured with IPsec.

FIGURE 3.1   IPsec tunnel from remote site to cloud data center

When operating in tunnel mode, special network gateways perform cryptographic processing in addition to the source and destination hosts. Here, many tunnels are created in series between gateways, establishing gateway-to-gateway security. When using either of these modes, all gateways have the ability to verify that a packet is real and to authenticate the packet at both ends.

Two types of encapsulation are used by IPsec. The first is referred to as the *authentication header (AH)*, and the second is called the *encapsulating security payload (ESP)*. Both AH and ESP provide security for the data on a network but have slightly different implementations.

- AH provides authenticity and integrity services. Authentication is provided by keyed hash functions that are called *message authentication codes (MACs)*. AH also has the ability to determine whether the packet has been modified in transit and has antireplay services for additional security.

- ESP is a protocol that defines how the IPsec protocol encapsulates the original IP packet and how it provides authentication, encryption, and confidentiality for the data inside the packet.

IPsec implements the most common services found in IT security, such as providing authentication, data integrity, data confidentiality, encryption, and nonrepudiation (which is a way to guarantee that the sender of a message cannot later deny having sent the message and that the recipient cannot deny having received the message).

Secure Sockets Layer

Secure Sockets Layer (SSL) and its successor, Transport Layer Security *(TLS)*, make up a protocol group that operates on top of TCP to provide an encrypted session between the client and the server. It is commonly seen on websites implemented as the Hypertext Transport Protocol Secure (HTTPS) protocol. Protocols on higher layers like HTTP do not need to be modified while still offering a secure connection. Although SSL/TLS is most often associated with secure web services, it can also be used to secure any TCP-based communications flow.

With an SSL/TLS security implementation, all that is exposed in the packet are IP addresses and port numbers. The rest of the packet payload is encrypted.

When a browser connects to a secure website and a TCP connection is made, the SSL handshake takes place and is initiated by the client's web browser. The browser then transmits to the server the SSL/TLS version, the encryption method it prefers to use, and, if using compression, what type to use. The server will select the highest version of SSL/TLS that it supports and agree to an encryption method offered by the client. If compression is to be used, it will also select a compression algorithm to use. When the basic handshake is completed, the server will send a certificate using *Public Key Infrastructure (PKI)* services to the client. The certificate must be trusted by either the client or a certificate authority the client trusts; a list of trusted authorities is stored in the browser.

After the client performs the certificate verification function to determine the web server is really who it claims to be, the client will generate a symmetrical key called the *session key* and then use the session keys exchanged for secure transmission of data. The SSL session is now established.

Now that you have a connection, every packet will be signed with a MAC. You can now ensure that the sender and receiver are in fact the originators of the data and not someone in the middle claiming to be the website or the client. The data cannot be modified by an attacker, and the attacker will not be able to read the data since it is encrypted.

Other Common Ciphers = ALGORITHM

A *cipher* is defined as any method of encrypting data by concealing its readability and meaning. Ciphers can range from the very basic to the highly complex. A simple cypher can realign data in the stream to hide its meaning—for example, replacing any character B with a number such as 7. Knowing the cipher at the remote end, you can reverse the process to deencrypt the data. Doing this for all letters in the alphabet would create a basic cipher.

In the modern world of computing and cloud data centers, more complex methods are employed that use a key and an algorithm that combines the key with the text. There are two basic types of ciphers: a block cipher and a stream cypher. They differ as to how the encryption is applied. With a *block cipher*, the data is broken up into blocks, and then the encryption process is run on each block. A *stream cipher* applies the encryption to each byte. Stream ciphers are common in symmetrical encryption.

So, with that introduction to ciphers in mind, let's investigate some of the most common ciphers found in the security world. AES = 256 STANDARD

- *AES* is the *Advanced Encryption Standard*. It is a symmetrical block cipher that has options to use three lengths, including 128, 192, and 256 bits. With encryption, the longer the key length, the harder and longer it will be to break the encryption. AES 256 is a very secure standard, and it would take an extremely long time and a lot of processing power to even come close to breaking the code. The very long 256-bit key is used to encrypt and decrypt traffic, and the same key is used in both directions. AES also implements multiple hash functions to further protect and encrypt the data. AES has been approved and adopted by many governments, including the United States and Canada, to encrypt sensitive data. AES has also been adopted as a standard by the National Institute of Standards and Technology.

- *3DES*, or the *Triple Data Encryption Standard*, was developed in 1977 and has largely been replaced by AES. 3DES is also a symmetrical cipher and is an extension of the DES standard, which was considered weak and could be easily compromised.

Three encryption keys of various lengths are used. The first key is used to encrypt a block of data, a second key is then used to decrypt the block, and a third key is used to encrypt it again. This triple encryption function on each block of data is reversed to decrypt the data.

- *RSA* is named after the developers of the protocol, Ron Rivest, Adi Shamir, and Leonard Adleman. RSA is an asymmetrical encryption implementation that uses a private key and a public key. PKI is the framework that uses protocols such as RSA for encryption. With PKI and RSA, the common implementation will be for an asymmetrical protocol using a public and private key pair such as RSA to set up an encrypted connection to exchange symmetrical keys. Then the symmetrical keys are used to perform bulk encryption and decryption since they are faster and require less processing.

- *DSA* stands for the *Digital Signature Algorithm*. It operates much the same way as RSA does but is slower than RSA for encryption but faster for decryption. Although DSA and RSA serve the same function and operate in much the same way, RSA is more commonly found in cloud implementations.

- *RC4 (Rivest Cipher 4)* is named after its developer, Ronald Rivest. It uses a shared key to encrypt and decrypt a stream of data. RC4 was commonly used to secure wireless connections and web transactions as an encryption protocol used in SSL. It has been found to be susceptible to compromise by hackers and is no longer in use. Most browsers and security implementations no longer support RC4.

- *RC5 (Rivest Cipher 5)* is the replacement for RC4. It is also a symmetrical block cipher algorithm that uses a variable-length key.

Security Certificates and Keys

In this section, you will be introduced to the area of IT security that concerns certificates and keys, which can be an extremely complex topic. For a greater understanding of security, it is recommended that you investigate CompTIA's Security+ certification. Certificate and keys offer security and encryption servers to many of the cloud services and also for user authentication. While there is a great deal of complexity underneath, the actual day-to-day operation of certificates and keys has been abstracted by the cloud providers for ease of use by their customers.

Understanding Public Key Infrastructure

A *public key infrastructure (PKI)* is a standardized set of roles, policies, and procedures used to create, manage, distribute, use, store, and revoke digital certificates and manage public/private key encryption. As the name implies, it is an infrastructure or a framework and not a specific protocol. Understanding PKI is a complex topic and again is beyond the scope of the Cloud+ certification exam. Here you will get an overview of what it is and why you use it in the cloud.

PKI provides for identity, authorization, and encryption services that are central to implementing security in the cloud. PKI is an industry-standard framework that provides authorization and enforces security policies.

With standard security models in the cloud, it is not enough to assume that everyone accessing the data is authorized and is who they claim to be. You must confirm their identity and make sure that security policies (such as which encryption protocols to use) are implemented to meet your security policies and procedures as well as to comply with regulatory requirements.

A PKI framework consists of five major parts, as shown in Table 3.1.

TABLE 3.1   Major components of a PKI framework

PKI service	Description
Certificate authority (CA)	Central authority of trust; authenticates the identity of individuals, computers, and other entities in the network
Registration authority (RA)	Issues certificates for use as permitted by the CA
Certificate database	Stores certificate requests issued and revoked certificates from the CA or RA
Certificate store	Stores issued certificates and pending or rejected certificate requests from the local computer
Key archival server	Stores the encrypted private keys in a highly secure certificate database in case the certificate database is lost and for disaster recovery

PKI is an encryption framework that uses a pair of cryptographic keys: one public key and one private key. A website or user will send their public key to the remote client; the recipient of the public key uses it to encrypt and transmit data. The owner then uses their private key to decrypt the data. Only the private key performs the decryption operation and is highly protected, while the public key can be freely disseminated.

Some of the common implementations of PKI are to control access and encrypt data across VPN connections, perform secure authentication, approve and authorize applications, protect data filesystem encryption, secure network traffic using IPsec, protect Lightweight Directory Access Protocol (LDAP)–based directory services, and meet security compliance laws. PKI is also used in two-factor authentication with smartcards and token-based systems. It protects traffic to internal websites with the SSL technology.

Cloud applications may also use the PKI certificates such as e-mail, databases, document signing, mobile device security, and many other applications.

In corporate cloud environments, PKI is commonly used to authenticate users trying to access data and to validate transactions.

PKI services have a well-deserved reputation of being difficult to understand and implement. However, with the explosion of cloud services, there are now PKI as a Service (PKIaaS) companies, which are cloud companies that allow you to use PKI managed services without the need to build and manage your own PKI implementation. There are also Cryptography as a Service (CaaS) cloud providers providing PKI services such as hardware and software tokens, authentication services, and encryption offerings.

Remote Access Security

Since your cloud data centers are by definition distant from the location that you will be accessing them from, you will need to access the operations, consoles, configuration consoles, dashboard, and a host of other cloud services remotely. This, of course, introduces potential security vulnerabilities that must be addressed.

In this section, We will address primarily the security of remote access as it pertains to managing your cloud operations. You will most likely use some sort of encrypted remote access VPN technology that you will learn about in this section. We will also discuss how to lock down your access locations and how to strengthen your remote access security posture.

Layer 2 Tunneling Protocol

L2TP is a communications protocol that is a common method to connect to a remote device over the Internet. Most VPN servers support L2TP even though it is an older protocol and not as widely used as it was in the past because it does not natively support encryption or confidentiality without using add-on application software such as the IPsec framework. L2TP is a combination of remote access protocols that were developed by Cisco Systems and Microsoft; L2TP was ratified as a standard in 1999.

Point-to-Point Tunneling Protocol

The *Point-to-Point Tunneling Protocol (PPTP)* is a Microsoft-developed protocol that has been depreciated and has been replaced by more current remote access technologies. PPTP allows a PC or network to access a remote network such as your cloud-based database. PPTP implements a TCP control channel with a Generic Routing Encapsulation tunnel to encapsulate PPP packets. PPTP is considered to be obsolete and now has limited support in most operating systems and network equipment.

Generic Routing Encapsulation

Generic Routing Encapsulation (GRE) is a standardized network tunneling protocol that is used to encapsulate any network layer protocol inside a virtual link between two locations. GRE is commonly used to create tunnels across a public network that carries private network traffic. For example, a hybrid cloud consisting of an interconnection over the Internet from a private to a public cloud may implement GRE tunnels. The effect of this interconnection is that the two clouds appear to be directly connected even though they traverse the public Internet.

GRE was developed by Cisco Systems.

Automating Cloud Security

Cloud security can be automated by combining many of the service offerings to architect complete systems for monitoring, reporting, and responding to security events.

For example, logging data can be collected and placed in a cloud storage system; then the files are read by a log file analytics application such as Splunk that may be offered as a cloud application service. Third-party and homegrown security operations can also obtain this monitoring data and run scripts that monitor for security threats. When events occur that require action, systems can be triggered and automation scripts run to take action without human intervention.

The scripts can be run on network management systems, intrusion prevention appliances or VMs, or microservices, as well as other sources such as custom applications.

Automation allows for rapid response to security events and can stop an attempted breach in progress as well as record all events to forensic analysis of the event. How to implement cloud security will be covered in more depth in Chapter 4.

Security Templates for Compute Platforms

In this section, you will learn about the security practices that are followed in an enterprise data center, as well as in any of the cloud deployment models, among other topics.

Securing User Accounts and Policies

User login information and rights given to default accounts should be disabled or have their passwords changed. Having default logins active on your systems leaves a potentially large security hole that, if left unattended, allows hackers to penetrate your system. Investigate to see what rights and permissions these default accounts have, and remove them if they are not necessary.

Many applications have user accounts for administrative users and for authenticating to the operating system. Any of these accounts should use strong passwords that are different from the original default passwords.

Password policies should be created and enforced, including specifying the number of times a password can be reused, the length, and the types of characters that can be used to prevent the use of short and weak passwords. Also, specify how many days the password can be in effect. Many operating systems ship with the ability to define and enforce user credential policies.

Disabling Services That Are Not Used

One of the basic tenets of securing a network is that if you do not need it, turn it off. When you install a new operating system, many applications' services that you will never use may be enabled and running and may expose your system to a malicious attack.

To *harden* the system, you must determine which ports and services are running on the machine and investigate whether they are required for the server's purpose. If the service provides no use or value, it should be shut down to make the server as secure as possible.

Both Windows and Linux may have services running that are enabled by default and may be of no use to you.

Hackers will often use a network scanning or mapping utility to determine which TCP ports are open and base attacks on the data obtained from network scans. The fewer ports and applications you leave active, the more secure the server will become. Although firewalls are also important to block network reconnaissance and attacks, it is best to harden the operating system in addition to the network perimeter.

Operating system vendors will often publish white papers and checklists that can be followed to harden their systems. They may also offer specific releases that have already been hardened for specific use cases. For example, an operating system may originally load with unneeded services such as printing, various networking services such as DHCP, and a web or FTP server enabled. These services expose the operating system to potential malicious activity. If they are not needed, they should be disabled so there is no longer any exposure for attacks on those entry points.

Host-Based Firewall Security

Hardware-based perimeter firewalls are a mainstay of any security implementation and provide a first line of defense as well as segmentation in the cloud. Although these are absolutely critical for a complete security implementation, the firewall security functions can also be run directly on the cloud servers using installed firewall software. In fact, many operating systems have firewalls preinstalled as part of the release.

A host-based firewall software can then be configured with rules or policies that allow connections only to the applications it is hosting and from known source networks.

Antivirus Protection

If your system has the ability to run an antivirus software package, it is critical that you install it on the operating system. Antivirus software is an application that runs on a computer that can identify and remove viruses or malicious software from a system. Many appliances and network equipment will not support this capability, but most operating systems do, and you need to install and keep up-to-date antivirus software to protect these systems.

Keeping Your Servers Up-to-Date by Applying the Latest Patches

There seems to be a constant release of patches and fixes for operating systems, applications, and system firmware to address bugs and vulnerabilities. When a security deficiency is found, hackers can be quick to exploit the system before it has had patches applied to it. The security administrator must follow, validate, and install critical security patches in a timely manner to prevent a breach.

Many systems can be configured to automatically detect and install patches, which can be both a blessing and a curse. It is generally preferable to investigate patches and test for stability and install them during a maintenance window.

Vendor support sites, automation software, operating systems utilities, and e-mail subscriptions can be tracked to keep up with updates that are required.

Shutting Down Default Accounts

Applications and operating systems often have default accounts that are required for initial configuration and ongoing interprocess communications. The user documentation will often publish what username and password are to be used to access these systems and how to make configuration changes. This may be an initial requirement, but it is also a massive security hole. You must disable all applications and operating system default accounts or change the username and password to prevent a breach.

Networking appliances such as switches, routers, load balancers, and firewalls should also be checked. Network management using *Simple Network Management Protocol (SNMP)* may come activated with well-known community strings that are wide open for exploitation.

Access Control

In this section, you will learn about access and authorization of your cloud-based operations. Access control includes many different areas of security. You will learn about object access, which includes not just users and groups of users but also machine-to-machine authorization and security at the network and storage levels as well as the services in the cloud.

You will then learn about security as it applies to service models and learn more about the authentication process.

Accessing Cloud-Based Objects

A cloud *object* can be a file stored in a storage system, a virtual machine, a load balancer, or any other system running in the cloud. An object is an item that can be accessed and manipulated in the cloud.

Controlling who can access objects and what actions they are allowed to take is a critical component of maintaining proper security in the cloud. In this section, you will learn about the authorization and access to cloud-based objects.

The Authorization Process

When a user logs into a cloud-based management system, the first step is to identify who that individual is, which is defined as the *authentication process*. Once the user has been identified, or *authenticated* as it is commonly called, you can move to the second step of granting them a list of authorizations that define what services and objects they are allowed to access and what they are allowed to do. Authorization extends beyond users to services such as servers being granted access to a storage array or an application being authorized to read and write to a SQL database. By defining granular rules in the authorization process, effective security policies can be implemented in your cloud deployment.

Many cloud providers allow an online assessment of your authentication and authorization configurations. An automated script can be run that compares your configuration to industry best practices and generates a report that can be used to align your configurations with the recommendations.

User Accounts

User accounts are created for each and every user who needs to gain access to the cloud objects and resources. A user account is usually associated with an individual person but could be expanded to include other objects such as servers or applications that need to authenticate with the system. The preferred practice to authorize users is to place them into groups, as we will discuss in the next section. However, depending on your needs and requirements, object rights can be assigned directly to each user in most cloud management systems.

Once the user is created, the administrator can assign rights and grant access to the user object, which will define the authorizations granted to the user.

User Groups

User groups are containers that rights are assigned to. They make management more effective and streamlined than managing a large number of individual user accounts. The trick is to create a group for each use case that is needed. For example, groups can be created for the following: server, database, network, and storage administrators. Once the groups have been created, rights for the group that are required to access and manage objects are assigned to the group.

Users who need authorization to access or manage systems in the cloud can then be placed into the appropriate group for that function. You manage the group and add or remove users to that group as required.

Compute System Access Control

Authorization can be granted for your compute systems in the cloud, meaning the virtual machines or applications running on the VM. Each virtual machine can have defined security access that outlines who or what is authorized to access it, which can include users or other computers and applications. Many cloud providers offer security groups and allow or deny access to the compute system and can be very granular by allowing access to be defined down to the application level. Groups, users, and objects can be defined for different levels of authorization to access the systems.

Network-Based Access Control

Network-based access control enforces who can connect at the network layer instead of the server or application level. Services such as requiring a login to gain access to the network and access control lists that are security policies that either allow or deny an IP address range or port number are common examples of network-based access control.

It is a common cloud security practice to use a layered security approach that implements security at all levels including the network for a broad definition of access and then define authorization policies at the server, storage, and application layers in a more granular fashion for a complete security implementation.

Storage Access Control

Just as there are access control policies that are defined at the network, server, and application levels, so is storage access controlled by the same techniques.

Access control to cloud storage resources can be at the volume or array level to define who or what systems can access the data or mount that volume. This can be done at the *Storage Area Network (SAN)* level with *Virtual Storage Area Network (VSAN)* or at the storage controller level with LUN masking. This is abstracted and hidden from the cloud consumer and implemented behind the scenes with automation systems.

Filesystem access control operates in the same manner that file permissions are granted at the operating system level in Linux and Windows-based systems. A cloud-based storage offering allows for granular polices that control access and what rights are granted for the system such as the creation, deletion, read, and write permissions.

Securing Services

Securing services such as load balancers, caching systems, domain name systems, and firewalls is a critical step in maintaining a secure cloud posture. Cloud management systems allow authentication and authorization systems to be implemented that work the same as for network, storage, compute, and application access. It is common to apply groups to the services and then place the users into the groups. For example, you might have a firewall in your cloud deployment and want to create a group called Firewall Admins to attach to the firewalls. Then you would place users who need to access the firewall for administration purposes into the Firewall Admins group.

Machine-to-machine authorization may also be required and defined with roles and authorization policies to granularly define object rights to services.

Cloud Service Models and Security

As you will recall from Chapter 1, there are three primary cloud service models that define what demarcation of services are offered by the cloud service provider.

The most basic offering is Infrastructure as a Service. In this service model, the service provider will be responsible for all cloud infrastructure up to the hypervisor level. The customer is responsible for the VM and higher, as shown in Figure 3.2.

FIGURE 3.2 IaaS security model

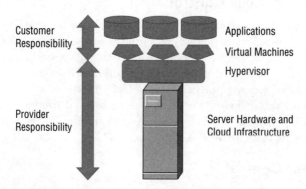

Platform as a Service offers the compute and operating systems as a service and allows customers to install their applications on the cloud platform. The security demarcation for PaaS is that the cloud provider assumes responsibility for security up to the operating system, and the customer manages the application and operating system configuration, as shown in Figure 3.3.

FIGURE 3.3   PaaS security model

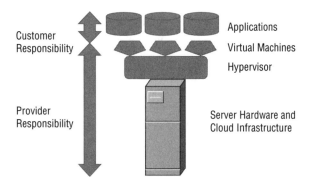

The Software as a Service model is where the customer of the service accesses application software that is owned and controlled by the cloud company, which has complete responsibility for the management and support of the application, as shown in Figure 3.4. All networking, processing, storage, and applications are offered as services in this model.

FIGURE 3.4   SaaS security model

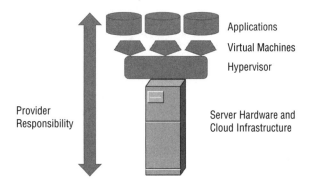

Cloud Deployment Models and Security

Chapter 2 introduced cloud deployment models and mentioned that a good understanding of the models is critical because they provide an overall structure to cloud computing. You also learned that deployment models are important to know not only for the Cloud+ exam but also for your day-to-day work as a cloud professional.

The primary deployment models are private, public, hybrid, and community. Security policies and responsibilities will vary based on the deployment model and each organization's specific definitions of who accepts security responsibility. However, you can assume that in a private cloud there is most likely one private organization that owns and operates the private cloud and would assume the responsibility for the operation.

With a public cloud deployment model, the security responsibility would be shared between the public cloud provider and the customer. The security demarcation would be defined in agreement with the provider and would vary based on the service model.

The hybrid deployments would be a combination of the two cloud models that are interconnected and would be defined based on both the service and deployment security policies.

Community cloud security would generally be the responsibility of the community cloud operator but can vary on a case-by-case basis.

Applying Access Controls

In this section, you will learn about user access control, which is the ability to identify users in your cloud environment. You can then apply access rights to define what they are allowed to do on the network. You will start by looking at granting rights based on an administrative user's role on the network. Then you will learn about the differences between mandatory and discretionary access controls. To add security, you must use several steps to log into a network; this is referred to as *multifactor authentication*, which will be covered as well. Finally, the concept of federations will be introduced and explained.

Role-Based Access Control

Role-based access control (RBAC) is a method in which access rights are granted to, or restricted from, users based on which roles they perform in an organization. RBAC uses different defined permission levels to assign routine activities and allows and restricts access to cloud resources based on these roles. The roles are defined based on the task, and users are then assigned to the roles. Based on the permissions allowed in the roles, the users will inherit those rights. What exactly is a role? It can be almost anything you decide to define it as. Many common roles are defined in applications, operating systems, and networking equipment.

Mandatory Access Control

The *mandatory access control (MAC)* approach is often found in high-security environments where access to sensitive data needs to be tightly controlled. Using the MAC approach, a user will authenticate, or log into, a system. Based on the user's identity and security levels of the individual, access rights will be determined by comparing that data against the security properties of the system being accessed. For example, if a user has rights to manage and configure the hypervisor in the cloud data center, the information in the user's profile may show that user as having hypervisor management rights. Based on this data, the account may be set up for only users with hypervisor management rights, and since they match, that user will be granted access.

MAC systems are highly controlled. The access is defined by strict levels of access that are common in secure environments such as defense or financial systems. A common implementation of a MAC system will allow fairly open access at the lower levels of data sensitivity, with tighter controls over the more sensitive data. MAC systems are centrally controlled using a defined security policy to grant access to a system or data. Users do not have the ability to change or overwrite this policy and grant access to other users.

Discretionary Access

Discretionary access controls differ from mandatory access controls by giving users the ability to grant or assign rights to objects and make decisions for themselves as compared to the centrally controlled method used by mandatory access controls.

Users with control over a system or data directory, for example, can use their discretionary access control rights to give other users or systems rights to those systems and directories. The discretionary approach allows users with the correct permissions to manage rights. These users own the objects and are allowed to make decisions on rights such as security, read-only, read-write, and execute on those objects.

Nondiscretionary Access Control

Nondiscretionary access control defines a set of rules to allow or deny access to an object, system, or service in the cloud. It is a method of access control that allows the objects to be accessed based on rules, privileges, and roles that define access.

Examples of nondiscretionary access include allowing access to a development server for certain hours of the day, granting a user complete control over a server fleet or storage system for administrative purposes, and enabling a select group of users to access a sensitive document stored in the cloud. Nondiscretionary access is the method used to define permissions of users' access to cloud resources. You will find that nondiscretionary access and role-based access are used interchangeably, and they can be considered to be one in the same in most all cases.

Multifactor Authentication

Multifactor authentication is an access control technique that requires several pieces of information to be granted access. Multifactor implementations usually require you to present something you know, such as a username/password combination, and something you have, such as a smart card, a fingerprint, or a constantly changing token number from an ID card.

An example of multifactor authentication is when you withdraw money from an ATM. The two-factor authentication includes something you have, which is your ATM card, and something you know, which is your PIN.

Since you have more than one requirement for authentication to access a system, multifactor systems are inherently more secure than single-factor systems such as a username/password combination.

Cloud vendors offer the option for two-factor authentication to access and administer your cloud deployment. This adds a second layer of access security and is a good security measure to adopt a multifactor framework. There are a number of companies that offer token generation hardware that is small enough to fit on your keychain and applications that can be installed on a smartphone.

When you log into your cloud management console or other services, you will be prompted for a token ID, which you will read from your token generator. You type in the five- or six-digit number along with your username and password to gain admission. Multifactor authentication is widely used in the cloud and corporate environments.

Single Sign-On

Single sign-on (SSO) is an approach that reduces the need to sign into multiple systems for access. SSO allows a user to log in just one time and be granted access rights to multiple systems. Using SSO, you can centralize the authentication of multiple systems into just one area, easing user administration significantly.

For example, a web server administrator may need to manage multiple web servers in the cloud simultaneously. Since all these web servers are under this administrator's control, you can create an SSO group called Web Administrators, and when an administrator logs into the servers, they are granted access to all servers in the group without having to log into each one individually.

Directory servers using LDAP are an example of SSO systems. You log into the directory services one time, and based on your rights, you are allowed to access systems in the network without any additional login requirements.

Single sign-on eliminates the need to remember multiple username and password combinations and saves the time of having to enter your authentication information repeatedly across a network.

SSO is also effective when terminating a session. When you log off, the directory services will log out, or disconnect you, from the multiple systems you were accessing.

Summary

Security and encryption technologies can be complex topics. We suggest reading this chapter several times until the concepts are clear. The topic of security is prominent in the cloud community, and CompTIA has a strong emphasis on security on the exam. It is important to understand security, encryption, authentication, and authorization.

This chapter started out with a macro view of the topic of cloud security. You then learned about the need for compliance and what compliance really is by exploring many regulations that apply to private industry and government organizations. Then you learned about developing security policies, meeting these requirements, and performing audits to ensure compliance.

Encryption of your data was the next topic; you learned about a lot of heavy topics such as IP Security, various encryption technologies such as SSL and AES, and the concepts of public and private keys.

Next remote access was introduced, and you learned about the various ways to access the cloud deployment from your remote site. Many of the VPN technologies were explained, with an emphasis on the security aspects of remote access.

The steps required to harden your cloud deployment are critical in maintaining a strong security posture. You learned how to make your deployment more secure by securing user accounts, disabling unused servers, implementing firewalls, installing antivirus applications, keeping your patches up-to-date, and disabling default user accounts.

The chapter concluded by discussing user access, specifically, the authentication and authorization of users and systems. Many different types of access technologies were explained such as role-based, single sign-on, and groups. You then learned how to secure various objects in the cloud such as VMs, storage assets, and networks.

Exam Essentials

Know about cloud security compliance.   Know that a company's security policy is an internal document that outlines its security posture and lists all topics related to security.

Understand that companies must meet certain regulatory compliance statutes.   Know that HIPPA compliance is required for the processing and storing of medical data, that PCI-DSS compliance is required for credit card processing, and that there are a range of U.S. federal cloud requirements such as DIACAP, FedRAMP, and FIPS 140-2.

Understand compliance audits.   Know that even if a cloud provider is compliant with a requirement, your organization must still meet those requirements on its hosted applications and submit to a compliance audit.

Be able to identify data encryption types and techniques.   Know what IPsec is and the components that are included with it. Understand ciphers, the public key infrastructure, encryption types, and common implementations of encryption technologies such as web browsers using SSL and VPNs using IPsec.

Know the various remote access technologies.   Common remote access protocols include L2TP, PPTP, and GRE.

Understand the devices that need to be hardened in your cloud fleet.   Disable all unused services, deploy a firewall, implement antivirus protection, keep your servers patched and up-to-date, and shut down default user accounts.

Be able to explain and identify authorization processes.   Know what users, groups, compute systems, access control, and network-based and storage access control is. Be able to explain how to secure network services such as load balancers, firewalls, and DHCP servers.

Know who has security responsibility for the various cloud services' models. For Infrastructure as a Service, you have full responsibility from the operating system up to the application level, and the cloud service provider maintains responsibility from the hypervisor down to the cloud data center infrastructure. Platform as a Service allows the cloud service provider to take responsibility for all IaaS services plus the operating system. For Software as a Service, the cloud service provider takes security responsibility up to the application level. However, it is important to understand that ultimately the cloud customer, which is you, is ultimately responsible for your data and for meeting compliance requirements.

Know the different types of access controls. Be able to identify and understand the many types of access control including mandatory, discretionary, nondiscretionary, multifactor, and single sign-on.

Written Lab

Fill in the blanks for the questions provided in the written lab. You can find the answers to the written labs in Appendix B.

1. Multifactor authentication must include something you _KNOW_ and something you _HAVE_

2. A _SECURITY POLICY_ is the document that defines your company's cloud controls, organizational policies, responsibilities, and underlying technologies to secure your cloud deployment.

3. _DISCRETIONARY ACCESS_ controls give users the ability to grant or assign rights to objects and make decisions for themselves as compared to the centrally controlled method.

4. _SSO SINGLE SIGN ON_ is an approach that reduces the need to sign into multiple systems for access.

5. A _CIPHER_ is defined as any method of encrypting data by concealing its readability and meaning.

6. _AUTOMATION_ allows for software scripted responses to security events and can stop an attempted breach in progress. These systems can provide hands-off recording of all events to forensic analysis of the event.

7. A cloud _OBJECT_ can be a file stored in a storage system, a virtual machine, a load balancer, or any other system running in the cloud and is an item that can be accessed and manipulated in the cloud.

8. Public clouds implement a _SHARED_ security model.

9. A _PKI (CA)_ is a standardized set of roles, policies, and procedures used to create, manage, distribute, use, store, and revoke digital certificates and manage public/private key encryption.

10. In the _SAAS_ service model, the cloud service provider assumes security responsibility up to and including that application level.

Review Questions

The following questions are designed to test your understanding of this chapter's material. For more information on how to obtain additional questions, please see this book's Introduction. You can find the answers in Appendix A.

1. Harry is investigating cloud service models and wants to outsource the security responsibility to the cloud company and not have to take responsibility for maintaining and patching the operating systems. Which service model will meet his requirements?

   A. IaaS

   B. PaaS

   C. SaaS

   D. CaaS

2. What is the name of the process when a cloud administrator uses his token, username, and password to log into the cloud console? (Choose two.)

   A. Authorization

   B. Two-factor

   C. Authentication

   D. Role-based access

3. Robert has been tasked with creating an access control solution for his company's fleet of servers in a hybrid cloud configuration. He has been asked to define the required tasks and then to put users, groups, and servers into this task-based implementation. What type of access control should Robert deploy?

   A. Mandatory access control

   B. Nondiscretionary

   C. Roles

   D. Multifactor

4. What is a report for the public disclosure of financial controls and security reporting that does not contain sensitive and technical information called?

   A. SOC 1

   B. SOC 2

   C. SOC 3

   D. ISO 27001

   E. FIPS 140-2

5. What is the National Institute of Standards and Technology publication that coordinates the requirements and standards for cryptography modules?

   A. PCI-DSS

   B. FIPS 140-2

   C. ISO 27001

   D. FedRAMP

6. What is a compliance requirement to be certified to meet the U.S. Department of Defense security requirements for contractors working with the U.S. Department of Defense?

    A. FedRAMP

    B. DIACAP

    C. FISMA

    D. 123

7. Mary's boss has asked her to investigate moving the company's medical records to the cloud. What compliance mandate must the cloud provider meet for Mary to recommend deploying her company's operations to the cloud?

    A. SOC 3

    B. HIPAA

    C. MPAA

    D. ISA 2701

8. Sue is preparing a change management process to harden various services running in her cloud fleet. What are common services that she is preparing to harden? (Choose three.)

    A. Firewalls

    B. Load balancers

    C. MySQL

    D. Linux virtual snapshot image

    E. DHCP

9. Harry is the cloud administrator for a company that stores object-based data in a public cloud. Because of regulatory restrictions on user access to sensitive security data, what type of access control would you suggest he implement to meet his company's security policies?

    A. Mandatory access control

    B. Nondiscretionary

    C. Roles

    D. Multifactor

10. Christina is investigating obtaining compliance for her employer, which is a large public cloud company. She has been asked to provide a report on the process to enable her company to host a large U.S. federal government database. Which compliance certification is she investigating?

    A. HIPAA

    B. FedRAMP

    C. DIACAP

    D. FISMA

11. What is the process document that outlines your company's responsibilities in safely deploying your fleet of servers in the public cloud?

    A. DIACAP

    B. Security policy

    C. Service level agreement

    D. SOC-2

12. Hank goes to his local bank and inserts his card into the ATM and then enters his PIN on the keypad. What type of authentication is he participating in?

    A. SSO

    B. Two-factor

    C. LDAP

    D. User based

13. You work in the financial services industry and are required to encrypt your data at rest in the public cloud to comply with securities regulations. You want to implement a strong encryption protocol that is widely approved by industry best practices. Which one of the following meets your requirements?

    A. 3DES

    B. RSA

    C. AES-256

    D. Rivest Cipher 5

14. Single sign-on services allow a user to log into the system one time and be granted device access without having to perform multiple system authentications. What two technologies enable SSO systems? (Choose two.)

    A. PKI

    B. LDAP

    C. AD

    D. Roles

15. Martha is learning about storage access control to secure her cloud storage assets. She wants to know what low-level security methods the cloud provider is using on its storage area network and storage head end controllers. What two technologies is she learning about? (Choose two.)

    A. ACL

    B. VSAN

    C. PKI

    D. LUN masking

    E. Discretionary access

16. Sarah has been tasked to implement a strong user authentication strategy to secure dashboard access to her SaaS cloud services. She wants to use temporarily issued tokens to prevent unauthorized users from accessing her cloud administrator's account. What type of authentication would you recommend that Sarah implement?

    A. Multifactor

    B. Mandatory access control

    C. Roles

    D. Nondiscretionary

17. Brad has been tasked with encrypting data in flight into his e-commerce presence in a community cloud. He is investigating a standards-based secure solution that web customers can easily implement to ensure secure transactions. What is a good solution that you would recommend to Brad?

    A. AH/ESP

    B. AES 256

    C. SSL

    D. IPSec

18. You have been asked to investigate cloud-based VPN access from your corporate data center that offers data integrity and confidentiality. Your manager does not want to incur the costs of a dedicated circuit to the cloud provider. What connection protocol would you suggest be implemented that can offer a secure connection across the unsecure Internet?

    A. AES

    B. SOC-3

    C. IPSec

    D. RC5

19. Bob is compiling a list of security tasks to implement to harden his public cloud posture. What are four recommendations you would suggest? (Choose four.)

    A. Install antivirus protection software on public-facing servers.

    B. Shut down unused services.

    C. Nothing; the cloud provider offers infrastructure security.

    D. Implement a host-based firewall or security groups.

    E. Allow all storage volumes' authenticated users full access.

    F. Disable all default accounts.

    G. Grant ephemeral ports access to the DMZ.

20. Jill is planning on optimizing and controlling user access by implementing a technology that will allow access to all allowed systems at the time of user authentication. She is implementing the LDAP protocol to enable this service. What is she planning on deploying?

    A. Token-based 2FA

    B. SSO

    C. RSA

    D. Nondiscretionary

Chapter

4

Implementing Cloud Security

THE FOLLOWING COMPTIA CLOUD+ EXAM OBJECTIVES ARE COVERED IN THIS CHAPTER:

✓ **2.3 Given a cloud service model, implement defined security technologies to meet given security requirements.**

- Data classification
- Concepts of segmentation and micro-segmentation
  - Network
  - Storage
  - Compute
- Use encryption as defined
- Use multifactor authentication as defined
- Apply defined audit/compliance requirements

✓ **2.4 Given a cloud service model, apply the appropriate security automation technique to the target system.**

- Tools
  - APIs
  - Vendor applications
  - CLI
  - Web GUI
  - Cloud portal
- Techniques
  - Orchestration
  - Scripting
  - Custom programming

- Security services
  - Firewall
  - Antivirus/anti-malware
  - IPS/IDS
  - HIPS
- Impact of security tools to systems and services
  - Scope of impact
- Impact of security automation techniques as they relate to the criticality of systems
  - Scope of impact

Implementing Security in the Cloud

This section focuses on data classification, the segmentation of storage, and compute resources, encryption and multifactor authentication. Then you will learn about meeting regulatory and compliance requirements.

Data Classification

Data classification organizes data into different tiers or categories for the purpose of making data available as required and to meet regulatory requirements, mitigate risks, and secure data. For example, classification can be used to identify sensitive data and to mark something as requiring encryption.

Data can be organized into any defined category and managed according to that classification's needs. *Metadata* is data that is attached to a file and can be thought of as a tag that explains, categorizes, or classifies the data. This metadata allows data to be tracked as a group for it to be efficiently searched and can reduce duplication of like data that can help reduce or even eliminate storage requirements. Tagging increases security and makes for efficient searches of the data. Many metadata tags can be applied to data and are usually in a type-value format where a tag type is defined and then a value is given for the type. For example, a type could be *public*, and the value could be a country such as *Germany*, so the pair would be *public: Germany*. Public cloud vendors offer classification for accessing data and allow you to assign metadata based on your needs.

A common classification need is based on the sensitivity of the data, such as levels of confidentiality or importance. If your organization were to classify its data into three security categories such as Restricted, Private, and Public, then the appropriate level of security policy could be applied to each classification. Public would require the least amount of security followed by Private, to which your organization would need to apply additional security policies. With the Restricted category, your company's security policies may require highly restricted access to encryption in transit and at rest to meet any compliance requirements such as HIPPA, SOX, or PCI-DSS.

Classifying data can be an involved process depending on your policies. Each organization must be able to define what criteria is used to classify its data and then how to apply policies based on each classification. Employees may need to be trained on how to identify and classify data and implement the required security standards required for each classification level.

Classification policies need to be clearly outlined in your company's data policy documents and any documentation that is needed for regulatory compliance. Polices should explain the types of classifications, how they are determined, and what data belongs in each category. Policies should also include the security operations required for the data; how it can be transmitted, received, backed up, and stored; and what the risks and penalties are if there is a security breach.

Data classification also allows organizations to manage large amounts of data in their cloud storage systems. Classification allows an organization greater and more precise visibility of what the data is and how it is stored, accessed, and protected.

It is also important for you to revisit your classification policies and implementations on a regular schedule to determine whether there is a need to reclassify that data as its status may have changed over time.

Segmenting Your Deployment — *SEGMENTATION (SECURITY)*

Cloud segmentation is the process of dividing your cloud deployment into sections to allow for granular security polices to be applied. By applying segmentation to your cloud deployment, you can implement a multilayered security approach that aligns with a defense-at-depth security model.

Cloud networks can be segmented into functions, and then security policies can be applied between each segment. Segments can include the public-facing web servers and then an additional segment for the application layer and a third for the database. Other segments may include dedicated storage, backend management and services, and a DMZ. By creating multiple segments, greater security and controls can be applied to the flow of data into and out of each segment. A strong security posture on the cloud network periphery is critical to defining who you allow into and out of your network, and it defines how your network defenses are configured. Security is applied using network access control lists, security groups, users, user groups, roles, and firewall configurations that are designed to meet your company's security requirements. These security policies protect, for example, data in storage systems, databases, and application servers from unauthorized access.

Networks can also be segmented by creating more than one virtual private cloud and interconnecting the VPCs with security policies in place to define the permit/deny rules of the traffic flow between the VPCs. In this approach, each VPC can be dedicated to a specific function such as production workload or development and be isolated from the other processes running in your cloud deployment.

Cloud networks are also segmented in IP subnets, which allow like functions to be placed in a subnet and a policy to be applied to traffic flow allowed inside and incoming and outgoing from each subnet. Also, subnets can use either public IP addresses that are reachable from the Internet or private IP ranges, which allow some degree of security since they are not reachable from the Internet without a NAT gateway. For the sake of completeness, we should mention protected subnets, which are the same as private subnets but are

100 percent isolated from the Internet since a protected subnet does not have access to a NAT gateway to access the Internet.

Network segments should be spread across multiple cloud data centers for survivability and resiliency. This type of deployment is often referred to as a *multi-availability zone architecture*.

Storage Segmentation

Storage segmentation is used to separate cloud data stores and storage offerings to meet a customer's requirements. Using the cloud provider's provisioning tools, multiple storage arrays can be launched to allow for any type of storage requirements. For example, a database that requires very high read-write I/O operations will best be served using a storage media that utilizes solid-state drive hardware and is optimized for a high rate of I/O operations, while another database may have a low read-write requirement and could make use of standard magnetic drives at a substantially lower cost. If the data is classified to be archived for long-term storage to meet regulatory requirements, then significant cost savings can be realized using lower-cost long-term storage instead of a fast-response online storage offering.

Storage volumes may also be segmented by OS where there are Linux and Windows storage segments that can restrict the appropriate operating system and filesystem access or can be classified by durability and reliability metrics.

Storage segmentation also addresses what type of storage system is needed. The three primary storage types are file-, block-, and object-based storage. Each meets different storage use cases and needs.

Storage systems connected to a virtual machine can offer *durable storage* or *nondurable storage*. If the virtual machine is deleted or stopped, nondurable data will be lost. This is sometimes referred to as *ephemeral volumes* in that it gets deleted when the associated VM goes away. Durable storage volumes will not be deleted and as such retain data even if the virtual machine is stopped or terminated.

Compute Segmentation

Computing segmentation refers to the grouping of compute resources in an isolated network that allows for local connections and enhanced security. It is a cloud best practice to place compute, or virtual machines, into an isolated subnet and configure access control on traffic into and out of the segment.

Internet-facing web servers can be segmented in your cloud deployment with public-facing access that has filters applied that only allow common web access protocols, such as HTTP and HTTPS. On the back end of the web segment is often a fleet of application servers that are placed in a second segment that again has access security that allows only connections from the upstream web servers and not the public Internet. Below the application servers is a third segment for databases with a similar security configuration except that access to the database is limited only from the application servers. This is commonly referred to as *three-tier architecture* and is usually found in web hosting designs.

Other applications that make use of segmenting compute resources is big data hosting in the cloud. A big data configuration will often implement a very large fleet of virtual machines, which can number into the hundreds and sometimes the thousands of servers. There is heavy and delay-sensitive traffic loads between the big data servers. By placing all big data servers into their own compute segments, the high network I/O needs can be addressed and the security needs defined for the segment.

Implementing Encryption

Many regulations and corporate policies require that data be encrypted not only as it is transmitted across the network but also when it is in a storage system, or often called *data at rest*. Also, some database products allow for encrypted data to be processed in a database in real time.

There are many technologies, frameworks, and techniques to encrypt data with a focus on data as it passes across the Internet to the cloud data center. However, data can also be encrypted in the storage arrays for added protection using the same or similar encryption techniques.

Regulatory agencies, governments, and corporate policies may require the encryption of stored data. For example, data may be required to be encrypted in such areas as the storage of finance and healthcare records. Performing the encryption function may add a delay because of the increased processing requirements required to encrypt the data. This overhead may slow the storage read and write operations. Encryption overhead is a trade-off that must be made to satisfy legal or corporate requirements. High-end storage controllers have options to perform the encryption on data at rest as well as the server operating systems and storage subsystems. These controllers may implement coprocessors using special silicon chips called ASICs to offload the compute-intensive encryption from the core CPUs for greater efficiency.

The actual implementation and configuration of encryption can be as simple as a checkbox on a web control panel when configuring a service. Many cloud providers have extensive automation systems in place that abstract the complexity and hide the sometimes highly complex configurations from their customers.

Encryption is commonly implemented on storage systems and databases in cloud computing data centers. The cloud provider may require that encryption be implemented at the time of creation of the storage system or database. The only way to add encryption after you have brought up your services may be to create a new encrypted deployment and then migrate the data over from your original nonencrypted deployment. Most regulatory structures such as PCI and HIPPA require that the storage data also be encrypted when making backup and archived copies and that each storage drive must be tracked and its location known at all times.

When data is being transmitted, often called *in-flight*, over an insecure network such as the Internet, encryption becomes very important. There are many VPN and access encryption protocols that were introduced in Chapter 3. For web connections, the Secure Sockets Layer and Transport Layer Security implementations are the most common. VPN connections will use the IPsec framework for a flexible framework of encryption options.

Applying Multifactor Authentication

In Chapter 3, you learned that *multifactor*, or two-factor, authentication includes something that you have, such as a one-time token generator, and something that you know, like a PIN or password. Figure 4.1 shows an example of a multifactor login dialog.

FIGURE 4.1   Multifactor authentication login screen

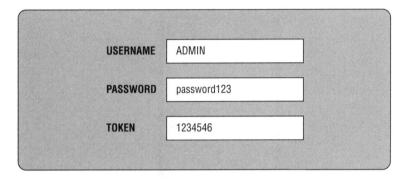

The identity management console in a cloud configuration dashboard allows you to configure user accounts. When setting up a user, there will be a dialog box that allows you to define your user authentication profile. This is often as simple as clicking the multifactor checkbox to enable the feature and identifying the authentication vendor. There are also options to use Application Programming Interfaces (APIs) and command-line interfaces to script the MFA configurations.

When configuring multifactor authentication in a cloud's identity user account system, there are several different options for MFA system vendors to select from.

Hardware tokens are popular devices that allow you to access your authentication token; they are small devices that usually fit on a keychain and have small screens that display a changing ID number. This ID token is usually valid for only a few minutes at most and needs to be typed into the authentication dialog box along with your username and password.

Hardware-based token systems are available from several different global suppliers such as Gemalto and RSA. As shown in Figure 4.2, a hardware-based tried-and-tested combination used by countless organizations is the hardware key fob (something you have).

FIGURE 4.2   Hardware-based multifactor authentication token

There is also a software version of the one-time password token generator that can be installed on laptops, tablets, or smartphones. This type performs the same function as the hardware keychain version, but instead of having to carry around another device, you can just pull out your smartphone and access your token. Figure 4.3 shows an example of a one-time password token generator.

FIGURE 4.3   Smartphone-based multifactor authentication token

Regulatory and Compliance Issues During Implementation

The cloud offers many advantages over the traditional compute model including rapid provisioning, the ability to dynamically add capacity, minimal capital expenditures, lower operational costs, and access to advanced technology that has traditionally been available to only the largest corporations or companies with large technology budgets. With all of these advantages come a few challenges when implementing your operations in the cloud. As you have learned in this chapter and in Chapter 3, you are responsible for all regulatory and security compliance requirements for your cloud deployment. Even though a cloud provider may be compliant for a specific regulation, this does not absolve you of also having to meet those same requirements on the cloud's platform. Being compliant with all laws and regulations that apply to your deployment is your responsibility and not the cloud provider's.

When implementing your operations in the cloud, it is best to plan to meet all compliance issues from the beginning of the project so that your migration is not delayed with unforeseen compliance requirements. Planning for compliance should start when defining your original requirements and proceed though the design, implementation, and validation phases. After the deployment, extensive testing and validation must be performed to ensure that your migration is working as expected and all compliance configurations are operational. Often there are reference designs available to guide you on creating the proper architecture to meet specific regulatory requirements. Many third-party agencies and service providers are also available to assist in the process of meeting your specific regulatory requirements when migrating to the cloud. Only after all of the planning, implementing, and validations have been completed is it advisable to proceed to compliance testing with the regulatory authorities.

Automating Cloud Security

With the virtualization of all cloud resources, there have been many software capabilities that were developed to create, monitor, configure, and remove services deployed in the cloud. Given this capability, it is possible to automate much of your ongoing cloud security operations.

Security automation can allow code to replace many of the processes that had to be performed manually in the past. Scripts can be implemented to apply security policy and configurations to new devices such as virtual machines when they are created. This allows for a uniform and consistent security policy for your organization. With the extensive monitoring and reporting capabilities of cloud operation centers, event triggers can be defined for security events that can, in turn, call software automation processes to address the alarm.

Applications can be designed with security in mind, operating systems have the ability to automate updates with patch management software, and network security and monitoring systems generate log files and alerts that can be used to instigate an automated security operation.

Many security service providers have already done the background automation work to implement industry best practices and offer their systems as a service to cloud customers with many different types and levels of service offerings.

Automation Tools

In this section, you will learn about the components and technologies available to create automation tools. The most important is a programmatic interface that is largely hidden in plain sight and is used daily even if you are not aware of what is going on behind the scenes. In almost every case, anytime you make a configuration change on any cloud-based object, whether it is using a web GUI or a command-line interface, you are actually communicating with the device via what is known as an API.

You may often hear the cloud described as one big programmable interface by those who have worked with it for many years. That description may be the most descriptive cloud definition out there! The cloud is a programming language between many different platforms and applications. Automation is the glue that makes all the cloud economics and operations possible. By implementing a well-defined and agreed-upon set of software interfaces that allow devices to intercommunicate with each other, the magic of cloud computing can happen.

Application Programming Interfaces

An *application programming interface (API)* is a defined means to programmatically access, control, and configure a device between different and discrete software components. The API defines how software components interact with each other. APIs provide the means to enable automation of the complete stack from the physical devices to the applications and everything in between. Without APIs, there can be no automation!

APIs support defined standards to ensure interoperability. Each device or system that supports APIs will publish its interface programmability in detail, which allows software developers to write to the interface of the device for automation. The most common protocols used to access a device's API interface are the *Representational State Transfer (REST)* protocol that communicates between devices using HTTP/HTTPS. The data format is either *JavaScript Object Notation (JSON)* or *Extensible Markup Language (XML)*. A common coding language for automation is *Python*. There is a wide variety of preconfigured automation scripts that are available on the web and from the cloud vendors. A popular website for sharing automation information and examples of scripts is GitHub.com.

Software languages and how they are implemented are well beyond the scope of the Cloud+ exam. However, the authors urge you to learn the basics of programming and automation as it will be invaluable in your work with cloud technologies.

Vendor-Based Solutions

Vendors and suppliers of virtualized cloud services offer internally developed automation tools and configuration examples as part of their offerings. The solutions may be offered by the cloud provider or the original software developer for free or for additional charges in a premium package of software and services.

Vendors will publish a document detailing their API interfaces and how to interact with their products programmatically for automation and management. Other solutions may include a custom web interface or a locally installed client application that interacts with the remote cloud service or device.

Command Line

For those of us who are old-school, we continue to use a *command-line interface (CLI)* over other utilities such as the more popular web-based configuration capabilities now deployed in the cloud. A command-line interface is a text-based interface tool used to configure, manage, and troubleshoot devices. The command-line interface allows devices to be automated though configuration scripts. Users who become familiar with the CLI interface of a device are proficient in extracting detailed and specific data and effective configurations much more quickly than is possible when using a web browser.

Web Graphical User Interfaces

Most cloud user interfaces found in production today are based on web browsers because of their ubiquity and functionality. A *graphical user interface (GUI)* is a web-based interface that is usually your first introduction to a cloud provider's system. The GUI serves as its primary interface's front end. As you learned earlier, the web interface is a front end to an API that actually accesses the devices.

Using a web browser, you will log into the cloud management console that will allow you to create, manage, and monitor almost all of the common requirements of a cloud consumer.

Portals and Dashboards

There are also machine-to-machine or application-to-application alerts. A common dashboard published by cloud companies shows the health of the operations in real time and is accessed using a web browser, as shown in Figure 4.4. One important use of alerting is for automation of troubleshooting, where a management application can alert an application to perform troubleshooting and problem resolution based on the issue reported from the management application.

FIGURE 4.4   Dashboard applications show cloud health reports using a browser.

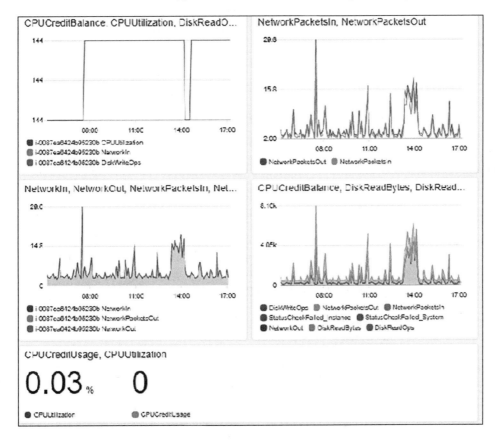

Techniques for Implementing Cloud Security

Each cloud provider will offer its own cloud security package based on its shared security model. As you have learned, the shared responsibility model defines the areas you will secure and what sections the cloud provider assumes responsibility for.

There are several well-defined approaches to follow when implementing cloud security. The first is the use of orchestration systems that offer automation for the security overlay of your cloud as a core component. Another common method of implementing security is to run preconfigured scripts that apply policy and security configurations. The final implementation technique discussed in this section is using a customized approach with specific tools designed for cloud security.

Orchestration Systems

Orchestration systems are software packages or services that automate cloud security in a single package. Orchestration can provide cloud asset discovery that can be scanned, and a vulnerability assessment can be completed on all of the cloud services. Additional services include compliance management for the many different regulatory compliance requirements you may be required to meet. Some orchestration systems may include software modules for logging, intrusion detection and prevention, and any number of other products designed to add additional functionality to the application.

Orchestration systems are part of a cloud provider's basic offerings and are most often included at no charge as they are often a requirement to launch your cloud services. Orchestration systems may be middleware that has a web front end visible to the cloud customer and the APIs to interface with the virtual services in the cloud on the back end.

Most large network management software companies offer commercial orchestration systems. There is a robust open source community offering popular packages such as Chef, Docker, Puppet, and OpenStack. *Managed Security as a Service (MSaaS)* companies that you can contract with have their own orchestration systems.

Script-Based Services

Scripting is a method of running configuration commands in the cloud to automate cloud deployments and security services. Scripts can be run on a virtual machine at startup to apply updates, install applications, and automate the cloud security deployment. Scripts can be run based on time of day using a CHRON function or based on an event trigger from network management systems. It is a common practice to deploy a management, or *jump server*, in your fleet of compute instances in the cloud. The jump server can be left up and running at all times and used for management tasks such as running automation scripts.

Customized Security Implementation Approaches

Many cloud vendors and equipment suppliers will offer internally developed applications to implement security in your cloud deployment. For example, a firewall company may offer a configuration and management application based on a technology such as Java or a web front end to an API on the firewall. These specialized interfaces are useful in implementing cloud security as they are closely integrated with the vendor's product set. A firewall vendor may deploy a virtual firewall in the cloud as a service and integrate custom configuration applications into the cloud provider's management platforms. Many times the vendor's customized systems are hidden from the cloud end user because they interface with a web front end.

Security Services

In the security world, services are often used interchangeably with applications or devices that perform a specific security function or service. Cloud-based security services include devices such as firewalls, intrusion detection and prevention systems, and host-based intrusion systems.

There are many other security services such as authentication, authorization, and accounting services; security key management; inspection services that scan and report on security configurations; denial-of-service deflection offerings; and classification services. In addition to this long list of security services, the fast pace of the cloud marketplace means that new offerings are constantly being introduced and existing services are being enhanced and expanded.

Firewalls

The device that is central to any security implementation is the network firewall. A firewall will be installed inline in a network so that all traffic must pass through it as it transits from one network to another. Firewalls will have rule sets, or policies, configured that will either permit or deny traffic to pass. Firewalls also have advanced algorithms that monitor not just each packet individually but the session for additional capabilities and security. Firewall placement is an important consideration when designing your cloud security structure. Firewalls are often placed at the border of a network—between your cloud site and the Internet, for example—and are called *perimeter*, or first line of defense firewalls, as shown in Figure 4.5. Inside your cloud infrastructure, firewalls are used to segment the network and to isolate critical systems from the rest of the network.

FIGURE 4.5   Firewalls define what traffic is allowed in and out of the network.

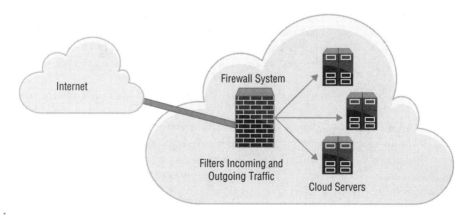

While network firewalls are almost always hardware-based, there are virtualized firewalls that run as a VM on a hypervisor, inside either the hypervisor or firewall software that can be installed on the server operating system to protect each individual server from attack.

Antivirus and Malware Prevention

Antivirus and malware application software plays a critical role in the virtualized world of the cloud just like it does in the corporate data center or at home. Regardless of where your systems are deployed, it is critical that you take the needed steps to protect them.

Protection software can be purchased in the marketplace from the same antivirus companies and in the same manner as you are currently doing. Some cloud providers offer antivirus and malware protection services, and if you hire a third-party managed security provider, it will most likely offer the service as part of its standard product portfolio.

Intrusion Detection and Prevention

Intrusion detection and prevention services play as important of a role in the cloud as they do in the private cloud or corporate data center. A complete security posture includes either an IDS or IPS implementation. As you learned in Chapter 2, intrusion detection systems (IDSs) and intrusion prevention systems (IPSs) are similar in that they are used to monitor network traffic looking for suspicious activity. Both solutions can detect, in real time, suspicious activity on the network.

Intrusion systems monitor traffic looking for signatures of network activity that indicates an intrusion based on predefined rule sets that are kept up-to-date by the IDS/IPS vendors. The intrusion detection system will alert a management system or can be configured to send out e-mails or text notifications if an attack is discovered. However, the intrusion detection system will not take action to remedy the situation—it only monitors and reports.

The intrusion prevention system is more advanced than the IDS and can actively take measures to mitigate the attack with configuration scripts and methods to stop an attack that is underway. The IPS communicates with network devices such as routers and firewalls to apply rules to block the attack.

Most cloud providers will manage their own internal IDS/IPS systems as part of their security posture in the shared security model. Managed security-as-a-service vendors will offer intrusion systems either as part of their base offerings or as an add-on service. IDS/IPS software companies offer cloud-based versions of their commercial products with the advantage of templates that can be used to ease the install, configuration, and management of IDS/IPSs.

There are IDS/IPS open source offerings available from Snort, Suricata, Tripwire, and many others.

Scripts and automation tools can be used to install, monitor, and maintain these systems. Also, it is important that you create or enable existing scripts and the ability to pull down from the vendor security heuristics files and updates.

When implementing IDS/IPS security in the cloud, it is best to investigate your options early in the planning process as offerings can vary widely. If you must meet a regulatory or corporate compliance requirement to implement intrusion systems, make sure that it is addressed early in the planning and design stage.

Sensors are offered as a native option, or customers can install their own implementations. Many preconfigured virtual machine images of popular commercial and open source IDS/IPS offerings are available on image marketplaces. These can be especially useful as many intrusion detection and prevention vendors offer a try-before-you-buy option that also offers commercial support agreements.

Malware detection systems follow the same model as intrusion systems and should be installed on susceptible servers and systems in the cloud just as they would be in a commercial data center. Companies such as MetaFlow offer malware prevention and detection services that are designed for cloud-based operations and can even be deployed at the hypervisor level. Be aware that the cloud service provider most likely also has a malware security presence and may stop such code from even reaching your fleet of cloud servers.

Host-Based Intrusion Systems

Host-based intrusion detection systems perform the same security functions as network-based systems but run exclusively on each host computer or hypervisor. With IaaS deployments, you will have full control over the operating systems and their configurations in your deployment. This gives you the ability to install your preferred HIDS applications. For PaaS and SaaS, host-based intrusion detection and prevention systems will be the responsibility of your cloud service provider.

A hybrid option is available in the marketplace that includes software agents that are installed in each host system and a central controller for IDS/IPS management of the fleet of cloud servers offered from companies such as IBM/ISS, Tripwire, OSSEC, and Verisys.

Host-based intrusion systems can report on the state of the virtual machine at the time of the attack, which programs were affected, and what systems or services were started or modified; they can also capture log files and memory states. Host-based intrusion systems are valuable security tools for managing compliance to your security policies and gathering forensic data in the event of a security breach.

Physical Security of Cloud Systems

Security has a critical role to play in any IT deployment, and the cloud is no different. It is just a different deployment model. The critical need to protect and secure systems remains the same regardless of where the compute systems reside.

The cloud provider will ensure that it has secured its infrastructure and facilities. Data center personnel will be screened and only allowed in data center areas where they have a need to be. Security includes physical privacy as most cloud data centers are inside of nondescript buildings with no company markings and the cloud provider taking measures to keep their operations confidential. Since insider attacks are common in IT, the providers take all the steps necessary to mitigate the risk, including doing personnel background checks and monitoring for suspicious activity.

The security impact extends beyond the physical facilities. For example, the data stored in the cloud and the need to strengthen the security posture of all services, operating systems, programs, and networks in your cloud deployment must be addressed. Security also includes disaster recovery, business continuity, and, above all else, protecting the data.

Automation Impact on Critical Systems

Automation will relieve cloud engineers of repetitive tasks and allow for unified deployments and for rapid response to events. In the virtualized world of cloud computing, automation is a critical component to any cloud operation. Automation will continue to evolve, advance, and take an even greater role in cloud computing as the technologies become more mature and operational experience is gained with today's deployments.

Monitoring and management system scan trigger on events and alarms that indicate an anomaly in the operation of the cloud infrastructure. These triggers can initiate automated scripts that correct the issue without human intervention, or they can alert the operations staff of the issue. Automation systems are always running in the background of the cloud data center to maintain the uptime of all physical and virtual devices.

Summary

The Cloud+ exam has a strong security focus, which makes this a critical chapter to understand before taking the exam. The chapter focused on the implementation of security in the cloud.

You learned about data classification and how it is used, as well as that classification serves many purposes including compliance, security, and lifecycle management. You learned that by segmenting your cloud deployment into sections, security polices can be applied to each segment or area, which allows for a granular security deployment. You learned how to segment the network, storage, and compute resources and then were given an overview of how security can be applied to these segments.

Encryption technologies have a central role in security. The chapter covered the implementation of encryption and the many frameworks and encryption types that are common in the cloud. You learned about encrypting storage systems, databases, and data as it is being sent over a network. Encryption as it applies to regulatory requirements was also discussed.

Multifactor authentication allows you to have a greater level of sign-on security to cloud services. It requires you to have both something you know and something you have to be able to authenticate to your cloud services. Beyond the common username and password combination, multifactor authentication adds the requirement to enter a rotating number that is present on a hardware device on your keychain or as an application on your phone or laptop. If you do not have access to the token generator, you will not be able to log into the network; this adds an additional layer of security.

Many cloud customers will be required to meet various regulatory requirements for security depending on the market or country they are in. The importance of implementing compliance early in the design and implementation phase was discussed.

Cloud computing has evolved and grown based on its programmability, which allows for the automation of tasks. The ability to achieve conformity and uniformity in the cloud security implementation is greatly enhanced with the use of automation. It is important to understand APIs, what they are, and how they are used as they are the central programmability interface for cloud services and objects. While it is not required for you to be a programmer, knowledge of common languages used in automation is important. REST, JSON, XML, and Python are all commonly found in the cloud automation space.

In addition to APIs, there are many overlay applications that abstract the coding needed to communicate with a device using an API. Web-based front ends and vendor applications are available for ease of use in automating and configuring cloud resources. Portals and dashboards are often made available by cloud vendors; they offer a graphical view of your deployment and can be customized with a focus on security monitoring.

Orchestration systems, scripting, managed security service providers, and customized or proprietary designs are techniques used for implementing cloud security. Each topic was introduced and explained.

Security services can include many different types of systems and applications. For the exam blueprint, we included firewalls and intrusion detection and prevention systems for both the network and the host; you also examined virus and malware implementations.

Finally, the impacts that may occur when implementing security were discussed, and we ended with a short section on how automation may impact your cloud-based systems.

Exam Essentials

Know what data classification is.   Data classification is the organization of data into different tiers or categories for the purpose of making data available as required and to meet regulatory requirements, mitigate and manage risk, and secure data. Data can be organized into any defined category and managed according to that category's needs. Metadata is data that is attached to a file and can be thought of as a tag that explains, categorizes, or classifies that data. Metadata allows the data to be tracked as a group and be searched and can reduce duplication of like data that can help reduce or even eliminate storage requirements.

Understand segmentation of cloud resources.   *Cloud segmentation* is the process of dividing your cloud deployment into sections to allow for granular security polices to be applied. By applying segmentation to your cloud deployment, you can implement a multilayered security approach that aligns with a defense-at-depth security model.

Know how to implement encryption in the cloud.   The subject of encryption and the many ways it is applied can be an incredibly complex topic. For the exam, know that there are regulations and corporate policies that require data be encrypted not only as it is transmitted across the network but also when it is in a storage system. Be able to read scenario-based questions and determine the encryption application that is applicable to the question.

Understand multifactor authentication.   For the exam, know that multifactor authentication includes something you know (username and password) and something you have (a rotating numerical token). When authenticating to systems, you will be prompted for a username and password and also be asked to type in the number given on the rotating token generator. Multifactor authentication offers a higher level of security than using a simple username/password combination.

Understand and differentiate regulatory compliance issues as they relate to the implementation of cloud security.   For the exam, be able to answer questions related to the implementation of regulatory and compliance requirements and that it should start early in the planning process and follow through the design, implementation, and validation phases to ensure a successful compliance verification experience.

When implementing your operations in the cloud, it is best to meet all compliance issues from the beginning of the project so that your migration is not delayed with unforeseen compliance requirements. There may be scenario-based questions about specific industries or laws, and you should be able to answer that they are related to compliance.

Know the basics of automation and programmable interfaces.   For the virtualization of resources, there are many software capabilities that were developed to create, monitor, configure, and remove services deployed in the cloud. Given this capability, it is possible to automate much of your ongoing cloud security operations. Security automation can allow code to replace many of the processes that had to be performed manually in the past. Be able to identify exam questions that reference APIs, REST, CLI, or other automation programmability interfaces. You do not need to know how to program, but you do need to be able to identify the interfaces and have an understanding of how they are used.

Identify the different ways that security is implemented.   You may be required to identify the different methods of how security is implemented. Examples are using orchestration systems, scripting techniques, and customized automation systems.

Know security services.   For the exam, you should understand the basic operations of firewalls, intrusion detection and prevention services, host-based intrusion, and common virus and malware software implementations. Be able to differentiate between the different types of intrusion applications.

Written Lab

Fill in the blanks for the questions provided in the written lab. You can find the answers to the written labs in Appendix B.

1. The process of organizing information into different tiers or categories is referred to as
   _____.

2. Dividing your cloud fleet of servers into smaller discrete areas for the purpose of applying a granular security policy is known as _____

3. Data that is obfuscated on a RAID 5 storage array is __AT REST_____ encryption.

4. Multifactor authentication includes something you __KNOW__ and something you __HAVE__.

5. Hands-off programmatically driven cloud configuration change is commonly referred to as __AUTOMATION__

6. __API__ allow for a defined machine-to-machine software interaction to enable automation.

7. The __GUI_____ is a user-friendly front end interface to a service's APIs.

8. Network-based __IPS_____ take active security breach counter-measures.

9. Cloud-based security places a load on a virtual machine's __CPU__.

10. Security __automation__ can allow code to replace many processes that had to be performed manually in the past.

Review Questions

The following questions are designed to test your understanding of this chapter's material. For more information on how to obtain additional questions, please see this book's Introduction. You can find the answers in Appendix A.

1. Robert has been tasked to create a security implementation that segments his employer's e-commerce design to allow for policy enforcement. What are some of the areas that he is investigating? (Choose three.)

   A. Network

   B. Automation

   C. Storage

   D. Compute

   E. APIs

   F. JSON/XML

2. MFA tokens can be obtained where? (Choose two.)

   A. Python app

   B. Smartphone app

   C. Automation systems

   D. Keyfob

   E. Cloud vendor management dashboard

3. Hank just completed running some security automation scripts on his new fleet of application virtual machines. After applying intrusion detection, virus, and malware protection on the Linux images, he notices an increase in which VM metric on his management dashboard?

   A. DMA

   B. BIOS

   C. CPU

   D. IPSec

   E. I/O

4. What technology was instrumental in the growth of cloud services?

   A. XML

   B. Python

   C. Automation

   D. Authentication

   E. Scripting

   F. workflow services

   G. Encryption

5. Carl is planning his cloud migration and must meet HIPPA requirements for confidential storage of cloud data at rest and in use in the cloud. What services must be addressed by Carl? (Choose two.)

   A. Virtual private network

   B. Storage

   C. Client-side

   D. Database

6. What is a common cloud-based GUI used to get an overview of your security operations?

   A. Puppet automation

   B. Gemalto system

   C. Dashboard

   D. Vendor-based security appliance

7. Who does responsibility for stored data integrity in the cloud belong to?

   A. Cloud provider

   B. Compliance agency

   C. Cloud customer

   D. Shared responsibility

8. What are complex software systems that automate cloud operations and are offered by companies such as Chef and Puppet called?

   A. Authentication

   B. Federations

   C. Orchestration

   D. Ephemeral

9. RESTful APIs using XML and JSON on southbound interfaces can be used to orchestrate and automate what cloud-based services? (Chose all that apply.)

   A. Firewalls

   B. Load balancers

   C. Virtual machines

   D. DNS servers

   E. Durable storage volumes

10. Jim has a critical server in the application tier of his cloud-based deployment. He is looking at a device-specific security solution to add defense-in-depth capabilities to his currently deployed network-based security defenses. He has been researching ways to mitigate potential hacking attempts. What is a good solution for him?

    A. DMZ

    B. IDS

   C. IPS

   D. Classifications automation

   E. HIDS

11. A constantly changing six-digit numerical token is used in what type of cloud service?

   A. XML

   B. TLS

   C. SSL

   D. MFA

   E. JSON

12. A web-based dashboard is being deployed by your company. Hank has been tasked to develop the application but is concerned that the application must pull data from many different cloud locations and devices. What is a good interface for him to use to meet his requirements?

   A. Python

   B. XML

   C. API

   D. SNMP

   E. TLS

13. Samantha has been tasked to meet FedRamp compliance for her customer's new contract. Where should she integrate compliance in her project? (Choose four.)

   A. Hand-off

   B. Design

   C. Implementation

   D. Automation rollout

   E. Planning

   F. Validation

   G. HIDS

   H. JSON/XML scripting

14. Sharon is investigating a standards-based construct to enable automation on her load balancers. What is a good lightweight data-interchange format standard that is easily readable and for computing systems to parse and to generate? (Choose two.)

   A. XML

   B. JSON

   C. REST

   D. Python

15. Mike has been investigating multiple hacking attempts on his cloud e-commerce web servers. He wants to add a front end with a service that actively takes countermeasures to shut down the hacking attempts. What application would you suggest that Mike deploy?

- **A.** DMZ
- **B.** IDS
- **C.** IPS
- **D.** RAID
- **E.** HIDS

16. Hank works in his e-commerce company's IT security group and has been tasked to investigate options that will allow customers to securely access their personal records stored on the cloud deployment from their smartphones. What is the most common in-flight e-commerce security posture on the market?

- **A.** MD5
- **B.** SSL/TLS
- **C.** IPsec
- **D.** VPN

17. Storage that does not survive a virtual machine removal is referred to as what classification? (Choose two.)

- **A.** Durable
- **B.** RAID
- **C.** Ephemeral
- **D.** Nondurable

18. Cloud segmentation enhances security for cloud-based applications. What services is it a best practice to segment?

- **A.** Python
- **B.** Compute
- **C.** RAM
- **D.** VPN

19. What is a long-standing text-based interface that is used to configure network services both locally and remotely?

- **A.** GUI
- **B.** CLI
- **C.** REST
- **D.** SNMP
- **E.** API

20. Your company has purchased a specialized intrusion prevention system that is virtualized and designed for cloud-based network microsegmentation deployments. When reading the documentation, Sam notices a link to download a Java-based application to monitor and configure the IPS. What kind of automation system is this?

   A. CLI

   B. GIU

   C. Vendor based

   D. API

   E. RESTful

Chapter

5

Maintaining Cloud Operations

THE FOLLOWING COMPTIA CLOUD+ EXAM OBJECTIVES ARE COVERED IN THIS CHAPTER:

✓ **3.1   Given a cloud service model, determine the appropriate methodology to apply given patches.**

  ▪ Scope of cloud elements to be patched

    ▪ Hypervisors

    ▪ Virtual machines

    ▪ Virtual appliances

    ▪ Networking components

    ▪ Applications

    ▪ Storage components

    ▪ Clusters

  ▪ Patching methodologies and standard operating procedures

    ▪ Production vs. development vs. QA

    ▪ Rolling update

    ▪ Blue-green deployment

    ▪ Failover cluster

  ▪ Use order of operations as it pertains to elements that will be patched

  ▪ Dependency considerations

✓ **3.2   Given a scenario, apply the appropriate automation tools to update cloud elements.**

  ▪ Types of updates

    ▪ Hotfix

    ▪ Patch

    ▪ Version update

    ▪ Rollback

- Automation workflow
  - Runbook management
    - Single node
  - Orchestration
    - Multiple nodes
    - Multiple runbooks
- Activities to be performed by automation tools
  - Snapshot
  - Cloning
  - Patching
  - Restarting
  - Shut down
  - Maintenance mode
  - Enable/disable alerts

✓ **3.3   Given a scenario, apply an appropriate backup or restore method.**

- Backup types
  - Snapshot/redirect-on-write
  - Clone
  - Full
  - Differential
  - Incremental
  - Change block/delta tracking
- Backup targets
  - Replicas
  - Local
  - Remote
- Other considerations
  - SLAs
  - Backup schedule
  - Configurations
  - Objects
  - Dependencies
  - Online/offline

In this chapter, you will learn about the maintenance and ongoing operations of your cloud deployment. You will learn about the various software services and systems that will require regular and ongoing patches and version support and about the various methods and operational approaches of performing regular patches.

The primary enabling technology of cloud computing is the automation of operations accomplished with advanced orchestration software and the virtualized infrastructure of the modern cloud data center. These automation systems are also enabled to perform ongoing maintenance and support of cloud data centers.

This chapter will also cover storage backup operations by discussing the different storage backup types and targets and the operational aspects of backing up your cloud storage systems.

Applying Security Patches

All software has bugs that must be patched to prevent bad things from happening. When new bugs are discovered, the details are often published or leaked to the media. People with less than wholesome intentions can use this information to craft exploits by taking advantage of these bugs with the knowledge that most systems are out-of-date and not protected.

With this in mind, it is important to keep on top of the security landscape and have a planned approach to patch management. This section will focus on the subject of securing your cloud fleet of servers and services as it relates to keeping your systems up-to-date.

As part of a shared security model, the cloud provider will secure the infrastructure, and the cloud customer will be required to address security concerns based on the service model they are operating under. A complete patch management approach must be developed, implemented, and adhered to in order to prevent a security breach.

Cloud Element Security

When discussing security in this chapter, I will break it down based on elements in the cloud that may require patches to be installed to mitigate security concerns. While this is not anywhere close to a complete list of devices or services, I will discuss patching hypervisors, VMs, appliances, networking components, applications, storage systems, and clustered devices, which cover a large swath of cloud systems.

Hypervisors

As you now know, a hypervisor is the virtualization software running directly on top of the server hardware that enables the hardware to be virtualized into pooled resources that are, in turn, allocated to virtual machines. This is of course critical software that is often hidden from sight but at the core of a virtualized data center.

Since there are many virtual machines running on each hypervisor and given that the hypervisor is a core component of the server, most, if not all, operations on the hypervisor will require that it be taken offline when patching or upgrading takes place. To prevent the disruption of the operations of every virtual machine running on top of the hypervisors, each VM will need to be migrated to another server prior to performing any patches on the hypervisor.

Once all active services have been migrated off the server, then patching can be performed on the hypervisor while it is offline. Hypervisor code will require periodic maintenance to address security vulnerabilities, fix feature deficiencies, and add functionality.

Virtual Machines

VMs will require patch management as well; this can be accomplished with automation software that tracks patches and that can download, implement, and validate the installation of the patched VMs automatically. Also, snapshots and cloned images can be used to create a master copy of a virtual machine with all the required patches installed and tested. These cloned images can be used as the master template when updating VMs.

Virtual Appliances

Just as VMs require a patch management process to ensure they are kept up-to-date and secure from exploits, virtual appliances need to be patched as well. A virtual appliance is often a specialized application running on a version of Linux, so it has its own set of deficiencies and vulnerabilities that require ongoing patch management.

A virtual appliance may be a managed cloud provider service, and as such, it will be the provider's responsibility to keep all the managed appliances up-to-date. However, in the cloud marketplaces, many appliance vendors' offerings (including firewalls, load balancers, and IDSs/IPSs, for example) license their products to you, so it is your responsibility to perform the ongoing maintenance of these applications. Most offer support agreements that allow access to vendor support forums, technical support teams, and software updates.

There are many different virtual appliance offerings from many different companies. Each vendor offering virtual appliances will have its own security and patch management offerings based on its own product offerings.

Network Systems

Network systems such as firewalls, IDSs/IPSs, load balancers, routers, and DNS servers are offered as managed services by most cloud providers and are also available for you to install and manage yourself. The entity with control of the system will have responsibility for keeping the devices up-to-date with the current security packages. It is imperative that if you are responsible for any of the network elements that you keep them up to current revision levels. This is required because most network elements sit at the core of your cloud fleet of servers, and most data passes over the network. If the network can be compromised, then a malicious hacker may be able to use the network to attack all of your systems.

Applications

The application or development teams will generally be responsible for patching and maintaining systems at the application level. If you are purchasing a Software as a Service solution from your cloud provider, then the provider will assume responsibility for maintaining and ensuring that the applications are current and secure.

However, if the application was developed internally or you are running an IaaS or PaaS service, then you will be responsible for application maintenance.

Many applications will check automatically with a central repository to make sure they are current, and if they are not, they can download and either install the update or prompt you that there is an update available and allow you to manage the process.

Automation software such as Puppet or Chef can also patch applications if configured to do so. Automated scripts can also be run on the servers that check for and install application updates.

Storage Systems

SAN Fibre Channel switches, storage controller heads, host bus adapters, and RAID controller software all go through the revision cycle just like any other system that runs on software. Because of their critical nature and need for constant uptime, storage systems are highly redundant. This allows for some flexibility in performing updates as one part of the storage systems can be temporarily taken offline for maintenance while the backup system assumes full operational responsibility.

Clusters

Clusters are groups of computers interconnected by a local area network and are tightly coupled together. Clusters can be configured in many different topologies depending on the use case and for the different solutions they are designed for. However, all clusters are designed for high availability, which can allow for installing patches with zero downtime. Depending on the capabilities of the cluster software, most individual components in a cluster can be taken offline without the need to take the whole cluster down. This allows for individual systems to be upgraded while the cluster is live. Another common approach is to upload the patch to a master or controller node in a cluster and have the cluster management software perform the upgrades internally.

Patching Methodologies

This section discusses the different types or methodologies of patching. Patching is an important requirement for ongoing cloud operational support. By making sure all of your systems have current patches installed, you reduce your attack footprint and protect yourself by addressing known bugs that may affect your operations. There are different approaches to take when patching your systems, and there are different types of patches for different requirements that you will explore in this section.

Patch management can be a rather complex topic area. It is suggested you work to keep all of your related systems at the same version, revision, or patch level. This will allow you to have a known baseline for you to operate on and to troubleshoot. There are applications that keep track of version levels, while some network administrators prefer to use a basic spreadsheet and manually track software version levels that are installed on platforms either on-premise or in the cloud.

Given that there are often a large number of patches released every week or month, it can become a chore to track them and decide which ones demand immediate attention to solve a critical issue and which ones are minor or cosmetic and can be safely ignored. You must also know the proper order to install these patches in.

It is helpful to classify the risk and to understand with a cloud-based shared responsibility model who is responsible for patching certain systems and who is not. Systems may sit behind a firewall or inside of a security group that may protect the system from an outside attack even if the patch has not been installed. The likelihood of an attack should be assessed, including how critical the system is. Is there a bigger operational risk installing the patch than leaving the system as it currently is? It usually comes down to how severe the threat is, the potential impact it may have on your operations, the probability you could get exploited by your unpatched systems, and the cost of time and monetary impact to recover if you were to be attacked by choosing not to install the patch.

Production Systems

Applying patches in the production environment is inherently risky. In addition, there are other steps to consider to make sure that a patch operation is successful.

Production updates will need to follow the change management process, and a plan should be developed that outlines the upgrade steps, the validation and testing process, and the plan if you need to remove or roll back the patch after experiencing undesirable results.

It is advised that all patches be tested in a nonproduction environment prior to a production rollout. If you have a large fleet of servers, it is recommended that you automate the process to ensure consistency. Many automation systems such as Puppet, Chef, Openstack, or Ansible allow you to automate updates. After patching, testing should be performed to ensure that it was applied successfully and the system is operating as expected. If there are any issues, you should have a rollback plan in place to restore the system to its original state.

There is a risk to patching production servers, but there may not be a choice depending on the severity of the bug that needs to be corrected. All precautions and due diligence must be performed up front to mitigate the risk.

To reduce the impact to operations when applying patches, have a well-architected network and ensure that production operations are not negatively affected. Redundant and high availability designs allow systems to be patched while others assume the workload.

Development Systems

Patching in the development system allows for full integration of system patches prior to QA testing and rollout of your applications or services. The DevOps team should evaluate the patches and integrate them into their product as soon as practical. This ideally allows for a better product release.

Quality Assurance

Updates should be validated by the software vendor, the cloud company, and your operations staff to determine how the patch will perform in production. It is important that you establish a quality assurance test bed that allows you to test the patch in your specific environment to identify dependencies, interoperability issues, unknowns, and, most of all, whether the update fixes the problem you are experiencing!

For the software vendor that has developed the patch, it is absolutely critical that the vendor performs a full suite of QA tests of the package. This will be to verify that the fix does in fact fix the issue it was intended to fix. There are also QA tests done to make sure that the fix does not interfere with other processes and that there are no memory or buffer issues experienced with the patched version of software.

Performing Rolling Updates

Rolling updates is the constant delivery of software updates or patches to operating systems or applications. Other terms that are synonymous with rolling updates are *rolling releases* and *continuous delivery*. Rolling updates are generally related to small but frequent updates. Rolling updates are common in the Linux world and are often delivered as a package accessed remotely over the Internet. A rolling update is performed sequentially with one system being patched at a time; when the first system's patch is complete, the next system is patched, as shown in Figure 5.1.

FIGURE 5.1   Rolling updates are performed sequentially.

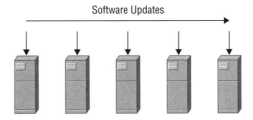

Software Updates

Blue-Green

Blue-green is a methodology that uses two configurations for production that are identical to each other. These deployments can alternate between each other with one being active and the other being inactive. One of the two identical environments is referred to as *blue*, and the other is called *green*. Each can handle the complete workload without assistance from the other. This allows you to implement, test, and validate software updates to the inactive side. Once this operation has been performed and you feel comfortable with the updates, you can make it active. The previously active side (which could be either blue or green) will now be inactive, and you have to perform the same updates on it. Blue and green are arbitrary names that are merely used to differentiate between two sides.

The blue-green model avoids downtime by supplying two identical deployments that allow you to operate while one is active and have the other on standby. Updating the inactive one does not affect the active one and allows for thorough testing before going live. The blue-green approach also works well for new application deployments in critical implementations with high uptime requirements or for critical customer-facing applications. Rollbacks are as fast as redirecting traffic to the standby. The downside it that this approach requires a massive fleet of servers since you must allocate as many resources in standby mode as you do for your production fleet of servers. Figure 5.2 illustrates a blue-green deployment.

FIGURE 5.2   Blue-green deployment

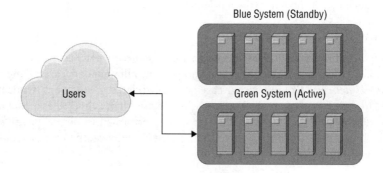

Clustering and Failover

A *cluster* is a group of servers operating in tandem that often appear as a single larger system. Clusters can be managed as a single larger system instead of many smaller servers grouped together. This allows for a central point of management that simplifies operations. You can manage a cluster as a complete system and not be concerned with all of the individual systems. Patches can be downloaded to the master nodes in the cluster, and they will push out and install the updates to all systems in the cluster. Depending on the system and its capabilities, a cluster can be upgraded while maintaining full operational capabilities less the reduced capacity of individual nodes being taken offline for upgrades. The devices in the cluster work together to support a high availability platform for applications and services, as shown in Figure 5.3. If any node in a cluster were to fail, other nodes would pick up the operations and continue without any downtime.

FIGURE 5.3   Cluster updates on each server with no downtime

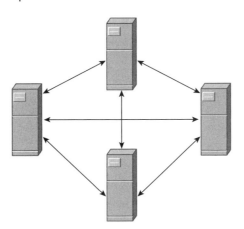

Patching Order of Operations and Dependencies

When applying patches, it is often important to apply patches in a certain order because of dependencies that are needed. When performing upgrades, it is sometimes common that various subsystem patches be installed before patching the main system controller and performing a restart because the main patch requires that other systems be at a certain revision level. System documentation or release notes will explain the steps and in what specific order they need to be performed. As you will learn later in this chapter, workflows can be constructed based on these update tasks, and the upgrade process can then be automated based on runbooks created from the workflow.

Any packages, especially on Linux systems, ship with package managers that abstract the dependencies and are applied without any user intervention.

Updating Cloud Elements

All software companies will experience deficiencies in their products, be required to make changes because of external events, or have to add new features or capabilities to remain current to receive vendor support or to remain in compliance with regulatory requirements. Let's take a look at the different types of patches and the role automation plays in updating systems with these patches.

Understanding the Different Types of Updates

In this section, you will learn about the various types of updates that are available and the problems they are intended to solve. During your career in cloud computing, you will find that these terms are often used interchangeably. This section will allow you to understand what the terms really are and how they should be used. Out in the field, your mileage will vary widely!

Hotfix

A *hotfix* is a software update type that is intended to fix an immediate and specific problem with a quick release procedure. A hotfix may be customer-specific and not released to the public or available to everyone. Many times a hotfix is a bug fix that has been made quickly and did not follow the normal quality assurance or formal release procedures since the intention is for a rapid deployment.

Because of the urgent nature of supplying a bug fix to a critical issue, a hotfix has a higher risk factor than other approaches to patching software. Testing the patch is usually quick using a subset of the full QA test suites. Installing a hotfix may introduce new and unknown issues into your environment.

The risk of installing a hotfix to correct a bug and introducing new problems must be weighed against not taking action and living with the bug until all testing has been completed.

Patch

A *patch* is an update that fixes a known bug or issue. The patch is a piece of software that is intended to update an application, operating system, or any other software-based system to fix or improve its operations. Generally, patches are synonymous with fixes for security vulnerabilities or any other type of operational bug. Patches do not offer feature enhancements but rather fixes or performance enhancements. Patches can be thought of as bug fixes or "improving usability and performance" or "removing an undocumented feature"!

Version Update

A *version update* is the process of replacing a software product with a newer version of the same product. Version updates can add new features, bring the system up-to-date, and provide a rollup of all previous patches to improve the product. Upgrading entails replacing the current, older version of the same product with a newer version.

Often a version update includes major feature enhancements and capabilities. As such, there may be a charge applied with the upgrade. Think of going between versions of operating systems from Linux, Apple, or Microsoft.

Rollback

A *rollback* is the process of returning software to a previous state. If a software update failed, did not correct the issue as expected, or introduced new issues that require you to downgrade the system to its original sate, then a rollback should be performed.

The process of performing a rollback is dependent on each system. If it is a VM, then a snapshot of the current VM could be taken prior to installing the patch, and if there is a need to perform a rollback, then the snapshot could be made active with the original instal-lation. Some applications and operating systems have scripts or utilities that allow the patch to be rolled back as needed. In other cases, it may be necessary to re-install the original software package to overwrite the patch.

The term *rollback* is also common when working with databases and refers to an opera-tion that can return the database to a known previous state to maintain database integrity. If there is a severe database issue, a rollback can be performed to a point prior to the issue being present.

Workflow Automation

Workflow automation defines a structured process for a series of actions that should be taken to complete a process. With cloud-based workflow services, special workflow applica-tions are offered as a managed service that creates a defined sequence of events, or *workflow*, with each procedure tracked and passed to the next process in the workflow.

The workflow reduces errors since it follows a defined sequence of events that ensures that all previous steps are completed before passing to the next step. This allows for consis-tency and eliminates human error.

Workflows can be created and used as templates for large system upgrades that automate the process of updating cloud-based systems in a systematic and predictable manner. If there are software dependencies that require one patch to be installed before another patch, for example, then a workflow can be created that tracks and verifies the order of operations have been completed before passing to the next workflow step. Think of a workflow as a flowchart that uses automation tools to carry out the process steps of the flowchart.

Runbooks

Runbooks are software processes that perform automated tasks and responses that simplify and automate repetitive tasks. Runbooks can be created to automate the installation of soft-ware packages or patches on your fleet of virtual servers in the cloud. Runbooks script and run repetitive automation tasks for any operation such as installing updates, responding to events or alarms, or performing routine system maintenance.

Multiple runbooks can be created, with each one dedicated to performing a specific automated task. When an event occurs, the automation and orchestration applications can execute a specific runbook to perform an action based on the event. For example, if a VM should fail, the management software could call a runbook that runs a series of diagnos-tics, attempts to restart the VM, tests for completion, and installs a new VM using a pre-defined image if the restart fails. If a new VM is created, a runbook could be used to install all updates and applications that are required.

Orchestration

Orchestration was introduced in Chapter 4 and defined as software packages or services that automate cloud security in a single package. Orchestration systems play a critical role in cloud operations that goes beyond just security to many other tasks such as the day-to-day maintenance of operations.

Orchestration systems coordinate and process tasks, functions, and workflows of cloud operations without the need for human intervention. Orchestration is often described as service-orientated architecture, automated provisioning, converged infrastructure, or dynamic data center. While there are many marketing terms and products, the definition remains the same.

These systems carry out processes as required to deploy new services and systems as well as responding to operational events such as a loss of network services that may necessitate switching to a backup system or calling programs to restart a failed system. Orchestration systems carry out the automated operations in the modern cloud that used to be done manually.

The main function of orchestration systems is to combine the multiple tasks that must be completed to accomplish an operation. These tasks are combined into a workflow that defines the order of events and steps needed to complete the operation. The orchestration system uses software systems and processes to carry out the workflow. Orchestration abstracts and hides much of the complexity of modern cloud systems and also reduces operational errors by executing tested cloud systems, scripts, workflows, or runbooks to make sure the systems are configured correctly.

Cloud providers usually offer a web-based or CLI interface as a front end to their automation systems. End users will not be able to directly access these systems but can input order or configuration requests that trigger the orchestration systems running in the background. The web front ends also act as a dashboard that allows you to monitor the activities in real time as the orchestration system carries out its operations. There are also APIs usually published for machine-to-machine communications to programmatically access these systems.

Virtualization Automation Tools and Activities

This section will address the various issues of patching cloud services and systems. You will learn about creating snapshots and clones of virtual machines. You will also learn about common practices to be aware of when performing maintenance such as turning monitoring off so as not to generate false alarms on systems undergoing routine maintenance.

Snapshots

A *snapshot* creates an instant-in-time image for rollbacks or backups. The process of taking a snapshot is usually performed with the management tools that are used to manage the virtual environment. The snapshot is a file-based image of the current state of a VM, including the complete operating systems and all applications that are stored on it. The snapshot will record the data on the disk, its current state, and the VM's configuration at that instant in time, as illustrated in Figure 5.4. Snapshots can be created while the VM is in operation and are used as a record of that VM's state. They can be saved to roll back to at a later time.

FIGURE 5.4   Virtual machine snapshot

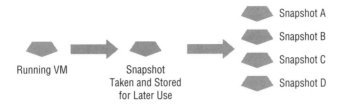

Running VM   Snapshot
                    Taken and Stored
                    for Later Use

Snapshot A
Snapshot B
Snapshot C
Snapshot D

VM Snapshot Creates an Instant-in-Time Image for Rollback or Backups

Cloning Virtual Devices

There is a second type of VM replication called *cloning*, as shown in Figure 5.5. Cloning is similar to snapshots but has a different use in managing cloud deployments. With a snapshot, an exact copy is made of a running VM. Cloning is different in that it takes the master image and clones it to be used as another separate and independent VM. Important components of a server are changed to prevent address conflicts; these include the UUID and MAC addresses of the cloned server.

FIGURE 5.5   Virtual machine cloning

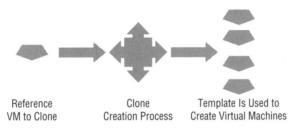

Reference   Clone   Template Is Used to
VM to Clone   Creation Process   Create Virtual Machines

Keep in mind that snapshots are used to restore an existing VM, and cloning is when you take a VM and use it to create a new and separate VM.

Patching Automation

There are automation tools that perform patching functions as a base service. The patching service can also be used to establish a versioning baseline that all systems should be operating at. The systems will download the patches from the software vendors, create all update scripts, and push the updates out to the virtual servers and applications on a predefined schedule. Also, validation, and if necessary, rollback functions are performed. Applications such as Chef, Puppet, Openstack, and Ansible are examples for automation packages that offer patching services.

The servers can also run scripts on a regularly scheduled time frame to check for and, if desired, install updates.

Restarting Systems

Cloud configuration front ends as well as automation systems using scripting or API calls can restart virtual machines as required. Restarts may be performed to upgrade code, to troubleshoot, or to meet many other needs. The restart process can be monitored through the management systems and dashboards that are offered by the cloud provider. Depending on the application and operation being performed, the dashboard may not be notified of a restart at the application level. The ability to notify the monitoring systems may depend on the management and reporting capabilities of the system that is being restarted.

Shutting Down Systems

In the same manner that systems can be restarted, they can be shut down. A shutdown may be desired if you choose to retain the VM and its applications but do not need it to be active. Most cloud providers will not charge you for a VM that is not active. So, having VMs that are shut down makes sense as a cost-saving measure that allows you to quickly bring fully configured computing capacity online later as needed.

Enabling Maintenance Mode

When performing maintenance on a server in the cloud, it is a best practice to put it into *maintenance mode*. When a server is undergoing maintenance, it may be in a state that it will not respond to health checks, API calls, SNMP, or any other means used to monitor its health by network management systems. This may cause false alarms and trigger automated troubleshooting systems.

When a server is in maintenance mode, the management systems will not respond to alarms from the server being down for maintenance. Maintenance mode suppresses all alarms, alerts, or nonresponsiveness that may occur because of a device being offline due to maintenance.

Enabling/Disabling System Alerts

Alerting allows a virtual server to send management data to monitoring systems informing them of either predefined or custom events. Alerts can be in the form of traps, logging information, or data generated by management software running on the server. In the cloud dashboard or management console, many cloud providers allow you to enable or disable the alerting system. When you initially create a virtual server, you may set alerting to be enabled for that VM, and the automation systems will create a managed object for that server in the monitoring systems. As discussed earlier, it is a best practice to disable alerts prior to taking a server offline for maintenance.

Storage Operations

In this section, you will learn about a critical aspect of ongoing operations in your cloud deployment. *Storage operations* means managing your data, its availability, and what you need to know about backup and restore operations.

Types of Backups

In this section, you will become familiar with the different types of backups and what the best use cases are for each one. Backups are a critical piece of your overall IT strategy and will usually be required for regulatory compliance and corporate policy.

Backups may be performed by the cloud provider as part of its service offerings and as a managed service. Cloud customers may also want to implement their own backup strategy to meet their specific needs.

There are many different types and variations of backups to meet the use cases and objectives you may need to meet. I will cover the most common backups that are objectives for the Cloud+ exam.

Image Backups

Image backups are copies of complete hard drive volumes. This technology is often called *disaster backup*, *cloning*, *ghosting*, *image backups*, or *block-level backups*. You use image backups to prepare for disasters resulting from losing VMs or to roll back an image after an update has failed or from a server that will not boot or is corrupted. Figure 5.6 shows the process of creating an image backup.

FIGURE 5.6   Image backup

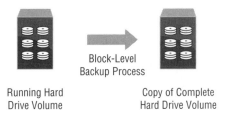

Running Hard   Copy of Complete
Drive Volume   Hard Drive Volume

File Backups

File backups, as shown in Figure 5.7, are what people normally think of when backing up a server or personal system. File backups are the storage of folders and files that you select with your backup software to copy to another storage location for later access if needed. File-level backups are generally smaller in space requirements, are more efficient, and have more options during restorations than complete image backups.

FIGURE 5.7   File backup

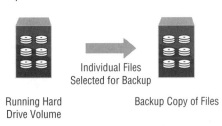

Running Hard   Backup Copy of Files
Drive Volume

Snapshots

Storage *snapshots* are a point-in-time copy of a storage volume or image that can be used as a backup to shorten recovery time objectives (RTOs) and recovery point objectives (RPOs).

There are several variations of snapshots; the two most prominent are the copy-on-write and redirect-on-write snapshots. The *copy-on-write* snapshot is based on reserved storage capacity that is required to store the snapshot of your data. When the snapshot is performed, it includes only metadata that contains information about where the original data is stored instead of storing the actual data. The primary advantage is that copy-on-write snapshots are immediate and have a minimal impact on storage operations. The snapshot will then track the storage volume by monitoring the storage blocks as changes are performed. When these blocks of storage data change, the original blocks of data are moved to the reserved snapshot storage area. This is done prior to the block of data being overwritten. The snapshot data is in sync with the time that the snapshot was taken.

A copy-on-write snapshot requires an original copy of the data and stores changes to the reserved storage. The advantage of the copy-on-write method is that it is compact and uses minimal backup storage space. However, there will be a negative effect on storage write performance as the original volume must store the backup data to the copy-on-write backup storage space prior to accepting the write request.

The *redirect-on-write* snapshot process takes a different approach. When a storage write operation takes place, the redirect-on-write snapshot will not store the new data over the existing block. Instead, it will create a pointer that tells the snapshot image where the original block is located on the original storage volume. These pointers allow a system accessing the snapshot to reference the data at the point in time the snapshot was taken and uses less storage I/O operations than a copy-on-write snapshot. This allows for a more efficient storage system with less overhead and a faster response.

Cloning

Cloning creates an identical copy of the data that may be a storage volume, a filesystem, or the logical unit number (LUN) on a storage area network (SAN).

Advantages of cloning include a complete image being available for restoration. Storage efficiency is very low as a clone takes as much storage space as the original source since all of the data is copied in the clone operation. There is also a performance hit with cloning in that there is overhead involved when writing data to the cloned copy from the source while the source is actively serving production storage operations.

Full Backups

A *full backup* is a complete copy of the backed-up data. Full backups are generally performed on a routine backup schedule with a series of smaller, or incremental, backups that are added to the full backup in the time between the full backups. Full backups offer the advantage of a complete and up-to-date copy of your data in one operation. They have the disadvantage of taking a long time to perform as all the data in a storage system must be copied instead of just the modified data from the last backup. Full backups also require a significant amount of storage capacity since the complete data set is copied in the operation.

Differential Backups

A *differential backup* uses the latest full backup as a source data set, and with each additional sequential backup operation the differential backup will identify and back up only the data that has been modified since the last backup was performed. This allows for an efficient and significantly smaller backup operation.

For example, let's assume you perform a full backup on Sunday and then do daily differential backups for the rest of the week. The first differential backup that runs on Monday will include the file changes made since the time of the full backup that was performed on Sunday. The next differential backup that runs on Tuesday will contain the changed data from both Monday and Tuesday and so forth.

A differential backup contains all of the changed data since the last full backup. This allows for faster restore times since the process takes only two steps, restoring the full backup and then restoring the most recent differential backup.

Incremental Backups

Incremental backups perform operations based on the change of the source data since the last incremental backup was performed. Incremental backups can be run, for example, on a nightly basis and capture the changes that were made since the previous backup was run the night before. This allows for an efficient backup operation since only the changes in the past 24 hours are stored on the backup media. Incremental backups are much less time- and resource-consuming than a full backup and are used to complement them.

One downside of using incremental backups is that the restore time objective can be longer since the last full backup must be restored, and then all of the incremental backup images taken since the last full restore would need to be retrieved and copied over the full restore to bring it up to the current point of the last differential update.

Tracking Block and Delta Changes

When a block of data on a storage device is modified, it will be flagged as having been changed since the last backup. When a backup operation is performed, if it is a full, incremental, or differential backup, the flag can be reset to indicate the data has been backed up. The tags indicate to the backup software if an operation needs to be performed or skipped because there were no changes. When the file is later modified, the flag will be set again to indicate that there were changes made to it since the last backup.

Backup Targets

The *backup target* is defined as the endpoint or storage system where the backup data is to be stored. Backup targets can store data as a live copy to be used by your applications like with replicas or can store data as a local storage array that can perform the function of a backup data store; alternatively, they can store data as a secondary system that can support a copy of your live data. Remote backups address the need for geographic separation of your backup data from your production systems.

Replicas

Replicas are backup copies of data that can be stored either locally or remotely that can act as alternative data stores from your main production operations. For example, with many popular databases, you can create one or more read replicas that can be stored in local or remote data centers. These replicas are updated in real time from the master, and the database can access them instead of the master replica. This allows for the database to scale and operate at very high read rates.

Other applications such as caching and content delivery services rely on replicas stored locally that were downloaded from a distant source location for enhanced performance.

Operating systems, storage management software, applications, and virtualization management systems offer storage replication where data that is stored in a local volume, LUN, or array is automatically replicated to another system for availability and redundancy purposes.

When a file is stored in the primary storage system, the replication software will automatically store the same file in another location, or replica.

Local Backups

Local backups are just as they sound; they are data in a local data center that is stored on its local primary storage array, and when a backup operation is performed, the data is backed up locally. The advantage of local backups is speed. High-speed Fibre Channel or Ethernet networks can be taken advantage of for fast backup operations. The disadvantage is that if something happens to that data center, all of your data could be compromised since the backup and primary data are all in the same location, as shown in Figure 5.8.

FIGURE 5.8   Local backup

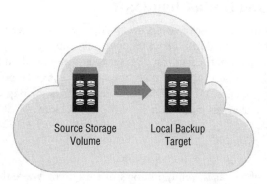

Source Storage Volume   Local Backup Target

Remote Backups

Remote backups are a preferred approach since they have the advantage of geographical separation. Many corporate and most regulatory requirements will specify that the backup data be located at a separate data center from the origin data center and that the two locations are geographically some distance apart from each other, as illustrated in Figure 5.9. Many cloud providers interconnect their data centers into regions and availability zones using high-speed, directly connected, fiber networks that allows large backup sets to traverse the data network between the data centers and makes remote backups feasible.

FIGURE 5.9   Remote backup

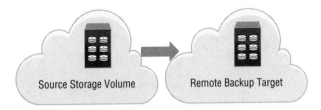

Source Storage Volume   Remote Backup Target

Backup and Restore Operations

In this section, you will learn about backing up your systems and stored data and the operations that make up successful backup and restore operations in the cloud.

Backup Service Level Agreements

Cloud service providers that offer backups as a managed service will publish service level agreements that outline their offered service levels for backup operations to the cloud consumer. Examples of the items that may appear in the SLA include a percentage of availability for backup and restore services, monthly uptime, or time that the service can be accessed and used. The SLA will also include details on the service and a statement of what is and what is not covered under the SLA. Basically, the SLA is a legal document that defines the boundaries of what the backup provider is and is not responsible for and the levels of support and discount credits if the SLA is not met in a defined time frame.

Scheduling

The *backup window* is the time available for the backup operation to run while the source storage system is either offline or lightly used. The backup applications allow you to define when the backup operation takes place and what type of backup is to be performed. For example, a full backup can be scheduled for 1 a.m. to 5:30 a.m. every Sunday, and then incremental backups on every other day of the week can take place from 1 a.m. to 2 a.m. The schedule and backup window must allow for enough time for the backup operation to complete and take into account the volume of data and the time to transport the data across a network and to write the data to storage media.

Backup Configurations

The configuration and management of backups will depend on the level of service you have purchased from the cloud service provider. Most cloud providers will offer storage as a managed service that allows you to define your backup and data lifecycle operations from a control panel. Once configured, the cloud provider will use automation and orchestration systems to carry out your backup requests.

The service provider backup options can be quite extensive and feature-rich. For example, you can define which storage tier to use to store your data, including frequently accessed data to rarely used data that must be archived but can be infrequently accessed. You can define the region or regions to store the data to meet regulatory or corporate requirements for the location of the data and geographical separation of the online and backup data. Most providers offer multiple encryption options for data at rest and for archival needs. You can manage your own encryption keys or, if offered, allow the cloud provider to provide key management services for encryption as part of your backup agreements.

The cloud management web interface, command-line interface, or APIs allow you to set up, monitor, and change your backup configurations.

Objects and Dependencies

In storage systems or databases, it is common to find that one object of data may be dependent on another to operate. A database table may be related to another and must be backed up and restored in order for each to work. The object cannot run independently without the other, upon which it is dependent. Most database management software with backup modules will track all dependencies and back up the data as needed to meet these requirements.

Many cloud storage systems are object-based and are not either a file or block storage system. Object-based storage is highly utilized at the large cloud companies as a fully managed and cost-effective service. These systems are often automatically backed up locally or between multiple data centers in an availability zone for redundant and durable storage. It is important to be aware of where and how your data is being stored, and while the information can be opaque, it is important to investigate and monitor for your own comfort level and to meet regulatory laws that pertain to how your data is stored and accessed.

Online vs. Offline

Online storage is a storage system that can be accessed at any time without the requirement for a network administrator to mount the media into a storage system. Online is the most common storage design, and with backups, this offers an always available method to store and retrieve data.

Storage locations define where the location of the stored data will be. Offline storage is commonly tape, DVD, CD, or removable portable devices such as USB drives.

Offline storage is storage that requires an administrator or tape jukebox to make the data available by inserting a tape or other media into a storage system for retrieval. Offline storage can be transported to remote storage facilities or stored in vaults for protection. The offline architecture allows the backed-up data to be safely stored in a secure location and is generally a cost-effective method to store long-term data that is infrequently accessed.

Summary

The ongoing maintenance and support of cloud deployments is a primary focus for many Cloud+ certified professionals. The world job market has a strong requirement for knowledgeable cloud support personnel as the transfer from private to cloud computing grows year after year. This chapter's focus was on many of the core topics of cloud maintenance.

The chapter started with a discussion of applying software patches to the most common cloud elements such as the hypervisor, VMs, network systems, applications, storage, and compute clusters. You learned about patching software and the different issues that need to be taken into account when patching production, development, and QA deployments. Patching methodologies were introduced including rolling updates, blue-green, and clusters. Even with the cloud provider being responsible for the maintenance of the cloud infrastructure, you must be aware of its operations and know what your maintenance responsibilities are and what systems fall under your management domain.

There are different types of software updates that cloud professionals will need to be familiar with, including hotfix, patch, and version updates. You also learned about removing these updates by performing rollback operations.

The cloud is like one big software platform with APIs to configure and control its operations. With hyperscale cloud computing, the massive numbers of ongoing changes taking place at any point in time is staggering. The only way that a modern cloud system can function is with the use of automation systems. This chapter reviewed workflow automation, runbooks, and orchestration systems as they relate to ongoing maintenance. You learned about the details of automated patches that must be addressed such as shutting down and restarting systems, why it is a good practice to put systems into maintenance mode, and disabling system alerts to prevent false alarms.

A critical part of ongoing operations is the protection and care of your user data. The different types of backups were discussed including snapshots, copy/redirect-on-write, cloning, full, differential, and incremental.

Next you learned about backup targets, replicas, and the advantages and disadvantages of local and remote backups. You then looked at service level agreements, the issues with scheduling backups, different backup configurations, and the differences between online and offline backup operations.

Exam Essentials

Know the common systems that need ongoing patch management.   The most common systems that are operating in the cloud are hypervisors, virtual machines, virtual appliances, software applications, and clustered systems. Also, networking components, such as switches, routers, load balancers, firewalls, NAT systems, and many others, will need to be patched to remain current and secure. Storage systems are also included here.

Differentiate between the different types of updates.   You can expect the exam to ask you questions about the different types of updates. An update procedure will be described in the question, and you will need to identify what type of update it is. It is important that you are able to distinguish the differences between these types such as blue-green, rolling updates, production, development, and QA.

Understand automation and the basic support operations that can be performed.   Automation systems play an important role in cloud computing. You need to know what runbooks, workflow, and orchestration systems are.

Know virtualization operations that are common in the ongoing support and maintenance of cloud operations.   Be able to answer exam questions concerning what a snapshot is and what its purpose is. Know the differences between snapshots, which are backups, and cloning, which is a master copy of an image that is used for repetitive deployments.

Explain the storage operations in ongoing cloud maintenance.   You can expect that the exam will test you on your storage knowledge as it is a critical component of all cloud operations. Know the types of backups and be able to identify questions that differentiate between full, differential, and incremental backups.

Differentiate between the different types of backup targets.   Prepare for scenario questions that may describe a particular backup target solution and be able to select the correct type. Replicates, local, and remote are all common target types.

Understand backup and restore topics.   Know that there are service level agreements that address backup operations, that backups can be scheduled for automated operations, and that service providers offer many different configuration options.

Written Lab

Fill in the blanks for the questions provided in the written lab. You can find the answers to the written labs in Appendix B.

1. The ~~blue green~~ model is a software deployment methodology that uses two configurations for production that are identical to each other.

2. A constant delivery of software updates or patches to operating systems or applications is referred to as a ~~rolling update~~.

3. If you experience undesirable results after deploying a patch to a fleet of VMs, you may be required to perform a ~~rollback~~ to withdraw the patch from operations.

4. ~~Snapshot~~ are used to restore an existing virtual server, and ~~cloning~~ is when you take a VM and use it to create a new and separate VM.

5. The endpoint or storage system where the backup data is to be stored is commonly referred to as the ~~backup target~~.

[handwritten: REPLICAS]

6. _____ are backup copies of data that can be stored either locally or remotely and act as an alternative data store from your main production operations.

7. A _____ *[handwritten: HOTFIX]* is a software update type that is intended to fix an immediate and specific problem with a quick release procedure.

8. A _____ *[handwritten: DIFFERENTIAL BACKUP]* uses the latest full backup as a source data set, and with each additional sequential backup operation, this type of backup will identify only the data that has been modified since the last backup was performed for backup and not the complete backup set. This allows for an efficient and significantly smaller backup operation.

9. When installing patches on a server and knowing that the server will be down and unresponsive for a period of time, it is important to disable _____ *[handwritten: SYSTEM ALERTS]* when performing maintenance.

10. A _____ *[handwritten: BACKUP WINDOW]* is the time available for the backup operation to run while the target storage system is either offline or lightly used.

Review Questions

The following questions are designed to test your understanding of this chapter's material. For more information on how to obtain additional questions, please see this book's Introduction. You can find the answers in Appendix A.

1. What backup type offers the advantage of a complete and up-to-date copy of your data in one operation?

   A. Full

   B. Differential

   C. Incremental

   D. Online

2. When applying a series of patches to your fleet of middleware servers in the cloud, you are concerned about the monitoring systems generating invalid alerts. What part of the server maintenance process would cause this? (Choose two.)

   A. API polling

   B. Rolling upgrades

   C. Shutdown

   D. Restart

3. What are common automation systems that are used for patch management? (Choose three.)

   A. Chef

   B. Cloudpatch

   C. Ansible

   D. DevOps

   E. Puppet

   F. Cloud Deploy

4. What type of software change is designed to address a known bug or issue and to bring a system up-to-date with previous bug fixes?

   A. Hotfix

   B. Patch

   C. Version update

   D. Rollout

5. What backup method is used to create a master copy of an image that can be used as a template to create additional systems?

   A. Full backup

   B. Snapshot

   C. Clone

   D. Replicate

6. What backup method creates a file-based image of the current state of a VM including the complete operating system and all applications that are stored on it?

   A. Full backup

   B. Snapshot

   C. Clone

   D. Replicate

7. To meet regulatory requirements, your company must provide geographical separation between active and backup data of certain medical records your company collects and processes in Germany. The requirements stipulate that the data cannot leave the country and must be in two or more data centers. As the cloud professional for your company, what recommendations would you offer to meet these requirements?

   A. Remote

   B. Offline

   C. Target

   D. Incremental

8. What type of software update may offer new features and benefits in addition to bug fixes?

   A. Hotfix

   B. Patch

   C. Version update

   D. Rollout

9. What deployment system offers a structured process for a series of actions that should be taken in order to complete a process?

   A. Automation

   B. Workflow

   C. Orchestration

   D. Application programmable interface (API)

10. These cloud-based systems abstract and hide much of the complexity of modern cloud systems and also reduce operational errors by executing tested cloud systems, scripts, workflows, or runbooks to make sure the systems are configured correctly.

   A. XML

   B. SDN

   C. Orchestration

   D. REST/API

11. When a server is undergoing updates, it may be in a state that it will not respond to health checks, API calls, SNMP, or any other means used to monitor its health by network management systems. This may cause false alarms and trigger automated troubleshooting systems. What can be done to prevent false alarms? (Choose two.)

   A. Put the system into maintenance mode.

   B. Edit workflow scripts.

    C. Assign a workflow to the orchestration rollout.

    D. Disable system alerts.

12. What type of software change is designed for rapid deployment and to correct a specific and critical issue?

    A. Hotfix

    B. Patch

    C. Version update

    D. Rollout

13. What type of backup system is intended to provide quick restore access if needed?

    A. VSAN

    B. FCOE

    C. Online

    D. Replica

14. What are tightly coupled computers that allow for software patching without incurring downtime called?

    A. Blue-green

    B. RAID

    C. Cluster

    D. Availability zone

15. Your IaaS cloud company has announced that there will be a brief outage for regularly scheduled maintenance over the weekend to apply a critical hotfix to vital infrastructure. What are the systems they may be applying patches to? (Choose three.)

    A. VM

    B. Load balancer

    C. Hypervisor

    D. NoSQL database

    E. Router

    F. E-mail server

16. You have been asked to update your entire fleet of Internet-facing web servers to remediate a critical bug. Your supervisor has agreed to operate under reduced computing capacity during the process but stipulates that there can be no downtime. What upgrade approach should you recommend your company follow to meet these requirements?

    A. Orchestration

    B. Rolling

    C. Hotfix

    D. Blue-green

17. Before a new patch is released to the public, the release manager at a large software development house has requested a report that shows the pass/fail data to verify that the fix does, in fact, work. He is requesting data about the issue it was intended to fix and the results of the tests done to make sure that the fix does not interfere with other processes and that there are no memory or buffer issues experienced with the patched version of software. What process is he verifying?

A. Rollout

B. Orchestration

C. Automation

D. QA

18. You company's primary application is critical to the power generation industry and must be highly available. When critical patches need to be installed, downtime is not an option that your customers can tolerate. You have designed a web architecture to take this into account and that allows you to have an exact copy of your production fleet that can be brought online to replace your existing deployment for patching and maintenance. What type of model did you implement?

A. Cluster

B. DevOps

C. Blue-green

D. Rolling

19. What type of backup operation is based on the change of the source data since the last backup was performed?

A. Full

B. Differential

C. Incremental

D. Online

20. What backup solution requires an administrator or tape jukebox to make it available by inserting a tape or other media into a storage system for retrieval?

A. SAN A/B

B. FCON

C. Cluster

D. Offline

Chapter

6

Disaster Recovery, Business Continuity, and Ongoing Maintenance

---

THE FOLLOWING COMPTIA CLOUD+ EXAM OBJECTIVES ARE COVERED IN THIS CHAPTER:

✓ **3.4 Given a cloud-based scenario, apply appropriate disaster recovery methods.**

- DR capabilities of a cloud service provider
- Other considerations
    - SLAs for DR
    - RPO
    - RTO
    - Corporate guidelines
    - Cloud service provider guidelines
    - Bandwidth or ISP limitations
    - Techniques
    - Site mirroring
    - Replication
    - File transfer
    - Archiving
    - Third-party sites

✓ **3.5 Given a cloud-based scenario, apply the appropriate steps to ensure business continuity.**

- Business continuity plan
  - Alternate sites
  - Continuity of operations
  - Connectivity
  - Edge sites
  - Equipment
  - Availability
  - Partners/third parties
- SLAs for BCP and HA

✓ **3.6 Given a scenario, apply the appropriate maintenance automation technique to the target objects.**

- Maintenance schedules
- Impact and scope of maintenance tasks
- Impact and scope of maintenance automation techniques
- Include orchestration as appropriate
- Maintenance automation tasks
  - Clearing logs
  - Archiving logs
  - Compressing drives
  - Removing inactive accounts
  - Removing stale DNS entries
  - Removing orphaned resources
  - Removing outdated rules from firewall
  - Removing outdated rules from security
  - Resource reclamation
  - Maintain ACLs for the target object

Implementing a Disaster Recovery and Business Continuity Plan

Cloud computing operations can be amazingly complex, as you have learned throughout this book. Failures can and will happen, often when least expected. It is important for you to expect that these failures are going to happen and plan for disruptions ahead of time so you can be ready when they occur.

Some outages, such as a web server failure, are relatively easy to plan for by implementing multiple web servers behind a load balancer. With the amount of virtualization in the cloud data centers, virtual machines can easily be replaced or moved quickly to new hardware platforms in the event of an outage. If a complete data center goes offline, then the complexity of recovery increases dramatically.

This section will discuss disaster recovery and business continuity.

You will learn about how to prepare for a disaster and the different architectures and reference designs for you to consider when creating a disaster recovery plan.

When a company's computing operations are migrated to the cloud, the cloud service provider will maintain hosting facilities that are designed and built to be highly resilient and to offer protection from service disruptions. Redundant systems for power, cooling, networking, storage, and computing are commonly implemented in the data center to reduce the frequency and probability of outages and to quickly recover critical systems in the event of an outage.

As you move computing operations to the cloud, it still remains your responsibility to plan for, and be able to recover from, any disruptions in the cloud computing center. Many types of natural disasters, such as weather-related events, may cause power or communication interruptions in the data center. Other events that may cause disruptions are key infrastructure outages, such as power and cooling systems, cyber-attacks, virus infections, critical service or equipment suppliers going out of business, or labor disruptions. This section will investigate the methods and concepts for recovering from a service disruption. You will learn the options available for proactive planning for an outage and investigate how to build resiliency into your cloud deployment.

You will also learn about deploying cloud operations, with business continuity as a design requirement, which will allow your operations to quickly recover in the event of a service disruption.

Service Provider Responsibilities and Capabilities

In this section, we will go over the responsibilities of the cloud service provider for disaster recovery and ongoing maintenance. You will learn about their capabilities, what is generally included in an Service Level Agreement (SLA), and the process of recovering from a disaster. There are many new terms associated with disaster recovery that will be introduced in this section, and it is important that you completely understand these because they are a focus of the Cloud+ exam.

Recovery Point Objective   *= AMOUNT OF DATA LOSS*

The *recovery point objective (RPO)* is the restore point you recover to in the event of an outage. Basically, the RPO indicated the amount of data that may be lost when restarting the operations after a disaster.

An example to help you understand the RPO is that if you have a database storing sales from your online e-commerce site and it is set to create a backup every two hours, then the RPO would be a maximum of two hours. If you had a disaster strike and as part of the recovery process you switched over to a backup site, the RPO would define how fresh the data would be at the new site. Generally speaking, if the site is used for financial or other critical transactions, such as healthcare, the RPO would need to be close to zero since losing any data could be catastrophic. However, if you had an outage on a noncritical system where losing recent data would have no impact, then the recovery point could be longer and not have any lasting negative effect on the business. When performing business continuity planning, the RPO plays a critical role in the design of the cloud computing architecture.

Recovery Time Objective   *MUST BE LESS THAN MTD*

The *recovery time objective (RTO)* is the amount of time a system can be offline during a disaster; it is the amount of time it takes to get operations back up and operational after a failure. When planning for business continuity, the cost of the downtime must be taken into consideration. Ask yourself what the impact to business operations will be if the cloud operations or a section of them were to fail. If the site is an active e-commerce operation during the busy holiday selling season, the outage can cost the company a large amount of lost revenue each minute the site cannot be reached by customers. In this case, the RTO would need to be a short amount of time. However, if the failure is a noncritical system that has no impact on operations, the RTO can be days or even weeks to bring the systems back online. As you can see, the RTO value will be a critical metric for your cloud business continuity design and operations.

Corporate Policies and Guidelines

The role that information technology plays in any modern corporation has become absolutely critical to the daily operations of any corporation. Many companies cannot function when IT services are offline.

As with any critical corporate operation, a business continuity and disaster recovery plan needs to be developed and approved by the company. This plan should outline all the operational and governance plans that make up a complete disaster recovery plan. This is much more than a technology document as it has a direct impact on a company's ongoing operations

MTD = MAXIMUM

and possibly even its survival. The executive committee and even the company's board will
need to decide the RPO and RTO objectives and build a plan around that. These metrics will
drive the decisions on the various disaster recovery approaches that can be implemented.

BCP
DR

There is an old saying that explains this well: "When you fail to prepare, you prepare
to fail."

The business continuity plan should not just include the restoration of network operations but may include topics such as moving into a new office space if there is a loss of access
to facilities because of natural disasters such as storms, floods, or earthquakes. Another
issue that may arise in a disaster is that many of the company's employees may not be able to
work for a period of time, so the company needs to plan how to operate in such a situation.

The first step in implementing any Disaster Recovery (DR) offering is to evaluate your organization's needs. Based on the needs outline, you can choose a cloud provider that offers the
specific services you require to meet your stated needs. Once you have these steps completed,
you can architect and implement an effective DR plan that meets your requirements and budget.

Once the disaster recovery plan has been implemented, it is absolutely critical to test
the design and effectiveness against the documents. This offers you a great opportunity to
uncover any unforeseen process or technical issues that need to be modified. Also, as time
goes on, your DR needs will most likely change and need to be modified. As such, it is
important to revisit your company's DR requirements over time, test, and adjust accordingly.

Cloud Service Provider Polices and Guidelines

Cloud providers have extensive disaster recovery planning and operational designs. They
must be prepared for any disaster to be able to offer their customers service level agreements that commit to defined recovery objectives.

All of the major public cloud provider's networks have been designed for recoverability
and survivability from the beginning. These designs are outlined in the cloud company's
offerings and are often used to gain a competitive advantage over other cloud companies.

When a company is preparing and designing its disaster recovery plan, it should work
closely with its cloud provider to understand their capabilities and limitations. These are
outlined in policy, compliance, and guideline documents offered by the cloud provider to
their customers. A cloud provider may also offer reference designs and case studies to assist
their customers in planning for a disaster.

Disaster Recovery Network Capacity

During a disaster, network capacity plays an important role in the recovery and restorations of corporate operations. Wide Area Network (WAN) circuit bandwidth and connectivity are critical components of any DR plan.

When the recovery site comes online, it must be designed for peak network capacity and
not get saturated with the new traffic of your recovered sites load. In addition to the site's
regular peak load, the possibility of exceeding your normal peak traffic should be considered. During a disaster, your site may need additional bandwidth provisioned for data
replication and backup; customers checking order status and suppliers may have a higher
interaction with your company, for example. You must address all possibilities for bandwidth starvation during a disaster event such as the replication of storage traffic consuming

so much network bandwidth that all other applications are starved for bandwidth. Do you want to consider implementing a quality of service (QOS) architecture or add bandwidth to address these issues? It is best to gain an understanding of any potential problems and deal with them well before you have a DR event and do not have the bandwidth in your network to handle the traffic!

Other network disaster recovery services that need to be addressed are Domain Name Services (DNS), Dynamic Host Configuration Protocol (DHCP), File Transfer Protocol (FTP), Active Directory, Remote Authentication Dial-In User Service (RADIUS), and Terminal Access Controller Access-Control System (TACACS). These services are well suited for a multisite deployment that offers failover in case of an outage. Also, the cloud service provider will usually offer a variety of network services that include these and others. Using the service provider's infrastructure may be a good disaster recovery option if you are already using its compute services and allows you to leverage the provider's extensive resources.

It is common for service providers to offer highly redundant network services that consist of data centers, sometimes called *availability zones*, that are interconnected with private high-speed and low-latency fiber connections.

Disaster Recovery ISP Limitations

A potentially critical issue in formulating and deploying an effective disaster recovery plan is to make sure that your Internet service provider (ISP) has the facilities that meet your requirements, and you have the correct services enabled so that the ISP does not present obstacles.

Issues to be addressed with the ISP include any charges that the ISP may place on you for bandwidth consumption and whether these are acceptable and in alignment with your expectations. Are there any monthly usage caps that you need to be aware of? These caps may cause the ISP to throttle or, worse yet, block the flow of traffic when exceeded. Is there enough ISP capacity to handle additional traffic load because of the DR event such as data backup and replication processes taking place?

Disaster Recovery Models and Techniques

One effective use of the public cloud is to use its resiliency, on-demand resources, and pay-as-you-go business model to implement a cost-effective disaster recovery plan. Public cloud regions and zones are designed for high availability and resiliency that can complement your company's disaster recovery requirements. The cost model and economics of this approach bring a complete and effective disaster recovery plan in the reach of even smaller companies that in the past may not have had the financial or technical resources available to implement a complete recovery. If your primary data center goes offline because of any number of events, such as a flood, earthquake, or any other type of disaster, the cloud can be used as your temporary backup data center. Also, one cloud site can back up another and is often automated if the sites are controlled by the same cloud provider.

Site Mirroring

Site mirroring can encompass multiple redundancy strategies that you will explore in this section. *Site mirroring* refers to the process of keeping the backup site updated so it is ready to assume the workload in the event of a primary data center failure. Site mirroring provides an identical copy of the original site's data and applications operating in standby at a remote site. By implementing a mirroring strategy, you can be better prepared to survive an outage event with little or no impact on your operations.

The cloud operations can be deployed in a *hot site* model where two fully redundant cloud data centers are in sync with each other, with the standby site backing up the primary in real time in the event of a failure, as shown in Figure 6.1. The hot site offers the most redundancy of any model. However, it is also the most expensive option and is used when having your cloud computing operations go offline is not an option.

FIGURE 6.1   Hot site mirroring

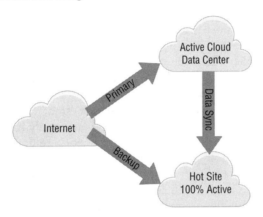

The *warm site* approach to recovering from a primary data center outage is when the remote backup site is offline except for critical data storage, which is usually a database. The warm site will host an operational database server that is in sync with the database server at the primary data center. This is sometimes referred to as the *candlelight design*. All other needed site infrastructure, such as servers, storage, load balancers, and networking, are either offline or not provisioned until the warm site is brought online after a failure at the primary data center, as shown in Figure 6.2. There will be a delay during the transition process, which will have an effect on operations.

FIGURE 6.2   Warm site

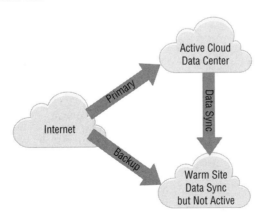

The warm site model is similar to the hot site, except there will be more work involved in the cutover process and usually much more time will be needed before it becomes operational and takes over processing from the failed primary site. There is also a lot of planning and testing that needs to take place ahead of time to ensure that you can quickly bring the warm site online. The warm site approach is more cost effective than the hot site solution as you are not being charged for services that are not active. The time to restore objectives is much less than a cold site but, of course, higher than a hot site. However, the hot site approach will not lose data as compared to the warm site since it is designed for a short RTO. With the warm site solution, transactions will not take place during the time the primary data center goes offline and the warm site comes up. For many cloud customers, the warm site is a good compromise between the expense of supporting a hot site and the extended downtime incurred with the cold site approach.

The *cold site* model is where a backup data center is provisioned to take over operations in the event of a primary data center failure but the servers and infrastructure are not operational until needed. A cold site facility is not ready to take over operations from the primary data center usually for a very long time. The cold site facility may not have any servers or infrastructure installed, so to recover from an outage, the cold site approach will need significant amounts of installation and preparation before it is ready to be utilized. This effort means it can take a long time for a cold site to come online. Figure 6.3 shows that the cold site does not have data replication or equipment installed. However, the cold site may be good for extended outages and is certainly more cost effective than the hot or warm site approach. The servers at the cold site must be installed and configured in the event of an outage at the primary data center. The cold site model of recovery means that all cloud operations will need to be brought online and configured at the cold site when the primary site has a failure. Automation tools in the cloud service provider's network may be used to accelerate the replication of the primary site's architecture, including servers, load balancers, storage, networking, and security, at the cold site location.

FIGURE 6.3   Cold site

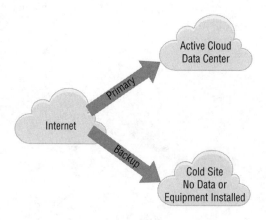

When deploying a cold site model for your business continuity planning, you must take into consideration that the time it takes to recover can be long, so a cold site solution may not be optimal for business-critical operations. For example, operational data such as databases will need to be transferred to the cold site and restored onto the database servers. This can take a long time, depending on the amount of data to send over a network and store in the storage arrays in the cold site data center. If the primary data center experiencing an outage is a mission-critical system, the monetary and goodwill costs can be very high, and the time it takes to recover from a cold site may not be a cost-effective solution.

When operating a popular e-commerce site during a holiday shopping season, for instance, even a short outage can cost an organization a large amount of lost revenue, so a warm or hot site should be considered as a more optimal solution. If the site is mission-critical, a cold site will most likely not be the solution that best meets your requirements. However, if the cloud operations are not critical or can be down for the time it takes to bring the cold site online, the cost savings of the cold site approach may be the best disaster recovery solution.

The advantage of using the cold site approach for recovery is that charges for the cold site will apply only when it is being used, which can be a significant cost savings to the business.

Replications SYNCHRONOUS / ASYNCHRONOUS

Replication is the transfer and synchronization of data between multiple data centers, as illustrated in Figure 6.4. For disaster recovery purposes and data security, your data must be transferred, or replicated, between data centers. Remote copies of data have traditionally been implemented with storage backup applications. However, with the virtualization of servers in the cloud, you can now replicate complete VM images, which allows you to replicate complete server instances, with all of the applications, service packs, and content, to a remote facility. Later in this chapter, I will discuss synchronous and asynchronous replication approaches and the advantage of each implementation.

FIGURE 6.4   Site-to-site replication of data

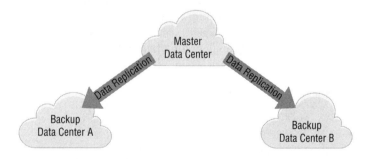

Applications such as databases have replication processes built-in that can be utilized based on your requirements. Also, many cloud service offerings can include data replication as an included feature or as a chargeable option.

Two primary types of replication are found in the cloud today: *synchronous replication* and *asynchronous replication*. Most synchronous replication offerings write data to both the primary storage system and the replica simultaneously to ensure that the remote data is current with local replicas. The second type of replication is asynchronous, where the data is written to the primary first and then later a copy is written to the remote site on a scheduled arrangement or in nearly real time.

Synchronous replication is the process of replicating data in real time from the primary storage system to a remote facility, as shown in Figure 6.5. Synchronous replications allow you to store current data at a remote location from the primary data center that can be brought online with a short recovery time and limited loss of data.

FIGURE 6.5   Synchronous replication

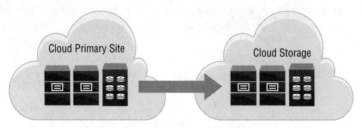

Real-Time Data Replication

Synchronous replications offer high availability for mission-critical applications by storing data in a remote site that can assume processing responsibility with current data from the primary site. When implementing a synchronous replication solution, disaster recovery hot and warm sites can be effectively implemented.

Asynchronous replication works off a store-and-forward model and is a cost-effective protection and backup solution. With asynchronous replication, the data is first written to the primary storage system in the primary storage facility or cloud location. After the data is stored, it is then copied to remote replicas on a scheduled basis or in near real time, as shown in Figure 6.6. Many asynchronous backup offerings can be implemented in the storage controller as an application such as backup software running on a server, as a cloud service offering, or even in the hypervisor itself, which allows complete virtual machines to be replicated to a remote site that can allow for a failover in the event that the primary location experiences a failure.

FIGURE 6.6   Asynchronous replication

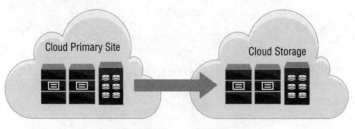

Delayed or Scheduled Data Replication

Asynchronous replication is much more cost effective than implementing a synchronous replication offering. Since asynchronous replication is not in real time, it works well over slower, wider area network links, where a certain amount of network delay is to be expected.

File Transfers

When preparing for, or during, a disaster recovery operation, there will be a redirection and possibly synchronization of user and operational data between facilities. The transfer of these files often takes place in the background and is controlled by automation systems. For the exam, it is important to know that these transfers are taking place in the background and are for the purpose of moving current data to the recovery facility.

Archiving Data

Protecting your data is critical for any recovery operations. Storage systems offer sophisticated data management techniques to protect you from losing critical data. When archiving data, the service may be provided by the cloud service provider with its storage or backup offerings. Many large cloud companies have extensive storage and backup systems that can archive and store data in a tiered approach both on-site or to a remote facility. *Data archiving* moves inactive data, or data that is no longer being used, to a separate storage facility for long-term storage. It can be more cost effective to store archived data in less expensive storage systems and still allow the cloud consumer access to that data for backup and retrieval as needed. Regulatory and company policies may require long-term retention of information. Archiving policies, often implemented in automated systems, allow these capabilities to be met and often at a low price since the data does not need to be immediately accessible. The process of identifying which information will be archived can be automated so that the data will be automatically identified and stored off-site without any manual intervention by using policies running on special archival software applications.

The off-site storage of data consists of storing data on less expensive media since fast read and write times may not be required. The off-site data can be accessed over the Internet or with a direct network connection. By sending data off-site from the primary location, the data can later be retrieved in case of a disaster; it also ensures that a duplicate copy is stored away from the primary data center for backup. The off-site storage media may be magnetic disks or optical or tape-based systems depending on the requirements and pricing.

There are companies in the market that specialize in the management, storage, and protection of backup information, which will relieve a company of the burden of managing off-site storage internally. Storing data off-site reduces the risk of data loss that could result in a natural disaster, in a catastrophic failure of the storage system, by human error, or via any other calamity. Storing a copy off-site is a sound business practice and allows you to recover operations should the primary cloud data center fail.

Third-Party Offerings

It should be noted that there are companies that offer consulting and management services aimed at assisting companies with their DR requirements. Management consulting companies have business continuity practices that assist companies with the process of developing and implementing a DR plan. This approach takes all legal, regulatory, industry, technology, and operational needs into consideration and develops a complete business continuity plan for your company.

With the hype of the cloud and every technology company now "cloud enabled," it should come as no surprise that there is such a thing as DRaaS—that's right, Disaster Recovery as a Service! With due respect, these companies have a large knowledge base and specialize in DR. They have models developed for the most common DR implementations and have the knowledge to architect custom design requirements.

Also, in the event of a disaster and when the need comes to implement your plan, their experience and assistance may be invaluable. With the DRaaS operations being at a different location from the disaster site, they are often in a better situation to perform the failover, testing, and restoration services than your company may be.

DRaaS may store fresh user data at the DR site and offer short RPO/RTO timeframes. These companies offer a high-value service to small and medium businesses that may not have the resources internally to develop and manage their own DR plan. Using DRaaS providers saves an organization from investing capital and resources to maintain and operate off-site DR systems.

One downside, or potential for concern, is that you really are placing a lot of trust in the DRaaS company. Potentially, the survivability and validity of your company's ongoing operations after disaster strikes rests with the DRaaS provider's capabilities and ability to execute. Can the DRaaS company meet the RPO/RTO objectives? Will the backup site function as planned? All of these issues require a high level of trust to be placed in your DRaaS and management consulting business partners.

Business Continuity

Business continuity is defined as preparing for a failure or outage and compiling the steps for a business to quickly recover to an operational state. This section will focus on business continuity specifically as it pertains to cloud operations and will discuss some strategies to protect against outages. The best defense against an outage is a solid plan for recovery. Business continuity is the ability of an organization to continue operations and be able to deliver products and services after an event that disrupts its operations. It includes the planning and preparation for a failure or outage and compiling the steps for a business to quickly recover to an operational state. A *business continuity plan* is defined as the creation of a plan with the recognition that there are inherent threats and risks that can have a detrimental effect on a company; it defines how to protect the company assets and to be able to survive a disaster.

Business continuity improves your organization's resilience against both man-made and natural disasters. It outlines the company's priorities and lays out a detailed plan of how the company is to respond in the event of a disaster. It determines and quantifies your company's priorities and urgent needs in the face of a disaster. Based on this collected information and devised framework, you can develop a detailed plan to carry out your company's objectives should the need arise.

Establishing a Business Continuity Plan

The first step in implementing any DR offering is to evaluate your organization's needs. Based on the needs outlined, you can choose a cloud provider that offers the specific services you require to meet your stated needs. Once you have these steps completed, you can architect and implement an effective DR plan that meets your requirements and budget.

Once the disaster recovery plan has been implemented, it is absolutely critical to test the design and effectiveness against the documents. This offers you a great opportunity to uncover any unforeseen process or technical issues that need to be modified. Also, as time goes on, your DR needs will most likely change and need to be modified. As such, it is important to revisit your company's DR requirements over time and adjust accordingly.

Determine Alternate Sites

The site placement for DR would include geographical separation from your primary location. You would not want the same hurricane or earthquake to take out your primary and disaster recover sites at the same time, would you? Most corporate governance documents will stipulate that their operational data center have a certain degree of geographical separation from the DR site so that one event will not affect both of them. This can be true when using the public cloud as a DR facility. The cloud provider will outline a regional area where it has a presence and also a number of smaller data centers in those regions that are often referred to as *availability zones*.

Other factors that determine which alternate sites are desirable include regulatory requirements, such as HIPAA or PCI compliance, or restrictions on data being stored in-country. The capabilities to meet these compliance requirements may also limit your options if the provider is not certified for compliance.

Define Continuity of Operations

What does it mean for your company when it contemplates business continuity? What are the operational requirements needed to function after a major event that disrupts operations? Your company must define these issues and many more as it prioritizes its operations and the steps that it must take to resume operations. These issues are well beyond a discussion of technology. The role of technology is to enable these requirements. As such, the managers, directors, and C-level executives must determine what is required for the business's continuity of operations and outline them in the document. Based on these requirements, business processes with the aid of technology can be used to carry out operational continuity.

Addressing Network Connectivity

Earlier in this chapter we discussed the issues, concerns, and requirements of network connectivity from both the cloud service provider and the ISP or WAN provider. Network connectivity requirements need to be investigated, and your current facilities upgraded, if necessary, to take into account your business continuity requirements.

The continuity plan should require that your network connectivity partners have the needed capacity and an SLA that outlines specifically what they guarantee to offer you in the event of a disaster recovery operation. Care must be taken to ensure that you are prepared for peak data usage and any additional network traffic beyond your normal operations such as data replications taking place.

Deploying Edge Sites

It is common for large public cloud vendors to offer *points of presence*, or local edge sites at locations around the world that allow them to have a presence but not a complete, fully operational data center in place. These are often called *edge facilities* and are placed at key locations worldwide or in the geographical areas covered by the service provider. Edge locations allow you and your customers the ability to connect locally to fast, low-latency connections at the DR location. They can also store, or cache, data at these locations for low-latency responses to local user requests.

Edge site deployments are usually straightforward to configure using the cloud provider's management dashboard and to deploy via the backend automation systems.

Procuring Backup Equipment

There may be a requirement for additional equipment depending on your DR design. If you are leasing data center space only, then you must incur all capital expenses for the IT equipment and software required for the backup site. This can be a significant expense because a complete, or nearly complete, image of your production network would need to be procured and implemented. The equipment required would include all servers, storage, network, software, and any other hardware or software needed to restore services. This is usually not very economical or easy to keep up-to-date as it requires that the equipment sit idle and unused; also, as your primary site undergoes constant maintenance upgrades, you would need to address the requirement of keeping your offline backup gear up-to-date, which needs to be stored at a remote location and may not be online.

Also, as you implement your DR plan, the issue of restoring operations services if your company's IT operations center goes offline must be addressed. You must plan not only for the data center operations being disrupted but also operations. Additional hardware and software may be required to replicate a network operations center at another location.

When procuring backup equipment, care must be taken to purchase and implement gear that can handle the anticipated workload. It may be temping, for example, to purchase a smaller server or router model since it is intended to used only for disaster recovery. However, the risk is that when the servers go online, they may not have the capacity to handle the workload.

Recovery Site Availability

What would happen if there was a disaster and the disaster recovery site could not be accessed? Well, that would be a very bad situation! When devising and implementing a DR plan, it is important that you consider all possible scenarios.

Also, if your DR plans require your IT staff to go on-site at the DR data center for implementation of your infrastructure, it is important that arrangements be made well ahead of personnel arriving on-site. Data centers by their nature are secure facilities, and no one can just pull into the parking lot and gain access to the data center floor. Not even close! Many cloud providers completely restrict anyone from entering their facilities. Others require a service ticket and employee clearance in advance to get access to the facility. You should also be expected to be escorted when in the facility and any equipment that you bring along to be inspected and approved before being installed.

Because of security concerns, data centers do not hang huge neon signs outside of their facilities flashing who they are! The cloud data centers are usually in nondescript facilities, often with no names on them, and seem to go out of their way to not be noticed. One give-away is the high fences, cameras, and floodlights. They look like secure fortresses! So, get a good set of directions before heading over to do your work.

Third-Party Disaster Recovery Vendors

There is, of course, a whole disaster recovery industry that has formed. Companies such as Sunguard Availability Services offer specialized data centers and operations designed specifically for disaster recovery. Other companies offer services that manage the complete disaster recovery process from start to finish.

Management consulting companies offer valuable consulting services for defining and implementing a company's business continuity and disaster recovery plan.

Establishing Service Level Agreements

An SLA outlines responsibilities and serves as a basic contract between you and the service provider. In this section, you will learn about the disaster recovery topics that are often out-lined in a typical SLA between you and the service provider.

A disaster recovery SLA will outline the fundamental issues of determining the busi-ness impact, performing a risk assessment, managing the risk, and planning for a disaster. Also, the SLA will include metrics such as the RPOs and RTOs for the services offered, and the SLA metrics are highly dependent on the type of offerings such as IaaS, PaaS, or SaaS. SLAs are used to determine the area of responsibility, and what part of the recovery is the responsibility of the provider, and what responsibilities the customer assumes.

As you learned earlier in this chapter, the RPO is the amount of data that can be lost because of an outage. The RTO is a measure of the amount of time a system can be offline during an outage. The SLA also outlines the levels of availability and response times when an emergency or critical event takes place.

The RTO and RPO metrics are used to create a measurable SLA that outlines to you when you can expect your systems to be back online after an outage. These SLAs are often dependent on the service offered and what level of support you have contracted for. For example, if the cloud provider is offering a managed database service, it would have a much greater responsibility and be accepting a higher complexity level of recovery if they were an IaaS provider and had responsibility for all of your running servers, applications, and other cloud services.

We should point out that while you would like all systems to instantly fail over and come online with little or no impact on your operations, this is generally not possible. In the event of a large-scale outage such as a data center losing power or a fiber cut isolating the data center, there are a lot of operations that must take place to move the workloads to a backup location. There will always be the possibility of data loss or an extended outage taking place.

The failover will require that the virtual infrastructure be configured or activated at a remote location and the data be current enough to meet the RPO. There are a lot of operations that must take place, and there are often dependencies where one section must be activated before the next steps in the workflow are addressed. For example, the servers and networking must be active before the database can be brought up and connected, the database must have current replicas, and so forth; one step must take place before another.

The SLA's agreed-upon levels can have variable costs associated with them. If there are very short RPO or RTO requirements, then additional resources and potential infrastructure will need to be allocated, which means a higher cost service to you for the solution.

Cloud Maintenance

Maintenance activities are a fact of life in any IT operation including cloud data centers. We have covered this subject throughout this book as it pertains to the various aspects of ongoing operations. This section will go a little deeper and explore the issues of maintenance operations and not the detailed technology maintenance requirements discussed earlier.

With the shared responsibilities between the cloud provider and customer, it is important to understand who is performing what maintenance when, and what the impact is going to be. With the highly redundant cloud data centers and an architecture designed for high availability, there are often maintenance activities that take place and have no impact on operations. If the cloud vendor is performing the maintenance, they will generally post the operation's notice on their maintenance dashboard or send out notification e-mails to subscribers that outline the work to be done, the time frames, and what the expected impact will be. It is common to see regular status updates when the operations are taking place and an "all clear" message when the maintenance event is completed.

If you are performing maintenance on your cloud deployments, it is advisable to follow the change management process you learned about in Chapter 2. If you are undertaking planned maintenance, the formal change process reduces the risk of the undertaking. If it is an unplanned event, then the objective is to get the systems operational and back into production as soon as possible with a review and post-mortem analysis after the excitement is over!

Establishing Maintenance Windows

Your IT operations group must create a change window strategy that clearly shows dates and times that changes are allowed to take place. These are driven by business operational objectives. For example, it you are a retailer, you would limit any changes leading up to and during the holiday selling season. Many companies have heavy compute operations during end-of-month or fiscal-quarter processing. In most cases, the change windows are open during times that have the least impact on your operations, which usually is overnight and on weekends.

Maintenance Interruptions to Operations

With the virtualization of the modern compute infrastructure, new VMs can be created and deleted at a rapid pace. This allows for a highly resilient infrastructure. Modern cloud data centers are designed to resist almost any failure scenario. However, you are responsible for the architecture of your cloud deployment. If you do not design a highly available infrastructure using best practices and reference designs from the start, you may be adversely impacted when performing maintenance.

In an ideal situation, you should have a design that allows for nonintrusive maintenance on different components. By implementing high availability and redundancy using failover and multizone designs, you can reduce interruptions to your operations when performing maintenance.

It is important to know what the impact of your scheduled maintenance is going to be and plan accordingly. You may need to proactively disable systems or notify customers, suppliers, or other interested parties prior to the maintenance event.

Maintenance Automation Impact and Scope

Chapter 5 introduced some of the automation technologies such as Openstack, Chef, Puppet, and Ansible and also covered general scripting operations. Automation really is a huge asset when it comes to cloud maintenance. You can prepare for the maintenance work well ahead of time and have it staged in the automation systems that are configured to automatically perform the operations during the maintenance window. Automation has been a real game-changer in the data center.

With automated maintenance, you can be assured of consistency of operations by taking a repeatable process and applying automation technology to have a consistent and repeatable maintenance function for your deployment.

Cloud dashboards allow for monitoring and sometimes configuring maintenance operations with the cloud provider. If you have regularly scheduled backups for your cloud storage volumes, you can configure the cloud provider to perform specific operations for you using its automation systems. When configuring the automation, you can define the maintenance window by day of the week and stop and start times. These values are added to the automation scripts, and the maintenance operation is performed by the automation systems.

Common Maintenance Automation Tasks

In this section, you will learn about many of the tasks that need to be performed during the ongoing operation of your cloud fleet of servers and associated systems. You will learn about how to manage log files, manage storage, and disable accounts. Also, this section includes many networking-oriented subjects such as firewalls, DNS, access control, and security rules.

Log Files Archive and Clearing

Most computing, storage, and networking gear generates system log files detailing ongoing events. There are many different types of system logs, from highly critical to informational. Store these logs in a safe area where they can be retrieved and reviewed in case of a device failure, when you're troubleshooting an issue, or when you're creating baseline and capacity planning projects. A syslog server can act as the central repository of logging information. Utilities are available that can search these syslog files to correlate events and look for malicious activity, among other tasks.

Logging information from all the devices being monitored and managed is sent to a central logging server and archived. By using a central logging server, you consolidate all of the logs generated and have the ability to review and audit the collected logging data. The central logging database allows you to monitor for performance issues and baseline analysis. Logging information is also used for security issues, such as investigating a breach or an attempted breach. Logging analysis allows you to view suspicious activity and follow the trail using the consolidated logging information. Log files will collect network, security, server, storage, and application events. The more data you can collect, the better view you will get of your environment. A determination should be made as to what systems and applications are able to generate logging information and what level of detail is desired. Most end systems can be configured to provide detailed logging data to the central syslog server for analysis, with the trade-off being the need for additional CPU, storage, and network utilization. You need to also decide whether the logging information should be encrypted during transmission and when on the storage systems, as well as whether the data should be stored in the cloud or at a remote location for security reasons. A lot of interesting applications have been developed to extract and analyze logging data. Big data applications can take a large amount of disconnected information and analyze trends and extract useful information about your systems, applications, and customers.

Another critical use of storing logging data is for regulatory compliance. Since it is your responsibility to comply with these regulations, collecting, analyzing, and storing logging information are critical tasks to the operation of many cloud customers. There may be a requirement for external audits to be performed based on the rules and regulations for your particular business. By retaining a complete history of logging information, you are better prepared if the requirement for an external audit ever arises. Each country and line of business will have different laws and regulations that will need to be understood and followed. It is often a good idea to involve your legal department in these issues when designing your logging solution.

Like many aspects of getting a cloud service up and running, the level and type of logging information must be defined and included in the service level agreement with the cloud service provider. Keep in mind that there will be logging data that needs to be collected both from areas under your responsibility and from areas controlled by your cloud service provider. It is also important that the format of the logging data be investigated in the predeployment engineering phase to make sure it is compatible with your logging and analysis applications.

Compressing Storage on Drives

Many organizations will include storage compression as part of their ongoing maintenance plans. The advantage of implementing compression to data at rest is that it can significantly reduce storage capacity requirements and, as such, reduce operating expenses since less storage space is required. Storage compression can compact the amount of physical storage space required to less than one-half the amount needed for uncompressed data.

Filesystem compression can be enabled to compress each individual file in a storage volume. This type of compression is best suited for long-term storage such as archival systems and not for operations that will require many read operations that necessitate that the data be constantly compressed and then decompressed, such as a database filesystem.

Compressing the complete storage array can be implemented by the storage vendors and is offered as a feature in the storage controllers and head ends. Storage array compression can operate at the block level below the filesystem.

Be aware that compression operations can decrease disk performance, and if you are planning on running a compression process on a previously uncompressed data set, it should be scheduled to run during a maintenance window so as to not impact the disk I/O performance of regular operations.

Managing and Removing Inactive Accounts

Ongoing maintenance requires that accounts that are no longer used be removed or disabled. This is a standard best practice that allows for a clean configuration and reduces your cyber-attack exposure.

Security service providers provide account management as a standard offering and can do an inventory of accounts, groups, roles, federations, and two-factor accounts. Based on defined metrics, they can take administrative actions such as disabling or deleting inactive accounts.

There are software products on the market that automate the process search and actions on unused accounts. With a complete logging solution, a global search can be performed to determine when accounts were last used and report them to automation systems for further actions.

Stale DNS Entries

In many cloud deployments, the DNS mappings from a device's name to its IP address can be dynamic as virtual systems are added and removed in the highly elastic environment of the cloud that includes autoscaling, dynamic mobile users, DHCP to DNS mappings, and Internet of Things devices. When a DHCP record ages out, it is supposed to remove the associated DNS record automatically. Unfortunately, there are times when old records entered by a short-term DHCP mapping do not get deleted and remain in the DNS database indefinitely.

Over time many DNS entries become stale and are no longer valid. Systems have been long removed, but their domain names and old IP address assignments are still configured in the DNS systems. Most of these are host, or "A" records that map a single host to a specific IP address. It is a good maintenance practice to review these mappings for consistency and relevancy. If they are stale, they should be removed as part of your ongoing cloud maintenance operations.

Decommissioning old DNS records will improve DNS performance and troubleshooting. Many DNS systems will have scavenger applications that can be run against the DNS records to identify and remove stale records. There are also software products on the market that can scan and clean DNS databases.

Orphaned Resources

Orphaned resources are cloud-based services that are left over when a service terminates and are no longer needed or used. When you enable cloud-based resources such as servers, storage arrays, load balancers, content distribution, DNS, databases, or any other offerings, you may find it to be a challenge to monitor and manage all of these resources. When a service is no longer being used or was enabled for a short period of time, it is all too frequently the case that the services do not get terminated properly and remain active and chargeable even if they are not being used.

In other cases, different groups in a company may not be aware that there are inactive resources available in the cloud belonging to other groups that are being billed to the company. In this case, they may provision new services that are redundant to already contracted services and thereby increase costs.

With a detailed knowledge of your operations, you can identify orphaned assets and either terminate them or redeploy them to active projects where they can be of use. Proper resource management can significantly reduce your cloud expenses and improve your company's bottom line.

Also, there are often underutilized resources that you are being billed for in your cloud deployment that can be combined with other systems to reduce the number of billed elements. There may be instances that have more CPU or RAM capacity associated than is required; this offers an opportunity to reduce costs by moving to a smaller instance size. Other common orphaned resources include unattached storage volumes and database tables and idle load balancers or cache systems.

Monitoring systems can identify these systems by setting search metrics or configuring reporting systems to list idle resources. Also, the cloud provider may offer an automated trusted advisor system that uses automation to review your account and make a series of recommendations on how to reduce your operational costs by properly managing your cloud resources. These systems generally do not make the actual changes but instead offer suggestions for you to implement a more efficient operation.

Outdated Firewall and Security Rules

As part of your ongoing maintenance of the cloud deployments, security should always be at the top of your maintenance list. Firewall rules are added as part of the normal change process as applications are added and the topology changes. The change management process typically focuses on adds, moves, and changes. There is much less focus on removing outdated, unneeded, or overly broad firewall policies. By performing regular reviews of your firewall rules, you can have a faster and more secure operation.

Over time, the firewall rule base can grow to become very large and hard to administer. Many of the rules become obsolete, are duplicates of others, or conflict with each other. To ensure that compliance audits are successful, realize better performance, and ensure the rules are effective, it is important that you clean up the rules on a regular basis.

Rules can be cleaned by either a manual or automated process that addresses the following areas:

- Analysis of the usage of each rule
- Analysis of traffic flows
- Duplicate rule identification
- Unused rule identification
- Overly broad and open rules
- Compliance test assessment suites
- Rule review and recertification
- Rule removal process

With a greater understanding of how your rules are being used, you are better able to manage and change the rules to meet your specific requirements and remove the rules that are no longer valid or pose a security risk. This process can be manual, or automated systems can be implemented.

Reclaiming Resources

Over time, as cloud resources are added and removed, it is common to find that many services are not completely removed or sit idle why you are being billed for them. Many automation systems will remove the base services and leave configurations, storage volumes, network systems, and other infrastructure configured. Applications and appliances that are no longer being used may sit inactive or be abandoned. These idle systems can result in significant charges from your cloud provider over time, and by identifying and taking action, you can achieve significant cost reductions for your company.

Many cloud companies offer advisory services that use automation to locate unused resources and report them to you so you can address them. Also, a manual process of inventory can be performed across all of your accounts or departments to see whether there are unused resources that can be redeployed to other parts of your operations.

When deleting cloud resources, it is advantageous to educate yourself about what specifically gets removed and what remains. As with most technology systems, there are trade-offs and compromises that are taken into account with automation systems. These systems may not always do what you expect them to do, and being aware of what is not removed when deleting services can save money and keep your cloud configurations from getting cluttered with unused services.

Maintaining Access Control Lists

Maintenance of network and system access control is critical to maintaining a secure cloud infrastructure. ACL maintenance follows the same pattern as firewall rule maintenance that was discussed earlier. ACL entries accumulate over time and may not be reviewed for validity as they remain in the device configurations. It is important to periodically review access control and remove any policies that are no longer needed or have become invalid.

A network ACL can allow or deny traffic into and out of a subnet. As servers are added and removed and as new services are deployed, the network ACLs need to be reviewed and updated as part of your ongoing cloud support operations.

Computer operating systems also have access control mechanisms that grant access rights to users for access to system objects such as storage volume directories and files, administrator rights, and so on.

Understanding your access control configuration will allow you to clean up any unused or overly permissive policies. This process can be either automated or performed manually but should be conducted on a regular schedule to allow for enhanced security and performance.

Summary

Disaster recovery is an important topic as it addresses the survivability of a company should an event occur that affects their IT infrastructure. You learned about cloud provider DR capabilities and key concepts such as restore and repair time objectives.

Preparing for a disaster requires extensive input and approval from your company's executive management. Based on the business continuity plan, you learned how to create a disaster recovery approach that meets those needs. You learned about many of the technical issues that need to be investigated when creating a complete DR plan including dealing with WAN and ISP issues, scaling backup equipment, and keeping the backup configuration synchronized with the live data.

Hot, warm, and cold DR site architectures were introduced, and the pros and cons of each design were discussed. The chapter discussed other DR technical operations such as transferring data in the background, archiving data, and recognizing the value that third-party providers offer in DR planning and execution. Continuity of operations includes connectivity and the use of edge locations, backup hardware and software, and service level agreements.

Next you learned about the practice of performing ongoing maintenance operations on your cloud deployment and all of the items that need to be addressed. The importance of maintenance windows and automation and the tasks involved are a day-to-day responsibility of a Cloud+ professional.

Finally, you learned about some of the critical topic areas of ongoing maintenance such as managing logging files; compressing data; managing user accounts; dealing with old DNS entries, orphaned services, and outdated security polices; and reclaiming idle resources.

Exam Essentials

Know the key concepts of disaster recovery.   For the exam, you will be expected to know the DR responsibilities of the provider and of your company. Understand what an SLA is and how it defines responsibilities. Know that the RTO is the time it takes to restore operations after a disaster and that the RPO is the point in time that data is recovered and restored.

Know what business continuity planning is and the components to be considered.   You may be asked about business continuity planning in a scenario that gives background information and you have to identify what the question is looking for. Know that the business continuity plan is a corporate document that defines the ability of a company to survive a disaster and that it is used to create a disaster recovery plan to meet those objectives.

Understand the key components of ongoing maintenance.   Know that a maintenance plan includes scheduling and maintenance windows. Understand that automation and orchestration can assist in repeatable maintenance operations.

Explain disaster recovery designs.   Study the DR models of hot site, warm site, and cold site and be able to distinguish the use cases for each one. Be able to identify the pros and cons of each approach.

Understand ongoing maintenance of different cloud services.   The exam objectives require knowledge of certain ongoing maintenance tasks that you are expected to know and identify. These include working with log files, compressing data, dealing with inactive accounts, working with stale DNS, and dealing with outdated firewall and access control policies. Other maintenance topics that you can be expected to know are orphaned and unused resources and how to identify and reclaim them.

Written Lab

Fill in the blanks for the questions provided in the written lab. You can find the answers to the written labs in Appendix B.

1. To allow data to be moved to long-term storage off-site, a _____ process is performed.

2. _____ as a Service companies perform failover, testing, and restoration services.

3. _____ is the ability for an organization to continue operations and be able to deliver products and services after an event that disrupts its operations. It is the planning and preparation for a failure or outage and the steps for a business to quickly recover to an operational state.

4. A __DISASTER RECOVERY__ SLA will outline the fundamental issues of determining the business impact, performing a risk assessment, managing the risk, and planning for a disaster.

5. Security service providers offer account management as a standard offering and can do an inventory of accounts, groups, roles, federations, and two-factor accounts based on defined metrics. This is referred to as managing and removing __INACTIVE__ accounts.

6. __REPLICATION__ is the transfer and synchronization of data between multiple data centers.

7. The __RPO__ is the amount of data that can be lost because of an outage, and the __RTO__ is a measure of the amount of time a system can be offline during an outage.

8. By using a central server, you consolidate all of the __AUDIT LOGS__ logs generated and have the ability to review and audit the collected data.

9. __ORPHANED RESOURCES__ are cloud-based services that are left over when a service terminates and are no longer needed or used.

10. Data systems such as databases or storage volumes can be deployed in multiple data centers for fault tolerance. Implementing an __SYNCHRONOUS__ replication system will ensure that the data remains synchronized at all times.

RECOVERY POINT OBJECTIVE
RECOVERY TIME OBJECTIVE

Review Questions

The following questions are designed to test your understanding of this chapter's material. For more information on how to obtain additional questions, please see this book's Introduction. You can find the answers in Appendix A.

1. Data replication is often used to store copies of real-time data in remote zones. When there is a need to have the master data immediately updated, and then on the backend, update the remote zones, what type of replication would you recommend your operations department to configure?

    A. Synchronous

    B. Asynchronous

    C. Volume sync

    D. Mirroring

    E. RAID 5

2. Sharon has been directed to put together a disaster recovery plan based on directives from her company's executive management team. The company's core business is operating an e-commerce website selling winter apparel with 85 percent of its revenue received during the holiday season. If there was a prolonged outage, it would put the company's ability to continue as a financially viable operation in peril. Sharon has been instructed to create a plan that will restore operations in the shortest amount of time possible. What DR model should she implement?

    A. Hot site

    B. Active/active

    C. Warm site

    D. Active/passive

    E. Cold site

    F. Rollover

3. Which disaster recovery metrics are used to create a measurable SLA that outlines to you when you can expect your systems to be back online and how much data loss you sustained after an outage? (Choose all that apply.)

    A. RSO

    B. RTO

    C. RPO

    D. DR

    E. VxRestore

4. These cloud facilities provide the ability to connect locally for fast, low-latency connections to the DR location. They can also store, or cache, data at these locations for very fast responses to local user requests.

   A. Region

   B. Edge location

   C. Availability zone

   D. Replication

5. Computer operating systems have mechanisms that grant rights to users for access to system objects like storage volume directories and files, administrator rights, and so on. What should you monitor to make sure that old or unused entries are deleted?

   A. Stale cache

   B. Access control

   C. MFA

   D. Dashboard

6. James has been directed by his employer's finance department that they cannot afford to lose any more than 30 minutes of data in the case of a database failure or other catastrophic event. James has updated his corporate business continuity plan and has had his cloud provider update its SLA. What was the metric that was changed?

   A. RSO

   B. RPO

   C. RTO

   D. DBO

7. To meet regulatory requirements, Jill must store customer transaction records for seven years. The data will most likely never be accessed after the second year and can be stored offline if possible to reduce storage costs. What type of storage operation can Jill implement to achieve her goal?

   A. File transfer

   B. Archive

   C. Replication

   D. Data store

8. Sharon is a network engineer for your firm and is investigating the WAN connection into the hot site. In the event of operations being moved to the backup location, she wants to make sure that the load capacity is available. What should she be most concerned about? (Choose two.)

   A. Traffic normalization

   B. Peak capacity

   C. QOS

   D. SLA

E. Packet loss and jitter

F. Bandwidth starvation

9. Cloud dashboards allow for monitoring and sometimes configuring maintenance operations with the cloud provider. If you have regularly scheduled backups for your cloud storage volumes, you can configure the cloud provider to perform specific operations for you using what backend systems?

   A. Replication

   B. Automation

   C. Synchronous

   D. Block chain based

10. What service provides permit and deny polices that require regular review to delete unused entries?

   A. DNS

   B. DHCP

   C. Firewalls

   D. Active Directory

11. Christina has been pinging a new web server by its URL and getting strange and seemingly unexplainable responses from unrecognized systems. She recalls that the new web farm is on a reclaimed subnet that was no longer in use in their cloud server fleet. What would you recommend she investigate to resolve the issue?

   A. DHCP

   B. Orphaned services

   C. Stale network access control lists

   D. DNS

12. During a disaster recovery switchover, what network services may need to be modified as part of a multisite failover to the backup site? (Choose all that apply.)

   A. RADIUS

   B. TACACS

   C. DHCP

   D. FTP

   E. DNS

   F. Active Directory

   G. None of the above

   H. All of the above

13. Mark has been reviewing disaster recovery planning, and after receiving direction from his company's board of directors, it has been determined that they can only withstand a maximum of 36 hours of downtime. Mark is updating his DR plan with this new metric. What part of the plan should he modify?

   A. RSO

   B. RPO

   C. RTO

   D. DBO

14. Jack is preparing to update his company's business continuity with details on its DR backup site. His plan is to have a facility ready with floor space, power, and cooling that has facilities for him to load in his server racks to restore service. What type of DR implementation is Jack deploying?

   A. Hot site

   B. Active/active

   C. Warm site

   D. Active/passive

   E. Cold site

   F. Rollover

15. Will is running his backup DR site in a DNS load balancing rotation for testing. He needs to ensure that the database in the DR facility is updated in real time and current with the production replica in the primary data center. What type of updates should he define in his primary data center servers prior to enabling DNS load balancing?

   A. Synchronous replication

   B. Asynchronous replication

   C. Volume sync

   D. Mirroring

   E. RAID 5

16. What DR location can be used to cache data close to your customer and ease access to your fleet of web servers?

   A. Hot

   B. Warm

   C. Cold

   D. Edge

   E. Zone

   F. Region

17. Jerry is doing a test cutover to his hot site as part of his company's ongoing disaster recovery preparedness. He notices on his WAN monitoring dashboard that there are peaks of traffic flow from the primary to his hot site. What is he seeing take place?

    A. Synchronous replication

    B. Asynchronous replication

    C. File transfer

    D. Continuity updates

18. Tom has been performing an ongoing inventory of his public cloud assets and has found a number of storage volumes, CPU allocations, VMs, and firewall instances that are not connected to any project and are not being used. What services is Tom collecting data on?

    A. DNS

    B. Stale services

    C. Orphaned resources

    D. Dashboard service

19. Hank is preparing a disaster recovery test drill in advance of the upcoming hurricane season along the Gulf of Mexico. His plan is to create a DR location in the Midwest and have a database server running at that location with a synchronously refreshed data replica. His DR plan calls for activating all other services in the event of a hurricane causing an outage at his primary data center. What model is Hank going to deploy to meet his requirements?

    A. Hot site

    B. Warm site

    C. Cold site

    D. Active/passive

20. Carl has been investigating stale records in his database that were added by other applications but never deleted or timed out after they were no longer in use. This mappings application is now causing issues with the server addressing and troubleshooting. What system is he looking at?

    A. SNMP

    B. DHCP

    C. DNS

    D. FTP

Chapter 7

Cloud Management

THE FOLLOWING COMPTIA CLOUD+ EXAM OBJECTIVES ARE COVERED IN THIS CHAPTER:

✓ **4.1 Given a scenario, analyze defined metrics to determine the presence of an abnormality and/or forecast future needed cloud resources.**

- Monitoring
  - Target object baselines
  - Target object anomalies
  - Common alert methods/messaging
  - Alerting based on deviation from baseline
  - Event collection
- Event correlation
- Forecasting resource capacity
  - Upsize/increase
  - Downsize/decrease
- Policies in support of event collection
- Policies to communicate alerts appropriately

✓ **4.2 Given a scenario, determine the appropriate allocation of cloud resources.**

- Resources needed based on cloud deployment models
  - Hybrid
  - Community
  - Public
  - Private
- Capacity/elasticity of cloud environment
- Support agreements
  - Cloud service model maintenance responsibility

- Configuration management tool
- Resource balancing techniques
- Change management
  - Advisory board
  - Approval process
  - Document actions taken
    - CMDB
    - Spreadsheet

✓ **4.3   Given a scenario, determine when to provision/ deprovision cloud resources.**

- Usage patterns
- Cloud bursting
  - Autoscaling technology
- Cloud provider migrations
- Extending cloud scope
- Application life cycle
  - Application deployment
  - Application upgrade
  - Application retirement
  - Application replacement
  - Application migration
  - Application feature use
    - Increase/decrease
- Business need change
  - Mergers/acquisitions/divestitures
  - Cloud service requirement changes
  - Impact of regulation and law changes

✓ **4.4 Given a scenario, implement account provisioning techniques in a cloud environment to meet security and policy requirements.**

- Identification
- Authentication methods
  - Federation
    - Single sign-on
  - Authorization methods
    - ACLs
    - Permissions
- Account life cycle
- Account management policy
  - Lockout
  - Password complexity rules
- Automation and orchestration activities
  - User account creation
  - Permission settings
  - Resource access
  - User account removal
  - User account disablement

Introduction to Cloud Management

Cloud management involves making sure that your cloud deployment is optimized for your applications, meets performance agreements, is secure, has no faults or alarms, is configured correctly, and is collecting accounting data.

Many components and services come together under the umbrella of cloud management. In this chapter, you will learn what cloud management is, how it is implemented, and who has responsibility for network management. Traditional network management tools have been extended and adapted for cloud-based services, and at the same time, many new products and services have been introduced that specifically address this new and fast-growing market. In addition to the traditional information technology management providers, many investments have been made by startup companies that are developing products and services for this market. The definition of network management is very broad, so let's drill down and look at the components that encompass a complete network management solution. The basic architecture consists of one or more network management operation centers housing systems that monitor and collect information from the devices hosted in a private or public data center, as shown in Figure 7.1.

FIGURE 7.1   Basic network management topology

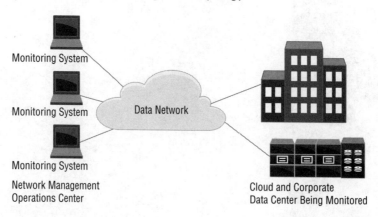

Cloud Metrics

To effectively operate, monitor, manage, and troubleshoot your cloud operations, it is critical to gather cloud metrics and operational measurements in real time. Cloud metrics include many different types of measurement information that can be collected from the many services and devices operating in the cloud. The definition of the term *cloud metric* is not all that specific, and even the standards bodies do not offer much help in defining what a cloud metric really means. However, a *metric* is a standard of measurement that defines the conditions and the rules for performing a measurement and for understanding the results of the measurement.

To better understand cloud metrics, Table 7.1 lists examples of the different objects that can be recorded and logged as part of your cloud management operations; these are just a small sample of the hundreds or even thousands of objects that are available for measurement.

TABLE 7.1 Cloud metric examples

Metric	Description
Availability	Percentage of service uptime; total uptime vs. total time
Database utilization	The measurement of database activity usually measured in I/O requests per second
Horizontal server scalability	Server capacity additions to respond to increased server workload. Adding additional servers to expand workload processing capability
Instance initialization time	The time required to start a new compute instance.
Mean time between failure (MTBF)	The life expectancy of a hardware component; how long it is expected to operate before a failure
Mean time system recovery (MTSR)	The time for a resilient system to complete a recovery from a service failure
Mean time to repair (MTTR)	The time required to repair a damaged hardware component
Mean time to switchover (MTSO)	The time required from when a service failure occurs to when the backup system assumes operations
Network capacity	The available network capacity usually measured by bandwidth

TABLE 7.1   Cloud metric examples *(continued)*

Metric	Description
Outage time	The total time of a single outage, measured from when the outage began until it ended
Reliability	The measurement, usually as a percentage, of successful service operations compared to the total number of operations
Response time	The time to complete an operation
Server capacity	Server capacity usually measured as the total number of CPUs, CPU frequency, and RAM and storage capacity
Storage scalability	The amount of storage that can be added to increase capacity because of increased workloads
Storage total capacity	The measurement of storage device or volume capacity
Task runtime	The time to run a task from the task request to task completion
Vertical server scalability	Server capacity fluctionations of capacity in response to workload fluctuations. The addition of resources or expansion of an individual server
Web server utilization	The measurement of load on a web server. Usually measured in requests per second

With the collection of metrics and using that data to trigger orchestration systems, you can use thresholds to react to events at all layers of your cloud deployment. This allows you to be proactive in your cloud management operations.

Monitoring Your Deployment

The ability of your organization to monitor your cloud deployment is critical to your ongoing operational success in operating in the cloud. You simply must have visibility into your operations to be able to effectively manage them.

Cloud management requires detailed knowledge of your operations. The way you acquire this information is by constantly monitoring your cloud services and making informed decisions based on the data collected.

Your monitoring operations can be completely automated, and most services offer flexibility on selecting what metrics to monitor and at what granularity.

Baselines

In an earlier chapter, I discussed the importance of establishing baselines when you are determining the optimal size of the virtual machines required when migrating servers to the cloud. Baselines also are used to determine what is considered to be not normal operations. You can use your baseline statistics as a reference, and if a counter has a variance above or below that value, it will be considered out of variance and may need to be investigated.

You can use baselines as a threshold to notify the network management or monitoring systems. To get a baseline measurement of a cloud resource you are using, you will set a sampling interval that is not so short as to monopolize bandwidth, storage, and other resources but also not so long of a sampling time window where the information becomes inaccurate. When you have your baseline established, you can then determine what deviations from this are considered normal and what would require an investigation or a support incident.

For example, if CPU utilization on a database server is expected to run in the 70 percent range when averaged over a 10-minute interval, you can configure the application to create alerts when the server is averaging 95 percent CPU utilization. These values can be tailored to the requirements of your organization, of course. You can also use the monitoring and alerting functions of the application to determine the baseline and then use the baseline as your reference point to determine what is to be considered out of range. This is referred to as the *variance*.

With help from performance monitoring software and services, you can use the collected data to provide trend analysis and capacity utilization information graphed over time. Historical data can be stored and used for future change management implementations. The network performance monitoring and management applications can also generate real-time data that can be stored for trend analysis.

Some network management tools have network discovery capabilities that can automatically document the cloud deployment's architecture and configurations. This feature can then use the baseline to dynamically track changes to the cloud over time.

Anomalies

Once you determine what is considered to be your baseline during normal operations, you can use that as a reference to determine what is considered to be an *anomaly* or a system that reports metrics that are either above or below your expectations. By trending the data, you are able to spot potential issues in your deployment or the data can be used in analytics systems to predict future requirements and capacity needs.

Being able to identify anomalies using cloud monitoring systems has many benefits. For example, you are able to use notification systems to alert systems and users of a critical issue, and automation and orchestration systems can act on reported anomalies and correct the issue, sometimes before they have an impact on service"s".

If a user's mailbox is reaching capacity, for example, the monitoring systems can be configured to add capacity before it fills up and rejects incoming e-mails. Other examples include network capacity issues or drops that are beyond your baseline references. A server's memory usage may be considered normal if it runs at 75 percent capacity of 16GB of RAM; however, if it suddenly spikes to 100 percent for more than the defined three minutes you have determined to be abnormal, you will be notified and can take action on the anomaly.

Alert Methods

When the cloud monitoring applications detect an event that requires attention, the question becomes "How do we let everyone know what is occurring with so many different devices, each with different interfaces?"

In cloud systems, there is often a managed notification service that addresses these issues. Figure 7.2 shows an example of a notification system.

FIGURE 7.2   Cloud notification system

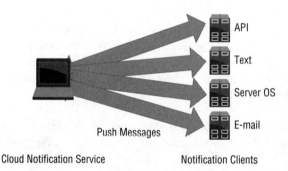

Triggers can be identified in many different devices and applications including data collected by the monitoring systems. When the alarm threshold is triggered, or reached, the event can be sent, or published, to a notification service that you access as a service from a cloud provider. This alerting method is referred to as a *push service* as it sends the events to the subscribed endpoints as they occur.

Many different devices and services can be subscribers to the events queue that the notification system publishes. The push notifications support a large number of options such as texting; e-mail; messages to Apple, Google, Amazon, or Windows operating systems; service queues; Application Programmable Interfaces (API) calls; the ability to run a script on a server; and many other operations. The notification services offer a single event to many different devices that can act upon the received information.

Alert Triggers

To create an alert, you must first decide what metrics to measure and define what value is falling out of your baseline. You also must decide whether the issue is critical enough to send an alert. If the event is deemed to be critical, alerts can be generated by configuring a *trigger.* Alerts can also be generated in the case of a service outage or if a device is no longer responsive.

The cloud management console will allow you to configure thresholds that are considered to be outside your baseline. The thresholds can be a wide variety of different values such as percent utilization, number of read or writes, packet drops, latency values, or any possible measurable metric available. It is common to smooth the reading out to prevent false positives by measuring the value over a lengthy period of time. For example, if you are monitoring the performance of your fleet of web servers, you may want to monitor the CPU utilization over a period of time. If the CPU average is more than 90 percent for 8 minutes, for example, you can create a trigger to alert your orchestration system to add additional web servers to your load-balanced deployment and not be concerned about shorter periods of high CPU utilization. It is a common practice to monitor the alert thresholds and adjust them over time. This will prevent you from taking actions prematurely or waiting too long after a critical event occurs before taking action. If you perform an action based on a premature alert, you risk acting on a false positive event. If you spin up new resources, you will be charged for these services even if they are not needed.

Collecting Log and Event Information

SCM

Log and events are constantly being generated by a large number of objects and services in your cloud fleet of devices. It should be apparent that there needs to be some way to collect, store, and analyze this data. In Chapter 6, logging was discussed, and you learned that event information is sent to syslog or logging servers where the data can be analyzed and archived.

By integrating cloud logging into a centralized logging collector, monitoring systems can see the whole complete picture of your remote public and local private cloud operations in one place.

Event Correlation

Event correlation is the method, or process, that makes sense out of a large number of reported events from different sources and identifies the relationships between the events.

Intelligent management applications have the ability to look at all the reported events from many different sources and correlate, or determine, how they are related to each other. A single event can trigger a flood of alert messages that need to be sorted through to determine what was the trigger and which of the other events were just in response to the main event. The larger and more complex the network becomes, the more log messages are generated and the greater the need there is to analyze the data with intelligent applications.

For example, assume that someone in IT operations configured a network access control list that blocked an application server from reaching a backend database on your e-commerce site. This would probably trigger a lot of alarms that are outside of your baseline metrics! You would be getting nonresponse alerts from the web servers trying to access the database, the application servers would report timeouts from the database server, and the network would show deny operations based on the Network Access Control List (NACL) that was defined. The database may even report that there had been zero table read or write operations and so on. All

UDP =tcp= 123

of these alarms are written to the logging server and need to be analyzed and reviewed to determine what is happening so the root cause can be identified and the service restored.

Using event correlation, all the events in the logging system will be scanned and processed to identify the root cause of the application server not being able to reach the database. Most of the alarms are generated not because they are the fault but, rather, were affected by the original fault event. In this case, the incorrectly inserted access control list statement that blocked the communications was identified by the correlation application as the root issue, and all of the other alarms were because of this incorrect database deny rule.

As you can see from the example, event correlation is a valuable tool to have! It can be time-consuming and error prone to manually sort through hundreds or thousands of log messages trying to find that one event that caused the issue.

Forecasting required resources

After you have collected statistics of your network and established a baseline of your operations, you can use this data to forecast what cloud resources you will be required. Accurate baselines are invaluable reference points for the ongoing management of your cloud operations. Any object that you track can be analyzed for trends in resource utilization and, based on this data, you can either manually, or dynamically, add and remove resources to your cloud operations. This allows you to identify potential resources limitations in time to add or remove them before they impact your operations.

Matching cloud resources to the forecasted requirements

Based on the forecast of resources you require in your clod deployment, you can either upsize and increase or downsize and decrease your resources to align with the forecast. Many cloud companies offer automated services that track object metrics you define and either add or remove capacity as required. This can be a fully automated process that operated in near real time. This allows for a fast response to changes in cloud computing demands. For example, if a web server in a public cloud begins to run out of memory, the management and monitoring systems will trigger an event and dynamically add additional memory. When the usages later decreases the memory can be removed to save the expense of paying for memory that is no longer needed.

Upsizing and downsizing your cloud operations can also be a manual process that is tracked by them management systems monitoring your operations. When data is collected over a period of time, you can determine trends that allow for informed capacity forecasting. Based on the trending data, you can plan to add or remove resources as your needs require.

Event Collection Policies

When configuring your event collection requirements, the repetition required to define all the logging definitions for each device and enter them manually or add them into the automation systems such as scripts of orchestration systems can be a large administrative task.

Many cloud configuration systems allow for policies to be defined and applied to objects. For example, a policy can be created to send a syslog message when a storage volume reaches 75 percent capacity. Once the policy has been created, it can be reused and applied to all the storage volumes as they are created or migrated. Event policies reduce the amount of management overhead and enforce consistency in your deployments.

Event Dissemination Policies

Logging systems can be surprisingly feature-rich given all the capabilities that have been added over the years. Policies, or rules, can be created to forward event information in a fan-out design to systems that may benefit from the data.

A policy can be created for event families, or types can be forwarded, or disseminated, to systems that require that data. For example, a big data application may be interested in knowing which geographical locations around the world access which specific files on your website at specific dates and times. A dissemination policy can be created to forward the relative logging information to the big data cluster for analysis.

The ability to define and manage the dissemination of specific data will depend on the capabilities of the cloud service provider management utilities and services. What started out as a basic service offering that generated and stored logging data has now expanded its capabilities to include advanced feature sets such as collections, forwarding, and advanced reporting systems. The enhanced capabilities allow you to better manage the logging information and to be able to manage a more secure operation. There will be a trade-off in the amount of information gathered compared to the associated costs you will incur from the provider and the management overhead of storing and analyzing the collected data. It is recommended that you collect only the data that is required by policy. The regulatory and compliance mandates that require the detailed logging information and these advanced features allow you to better manage your logging data.

Cloud Support Agreements OR SLA

Cloud companies have a lot of variations and options in their support offerings. It is typical to offer a base Tier 1 offering free of charge that entitles the customer to basic e-mail support, online forums, documentation, and limited response time commitments.

Beyond the basic free support options offered to all customers, the cloud providers have chargeable or premium offerings with higher support levels.

As an example of some premium support plans, you may select from tiered offerings to meet your support requirements. Added features will include guaranteed response times, enhanced and customized dashboards that give you the big picture of the status of your operations, and direct access to customer support engineers on the phone or via e-mail. The premium services may also allow you to select service windows that meet your operational needs such as Monday through Friday 8 a.m. to 5 p.m., 24/7 plans, or customizable maintenance windows with different response time options based on the severity levels you are experiencing.

Standard Cloud Maintenance Responsibilities

The responsibilities for cloud maintenance will be detailed in the service level agreement (SLA) or, for a private cloud, internal corporate operational documents.

The public cloud maintenance approach will use the shared responsibility model where the cloud provider outlines its responsibilities and what you are responsible for. The responsibilities fall along the cloud service model. For example, for IaaS systems, the cloud provider is responsible for all infrastructure but not anything higher up the stack such as the operating system and applications, which you would be responsible for. Continuing, the PaaS offerings have the cloud provider also taking on responsibility for the operating system, and you will assume responsibility for any applications or services running on the operating system. With the SaaS approach, service providers have the greatest maintenance responsibilities because they also assume maintenance for the application and everything below, including the operating systems and all infrastructure.

As discussed, the specific responsibilities will always be provided in the service level agreement.

Configuration Management Applications and Tools

There are many tools for managing the cloud. *Configuration management* tools create a central repository where configurations can be stored and archived. These systems also track any changes that were performed and who made the change. This is especially helpful for troubleshooting and regulatory compliance.

If there is an anomaly or outage in your operations, the cloud configuration management system can be consulted to see what changes were implemented and may even have the capability to perform a rollback operation.

Cloud companies will usually offer the configuration management service as a separate feature at a nominal cost.

Change Management Processes

The details of the change management process were explored in Chapter 2. As a review, change management is the process of managing all aspects of the ongoing changes, upgrades, repairs, and reconfigurations. Change management involves planning and managing changes to minimize any disruptions of service.

Change management outlines policies and procedures and provides a standardized process to follow, including recording the change, planning for the change, testing, documentation, approvals, evaluation and validation, instructions for backing out the change if needed, and post-change review if desired.

A change management procedure usually includes the name of the requester, what the change is going to be, and the reason or justification for making the change. Other areas include a description of the expected result of making the change and what risks are involved. You must also outline what resources will be needed and coordinate the activities of the various groups involved in the change. A list of individuals responsible for the various aspects of the change, including the design, configuration, deployment, and validation steps, must be prepared. There also needs to be an investigation into other changes that are taking place to make sure no conflicts exist between those changes and yours. Also, if one change requires another change to take place before it can be implemented, the change sequences will have to be coordinated.

Change Advisory Board

A critical piece of the change management process is a group commonly referred to as the *change advisory board*. The change advisory board supports the change management team by reviewing, sequencing, and approving changes that have been requested and determining the priorities and adequate planning for all upcoming changes. The primary goal of the CAB is to manage risk and ensure that the changes are necessary and are properly planned.

Change advisory boards advise change teams on guidelines and priorities, assess the changes, and make sure that all order of operations are addressed. They approve the time windows and ensure that adequate resources are assigned to the change. They may perform a post-implementation review to determine whether there can be any process improvements, or they may do a post-mortem of a failed change.

Change Approvals

The *change approval* process is dedicated to approving or denying all change requests submitted by your organization's IT operations. This oversight reduces the risk of implementing changes and acts as a formal step in your company's operations plans.

Generally, the change advisory board will meet with all parties that have submitted change requests for upcoming change windows. Each change request will be reviewed and discussed; if there are no issues, then the change will be approved for the time stated in the ticket or work order.

Document Action and Back-Out Plans

All change request documents must include a detailed plan on the steps to be taken, if required, to back out the changes. The plan can include all CLI commands or web GUI input and the expected output. If verification fails, the same change request document must outline specifically how to back out the change and verify that it has been removed. Remember, maintenance windows can be short, and your systems must be fully operational at the end of the allocated maintenance time. There will be no time to do any research; you must have everything documented before beginning the change.

The configuration management database (CMDB) is a family of applications designed to track inventory and configurations of your deployment. The CMDB can automate your change management steps in an archived online database. Many cloud providers offer applications that automatically backup and inventory your cloud resources. They can also allow you to add fields such as change documentation and roll-back, or back-out plans to the database.

If an actual CMDB system is not feasible, or overkill for the sized of your operations, a simple spreadsheet may be all that is required. Using a standard spreadsheet, you can record and track your actions taken, and add columns as desired to add detail to your documentation. The key point is to use whatever application works best for your operations but to always track and document your changes.

Adding and Removing Cloud Resources

Over time, and as part of the ongoing operations of your cloud deployment, resources will be added and removed to tune and maintain your cloud presence. In this section, you will learn about managing your resources.

Determining Usage Patterns

Usage patterns can be based on your collected metrics and baseline data. Also, a complete and up-to-date set of documentation can help in planning and understanding the details of your deployment and traffic flows.

Cloud monitoring and management applications allow you to view trend graphs of usage over a defined timeline. Also, logging data can be viewed with analytics software to determine detailed usage patterns based on your requirements.

Bursting

Cloud bursting is a hybrid model that is most commonly found in private cloud deployments that are designed to use public cloud processing during times of increased load. This is often an economical approach to accessing additional resources when required. Your company does not need to make capital investments for infrequently used reserve capacity. When your local resources are at capacity, the pay-as-you-go model of the public cloud can be utilized, and the additional capacity can be used and billed for when it is needed. Then it can be deleted and no longer charged for when activity returns to normal, and the private data center can handle the workload without the added, or burstable, capacity.

Migrating Between Cloud Providers

In a hybrid cloud, more than one cloud service is utilized. Given that all the cloud providers' data centers are virtualized operations, is it possible to move workloads between them? The answer is often a definite "maybe" or "it depends"!

This requires some background research and engineering to pull off. Where there is commonality between service providers, there are also proprietary implementations that may prevent a simple migration between cloud providers. Generally speaking, the higher up the stack you go, from IaaS to PaaS to SaaS, the more difficult it will be to migrate. With IaaS, most of the cloud operations are under your direct control, which gives you the most flexibility to migrate. However, if the cloud provider controls the application, you may not have many options to migrate.

There are companies and software applications that specialize in migrations between cloud providers and that make sure all the formats and configurations are compatible between the providers.

It's also important to review the financials involved in a migration to make sure you do not have any long-term contractual commitments with the cloud provider you are migrating away from and are not forced to pay for stranded resources.

Scaling Resources to Meet Requirements

Again, one of the primary benefits of the cloud is that cloud computing enables a utility business model that charges you only for the resources you consume. This model enables you to scale your cloud fleet to meet its current workload and be able to add and remove capacity as needed. This ability to scale enables financial savings as you are no longer paying for resources and systems when they are not being used.

In this section, you will learn about some of the options available, and techniques used, to scale resources to meet your current workloads.

Cloud Bursting

I discussed *cloud bursting* earlier in this chapter, and you learned that it is the model where a primary data center carries the current compute load, and when additional capacity is required, a remote cloud can assist with the load. Basically, one cloud is primary and can "burst" to a backup cloud if additional capacity is required to meet a peak demand situation.

↑ SCAUNGUP

Scaling Up and Scaling Out

Adding capacity to your cloud deployment is referred to as *scaling*. To scale your cloud, you decide whether you need to scale up or scale out.

Scaling up, or *vertical scaling*, will add resources such as CPU instances or more RAM. When you scale up, you are basically increasing your compute, network, or storage capabilities, as shown in Figure 7.3. Many applications, such as databases, will perform better after a system has been scaled vertically. For example, a system that is CPU bound will perform better when scaling up with additional CPU cores. The same is true with applications that benefit from more RAM or higher Local Area Network (LAN) throughput.

FIGURE 7.3   Vertical scaling

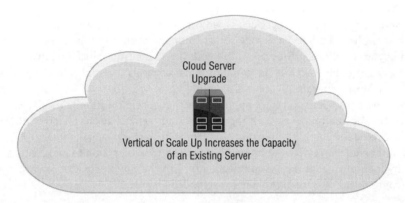

Scaling out, or *horizontal scaling*, adds more nodes instead of increasing the power of the nodes, as shown in Figure 7.4. So, with horizontal scaling, you will choose to add more servers to the existing configuration. This is a common scenario because the cloud data center uses cost-effective commodities or white-box servers. With horizontal scaling, you need to run applications that are distributed and are designed to work in parallel with each other. With a busy cloud website, horizontal scaling works well by adding web servers to handle the additional workload and implementing a load balancer to distribute the load between the many web servers. This arrangement is more efficient and reliable than a single server that has been scaled vertically by adding more LAN bandwidth, CPU cores, and RAM to handle the additional web load, but it is still a single point of failure.

FIGURE 7.4   Horizontal scaling

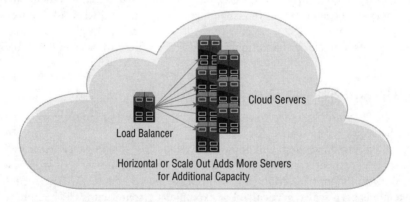

It is important to check the cloud provider's offerings and what options it offers when you are deciding whether to scale vertically or horizontally. The provider may offer better pricing options for multiple smaller systems than an equivalent larger system. The larger VM is a single management point as compared to multiple horizontally scaled systems, but it is also a single point of failure. When deciding to use the horizontal approach, you must consider that you need to manage more systems, and the distributed workloads between the systems may cause some latency that is not found in a single larger server. There is also a third option, referred to as *diagonal scaling*, which is a combination of scaling up to more powerful systems and scaling out by deploying more of these scaled-up systems. It is common to use horizontal scaling combined with load balancing on the Internet-facing web tier and vertical scaling for the backend databases, since many database applications operate more efficiently on a single larger server than multiple small servers. Choosing the best approach usually comes down to each particular use case, the application capabilities, and the cloud provider's pricing structure.

Reducing Capacity

Just as you are able to add capacity and scale up, it is also easy to reduce the cloud capacity needs after they are no longer needed. The ability to reduce capacity is normally defined in the scaling policies that monitor system utilization over time. For example, if your workload decreases after a scaling or cloud burst event, you may set the metric to be if the web server's CPU utilization remains below 50 percent for 5 consecutive minutes. When this is triggered, the scaling application will use the cloud orchestration systems to remove unneeded servers and reduce both capacity and cost.

Scaling in the Hybrid-Based Cloud

Most clouds today are based on the hybrid model, and single cloud deployments are becoming increasingly uncommon. Some organizations may have many clouds under their management based on their varied needs and use cases. Hybrid cloud scaling uses the additional capacity of another cloud for scaling; this is by definition cloud bursting and has been reviewed earlier in this chapter.

Community Cloud Scaling

A community cloud is a cloud where users with common interests or requirements access shared resources. These specialized cloud providers offer a wide array of different services and can be vastly different in their offerings and capabilities. As such, the ability to scale using a community cloud will be highly dependent on the capabilities of each individual community cloud provider.

However, it is helpful to remember that all clouds are, at their core, automated data centers controlled by software. So, if it is a community, public, or private cloud, the underlying capabilities are largely the same but may be different in scale and orchestration capabilities.

Scaling the Public Cloud

The public cloud is generally where the hyperscale data centers are, and massive scaling takes place. The business model is a pay-as-you-go utility service designed for large-scale deployments. Some of the larger public cloud providers can scale to thousands of servers on demand and offer many pricing options to meet your requirements.

Public cloud utilities, applications, and orchestration systems are designed for elastic computing operations. These tools and features are used to differentiate themselves from their competitors and make scaling easy to implement for their customers.

Scaling the Private Cloud

Private cloud scaling can be more difficult to implement depending on the scale of the data centers. If there is sufficient reserve compute capacity, then the automation and orchestration systems can be implemented just as they are in the public cloud. However, most private operations do not care to have the excess compute capacity sitting in a rack, powered up, and not being used. This is a large additional cost to a company that may be better served using a cloud bursting design.

Elasticity

The ability to automatically and dynamically add resources such as storage, CPUs, memory, and even servers is referred to as *elasticity*. This is done "on the fly" as needed and is different from provisioning servers with added resources that may be required in the future. This allows cloud consumers to automatically scale up as their workload increases and then have the cloud remove the services after the workload subsides. With elastic computing, there no longer is any need to deploy servers and storage systems designed to handle peak loads—servers and systems that may otherwise sit idle during normal operations. Now you can scale the cloud infrastructure from what is the normal load and automatically expand as needed when the occasion arises.

Extending the Scope of the Cloud

As part of your ongoing operations, it will likely be advantageous to add new features and capacity to your deployment. This is often referred to as *extending the scope*, and with the dashboard management and configuration systems most cloud providers offer, the extensions are very straightforward depending on what you want to accomplish.

Cloud providers are constantly releasing new products and enhancing existing offerings. There are a lot of new capabilities to take advantage of, and it is a natural progression to expand your scope of solutions to enhance your operations.

Understanding Application Life Cycles

All information technology hardware and software will have a normal cycle of usefulness. This is often referred to as the *application life cycle* and is the management of a software application from the initial planning stages through to its retirement. In this section, you will learn about the complete cycle as you most certainly will work with it in your career as a cloud engineer.

The life cycle process breaks the phases of an application into units such as deployment, upgrades, retirements, replacements, migrations, and feature additions or deletions as well as removal.

Deployments

The deployment phase of the application life cycle includes one or more of the following: The solution architects must determine the software requirements and work with the development team if required, and other items in the deployment phase may include coding, testing, configuring, and validation.

Upgrades

As was reviewed in Chapter 5, upgrades are a natural part of an application life cycle, and there are many different types of upgrades and patching that can occur. It is important to remember that software will most likely undertake many upgrade cycles over its lifetime, and each upgrade will need to be managed through the change management process.

Migrations

When a new application is brought online, there may be a need to migrate or move data from an older application or data store. Migrations need to be project-managed and controlled as part of both the life cycle and change process. If the applications are significantly different, the format of the user data may need to be modified as part of the migration process.

Feature Additions and Deletions

An application will undergo upgrades and modifications over its lifetime. Some will be to resolves issues through the patching process, and others will be to add new features as they are released. While less common, features can also be removed to save money by not paying for unused license fees.

Replacements

Over time applications will be replaced, and the process of project management to assist in replacing the existing application with a new or different approach must take place. This is a normal part of the lifecycle process.

Retirements

Applications will, at some point, be removed after having their data migrated to a new system or replaced. This is the end of the complete life cycle, and it will most likely start over with the deployment of a replacement application.

Corporate Changes

Over time, there are often ongoing changes to your corporation and its cloud computing requirements. Corporations can be constantly changing entities as they grow and shrink in size, and as they enter and exit markets, there may be legal or regulatory changes they must contend with. There can also be mergers and acquisitions that can have a major impact on their IT and cloud operations.

With a pay-as-you-use-it model, you can design and deploy a test bed for the new compute operations and then tear it down when it is no longer needed. The cloud allows for a cost-effective way of testing new designs since there is no large capital expenditure required to build a test site.

Mergers, Acquisitions, and Divestitures

Probably the most disruptive event that can happen to a corporation is that of a merger, acquisition, or spin-off of an operation. These will usually necessitate a sizable and potentially disruptive impact on its IT operations.

You should be prepared to work with new groups and departments to look at how the other company's cloud deployment is architected and what options are available to integrate them. Applications may be duplicated, and there could be efficiencies gained by integrating them.

This is usually a large and sometimes complex undertaking where attention to detail is your key to success. All interested parties must participate in this project management undertaking, and care must be taken to achieve success.

Cloud Service Requirement Changes

Cloud services can include many different offerings that a cloud provider sells. For example, services such as firewall or load balancer capabilities may change over time, compute services are constantly being added, and your requirements may change over time. Pricing for new services may be preferred to the older offerings you are operating on and that the cloud provider wants to depreciate.

It is recommended that your company keep up-to-date on new services, feature additions, pricing models, and trends in the cloud to see whether you can gain a competitive advantage and introduce efficiencies to save money on the new systems.

Be aware that these new offerings and changes to existing offerings can change at a rapid pace. Every week it seems, the cloud companies announce a bewildering number of new products and features!

Regulatory and Law Changes

Of course, there is always going to be changes on the legal and regulatory landscape, this is an important area to keep track of as changes can have a direct and long lasting impact on your operations. Also, if you are a regulated entity, you may be audited for compliance, and if you fail, it could have a devastating effect on your operations.

Depending on the changes, there may be no effect to your operations, but the cloud provider may need to make changes in their infrastructure or you may be responsible for the implementation of the change. It is important to coordinate and track changes of this type as required for business continuity.

Managing Account Provisioning

There seems to be an ongoing and seemingly never-ending stream of account changes. This can be because of users arriving or leaving your company or the addition of contractors or short-term agreements that require users to access systems.

The request for account provisioning may come from human resources, the project manager, or any number of other sources. Each account will need access rights to varied services, and all of this data must be entered into a directory service or cloud user database. This can be a manual process or automated with orchestration systems or by establishing confederations of user account systems.

Account Identification

Cloud accounts will have different methods to identify them that may include a domain name, an incomprehensible long number string, or a user-defined identification number.

It is important that the root account manager for the account keep detailed records of each account for management and billing purposes. Also, it is common for a single corporation or entity to have many different account databases, with the same or multiple cloud companies, and it can become difficult to manage that many different accounts. To rectify this, some cloud providers are able to consolidate a large number of accounts owned by a corporation for single billing and other global management services such as DNS.

Authentication

Authentication was a topic that you learned about in Chapter 2, and we will do a quick review here.

Authentication is the process of determining the identity of a client usually by a login process. When you authenticate a user, you determine the identity of that user and can authorize or grant permissions to cloud resources by either allowing or denying access to specific resources.

User authentication usually consists of a username and password combination or some variation of that, such as a token or biometric access method. Cookies can be used for web access to identify and authenticate a user connecting to your website.

Federations and Single Sign-On

You also learned about federations and single single-on in Chapter 2. Here We will give a quick review as it is listed as an objective for this section.

When you have different organizations, the limited capacity for locally-defined users can exceed the capacity of the cloud provider's limits. Or you want to use your internal directory system so that the federated approach will meet your requirements.

A federation includes external user systems, primarily Active Directory, as a user repository for your cloud user accounts. The federated approach can eliminate the need to keep two sets of user account data and also allows your cloud deployment in be accessed by other groups or companies that integrate with your user accounts using the federated approach.

A single sign-on architecture allows for your users to authenticate just one time with the cloud and be able to access all of the services they have rights to without having to log into each one individually. SSO allows you to centralize authentication systems into a single system and eases administration as you do not have to manage multiple accounts for the same user. Directory systems using the Lightweight Directory Access Protocol (LDAP) are an example of SSO systems where you log into the directory services just one time, and based on your rights, you are allowed to access systems in the network without any additional login requirements. Single sign-on eliminates the need to remember multiple username and password combinations and saves the time of having to enter your authentication information over and over as you log into different systems.

Authorization

After a user has supplied their login credentials, which is usually a username/password combination, the cloud will have a positive identification and be able to reference the functions they are allowed to perform and the systems they are allowed to access. This is known as the *authorization process*.

Access control systems will assign specific roles and duties to users or groups of users. For example, database administrators can be given full access to manage a database application but be restricted from performing VM or storage operations.

Access Control List Authorization Methods

The access control list for user authorization may share the same name as a network ACL, but, here, we are referring to what authorization a user is granted after being authenticated, or logging into, a system or directory.

Access control systems are user configurations that grant roles and duties to users or groups of users and also systems such as VMs, applications, and storage volumes.

Permission-Based Authorization

A user can be granted permissions after they have been identified through the authorization, or login, process. The permissions may be the cloud provider's identity and access management systems, a directory service accessed through a federation, user accounts accessed via LDAP, or local access control systems on the cloud user base, or a system such as a virtual machine with local access control that is independent from cloud-based authentication systems.

Managing the Account Life Cycle

As you learned in maintaining user accounts in Chapter 6, it is important to keep track of all user accounts and, if necessary, delete or modify them as needed. In this section, we will expand on that and review the account life cycle.

Policy

When creating or managing an account, a policy can be defined and applied that defines access rights, any time limits, and groups to which the user belongs.

Lockout

A lockout policy can be applied to an account that defines the parameters that create a lockout event. It is most common to apply a lockout policy to failed login attempts. For example, you can define a policy where four failed login attempts in five minutes will disable an account for thirty minutes. A lockout policy will most likely be defined by your information security group, and you may be asked to create and apply the policy as part of your duties.

Password Complexity

Another policy that will most likely be defined by the IT security groups is that of password complexity and reuse. Passwords that are too short or basic or are in place for a long period of time are security risks. The IT security group will most likely be the ones that dictate the complexity of the password and its life cycle.

For example, a password may be required to be a nondictionary word that is eight or more characters in length and contain at least one uppercase letter and a special character. It is also typical to have a rotation policy that requires you to create a new password on a regular basis such as every 30 days, for example.

To configure password complexity policies, the cloud configuration interface will have fields for these in the user or server login configuration dialog boxes.

Account Automation and Orchestration

Accounts can be managed with automation systems that use scripts to access device APIs that allow machines to automate cloud configuration functions. As discussed throughout this book, the cloud can be looked at as one big programmable device! As such, any feature or function that you configure with a web interface or a CLI is actually just a front end interface to an API. This is an important concept to understand. All automation and orchestration systems are scripted, and often reused code is used to control the cloud deployment.

User Account Creation

Account creation can be automated to prevent the laborious task of entering into the user database a large number of individual accounts. User data can be collected in many different manners including a web form.

For example, your e-commerce website may have an area for new users in its user login screen. The new user data can be collected, and on the backend a RESTful API script can be generated to create the user account at your site. Batch accounts can be created by accessing a database of new users such as students signing up for a new class you are offering this fall where all student data was previously collected in a SQL database.

User Permission Settings

Users can be granted permissions at the account level to perform a wide array of operations. The capability to manage cloud operations may allow the administrator to add, remove, or modify user accounts and permissions.

User permissions can be defined at the user level or by making the user a part of a group and assigning permissions to the group.

Resource Access Definitions

User accounts can allow access to approved resources, and these permissions contain any number of rights such as read/write permissions for a storage volume and access to run certain applications. Access permissions can be defined, and you can specify details on what functions the user is allowed to perform.

Removing Accounts

Part of a solid IT security operation is to remove any accounts, polices, or services that are no longer active. In Chapter 6 you learned about user account maintenance and the importance of tracking and removing accounts that will no longer be used. There are management applications that can assist in the identification of accounts that need to be removed. Also, automation systems can be employed to automate the accounts flagged for removal.

Disabling User Accounts

There is also an option of disabling a user account in many cloud management consoles. The ability to disable an account can be helpful in situations where the account will need to be re-activated at a future date and does not need to be deleted. Account disablement can be managed in the same manner as other account operations with a web front end or with the use of APIs for scripted and automated processes.

Summary

This chapter focused on the management operations of your cloud deployment. The subject of collecting monitoring and management data was covered. Once the data has been collected, a baseline can be determined by monitoring key data measurement points over a defined period of time. The baseline information can be used to determine future expansion and growth of the cloud. Also, if a system deviates too far from what is considered to be normal, which is the baseline, a trigger can be created to alert that there may be a problem. You learned about notification systems that process the alerts and distribute them to users and systems using such channels as text, e-mail, and API calls.

The chapter also went into detail on determining whether your resource allocations are correct and the options available to add or remove capacity. Support agreements are critical for ongoing management of your cloud fleet. You learned about cloud providers' support structures and responsibilities.

Configuration and change management are ongoing cloud management tasks. In this chapter, you learned about backing up and recording your device configurations and what the change management process is, as well as the roles that the various groups and processes play in making sure that changes are implemented properly and that the risk of an error is minimized.

Your cloud fleet will most likely be dynamic and require constant changes as your needs expand and contract. You became familiar with usage patterns and how cloud bursting works and what its advantages are. Autoscaling systems allow you to add and remove resources based on measured loads and to automate your operations by taking advantage of the elasticity features of the virtualized cloud data center.

An important topic is application lifecycle management. You were introduced to the concepts of lifecycle management and the stages that are common as an application is designed and deployed, through upgrades and ultimately retirement.

Cloud management will be driven by changing business requirements. Business disruptions such as mergers, acquisitions, and spin-offs all can have major impacts on cloud management. Other business-related topics include regulatory changes and how new laws may impact your operations and require that you make changes to meet new requirements.

The topic of user account management was revisited and expanded upon. You learned about identification and authentication, what a federated system is, and the advantages that can be gained by accessing user data using an external directory. User access control and permissions are defined to determine what systems a user or system can access and what actions they are allowed to perform on the system. Single sign-on, password management, user account creation, and disablement ended this chapter on cloud management.

Exam Essentials

Know what a metric is.   Know that a measurement is a metric and can be any number of objects that you select to monitor such as CPU utilization or disk reads. By collecting metrics, you can determine trends in your usage. The exam may give a long scenario-based question that can be solved by focusing on metrics and what they are used for.

Understand baselines and anomalies.   A baseline is what is considered to be normal operations, and values above or below the baseline are considered to be anomalies. There may be questions that test you in your knowledge to distinguish between the two terms.

Know alerting, methods, and, triggers, and notifications.   Alerting is the process determining that there is a value out of variance and notifying either people or machines that an event has occurred and needs attention. Know what event triggers are and how basic notifications work.

Understand cloud management support agreements and responsibilities.   Cloud companies offer a basic support plan that is usually free of charge but limited in scope. Premium service agreements are offered with varying levels of support commitments. You may be asked a question on who is responsible given a scenario of an outage.

Know what change and configuration management is. Configuration management is the tracking and documentation of ongoing changes to device configurations including what changes were performed, by whom, and at what time. Change management is a complete process that monitors and manages all changes that are made to your cloud fleet. For the exam, understand the role of the change advisory board and the approvals documentation that are part of an effective change management plan.

Understand resource management. You may be asked about migrating between cloud providers or how you would address issues where you need to either add or remove cloud computing capacity. Know the various ways to scale, such as cloud bursting, scale up and out, and scaling issues with the various cloud deployment models.

Know what the application life cycle is. For the exam, you should be able to answer questions that outline the life of an application from its initial design, deployment, updates, migrations, feature changes, replacement, and finally retirement.

Know about how corporate changes can affect the cloud. Corporate mergers, acquisitions, spin-offs, legal, and regulatory changes may be presented in the form of a long scenario question that requires you to select the specific corporate issue to resolve.

Understand user accounts. User account management includes authentication, authorization, federations, and single sign-on systems. Other topics that are fair game for the exam include account management such as new users, password complexity, polices, removing old accounts, and permission settings. User accounts are an important part of ongoing cloud management, and you should expect several questions that test your knowledge of the topic.

Written Lab

Fill in the blanks for the questions provided in the written lab. You can find the answers to the written labs in Appendix B.

1. A Metric is a standard of measurement that defines the conditions and the rules for performing the measurement and for understanding the results of a measurement.

2. Using metrics data to trigger Orchestration systems, you can use thresholds to react to events at all layers of your cloud deployment.

3. Once Harry has determined what is considered to be a baseline during normal web server operations, he can use that as a reference to determine what is considered to be a anomaly or a system that is reporting metrics that are either above or below his expectations.

4. If the event is deemed to be critical, alerts can be generated by configuring a Trigger.

5. As a general rule, the cloud providers will be responsible for the underlying Infrastructure and if it is not defined in the SLA, it will be your responsibility to maintain.

6. ___Change___ ___Management___ is the process of managing all aspects of the ongoing upgrades, repairs, and reconfigurations.

7. The management of a software application from the initial planning stages through to its retirement is referred to as ___Lifecycle___ ___Management___

8. Users can be granted ___Permissions___ at the account level to perform a wide array of operations. The capability to manage cloud operations may allow the administrator to add, remove, or modify user accounts and the services they are allowed to access.

9. Enforcing password ___Complexity___ may require a nondictionary word that is eight or more characters in length and contain at least one uppercase letter and a special character.

10. All change request documents must include a detailed formal plan on the steps to be taken to implement, and if required, ___back out___ the changes.

Review Questions

The following questions are designed to test your understanding of this chapter's material. For more information on how to obtain additional questions, please see this book's Introduction. You can find the answers in Appendix A.

1. Carol is collecting information on objects to monitor in her community cloud deployment. She is interested in establishing a baseline to produce a trend analysis report. What are some objects that she could natively monitor? (Choose all that apply.)

   A. Availability

   B. Instance initialization time

   C. Task runtime

   D. Total storage capacity

   E. MTBF

   F. None of the above

   G. All of the above

2. TipoftheHat.com's IT department wants to know what its normal day-to-day web hit count is so it can plan for the upcoming holiday selling season. Jim's job is to measure the incoming web requests and graph them against delay and missed connection counts. What type of data set is Jim producing?

   A. Metric

   B. Variance

   C. Baseline

   D. Smoothing

3. Elaine works in IT security and is reviewing user count policies. She needs to strengthen passwords by enforcing a mandatory minimum of a nondictionary word that is six or more characters in length, contains at least one uppercase letter, and contains a special character. What is she defining?

   A. Object access

   B. User policy

   C. Complexity

   D. SSO

   E. Federation policy

   F. Firewall zone rules

4. Donald has been tasked by the IT security group in his company to prevent dictionary login attacks to the company's VMs running in a private cloud at a remote data center. You have been brought in to offer him advice to deter the random but steady login attacks. What would you recommend be enabled to help prevent this type of cyber-attack?

   A. Object

   B. SSO

    C. LDAP

    D. Lockout

    E. Access control list

5. Christina is configuring her public cloud object storage bucket for granular access from a new Linux VM. She wants to set the permissions on the storage system. What would you recommend?

    A. Access control list authorization

    B. Federations

    C. Permission-based

    D. SSO

6. Liza is reviewing the maintenance responsibilities between her company and its public cloud service provider. She notices that the cloud provider takes responsibility for the operating system, and she needs to assume responsibility for any applications or services running on the operating system. What type of service model is she operating under?

    A. IaaS

    B. PaaS

    C. SaaS

    D. XaaS

7. Dawn has been working in the NOC and has been tasked with performing a root-cause analysis on a recent outage that affected the middle tier web stack in a private cloud. She is looking at the log files generated and notices that there are more than 430 logs that were generated around the time the site failed. What function does Dawn need to perform to distill all of these log files into a meaningful report?

    A. Baseline

    B. Event analysis

    C. Event correlation

    D. Logging

8. To increase TipoftheHat.com's security posture, Allison is reviewing her company's user accounts that access the fleet cloud resources. Allison notices that the summer interns have left to go back to school but their accounts are still active. She knows they will return for the winter corporate announcements and new products rollouts to assist in the project over winter break. What would you suggest Allison do with these accounts?

    A. Do nothing.

    B. Delete the accounts.

    C. Disable the accounts.

    D. Change the resource access definitions.

    E. Modify the confederation settings.

    F. Change the access control.

9. To make sure that all users are allowed to access only approved resources, Marie is auditing her public cloud identity systems. She wants to control specific access and operations. What is Marie defining?

   A. Federated access

   B. Resource access definitions

   C. User permissions

   D. Access control lists

10. To promote consistent cloud monitoring and to reduce configuration overhead, Lisa has created a number of policies to obtain baseline data. What type of polices is Lisa creating?

    A. Collection

    B. Dissemination

    C. Notification

    D. Publishing

11. Matt is preparing for an upcoming promotion his company is offering during a major soccer game. He needs to determine his options to add capacity to his company's web server farm so it can handle the anticipated additional workload. You are brought in to consult with him on his options. What do you recommend as possible solutions? (Choose three.)

    A. Vertical scaling

    B. Horizontal scaling

    C. Edge cache

    D. Cloud bursting

    E. Core elasticity

12. Bob is configuring an event notification service and notices that there are many different devices and services that can be subscribers to the notification system's published events queue. The notification services offer each event to be sent to a fan-out of multiple devices that can act upon the received information. What are examples of the notification server's receivers? (Choose all that apply.)

    A. Windows OS

    B. Android

    C. APIs

    D. Service queues

    E. Launch scripts

    F. All of the above

13. Samantha has been monitoring her cloud web server dashboard and notices that the CPU utilization on her company's database servers has been consistently at more than 80 percent utilization. She checked her baselines and reported that 57 percent utilization is normal. What is she noticing?

    A. Deviation

    B. Variance

C. Triggers

D. Baseline imbalance

14. Mindy has a SQL database back end that runs on a multi-CPU instance that has reached 100 percent utilization. The database supports a single server. What options does she have to support the requirements of this database?

A. Horizontal scaling

B. Vertical scaling

C. Pooling

D. Bursting

15. What is the ability to automatically and dynamically add additional resources such as storage, CPUs, memory, and even servers referred to as?

A. Bursting

B. Pooling

C. Elasticity

D. Orchestration

16. Ethel is the network architect for a hybrid cloud operation and has interconnected her private cloud to a community cloud in another province. She is investigating using the community cloud to supplement her private cloud operations during end-of-month processing. What operation is she going to perform?

A. Elasticity

B. Bursting

C. Vertical-scaling

D. Autoscaling

17. George and Wendy are working together as cloud engineers to combine two like systems into one. What type of activity would necessitate this? (Choose two.)

A. Merger

B. Acquisition

C. Divestiture

D. Bursting

E. SARBOX

F. HIPAA

18. Allison is preparing to modify a network access control list and add three firewall rules to her private cloud HR systems. She is planning on submitting a detailed plan to accomplish these tasks. What process is Allison following?

A. Cloud automation

B. Change advisory

C. Change management

D. Rollout

19. What does the application life cycle include?

   A. Deployments

   B. Upgrades

   C. Migrations

   D. Retirements

   E. None of the above

   F. All of the above

20. Dimitry has been tasked to develop a cross-cloud provider migration plan as part of his company's business continuity plan. As he assesses the feasibility of migrating applications from one public cloud provider to another, what does he find is the service model that has the most lock-ins and is the most complex to migrate?

   A. IaaS

   B. PaaS

   C. SaaS

   D. XaaS

Chapter

8

Cloud Management Baselines, Performance, and SLAs

THE FOLLOWING COMPTIA CLOUD+ EXAM OBJECTIVES ARE COVERED IN THIS CHAPTER:

✓ **4.5 Given a scenario, analyze deployment results to confirm they meet the baseline.**

- Procedures to confirm results

  - CPU usage

  - RAM usage

  - Storage utilization

  - Patch versions

  - Network utilization

  - Application version

  - Auditing enable

  - Management tool compliance

✓ **4.6 Given a specific environment and related data (e.g., performance, capacity, trends), apply appropriate changes to meet expected criteria.**

- Analyze performance trends

- Refer to baselines

- Refer to SLAs

- Tuning of cloud target objects

  - Compute

- Network
- Storage
- Service/application resources
- Recommend changes to meet expected performance/capacity
  - Scale up/down (vertically)
  - Scale in/out (horizontally)

✓ **4.7 Given SLA requirements, determine the appropriate metrics to report.**

- Chargeback/showback models
  - Reporting based on company policies
  - Reporting based on SLAs
- Dashboard and reporting
  - Elasticity usage
  - Connectivity
  - Latency
  - Capacity
  - Overall utilization
  - Cost
  - Incidents
  - Health
  - System availability
    - Uptime
    - Downtime

In this chapter, you will learn about the importance of measuring the performance of your cloud deployments and how to go about determining what you consider to be a normal operating condition. Once a good *baseline* is determined, then you can track operations and determine whether your services are operating beyond your parameters and take corrective actions. It is important that you collect actual measurements from your real-world operations and not estimate or simulate the baselines. This is done by setting parameters, or *metrics*, on measurable components. These components are called *objects*, and you can define the measurements that are sent to monitoring systems to collect data trends over time. With this information at hand, you can have good solid information to base the health of your deployment on.

A cloud service provider outlines their performance metrics in the service level agreement, and it is your responsibility as a Cloud+ professional to monitor your systems to make sure that the SLA performance metrics are being fulfilled.

Baselines and performance monitoring are also used in capacity planning to determine whether you require additional cloud capacity based on usage and consumption information collected over time. For example, as connection counts increase on a web server farm, it is important to know if you need to add CPU, memory, or network capacity. With a solid baseline and trending data, you can effectively plan to add capacity before you experience performance issues.

Measuring Your Deployment Against the Baseline

To determine whether your cloud services, whether they be servers, storage, security, databases, load balancers, or any of the other many cloud services offered, are performing as expected, you must know what normal is. Let's start this chapter by setting up your baselines so you can know what is considered to be normal operations and what is out of your expectations.

By following widely recognized best practices for performance measurements, you can fine-tune your cloud operations to achieve the performance levels you require to operate your business.

Object Tracking for Baseline Validation

When deploying and operating your fleet of cloud servers and services, you will, from time to time, encounter performance issues. By identifying and tracking various monitored statistics from manageable objects, you collect statistical data over a period of time. This data will then be used to construct a view of what is considered normal operations. These metrics, or baselines, provide valuable historical data of what is considered to be normal operations and assist in troubleshooting performance issues. By tracking objects over time, the data allows you to compare your current measurements to the baseline to see whether there are any deviations in the measurements that could be a cause of performance issues.

Figure 8.1 shows how a monitoring station collects metrics from objects in the cloud.

FIGURE 8.1   Cloud object tracking

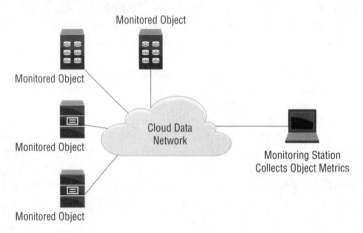

When architecting your device tracking to collect data for a baseline and ongoing operations, decide what your requirements are. That is, what do you need to measure? If you are deploying web servers, for example, then you may want to track VM CPU utilization, memory usages, requests per second, and response times from the backend applications. It is important that you think this through and measure what you need, but not so much that you get flooded with data. Be aware that monitoring adds a processing load on the managed devices, so measure only what is needed at appropriate time intervals, such as one or five minutes.

The objective here is to get a detailed and comprehensive collection of data so you can document what your performance requirements are. This allows you to scale your cloud fleet to the correct size so you do not pay for capacity that is not required or have too little capacity that performance or response times suffer.

Scripts can be utilized on servers that collect the needed data and then store the object metrics in a cloud management platform using API calls. Also, most cloud-managed services have object-reporting built into them, and you are allowed to select what you want monitored as part of the cloud service offerings.

Application Versions

For proper baseline documentation, it is important that you make valid and meaningful comparisons between baselines. Part of this is making sure you track all versioning of applications and also operating systems and device drivers if needed. If there are significant internal performance differences between application versions, it may render your baselines invalid and require that you create a new, or updated, baseline measurement to account for the new version of your application.

CPU Usage

Many applications are CPU bound, which is to say their performance depends on the amount of CPU resources available. One of the most common cloud objects that are tracked is the percentage of CPU utilization, as shown in Figure 8.2, since it has a direct impact on systems' performance. This metric is available at the hypervisor level and can automatically report usage to management systems with no scripting required.

FIGURE 8.2   CPU usage reporting

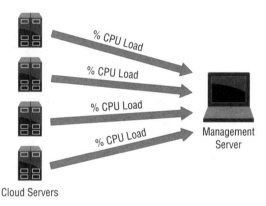

CPU usage can be tracked over time to identify trends, peak usage, and any anomalies that can provide invaluable information to you for troubleshooting and capacity planning.

Enabling the Audit Process

For regulatory or corporate compliance requirements, you may be required to implement an ongoing auditing process and retain the data for record retention requirements. This process will be specific to the application or cloud provider. In the cloud configuration dashboard, most providers will offer as part of their metric-monitoring applications a reporting application that meets the various regulatory requirements they are in compliance with. It is a matter of implementing and enabling the auditing feature to meet these requirements.

Management Tool Compliance

The cloud providers will offer their own management tools and also make accommodations for you to implement your own tools or those of a managed service provider. If there are compliance requirements for the various management tools, they will be outlined in the cloud provider's documentation as to what compliance requirements they meet. If there are special requirements for HIPAA, SBOX, PCI, or other industry requirements, it is your responsibility to make sure that the chosen management tools meet what is required by these regulations.

Network Utilization

Congestion across the network can cause major performance degradation. High network utilization leads to dropped data packets and retransmissions that cause high network latency and poor response times. It is important that you consider network infrastructure performance as a critical part of your metrics and benchmark process.

Network performance measurements are common across all cloud service and deployment models and include the following metrics:

- **Capacity:** The end-to-end metric for maximum available network bandwidth available and utilized capacity, or rate, from source to destination. Capacity is a function of the cloud provider's connections to the Internet and other service providers. While you will have little or no control over it, you should track it for SLA compliance and troubleshooting purposes.

- **Jitter:** The variable delay between packets from source to destination. Excessive jitter will cause buffering and unpredictable performance for real-time traffic such as voice and video networks.

- **Latency:** The time for a packet to travel from source to destination. Latency criticality will vary by application with voice and video requiring low latency and e-mail and file transfers more tolerant of delays.

- **Packet loss:** The percentage or number of packets that are dropped in the network. While a certain amount of packet loss is common in Ethernet-based networks, high packet loss can cause a noticeable performance impact. Protocols such as UDP do not retransmit compared to TCP, which does offer reliable connections by retransmitting dropped packets. Packet loss can have a notable effect on video and voice connections that rely on real-time communications. There are custom protocols in use that are designed for real-time communications that monitor network performance of the video or voice streams and adjust accordingly.

- **QOS:** Quality of service defines traffic priorities in the event of network congestion or impairments. By defining a QOS policy, you can prioritize critical or real-time applications over applications that can tolerate network impairments such as delay, dropped packets, or jitter. Tracking applications performance can ensure the QOS metrics are being honored in the network.

Patch Versions

As you learned in Chapter 7, keeping your cloud fleet of services patched to up-to-date versions is part of an ongoing cloud maintenance program. Versions are often included in the system's metadata or can be requested with API calls to the monitored device. VM monitoring scripts can be created to collect versioning data on the local machine and store it on the management server.

Some cloud providers will offer instances or installable code that allows the VMs to collect local metrics and download them to a management server. This allows you to collect object data such as CPU and RAM utilization as well as look at the OS and even application levels of the server.

RAM Usage

When RAM utilization reaches 100 percent on a server, the operating system will begin to access the swap file and cause a serious performance slowdown that affects all processes running on the server. Monitoring memory usage is one of the most critical objects to monitor and collect baseline data on.

Memory usage should be constantly tracked and measured against the baseline. If memory utilization begins to approach the amount of available memory available on the cloud server instances, you should immediately take actions to remedy the problem before you take a performance hit.

Adding RAM usually requires migrating to a larger VM instance and the associated downtime to perform the migration. The cloud providers offer a wide range of memory options to meet any compute requirement. I suggest you allocate more than anticipated RAM to your server deployments to reduce the need to perform system upgrades.

Storage Utilization

Cloud storage systems offer a wide array of options and features to select from. What is important here is that you configure managed objects for storage volumes and their utilization. Storage requirements will continue to grow, and by monitoring your storage operations, you can allocate additional capacity or migrate stored data to lower lifecycle tiers to take advantage of lower-cost storage options.

Another important storage metric is I/O operations. I/O may be a chargeable metric, especially for SQL database deployments. Disk read and write objects can be defined and tracked as part of your storage system baselines.

Applying Changes to the Cloud to Meet Baseline Requirements

In this section, you will learn about meeting baselines. As part of your ongoing cloud maintenance plans, you will be tracking your operations against your baselines and adjusting or troubleshooting the variations to these trend lines. To keep your operations in range of your established baseline, you will be making frequent or infrequent changes to your cloud deployments. Some changes may be minor, while others will be disruptive and incur system downtime in some cases.

Performance Trending

Once you have your baseline established, you will have solid data for what is considered to be normal operations of your cloud servers and services. Using your monitoring application (whether your own it or one is provided by the cloud company), you can now continue to collect performance metrics and compare that data against your baseline, as shown in Figure 8.3. This comparison will give insight into trends such as incoming connections, CPU usage, and any other objects you are tracking. You will be interested to see the increase and decrease of usage during hourly, weekly, or monthly time windows.

FIGURE 8.3 Collecting trending data

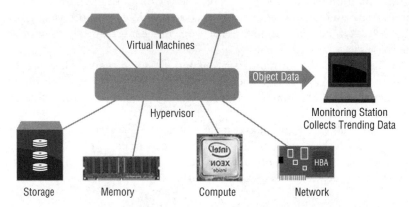

Trending data is crucial for planning resources to meet future demands. Utilizing trending reports, you can see which services may need to be replaced or scaled. This allows you to proactively manage your operations and correctly scale services before they become a performance bottleneck.

Baseline Validation

Is your baseline actually realistic or valid? That can be a critical question as your operations will be measured against that benchmark. It better be accurate!

The best way to validate your baseline measurements is to collect them over a long period of time to smooth out isolated events or short-term variations. Also, if it is an e-commerce web server, for example, were the measurements taken during the busy holiday season or during a slow cycle?

It may be helpful to compare your baselines against others that are in a similar operational state or use case. This can help to validate that your readings are what is expected and that there are no outlier measurements.

Compare and test all metrics collected including CPU, network, memory, storage, and any custom metrics with all available data to ensure your readings are in the range you would expect them to be in. As time goes on, you will achieve a stable set of operations that can be used to establish an accurate baseline.

Testing your deployment using simulations of load and application utilization can provide initial data on utilization rates to establish an initial baseline. After the testing runs, you can evaluate the data, make changes to any performance bottlenecks, and rerun the tests to validate the changes made.

After a system has been patched or upgraded, it is a best practice to run another validation to make sure the post-upgrade performance metrics meet your baseline measurements.

The best way to effectively measure and document a baseline validation during a system update or modification is to perform three benchmark validation tests.

- Pre-patch/pre-upgrade to get a snapshot of current baseline data

- Post-patch/post-upgrade to get performance data of the systems after modifications

- A comparison operation that measures the deltas between the pre- and post-reports

Service Level Agreement Attainment

As discussed in Chapter 2, the SLA defines key performance indicators that are the metrics selected to determine fulfillment of cloud provider performance guarantees.

Objects to be tracked should align with the SLA metrics. By collecting actual data, you can compare it to the offered service levels outlined in the SLA and ensure that the guaranteed metrics are being met.

It is up to the cloud customer to track the SLA metrics to ensure the guarantees are being met by the service provider. Effective monitoring allows you to accomplish this. However, just collecting large amounts of data is not sufficient; you must make sense of the raw data. Cloud management applications can process the collected data and present it in graphs and tables that make it easy to see the collected statistics in an easy-to-interpret format. The management applications can also export the data in Excel format and PDF reports.

As your business objectives change over time, it will become necessary to renegotiate SLA metrics that meet your new requirements. As part of your ongoing management processes, it is important to review the SLA on a regular schedule to make sure the SLA meets your operational requirements.

Review your baselines on a regular schedule and compare them to your SLA. Are they in alignment, and do they meet your current requirements? Are there critical metrics that are missing? Based on this information, you can discuss your new SLA requirements with the cloud service provider and add, remove, or adjust as needed for your current needs.

Once the new SLA has been agreed to and has taken effect, you can adjust your monitoring systems to measure compliance and alert you to trends or issues that do not align with the new agreement.

Compute Tuning

Should there be CPU starvation, you can be assured that your deviation from the baseline will be very noticeable! The only available solution is to either lower the load on the instance CPUs or add additional computing resources. Operating systems offer utilities that show how much CPU resources different processes are using. If possible, you can disable or shut down any services that are using up CPU cycles that are not needed.

If you are in the situation where you have tuned your server for optimal CPU resource consumptions and still are suffering from high CPU usage, then you may have no other choice but to upgrade your instance either vertically or horizontally to add CPU power. This will involve replacing your current machine image with that of a larger offering that has additional CPU capacity. Additional capacity can be added by either implementing a higher-performance CPU with higher clock speeds and a newer architecture or by converting to an image with multiple cores. This is known as vertical scaling. Performing vertical migration will involve some downtime to make the conversion. However, with the virtualization capabilities of the cloud, you can spin up a new, and larger, service instance; install and test your application; and have it validated before you go live with the new image and shut down the older image. The second option is to keep your existing deployment and add to it by implementing more servers of a similar architecture that run in parallel. This is referred to as *horizontal scaling* and will be covered later in this chapter.

Network Changes

When making deployment changes to networking performance issues, you need to understand what you can control and what the cloud service provider controls. Many of the networking parameters are global to the cloud and out of your area of authority. However, it is important to understand that making sure the network performs inside your baseline and SLA is your responsibility.

Cloud companies do offer solutions for network-intensive requirements. These include server images with 10 Gbps network adapters, a low-latency interconnection that places all of your servers on the same hypervisor for high-speed, low-latency interconnections, and the ability to group all of the servers in the same zone and subnet.

Storage Tuning

Baselines can be used to ensure that the storage systems meet your performance requirements and allow you to track changes over time. Storage systems are often monitored for I/O utilization from the host bus adapter to the SAN. Should there be excessive utilization, disk read/write performance will suffer, and the application's performance will degrade. The solution is to increase the bandwidth of the adapter on the VM. Using metrics that define what will be considered to be high utilization of storage network bandwidth over a defined period of time, automated actions can be performed to remedy the issue, or you can upgrade your machine image to one that is optimized for storage operations.

The monitoring system will receive and monitor log information from the VM, and for example, if disk I/O exceeds 80 percent utilization for a three-minute period, an autoscaling event will increase storage adapter bandwidth. When the utilization drops below your defined threshold, the bandwidth can be scaled back to its original value to save on costs.

A related issue is database read/write replicas. If a database is highly utilized, a single database replica may be bandwidth-starved and become a performance bottleneck.

This can be resolved by creating multiple read replicas on different storage volumes and balancing the server access across these replicas to distribute the load on the storage systems.

Service/Application Changes

Changing or upgrading services and applications may be required to add new capabilities and features that are beneficial or to maintain your cloud deployment compliance with changing regulations or corporate policy.

If you are implementing a SaaS solution, then the cloud provider will be responsible for any changes made to the application. They will most often notify you that a change is being made in the form of an update announcing new features or a maintenance upgrade that will be implemented. Cloud providers are constantly upgrading applications such as database offerings and collaboration services, for example, and this is a benefit to you as you can take advantage of the new features and capabilities offered.

Services such as load balancers, firewalls, DNS, identity management, and virtual private clouds also undergo frequent upgrades to keep pace with the competition and to add features. These services are largely the responsibility of the cloud provider and to your benefit as you get to take advantage of the new capabilities and offerings with little effort on your part.

Changing Operations to Meet Expected Performance/Capacity Requirements

As your cloud operations grow and evolve, so may your requirements for additional capacity and higher levels of performance. This will mean that you will be making changes to your deployment over time to meet your current and future capacity needs. In this section, you will revisit scaling and add details to the process now that you have a good understanding of monitoring and baseline management.

Vertical Scaling

You learned about vertical scaling in Chapter 7. In this section, the topic will be expanded upon, and you will learn the process to vertically scale your server to meet expanded workloads.

Some applications, such as many types of databases, are not designed to scale horizontally. You will need to scale to a larger machine image to increase resources for the application, as shown in Figure 8.4. The solution here is to configure monitoring metrics for critical server resources such as memory, storage, network and storage I/O and CPU. As you learned, these metrics can be collected and analyzed by monitoring applications and triggers configured to scale the virtual machine to a large instance type to handle the presented workloads.

FIGURE 8.4   Vertical scaling

Existing Server   Replaced by a
                                   Larger Capacity Server

When the scaling occurs, the existing machine is replaced with a larger instance type that you define. Depending on your requirements, you may add additional CPUs, memory, network bandwidth for storage, or LAN traffic. Be aware that you will effectively be replacing servers, so there will be downtime. This can be automated for dynamic scaling or performed in a maintenance window. With accurate benchmarks, you can see the trending data and scale before there are any performance issues. When the new server replaces the older image, the IP address will move to the new machine so that any DNS records of application settings do not have to be modified. Other operations involved in vertical scaling will be to mount storage volumes, put the new server image in the same security group, and assign user access rights to it to match the server being replaced.

As a general rule, you do not want to perform vertical scaling operations on a regular basis. The operations should be reserved for when it is absolutely required and you plan on staying on that instance for a long period of time. This is because of the disruptive nature of the upgrade.

Horizontal Scaling

Horizontal scaling is the process of adding cloud capacity by expanding your current server fleet by adding systems, compared to vertical scaling, which is replacing servers with a larger instance that meets your new requirements. Horizontal scaling works well for applications that are designed to work in parallel such as web servers, as shown in Figure 8.5. You keep your existing server instances and add more to increase capacity.

FIGURE 8.5   Horizontal scaling

Existing Servers   Horizontally Scaled Servers

A common way to automate adding machines to your operations is to configure the management application to monitor key metrics and respond when they are deviating from your baseline. For example, a fleet of web servers can be monitored for CPU utilization, and if they all exceed 80 percent over a five-minute window, you can trigger an *autoscaling* event. The monitoring application will initiate the loading and configuring of predefined web server images. You can define the number of VMs and configuration of the added capacity you require. The automation application will also add the new machines to a load balancer group, or DNS if needed, and put them into service. You can set up alerting to be notified of the event for awareness.

The autoscaling service can also be configured to remove the servers after the load has fallen below your defined metrics for a period of time to eliminate charges for unused capacity. Additional features offered are the ability to statically define time windows to add and remove capacity and to make sure that your server fleet maintains a minimum number of servers. If a server should fail for whatever reason, the autoscaling service can replace it with another.

Cloud Accounting, Chargeback, and Reporting

Cloud management includes accounting mechanisms for measuring consumption, billing, and generating management reports. In this section, you will learn about these nontechnical but important aspects of cloud operational management.

Company Policy Reporting

Companies will publish and manage IT polices; these policies cover a wide range of subjects including, but not limited to, how cloud services are consumed and accounted for. To effectively measure compliance, you will need to collect the required data and be able to process the information into effective reports.

Cloud providers are aware of policy reporting and offer services to assist you in collecting and presenting reports. These services are cloud-based and can be remarkably customizable. They are presented in a graphical format in a web browser dashboard. Also, the reports can be exported to Excel or PDF format, as shown in Figure 8.6.

FIGURE 8.6   Cloud reporting

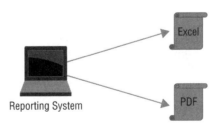

Reporting System

Reporting Based on SLA-Based Reports

As you have learned throughout this chapter, there is a close relationship between collecting data into baselines and then measuring them against your SLA to ensure compliance. Management services allow you to compare these two metrics and generate reports that can be used to analyze trends, identify problems, and store data for regulatory or corporate compliance purposes. These reports can be exported as discussed earlier, in many different formats including Excel and PDF documents.

Using the Cloud Dashboard

Cloud dashboards are incredibly useful and informative. It is common to display dashboards in operations centers or overhead in office environments to give an easy-to-read overview of operations. Dashboards are usually graphical and color-coded for quick notification of potential issues.

Dashboards are offered by the cloud providers, your internal monitoring and management applications, and any outside monitoring services you have contracted with. They allow you to define what you want to display and in what format. Dashboards are completely customizable and rather easy to configure. Once the dashboard has been defined, users with access rights can easily access them with a standard web browser.

Elasticity Usage

As you learned earlier in this chapter, one of the great benefits cloud computing offers is elasticity and the flexibility automation offers in adding and removing capacity. Elasticity events often incur charges and are also important to monitor to ensure that your cloud operations are scaled correctly.

Management applications can generate usage reports on a large number of events including elasticity. Metrics such as the event time and duration are recorded as well as details of the added capacity and utilization metrics that were collected after the scale-up or scale-down events occurred. Also, comparisons to performance and SLAs are important reports to generate to meet compliance with regulatory needs.

As with the other reporting types, you can generate the reports in formats that meet your needs.

Connectivity

Corporate management and various departments in your company will always be interested in how their operations are being accessed and who is connecting to their cloud presence.

Reports and graphical presentations can be created to show connections over time, location, new or returning visitors, what was performed (did they buy anything on your e-commerce site?), and how long they were visiting. This is valuable data for sales, marketing, and accounting.

Latency

Network delays and slowdowns can have an extremely negative effect on cloud operations. If an e-commerce site has high latency, many potential customers may give up and leave, causing lost revenue. Companies that rely on cloud-based services such as e-mail, databases, or any of the other many benefits of cloud computing will suffer productivity declines as they sit and stare at a screen that is not responding.

Latency in the network can come from many different sources; however, individual cloud bottlenecks all add up to latency, and the end result is frustrated employees and customers.

Metrics, benchmarks, SLAs, and proactive maintenance all come together to keep latency low and performance high.

Naturally companies want to track and report on how the cloud is performing, and latency is the big picture of performance. Reports can show latency globally and drill down to individual services such as a web server's response and database read-write latency.

Capacity and Utilization

Capacity and utilization reporting can include a wide range of metrics including storage, CPU, RAM, network, and so on. These reports are helpful in managing usage trends and change requirements. Accounting will be interested to see that the capacity purchased is being used effectively. As with the other measurements, capacity reports are customizable and offered in a variety of formats.

Incident and Health Reports

Tracking support services and impairments will give you insight into the overall reliability of operations, and the collected data can be compared to your SLA to ensure compliance.

Incidents can be defined by your company or the cloud provider as required. Incidents and health reports include trouble tickets opened, support engagements, and any event that causes degradation of your services.

Uptime and Downtime Reporting

A critical and bottom-line metric of any SLA is that of downtime. If you cannot access your cloud deployment, that is a critical event and must be tracked. Both the cloud provider and your operations center should track downtime and identify the root cause of what caused the outage. These reports can be analyzed to ensure SLA metrics are being met and to see if you have to change your architecture to design for higher reliability and less downtime.

Summary

This chapter focused on managing your cloud operations by establishing effective baselines, measuring performance, and understanding the importance of SLAs.

Baselines are created to establish what reporting is considered to be normal operations. By measuring critical components and utilization, data sets can be created and measured over time to determine how your cloud components are being used. With a well-established baseline, variations can be highlighted and used for identifying problems, the need to add capacity, if SLAs are being honored, and usage trends.

Baselines are a collection of metrics that are gathered from cloud objects such as CPU, RAM, storage, network, and any other service or component you deem important to measure. Baselines are a point-in-time view of operations and need to be constantly tracked as part of your ongoing operations. Baseline data allows you to analyze how your operations are performing, plan for growth, and generate reports for regularity or corporate compliance requirements.

The process of adding capacity by using cloud elasticity functions was introduced, and details were provided on autoscaling your deployments. Vertical scaling was expanded upon and is replacing a server with a larger, more capable system. Horizontal scaling takes a different approach and adds additional servers to your existing fleet for added capacity.

The importance of the service level agreements was introduced, and you learned about collecting operational data to measure SLA compliance. SLAs may need to be adjusted as your business needs evolve, and baselines may need to be modified to track new metrics included in the SLA.

Generating reports is an ongoing process for a Cloud+ certified professional. Reports are used to show utilization, capacity, billing, SLA attainment, latency, incidents, and availability. Reporting is flexible with the management applications offered by cloud service providers and monitoring companies. They are highly customizable and can be tailored for your internal corporate audiences and for regulatory or compliance needs.

Dashboards are visual reporting of cloud objects and services. A dashboard can be created to display graphs and charts of what you deem to be important. Dashboards are often displayed in network operations centers and user browsers to display real-time cloud statistics.

Exam Essentials

Know what baselines are and how they are created.   For the exam you may be given long scenario questions that pertain to measuring a system to determine its normal operational state, or the process of monitoring objects such as CPU utilization, and you must be able to identify that the question concerns baselines.

Understand service level agreements and what their purpose is.   SLAs are service provider documents that outline detailed performance metrics the provider guarantees to meet for their customers. Items such as downtime, latency, compliance, and division of responsibilities are all included. The exam may detail what is included, and you will be required to identify that it is the SLA that is being referred to in the question.

Know what objects and metrics are.   Objects are anything that can be measured and have data collected on. Metrics are the actual data. You may be given a long scenario question that, for example, asks about a performance issue of a server and how data can be collected and analyzed to determine what the problem is.

Differentiate between reporting options.   For the exam, know that there are many different types of reporting options available for management, marketing, accounting, and operations. Know that these may include policies, SLA attainment, elasticity, connectivity, latency, capacity and utilization, cost accounting, incidents, and availability. You may be asked to identify which reporting is being discussed in an exam question.

Understand the different ways to add capacity.   Given a scenario, you may be asked to identify a performance issue and determine what steps to take to remediate the problem. Know that scaling can be automated and that vertical scaling is expanding the capacity of a server and that horizontal scaling is adding servers to your fleet. Read each question carefully to fully understand what the performance issue is and the application requirements to be able to identify if vertical or horizontal scaling is the correct solution.

Written Lab

Fill in the blanks for the questions provided in the written lab. You can find the answers to the written labs in Appendix B.

1.   The _baseline_ measurements are used to detail resource usage under normal operations.
2.   A _metric_ is data collected from an object.
3.   Cloud components that data can be gathered from are referred to as _objects_.
4.   _Horizontal_ scaling is adding capacity by deploying additional servers.
5.   Reducing swap file usage can be accomplished by adding additional _memory_.
6.   Network delays and slowdowns are an indication of high network _latency_.
7.   The ability of cloud resources to scale up and down is referred to as _resiliency_ _elasticity_.
8.   The service provider outlines their performance guarantees in a _SLA_.
9.   _Vertical Scaling_ is the process of replacing a single machine image with a larger, more powerful image.
10.   For regulatory or corporate compliance requirements, you may be required to implement an ongoing _auditing_ process and retain the data for record retention requirements.

Review Questions

The following questions are designed to test your understanding of this chapter's material. For more information on how to obtain additional questions, please see this book's Introduction. You can find the answers in Appendix A.

1. When monitoring performance metrics on one of your servers, you notice that the server is utilizing 100 percent of the network bandwidth available to it. What modification could you make to the server that will most likely address the problem?

   A. Add memory to the system.

   B. Install a second network adapter.

   C. Update the network adapter's firmware.

   D. Install a second processor.

2. Which of the following is not a statistic that you would typically find in a server performance baseline?

   A. CPU utilization

   B. Disk transfer rate

   C. Network transmissions speed

   D. OS update history

   E. Memory utilization

3. What type of scaling involves replacing an existing server with another that has more capabilities?

   A. Horizontal

   B. Round-robin

   C. Elasticity

   D. Autoscale

   E. Vertical

4. Incident reports include which of the following? (Choose three.)

   A. Trouble tickets

   B. SLAs

   C. Scaling

   D. Support engagements

   E. Outages

5. Databases capacity can be added by scaling horizontally.

   A. True

   B. False

6. Cloud provider SLAs outline which of the following? (Choose two.)

    A. Device configuration

    B. DNS configurations

    C. Uptime

    D. Network performance

    E. Autocache

7. Reports are often provided to which interested parties? (Choose four.)

    A. Marketing

    B. Management

    C. Cloud provider operations

    D. Accounting

    E. Internal operation centers

    F. Customers

8. To collect metrics, you set up your management application to measure what?

    A. Database

    B. Server

    C. Hypervisor

    D. Objects

9. Reports are generated where?

    A. Hypervisor

    B. Databases

    C. Logging servers

    D. Cloud management and monitoring application

10. What is a visual representation of your current cloud operations?

    A. Operational matrix

    B. Management console

    C. Dashboard

11. Upgrading to a newer operating system may require that you update what?

    A. SLA

    B. DNS

    C. Baseline

    D. VPC

12. Capacity and utilization reporting often contains data on which of the following objects? (Choose three.)

- **A.** CPU
- **B.** OS version
- **C.** Volume tier
- **D.** RAM
- **E.** Network

13. Autoscaling can be configured to which of the following? (Choose four.)

- **A.** Add capacity.
- **B.** Configure time-of-day capacity.
- **C.** Generate metric reports.
- **D.** Remove capacity.
- **E.** Maintain a minimum number of servers.
- **F.** Track SLA objects.
- **G.** Perform patch management.

14. Cloud-based reports can be generated in which formats? (Choose two.)

- **A.** SQL
- **B.** PDF
- **C.** Python
- **D.** JSON
- **E.** Excel

15. What type of scaling involves adding servers to a pool?

- **A.** Horizontal
- **B.** Round-robin
- **C.** Elasticity
- **D.** Autoscale
- **E.** Vertical

16. Carl has noticed a slowdown in the response times of his SQL database and has been tasked to investigate the root cause of the delays. He has decided to configure his monitoring application to gather additional data on what may be the cause of the delays. What are some of the objects you would recommend he collect data on? (Choose three.)

- **A.** Read replica I/O
- **B.** Load balancer latency
- **C.** CPU
- **D.** Network packet drops
- **E.** Machine image
- **F.** SLA

17. Object tracking can be helpful in identifying which of the following? (Choose three.)
    A. Resiliency
    B. Trends
    C. Metrics
    D. ACLs
    E. Peak usage
    F. Anomalies

18. Rebecca is writing a change management plan to increase the processing abilities of one of her middleware servers. What components can she upgrade to increase server performance? (Choose three.)
    A. CPU
    B. SLA
    C. RAM
    D. Network I/O
    E. ACL
    F. DNS

19. Object tracking should be aligned with which of the following?
    A. VPC
    B. SLA
    C. RDP
    D. JSON

20. High-performance network clusters should share which the following? (Choose two.)
    A. Availability zone
    B. Group cache
    C. Identity group
    D. Hypervisor

Chapter

9

Troubleshooting

THE FOLLOWING COMPTIA CLOUD+ EXAM OBJECTIVES ARE COVERED IN THIS CHAPTER:

✓ **5.1 Given a scenario, troubleshoot a deployment issue.**

- Common issues in the deployments
  - Breakdowns in the workflow
  - Integration issues related to different cloud platforms
  - Resource contention
  - Connectivity issues
  - Cloud service provider outage
  - Licensing issues
  - Template misconfiguration
  - Time synchronization issues
  - Language support
  - Automation issues

✓ **5.2 Given a scenario, troubleshoot common capacity issues.**

- Exceeded cloud capacity boundaries
  - Compute
  - Storage
  - Networking
    - IP address limitations
    - Bandwidth limitations
  - Licensing
  - Variance in number of users
  - API request limit
  - Batch job scheduling issues
- Deviation from original baseline
- Unplanned expansions

✓ **5.3 Given a scenario, troubleshoot automation/ orchestration issues.**

  ■ Breakdowns in the workflow

    ■ Account mismatch issues

    ■ Change management failure

    ■ Server name changes

    ■ IP address changes

    ■ Location changes

    ■ Version/feature mismatch

    ■ Automation tool incompatibility

    ■ Job validation issue

Cloud computing can be complex! As you have learned throughout this study guide, there are a lot of different components and advanced technologies that make up the cloud. It is not uncommon to see a public cloud provider offering more than 100 different services. The combinations of all these offerings are practically limitless. With this flexibility and sophistication comes the reality that there are a lot of things that can go wrong. Not only can there be problems, there often are.

When your cloud deployment fails or is not operating as it should, your ability to troubleshoot and resolve issues will be called upon. The process of investigating and determining what the underlying problem is, and then resolving, is part art and part science. By understanding the details of your operations, referring to the proper documentation, and knowing how to use the tools and applications at your disposal, you can effectively troubleshoot and resolve any issues that you will encounter.

The objectives in this chapter cover common issues that, as a Cloud+ professional, you will be most likely to encounter. Complete books can be written on resolving problems with these services. However, for this exam, you will be introduced to the various issues you may encounter and then be expected to identify them in scenario-based exam questions. This chapter builds on the knowledge you have accumulated throughout this book, so knowledge of the many cloud services is expected before learning how to troubleshoot.

Examining Common Cloud Issues

While cloud issues can appear to be specific to one service, they can span across many different components and services in the cloud. In an effort to create some structure to troubleshooting, we have grouped some of the more common issues in this section. These broad categories act as pointers, or hints, to where a problem may reside. Also, when troubleshooting, eliminating these categories as the issue can help lead you to the issue.

Automation

What could possibly go wrong with a fully automated system where just the click of an icon unleashes a host of cloud automation scripts? Well, many things can go wrong! Not only that, automation often hides the complexity from the user and does not always report results to the person using these automated services.

The ability to troubleshoot automation-related problems comes down to whether you control the process or another party such as the cloud provider does. If the automated systems are part of the backend virtualization services embedded in the cloud provider's operations, then it is beyond your reach to troubleshoot the actual issue. However, when using these services, it is critical that you validate the end result is what you expect. Look at your original deployment plan and what you actually configured in the deployment and compare that to what you see as running services. If there is a discrepancy, go back and make sure that you requested what was actually deployed. Is there a difference between the input and the output? If the input, or requested, configuration is what you expect but the deployed services are different, it could very well be that the automation software did not work as expected. Log files can be collected on all API calls to a device or service; these can offer valuable information on the success or failure of the scripts used. A well-written script can also validate the changes and roll back if there was a script failure. Monitoring dashboards can also be configured to monitor the results of the automated systems in a graphical manner. Since it is most likely that you do not have access to the underlying automation code, your only real option here is to open a trouble ticket with the cloud provider for investigation. Also, the frequently asked questions (FAQ) or support discussion forums may have additional information on the issue you are troubleshooting.

If it was your organization that developed the automation applications, then you will have much greater flexibility in troubleshooting. Are there log files that were generated? Did the script fail before completion? Did an API call fail? By investigating the software and stepping through its execution, you, or your development team, should be able to identify the issue internally to your organization.

Cloud Interoperability

Interoperability between clouds, whether they be public, private, hybrid, or community, can expose a wide variety of issues that can trigger many hours of troubleshooting!

Cloud interoperability issues should be well investigated by the architect teams prior to deployment. Cloud provider documentation and testing often provide best practices and validated configurations. There are many vendor papers published with best practices for interoperability. The support forums can be invaluable as you may find discussions from other groups that are experiencing the same problems as you are and the results of other's troubleshooting. Also, the cloud companies often monitor or moderate these forums and can offer solutions to the issue you are experiencing. A good search engine and service provider documentation will go a long way in resolving cloud interoperability issues. Search for validated or reference designs that detail tested configurations and compare them to your deployment.

As much as possible, you should investigate where the source of the issue is located. This can be done by investigating log files and monitoring systems. Effective dashboards will also be a huge help here. Once you have a good idea of where the problem is located, you can localize your investigation to that cloud provider. For example, if you are wanting to move a virtual machine image from one cloud provider to another, all restrictions and caveats need to be identified to determine whether there are any interoperability issues you may run into. To troubleshoot issues like this, investigate the possibility of changing the format of the image at the source when you create it to match the destination or to see whether there are image conversions or import services offered by the destination provider.

Interconnections

Your connections to the cloud can test your networking troubleshooting skills. Most cloud providers offer VPN connections from your offices or data centers to their cloud data centers. These connections may drop and not reestablish or experience errors that cause retransmissions that degrade response times. The VPN console from the cloud company and the VPN system at your location can be investigated for status and log information that often points to the problem.

If the interconnection problems reside inside the cloud provider's infrastructure, such as connections between availability zones or regions, then you must rely on the cloud provider to resolve the issue. Cloud providers commonly post a health monitoring dashboard that offers a visual representation of any current problems they are experiencing.

Common interconnection issues are the encryption transforms matching. Are the security configurations the same on both ends of the VPN? Also, verify that your security certificates have not expired and that the link maximum transmission unit (MTU) is large enough to not cause fragmentation of network packets.

Language Support

This one can be a bit confusing; to clear it up, it is what programming languages are supported in your cloud services. This is more of a compatibility issue than anything else. The cloud provider will publish what it supports, and you must interoperate in that language.

Cloud automation and configurations generally support JSON, Python, and XML. Providers will publish this information online either in their technical documentation or in their FAQs. Pay special attention to any version requirements and ensure that you match what is supported.

Licensing

Licensing issues often manifest themselves as a sudden failure after everything has been working fine all year. After a quick investigation, you see in the log files that the application's license has expired!

The service model will determine how to start troubleshooting a licensing issue. As you learned, the IaaS and PaaS models allow you to install and run your own applications. Since you own the application, you are responsible for the licensing that allows you to use it.

With SaaS, the cloud provider is responsible for the application, and you pay for its use. As such, the SaaS provider is responsible for the software license, so the provider will manage all licensing-related issues.

You did follow best practices and document how licensing is managed between your company and your application vendor, right? This will be extremely handy when troubleshooting licensing-related outages. There can be a remarkable level of complexity when licensing application software. The vendors offer a bewildering number of options, and no two companies are alike. Software licenses for cloud deployments may be different than the structure for the same application running in your private data center. One may base its license on the total number of users, named users, or concurrent connections. It is common to find licenses for each processor that is used or the number of cores. There is more, licenses can also be based on actual usage measured by object monitoring.

License capacity can be measured in many ways, such as the number of users, total connections, named users, concurrent connections, or usage metrics. The license capacity responsibility is dependent on the service model. If it is an IaaS or PaaS model, you will most likely be responsible for the licensing, and if it is a SaaS model, the cloud service provider will take care of all licensing issues.

The bottom line is that you should track license consumption and keep ahead of capacity requirements.

Security certificates, while not specifically licensing, also expire. This can be a catastrophic event because any service, such as HTTPS, VPNs, storage, and communication encryptions and authentication systems that rely on the certificate, will also fail. Keep track of all certificate expiration dates and renew them prior to expiration!

Networking

Networking issues were introduced in the "Interconnections" section. To expand on network-specific issues, you need to store your log files in a syslog server so that you can compare information across multiple network devices. Cloud dashboards or in-house management or monitoring systems collect networking object metrics and are invaluable in reporting network problems.

Troubleshooting networking issues can be from either the ground up or the top down. A ground-up approach starts with the link-level statistics. Are there errors on the link? Is the link "up" and communicating with the remote device? Check networking operations as you move up the OSI stack from the physical layer to data-link, network, transport, and above. Check routing tables to see whether there is a path to the remote network. ping is a common troubleshooting utility, which you can use to see whether the remote is reachable. Another is traceroute, which follows a packet through the network from its source to the destination and can point to failures along the way. Check any access control lists or firewall rules that may be blocking traffic that you want to allow.

If you troubleshoot from the top down, you will start at the application and make sure that it is operational and able to communicate with the network stack. Work your way down from here until you verify that the data is reaching the network and being transmitted or whether there is a failure in the network stack.

Resource Contention and Starvation

As you learned in Chapter 8, a good baseline needs to be established so that you have solid data on what is normal. Once you have data on what is considered to be normal, you can monitor to see whether there are any issues with current measurements such as contention for resources. As your cloud activity grows, you may, at some point, run out of system resources. A resource starvation issue will usually manifest itself as a slowdown in performance as the application contends for what has now become a scarce resource.

Resource contention is conflicting access to resources such as CPU, network bandwidth, random access memory or storage. This leads to resource starvation where services are denied access to these pools.

To troubleshoot limited resource problems, it is helpful that you have set up object monitoring on critical systems and display the metrics on a dashboard. Also, thresholds can be programmed to trigger alarms when, for example, CPU utilization exceeds 90 percent for five minutes.

Common resources that may saturate over time are CPU, memory, storage, storage network bandwidth, and network capacity.

To resolve contention and starvation issues, it usually comes down to throttling the system consuming the resource or having to add capacity. If you add capacity, you can decide to use autoscaling to dynamically add or subtract resources based on current load or to manually upgrade virtualized resources for greater capacity.

Service Outages

If there is a service outage, you will certainly be in for some excitement! If the outage is in your network, it needs to be localized and all necessary resources brought in to resolve the issue. Companies often establish a "war room" where all the different groups that can assist in resolving the issue can congregate and collaborate to resolve the issue. War rooms may also have video, audio, and collaboration links with overhead displays to assist in troubleshooting. A service outage can include many different parts of your deployment, so you must be able to call in the groups or individuals who are responsible at a moment's notice. A good corporate response plan is needed in these cases.

Service outages can come from a wide variety of sources, some that are under your control and many that are not. If there is a power or carrier outage, you must rely on them to restore services. Storms or natural disasters can cause outages that may take time to restore. A good disaster recovery plan is essential because you may have to decide to fail over to your backup site if the outage is expected to last for an extended period of time.

Outages in the cloud are rare but certainly not uncommon. Public clouds are designed to be highly resilient to individual device failures. With the popular availability zone architecture, should an availability zone fail in a cloud region, the applications can be designed to automatically fail over to the backup availability zone with a minimal loss of service.

Cloud providers, as discussed, have extensive reporting systems that publicly disclose network heath and any availability issues in their network that they are currently experiencing.

Templates

Templates are software representations of network systems. By using these templates, you can deploy complete cloud systems at a single time. This allows you to implement "one-click provisioning" instead of deploying and configuring individual cloud objects. Templates can be helpful with automated deployments of virtualized systems. The template may use API calls to cloud services that have changed over time. It is a best practice to validate that your templates are current and operational so as to prevent them from failing when they are most needed.

Time Synchronization

Cloud services are often global in nature, which is to say resources can be in many different time zones. It is desirable to collect logging (syslog) information in a central server for all of your cloud objects. What happens if your devices all timestamp logging data in their local time zones? It's a huge mess.

The *Network Time Protocol (NTP)* allows all devices to synchronize to a central clock or time service. This ensures that all devices report the same times to allow for synchronization of logging information. It is important that you verify regularly that your cloud elements are synchronized with the NTP servers to prevent the drifting of device clocks. Cloud elements will have a command line, API, or GUI interface that shows if there is time synchronization.

Workflow

Workflow services will often be a collaboration of many applications coordinated by a workflow application running in the cloud. Workflow applications track a process from start to finish and sequence the applications that are required to complete the process. There will be a management console for the cloud-based workflow applications that are offered under the Software as a Service model. You can track individual jobs and see where they are in the workflow process and whether there are any errors. Based on this information, you can troubleshoot or restart the workflow.

Troubleshooting Cloud Capacity Issues

In this section on troubleshooting, you will learn about the limitations of the various cloud services, how to identify them, and what options are available to troubleshoot and resolve these types of issues.

Any system, whether it be hardware or software, will have a limit to its ability to handle a workload. This is its *capacity*, which can be defined as the maximum amount that something can contain, or in the case of cloud resources, the maximum limit of any object or service that is supported.

Cloud capacity planning was covered in the previous chapter and is the process of monitoring your operations and adding resources prior to them becoming exhausted. If you do not plan and add resources in a proactive manner, then you will, at some point, run into resource starvation and performance issues. You will learn about the more common problems you may find and how to troubleshoot them.

Capacity Boundaries in the Cloud

Every device or service will have a maximum threshold that, when exceeded, will fail, drop the requests, or slow down. Systems can, and do, get overloaded and often produce unpredictable results.

It is a common practice for cloud providers to publish the performance statistics of their services that also include maximum supported metrics.

A good baseline will show you your current capacity consumption and allow you to compare that to the maximum available. With this information, you can make informed decisions on managing your cloud operations.

You may have agreements with the cloud provider on the capacity level you have purchased and included in your Service Level Agreement (SLA). Should you approach the contracted capacity level, you can often purchase additional capacity and avoid any performance issues.

API Request Capacity

Application program interface (API) requests are usually a metered resource in the cloud. You will be charged for the total number of requests over time and have a maximum available capacity. API performance is often measured in requests per second. For example, a cloud service such as a database requesting writes to a storage object may have an upper limit of 100 per second. When the database writes exceed 100 per second, buffering may occur or additional charges could apply.

API requests are measured and can be tracked from baseline measurements to determine whether there is a variation. It may be as simple as adding to your contracted API capacity, or you may have to divide the requests across more than one interface.

To troubleshoot API issues, it is helpful to review your log files for any API-related errors or alerts. Also, monitoring applications can display actual compared to available API capacity.

Bandwidth

Server machine images allow for a selection of adapter speeds, usually offered in 1Gbps or 10Gbps options. Network I/O is a measurable object whose metrics should be included in your baseline documentation. If network bandwidth exceeds Local Area Network (LAN) adapter capacity, you are left with two options; the first is to reduce that load on the adapter or upgrade to a higher-speed network interface. For applications that require high-speed and low-latency connections, it is best to place all of your VMs on the same hypervisor and use machine images that have 10Gbps Ethernet adapters installed for maximum bandwidth.

Bandwidth capacity from the cloud to the Internet can be a potential bottleneck. Public clouds will own this part of the network including management and troubleshooting. If it is a private cloud, you may have greater control over bandwidth capacity and utilization. If so, it will be your responsibility to work with your network carriers to increase the speed of your existing connection or add additional circuits.

Network capacity starvation can lead to latency and degraded performance. Applications may time out, and for e-commerce sites, result in high customer dissatisfaction.

Cloud Batch Job Scheduling

Scheduling large cloud processing jobs can cause capacity issues in your cloud fleet. You will have your jobs scheduled ahead of the event, and this may entail purchasing compute instances on the spot, which may or may not be accepted. You can monitor the operation on your management servers to make sure that adequate resources have been applied for the batch job to run as expected. Troubleshooting may be required if the resources failed to deploy properly or the application failed. These issues can be reduced with offline modeling prior to deployment. The cloud's just-in-time metered service model allows you to test deployments ahead of them being placed into production and then to delete the test servers when the validation is complete.

Large batch reports are often run on databases residing in the cloud. The jobs can cause contention with the production database replicas. If this is the issue, your database may slow down and cause a chain reaction of performance issues. If this is the case, it is often a best practice to create a separate read replica and run batch jobs from that, which frees up I/O to be used by the primary production application.

Compute Resources

A finite number of CPU cycles is available. It is common for operating systems and applications to consume as much CPU power as possible. If it is there, use it! This allows for high-performance servers and applications with good response times. When you define your machine image, you request the speed of the CPU and number of cores. Prior to migrating to the cloud, it is helpful to get a measurement of the processing power used prior to the migration. If it is a new deployment, you may have to rely on vendor documentation or what others have experienced.

Operating systems have utilities that monitor CPU utilization at the VM level and also at the hypervisor level. This, of course, is a critical object to measure and track. With current measurements, deltas and trends can be determined from your baseline, and remediation can be performed prior to this becoming a serious issue.

In the event of CPU starvation, the only option is to either reduce what is consuming the resources, admittedly not always a viable option, or add CPU resources.

Network Addressing

IP addressing is another area where capacity plays an important role. When you configure your cloud deployment, one of the configuration points is the size of the network subnets that are determined by the IP address block's subnet mask. Make sure that you specify a subnet that is large enough not only for current requirements but also takes into account future growth.

The lesson here is to specify your subnets to have enough capacity that you will not exceed them in the future. Readdressing your devices is not anything you would ever care to do. However, you can usually add more subnets and route between them as a good solution.

When designing and assigning your network addresses, be aware that there may be reserved addresses that you cannot use. Some of these may be for the default gateway, DNS, NTP, or any number of services. These will be documented by the cloud provider.

Storage Capacity

One cloud resource that always seems to grow and grow is storage. Storage volume utilization can be tracked as a managed object, and triggers can be configured to alert operations at a predefined usage threshold. Managing storage capacity is a critical task; if a storage volume fills up, applications can fail, and data can be lost. Watch this closely!

To resolve storage capacity problems, you can migrate the data to a larger volume, or if you have elastic storage volumes, increase the capacity.

Variance in Number of Users

When collecting data for your baselines and ongoing operations, the number of concurrent users on the platform is a useful metric to track. Usage can show you how many users are visiting your site over time and display valuable information on peaks and valleys of usage by the hour, day, and month. Site activity can, of course, be an important measurement for planning additional capacity.

When troubleshooting cloud performance issues, the current number of users on the system can be an important indicator of load. When there are high user counts, you can track what parts of your deployment are most heavily used and track the load on all the devices to see where the congestion points are. Also, tracking users and the variance from your baseline is critical to managing software license models based on user counts. Many identity access control systems have maximum user hard limits that need to be monitored and managed.

Exceeding Your Baseline Measurements

In many ways, exceeding the baselines that you have created, monitored, and managed is a good outcome. When you exceed the metrics of the past, it can be a measurement of success in that your operations are growing and expanding. This is what you could call a "high-quality problem!"

Growing and expanding your operations is a measure of success. You just need to track and manage the growth. If you are proactive and deploy the needed modifications before any performance or capacity issues are realized, you are an effective Cloud+ professional!

By tracking your growth and comparing current workloads to those on your baseline measurements, you can be prepared to troubleshoot and manage you cloud fleet proactively. This chapter offers examples of common objects, services, and systems that you may need to troubleshoot. Be prepared and you can either avoid or be ready to troubleshoot cloud problems as they arise.

Expecting the Unexpected, Unplanned Expansions

As any longtime information technology professional will tell you, "Expect the unexpected, and you will not be surprised when it comes." Be prepared and have solid notes, diagrams, configuration documentation, and logs. Know how to quickly access them and make sure they are reachable during an outage. Think through and brainstorm with your co-workers various scenarios and how to quickly and effectively deal with them.

Growth in business operations or through mergers and acquisitions can challenge your expansion planning. However, the on-demand rapid provisioning model of cloud computing allows you to rapidly deploy additional resources to meet these needs. With clarity of what your deployment currently is and what you need to add, you can architect the changes and manage a smooth deployment to meet your new requirements.

Troubleshooting Automation and Orchestration

This section covers automation and orchestration service troubleshooting. You learned earlier in the chapter that oftentimes these systems are going to be out of your reach to troubleshoot and manage because they are controlled by the cloud service provider. If you are operating in a public cloud environment, then you should have more access to the underlying code to troubleshoot automated cloud applications.

You can compare the input to the output of automation and orchestration systems to determine whether what you requested was what was actually delivered. Based on the results of your troubleshooting, you can either open a trouble ticket with the public cloud company or work internally with your development teams to troubleshoot the issue.

Many of these systems are in the public software domain and supported with the open community model. If this is the case, you can be assured that if you are seeing a problem, many others are as well. Check the online support boards and discussion groups and participate in the resolution of the issue you are troubleshooting.

Process and Workflow Issues

Many problems can be traced back to process, planning, implementation, and validation deficiencies. These issues tend to get worked out over time as you gain experience operating in a cloud environment. In the following sections, you will become familiar with some of the more common process and workflow issues. With a basic understanding of these issues, you should be able to more effectively deal with them should they ever arise.

Account Mismatch

Accounts include users and groups that are defined in the cloud management console. Once a user is defined, the user can be either placed into a group of other users with the same job function, such as storage operators, or assigned privileges directly.

Should these privileges not match what is required for either the user or group of users to do their jobs, you may be called upon to troubleshoot the issue. You need to determine what rights are needed. Are they valid rights for these users and groups to assume, and are they correctly defined in the identity and access console in the cloud?

Since this can be a security issue, it is important that you make sure all of the approvals are in place and then verify, via the console, that the accounts are correctly configured for their intended roles.

Change Management Breakdowns

What happens when two changes are approved for the same night and the same time but the network guys take their downtime at the same time the server team is trying to install patches across the network? Well, nothing happens for the server team until the network engineers bring up the LAN so the servers can reach remote resources. This is just one of many examples of the hidden complexities of the change management process. There are many dependencies, and they all must be investigated to make sure that one operation does not have a negative impact on other changes planned at the same time.

As you have already learned, change management requires a written plan that includes all contingencies as well as participating in change review meetings to discuss upcoming changes. During the change window, you must be prepared to react to anything that can go wrong. For example, the server team must be able to react if the network is down and cannot access the needed files. If the team is in the middle of upgrading the servers and the network goes down, there needs to be a contingency plan to roll back any of the changes if required.

Afterward, action reports and reviews can be useful to discuss what went wrong, why, and what can be done to prevent a recurrence of the same issue from happening again.

DNS and Server Name Changes

Sometimes workflow problems are the subtle but important changes that need to be made but are easy to overlook. Once you forget these types of issues once, I guarantee that you will always remember them going forward!

DNS maps human-readable domain names to the IP addressing scheme used by the Internet. It's just like a phone directory that tells you Bob is at 555-1212. So, if you, for example, change a server's IP address or add a new load balancer to your deployment, there will be a DNS change or addition.

Since most services and users call the devices by their domain name, you must have defined the DNS entry. If you failed to make the DNS record entry, then the device will not be reachable unless you happen to know its IP address.

Keep this in mind when troubleshooting connectivity issues, primarily if there are time-outs or services that just never respond to connection requests. The nslookup utility really comes in handy for troubleshooting DNS problems; it allows you to query a DNS server using a command line where you enter the domain name and the DNS server replies with the IP address or an error message if there is no record. This allows you to see whether there is anything in the DNS server's database for that domain name or whether the information is inaccurate.

Incompatibility of Automation Tools

With so many components and with each service in the cloud being driven by software and automation, it is inevitable that there are going to be software compatibility issues. One moment everything is working fine, and then after the overnight changes, nothing seems to work. This can often be traced to incompatibility between orchestration or automation tools and the systems they are intended to communicate with.

When these types of issues are reported, it is helpful to query all the active parties involved to see what was changed since the systems reporting the error were last operational. It can often be traced to a patch being applied or an application being upgraded that caused the automation systems to no longer be able to communicate. Are there new API security requirements, or did the communications' interface change? Are there new user rights issues that require you to change your existing identity and access manager configurations? Sometimes a solid review of your logging files will provide information on where and what the issue is.

If you are using a public cloud service model, then the automation and orchestration systems will be out of your direct control as they are owned and managed by the public cloud provider. Your only real option is to open a trouble ticket to track the resolution with them. If the maintenance of the systems are in-house as is usually the case in a private cloud, then you can work with your internal development groups to troubleshoot and resolve the problem.

IP Address Changes

Changing your IP addressing scheme requires careful planning and a thorough validation after the changes have been implemented. You just learned about the importance of keeping the DNS records up-to-date. In addition to DNS, you must also verify that any access control lists that reference the old IP address be modified to reflect the new address. This is also the case for firewall rules and network routing tables. Also, the devices connected, such as servers or storage devices that have IP addresses assigned to their interfaces, will need to be reconfigured and tested. This project can often become a larger than expected undertaking.

A carefully outlined change management plan will be invaluable in defining the steps required during an address change readdressing project, including the testing and validation process and, if needed, how to back out.

Location Changes

Moving a deployment to another location can be completely transparent or a huge change management project! Most cloud providers have multiple availability zones in their cloud regions and can move services and servers automatically from one to the other should there be an outage. This level of resiliency is commonly automated in the SaaS model. If you are deploying your own applications, it is often up to you to design for changes. While every cloud provider is different, they all have methods and process to allow you to change locations with little or no impact to your production operations.

Should the plan be to move services from one region to another, then you can expect some downtime to shut down services in one region and bring them up in another. These types of changes should be well-planned and tested prior to implementing to make sure all goes well.

Possibly the most complex location change is migrating between service providers or deployment models. For example, moving from your company's internal data center to a public cloud's SaaS offering is a significant change. One of the advantages of the public cloud is the ability to turn up a test fleet of servers and then delete it when you are finished. You pay a minimal amount of money to build a test bed prior to deployment. You should take advantage of this flexibility and completely test your migration offline well in advance of making the changes. This allows you to fully plan and document location changes and helps to ensure a smooth transition.

Version and Feature Mismatch Issues

Many applications have dependencies on others. As you go through your change management process of applying patches, hot fixes, upgrades, and feature enhancements, you may encounter mismatch problems between applications.

The application vendor may have done regression tests as part of its quality assurance processes and then posted the test results for you to review. If there are any problems with versioning, you can tell well ahead of time and plan accordingly. Investigate all documentation and carefully read all release notes. A lot of planning up front here can save you from many problems later.

However, if you make changes to your cloud deployment and then your systems no longer communicate with each other or to the outside world with browser issues, for example, then you may have a critical situation that requires immediate troubleshooting.

Collect all log files and any symptoms and document what was changed and what the corresponding symptoms were. Make sure that all interested parties, such as the virtualization, networking, security, storage, or application teams, are involved in the troubleshooting. Also, check that all of the required features have been enabled and that their licensing requirements are valid.

Work Validation Issues

When performing a change management operation, you have learned that you must then test to make sure the change was implemented correctly and is operating as expected. This is commonly referred to as *validations*. This is an important operation as it is critical that the change management process is followed and that when systems get put back into production, they are operating as expected.

However, how do you know if the validation was accurate and complete in the first place? What if you performed the validation and learned after the system went live that there was a fatal flaw? The lesson here is that you need to make sure that the validation plan is complete, thorough, and accurate.

Testing for proper operation will include testing to make sure the intended fix or feature upgrade is now in place after the change. You can also ask the organization publishing the fix what their testing and validation methodology was. You can then incorporate their test suites into your validation documentation. A common practice is to also add tests to verify that what was originally working still works! Look at closely related features to the ones that you changed and run several tests to make sure they are operating as they were before the upgrades.

Peer review can be helpful when creating validation plans. It is a good practice to sit down with your peers and mark up the validation plans to constantly improve them. Over time you will build a library of validation test plans that are reusable.

Summary

This chapter covered troubleshooting and investigated many of the services and components that you may be called upon to troubleshoot.

There are hundreds of services available in the cloud, and most of them are interconnected, or interoperate, in a limitless number of combinations. To be effective in supporting and troubleshooting your cloud deployment, it is important that you have an in-depth knowledge of your systems, configuration repositories, diagrams, and extensive documentation. As you no know, this is a huge topic area that a whole bookshelf full of volumes discussing the subject could not completely cover. What is expected is that you have an awareness of the main troubleshooting areas covered in this chapter and be able to identify the key points discussed on the exam.

Common cloud issues that may require troubleshooting include automation, interoperability, interconnections, software language support, licensing, networking, resource contention and starvation, outages, template issues, time synchronization, and workflows.

All of these issues (and more) will require that the Cloud+ professional have an understanding of what these systems are, what they do, and how to resolve issues as they arise. You were given an overview of each and learned how to troubleshoot each one. Many of the troubleshooting techniques are universal so they can be applied to any cloud model of provider offerings. However, most cloud companies will offer their own interfaces and have different polices on what you can access and what is internal to the provider.

As your operations grow, it can be expected that what worked yesterday may not be sufficiently robust enough to work tomorrow. You learned about capacity issues and how to measure changes against your baselines. The capacity issues covered in this chapter include API request capacity, network bandwidth, batch job scheduling, compute resources, licensing, network address constraints, and making sure your systems can handle the required number of users accessing the system.

When the baseline measurements are consistently exceeded, actions must be taken to ensure your system has the resources needed to meet demand. How to determine where the capacity issues are using baseline comparisons and then adding resources to address the capacity shortage were outlined. There may be times when unexpected growth or unplanned expansions are going to need to be performed, and a solid understanding of these issues is necessary. This chapter discussed a basic plan on how to undertake cloud expansions.

Modern cloud systems are a marvel in their automation and orchestration capabilities. However, when automated systems fail or do not operate as expected, your job as a Cloud+ professional can get very interesting very quickly! You were given an overview of these software-based systems and what to look for in performing basic troubleshooting. You will most certainly come across issues with automation tools that do not work well with the services the automation systems are configuring. It was noted that automation and orchestration systems may be the responsibility of the cloud provider, and tips were given on how to proceed in these situations.

Cloud processes and workflows tend to get refined over time as you gain experience in your operations. Common topics include defining accounts to match your requirements, dealing with conflicts, and creating workflow sequences in the change management process. These are critical to understand and resolve to prevent a recurrence of the same issues. You learned about how to keep your DNS and server records up-to-date with changes such as IP address migrations.

Changes to your cloud fleet are a fact of life, and the change management process helps to lesson any problems by undergoing a structured planning process. Some of the changes may include moving your cloud operations to a new location or having to change the network address scheme to either segment the network or to expand. These can be rather drastic changes, and proper planning, including how to validate the changes, was introduced in this chapter.

Exam Essentials

Know the key concepts of troubleshooting. Keep up-to-date documentation of your network, backup of current configurations, and current diagrams. You may be asked questions about planning for outages or basic troubleshooting preparedness and what records you should have available.

Know the basics of common problems that require troubleshooting. While there are limitless issues that may require troubleshooting, for the exam be prepared for scenario-based questions that will ask you to select a specific service from multiple choices.

Explain capacity-related issues and how to identify and resolve them. The exam may quiz you on capacity starvation and verify that you know how to troubleshoot issues such as CPU, memory, network, licensing, API requests, or storage limitations and then how to resolve the problems once they have been identified.

Know how to identify and troubleshoot workflow issues. Workflows include account mismatches; failures in the change management process; and critical changes in IP, DNS, server names, or locations. The exam will present these topics as scenario questions where you are expected to identify the underlying issues.

Understand automation and orchestration. You will be expected to know how to validate that the automation and orchestration systems perform as expected and how to troubleshoot any problems. You need to understand that these systems are often the responsibility of the service provider and that you will need to rely on them to perform any troubleshooting.

Written Lab

Fill in the blanks for the questions provided in the written lab. You can find the answers to the written labs in Appendix B.

1. ___Templates___ are software representations of network systems.
2. ___NTP(123)___ _____ allows all devices to synchronize to a central time service.
3. ___Capacity___ can be defined as the maximum amount that something can contain or support.
4. In the event of CPU capacity starvations, you can either ___reduce load___ or ___add___ ___capacity___.
5. Expansion planning can be unexpectedly challenged by ___Mergers___ and ___Acqusition___.
6. DNS maps the ___Domain name___ to an ___IP___ _____.
7. After implementing a change, you should always ___validate___ that it is working as expected.
8. A centralized collection of device activity, known as ___log files___, assists in analyzing events during troubleshooting.
9. ___Configurations___ backups are valuable for quick restoration of a failed cloud service.
10. Proper network ___diagrams___ allow for a visual representation of your cloud deployment and facilitate troubleshooting.

Review Questions

The following questions are designed to test your understanding of this chapter's material. For more information on how to obtain additional questions, please see this book's introduction. You can find the answers in Appendix A.

1. Common cloud resources in your deployment that may saturate over time include which of the following? (Choose three.)

   A. RAM
   B. Power
   C. CPU
   D. Storage
   E. Monitoring
   F. IaaS

2. Connie has noticed an increase in the response time of the SQL database application she runs in her IaaS deployment. When comparing current results against her baseline measurements that she recorded when the database was deployed, she verified that there has been a steady increase in the number of read requests. What should she focus her troubleshooting on?

   A. Memory
   B. CPU
   C. Storage
   D. Networking

3. What are recommended procedures to take when preparing an outage response plan? (Choose three.)

   A. Configuration backups
   B. SLA
   C. Documentation
   D. Diagrams
   E. PaaS

4. Jeff has been monitoring resource usage increases in his web server farm. Based on trending data he has collected, there will be regular requirements to increase CPU capacity for his web servers as usage increases. Jeff wants to use the automation capabilities of his private cloud to automatically use the orchestration software to add CPU cores as required. What can he implement to automate this?

   A. Puppet
   B. Chef
   C. Docker
   D. Autoscaling

    E. SaaS

    F. OpenStack

    G. Resilient-scaling

5. Sharon posted a new software update to her company's popular smartphone application. After announcing the release, she has been monitoring her dashboard information and has noticed a large spike in activity. What cloud resource should she focus on?

    A. CPU

    B. Network bandwidth

    C. RAM

    D. API

    E. Storage

6. Jim has added a new group of users to his IaaS-based NoSQL database. What license requirements does he need to investigate to ensure compliance? (Choose all that apply.)

    A. Total connections

    B. Named users

    C. Current connections

    D. Usage metrics

    E. All of the above

7. Hank designed an application tier for his company's new e-commerce site. He decided on using an IP subnet that uses a /28 IPv4 subnet. He is planning for a maximum of 14 servers. You are brought in as a cloud architect to validate his design. What other devices may be on this subnet other than the servers that would also require IP address assignments? (Choose three.)

    A. SLA

    B. Default gateway

    C. DNS

    D. NTP

    E. API

    F. SNMP

8. Dale has been monitoring storage volume utilization and is writing a change request to add capacity. He has decided to automate the volume allocation size. What cloud feature can he take advantage of?

    A. SaaS

    B. API

    C. Elasticity

    D. OpenStack

9. Performance issues are measured by the load on a system. Which of the following should Jane be concerned about as she integrates her new marketing group into her PaaS cloud fleet?

   A. APIs

   B. Users

   C. Cores

   D. Licensing

10. Cloud capacity can be measured by comparing current usage to what?

    A. Orchestration

    B. Automation

    C. NTP

    D. Baseline

    E. APIs

11. SaaS orchestration systems are whose responsibility in the public cloud?

    A. Customer

    B. Provider

    C. Automation vendor

    D. DevOps

12. During a recent downtime window, the server team was applying patches to an application, and the networking team was upgrading a router's interface to 10Gbps. When the network was down for the upgrade, the server team complained that they could not download the needed software patches. During a post-downtime status meeting, it was determined that which process should be modified to prevent this from happening in the future?

    A. Orchestration

    B. Automation

    C. Change management

    D. API calls

13. Jerry is expanding a public subnet in his company's e-commerce site. After performing the address change for all of his public-facing web servers, he tested connecting from a bastion host located offshore. He was unable to connect. What does he need to change to allow the remote site to connect to the web server?

    A. NTP

    B. STP

    C. DNS

    D. API

14. What are software representations of a cloud network?

    A. Automation

    B. Templates

    C. Orchestration

    D. APIs

15. What application tracks a process from start to finish?

    A. API

    B. NTP

    C. Workflow

    D. Orchestration

16. Capacity boundaries can cause which of the following? (Choose three.)

    A. Application failure

    B. Latency

    C. API abends

    D. Request drops

    E. Workflow loops

17. API request capacity is measured with what metric?

    A. Total lookups per second

    B. Connections per second

    C. Burst capacity

    D. IOPS

18. Large batch processing jobs are common for which type of application?

    A. DNS

    B. NTP

    C. Databases

    D. Middleware

19. When configuring a machine image, what compute resources do you define? (Choose two.)

    A. Slots

    B. Cores

    C. Clock speed

    D. Threads

20. What determines the size of a group of servers sharing the same network range?

    A. Default gateway

    B. DNS

    C. NTP

    D. Subnet

Chapter

10

Troubleshooting Networking and Security Issues and Understanding Methodologies

THE FOLLOWING COMPTIA CLOUD+ EXAM OBJECTIVES ARE COVERED IN THIS CHAPTER:

✓ **5.4 Given a scenario, troubleshoot connectivity issues.**

- Common networking issues

  - Incorrect subnet

  - Incorrect IP address

  - Incorrect gateway

  - Incorrect routing

  - DNS errors

  - QoS issues

  - Misconfigured VLAN or VXLAN

  - Misconfigured firewall rule

  - Insufficient bandwidth

  - Latency

  - Misconfigured MTU/MSS

  - Misconfigured proxy

- Network tool outputs

- Network connectivity tools

  - ping

  - tracert/traceroute

- telnet
- netstat
- nslookup/dig
- ipconfig/ifconfig
- route
- arp
- ssh
- tcpdump
- Remote access tools for troubleshooting

✓ **5.5   Given a scenario, troubleshoot security issues.**

- Authentication issues
  - Account lockout/expiration
- Authorization issues
- Federation and single sign-on issues
- Certificate expiration
- Certification misconfiguration
- External attacks
- Internal attacks
- Privilege escalation
- Internal role change
- External role change
- Security device failure
- Incorrect hardening settings
- Unencrypted communication
- Unauthorized physical access
- Unencrypted data
- Weak or obsolete security technologies
- Insufficient security controls and processes
- Tunneling or encryption issues

✓ **5.6 Given a scenario, explain the troubleshooting methodology.**

- Always consider corporate policies, procedures and impacts before implementing changes
  - Identify the problem
    - Question the user and identify user changes to the computer and perform backups before making changes
  - Establish a theory of probable cause (question the obvious)
    - If necessary, conduct internal or external research based on symptoms
  - Test the theory to determine cause
    - Once the theory is confirmed, determine the next steps to resolve the problem
    - If the theory is not confirmed, reestablish a new theory or escalate
  - Establish a plan of action to resolve the problem and implement the solution
  - Verify full system functionality and, if applicable, implement preventive measures
  - Document findings, actions, and outcomes

In this final chapter, the focus will again be on networking and, specifically, the tools and techniques that you can use to identify and resolve network-related problems. In the previous chapter, I introduced network troubleshooting for interconnections, capacity issues, bandwidth, and addressing limitations.

I will go into much more detail in this final chapter and cover the many tools that can be used to gather information and resolve networking problems. While networking is a topic area of its own, for the Cloud+ exam you need to focus on the specific areas of networking that you will most likely encounter.

Security configurations and troubleshooting have become critical areas of concern for companies deploying services in the cloud. Throughout this book, I have discussed many different aspects of security. In this chapter, I will cover how to troubleshoot your security objects.

You will also learn about the processes of different troubleshooting approaches that will make you more effective as a Cloud+ professional.

Troubleshooting Cloud Networking Issues

Networking plays a critical role in the cloud just as it does for any data center or corporate operation. When the network is not fully functional, all of the services connected to it may be degraded or fail. With networks being the lifeline of any corporation, it is absolutely critical that you be able to quickly and effectively resolve issues with the network as they arise.

While CompTIA offers certification specific to networking, it also expects cloud engineers to be familiar with networking.

Cloud providers will be responsible for the core network in their facilities. This includes the connections to the Internet and high-speed fiber links that interconnect cloud zones and regions. The backbone switching and routing inside the data centers will also be managed by the cloud companies. The separation of responsibilities will be outlined in the service level agreement, with associated uptime commitments.

Depending on the cloud services you have implemented, you may be responsible for many network-related technologies such as IP addressing, Virtual Private Networks (VPN) or direct interconnections, local routing configurations, and network services such as Domain Name System (DNS) and dynamic Host Configuration Protocol (DHCP).

In the all too likely event of a network impairment or outage, you must be able to determine where the problem is originating from and who has the ultimate responsibility for resolution. In this section, you will learn about identifying issues as they arise.

Identifying the Common Networking Issues in the Cloud

A common networking issue covered on the exam is the IP addressing plan for your deployment. You must understand not only the actual IP address but also subnetting, understand what a gateway is, and possess a basic knowledge of routing. This section will introduce you to addressing, subnetting, gateways, and troubleshooting.

Network latency is the actual delay, or time, required for data to traverse across a network. While some delay is inevitable, if the network latency becomes too great, you will experience application issues. I will discuss latency in this section.

When a network becomes congested, you are able to configure quality of service (QoS) parameters that allow for the prioritization of certain traffic types over others. This section covers QoS as is required for the Cloud+ exam and as it pertains to cloud computing in general.

Network services such as Domain Name System servers, firewalls, and proxy systems play an important role in a well-designed network. You will become familiar with these services and gain a basic understanding of how to troubleshoot them.

At the lower levels of the cloud network, configuration and troubleshooting of Virtual Local Area Network (VLAN)/Virtual Extensible LANs (VXLAN) and frame size must be addressed. You will be given a basic overview in this section so you can be aware of the configurations of networks at the data-link layer.

Incorrect Subnet Issues

In the cloud or a private data center, application servers are commonly grouped together in the same IP subnet and VLAN. By architecting the network in this manner, you ensure that the devices can send data directly to each other on the network and not have to traverse a router interface to a remote network. This decreases the network workload and increases performance since all communications remain local.

For security reasons, when servers are grouped together in the same subnet, efficient firewall rules can be created to restrict and permit what traffic is allowed to and from the subnet.

The IP address contains two sections. The first bits in the 32-bit address block identify the network number, and the remaining bits are the hosts, or devices, inside that network. The addressing is flexible and can be adjusted using what is known as a *subnet mask*. The mask determines the total number of hosts on each network. All hosts will contain this mask information to determine which network they are on. The subnet masks must exactly match, or you will have network connectivity problems with the incorrectly configured resources.

Your documentation will contain your addressing scheme, show the subnets in use, and provide you with the correct subnet mask and address blocks. With this information, you can investigate the interface configurations and verify that the IP address, subnet mask, and default gateway are correct.

Incorrect IP Addressing

IP addressing is required for all devices connected to the network to be able to communicate. When deploying a new presence in the cloud, part of the engineering, design, and architecture process includes creating an IP address scheme. At implementation time, a validation test will verify that the addressing is configured correctly and is operational.

When IP addressing issues arise after a network has been deployed, troubleshooting should include asking whether there were any changes made recently. If so, investigate what was changed and whether that could have created the issues you are troubleshooting.

IP addresses must be in the correct range for the subnet they are residing on. If they are out of range, they will not be able to communicate with devices inside or outside of the network. Also, some addresses in the subnet will be reserved for networking services. This is especially true for the default gateway's IP address, which, by convention, is the lowest number in the range. The block range and reserved IP addresses are integral parts of your documentation.

One of the more common addressing issues occurs when two devices on the same network are configured with the same address. This is not valid as each device must have a unique address. Just think of the confusion if the same phone number were assigned to more than one person! The symptoms of duplicate IP assignments are intermittent communications. Using the ping utility, verify that you are getting a 100 percent response rate from a host on the same subnet. If it is anything less, investigate a duplicate IP address issue. You can also look at the ARP table and see if a MAC address mapped to an IP address changes to another address. This indicates that an IP address is assigned to two or more devices and is an invalid configuration.

Incorrect Default Gateways and Routing

The term *default gateway* can be misleading since a gateway is now called a *router*. But a default gateway is the IP address on the interface on the router on the local subnet that connects to the outside world. It gives computers on one network a path to other networks.

For example, a cloud web server that serves content to the Internet will reply by first sending the data to the default gateway router, which, in turn, forwards the data to the destination on the Internet.

Each device connected to the network must have knowledge of the router's address to send data to the outside world. This is commonly called the *default gateway IP address*. Your network documentation should include the IP address for its locally connected interface.

When a device is sending data to the network, it first looks to see whether the destination is local or remote. If the endpoint is local, the data is delivered directly to that device. However, if the reply is destined for a remote network, the server will not have any knowledge of where it is, other than that it is not local. In this case, the data frame is passed to the default gateway, or router, which, based on its routing tables, has knowledge of where to send the data.

When troubleshooting a networking scenario where you can use ping to connect to devices on the same subnet but are unable to connect to anything outside of the subnet, check the default gateway configuration on the local host and ping the default gateway's IP address. If you can ping the gateway, the local configuration should be good, and there is most likely a routing issue.

Network Infrastructure Troubleshooting

Generally, the infrastructure in the cloud data center is the responsibility of the cloud service provider. For example, power, cooling, physical security, and all other facilities-related components are owned by the cloud provider. With this separation of responsibilities, all infrastructure will be managed by the cloud provider.

It is common for cloud providers to publish uptime and status reports on a browser-accessible dashboard. These dashboard services allow you to monitor the status of all facilities for alarms and will outline any current issues the cloud provider may be experiencing.

Network Latency Troubleshooting

As defined earlier, *network latency* is the delay, or time, it takes for data to traverse a network. Delay can be important for applications such as voice and live video that will experience performance degradation in high-latency networks. For example, if the network imposes long delays that companies use for voice traffic, it can be difficult for the two parties talking on the phone to communicate. When applications and storage data are transitioned to the cloud, they must be accessed remotely. This contributes to congested networks that lead to delays because packets must contend for limited network bandwidth. Network response time becomes critical, and the latency in the network when accessing the cloud is a critical factor in network performance.

Electrons and photons in a network travel near the speed of light at 186,000 miles per second, which is the baseline speed of data passing through a copper wire or fiber-optic cable. However, if the data uses a satellite, significant delays will be incurred even at this speed because of the distances involved with going from the earth up to the satellite and back down again. There is also latency when the data must be buffered inside a switch or router as it is queued for transmission or processed for compression. The processing time to take a byte of data and serialize it to be transmitted and then reassembled at the remote location also adds to the latency. It is important to remember that you should calculate the end-to-end latency as your primary measurement and not the latency of each individual device in the patch from the source to the destination.

Many network management tools as well as integrated test capabilities in the network gear can track latency and even generate alerts if latency exceeds a predefined threshold.

Network latency is the delay incurred as a frame traverses the network. Each network device will receive the frame, compute a Cyclic Redundancy Check (CRC) error check, look up the exit interface, and send the frame out that interface. There are also delays in the serialization of the frame to exit the interface. When the frame passes through a firewall, it will be compared against the firewall rule set to determine if it is permitted or denied, and the data will be delayed during this process. If there is contention in the network, the frame may be buffered until network bandwidth becomes available. Quality-of-service policies may allow higher-priority frames to be forwarded and lower-priority frames to be buffered, which can also contribute to network latency. Figure 10.1 shows end-to-end latency.

FIGURE 10.1   Latency is an end-to-end network delay.

Network latency can vary widely in the cloud data center given the bursty nature of Local Area Network (LAN) traffic and orchestration systems constantly adding and moving VMs and causing constant changes in network traffic flows. In the cloud backbone network, higher-speed interfaces are deployed with link aggregation that can reduce latency.

In the data center, latency can be controlled, monitored, and managed to ensure that it does not affect applications or user experiences. However, outside the cloud data center on the Internet, latency can be a much larger issue and out of your area of control. With the increase in smartphones and mobile technology, latency can vary widely as you move from one cell tower to the next, for example.

Network monitoring systems and benchmarks will record standard latency and may also report current metrics. A simple ping test from the source device to the remote will report, as part of its standard output, what the end-to-end delays are across the network from the source to the destination and back again.

Domain Name System

There are many different network services in the cloud. These can include load balancers, firewalls, IDSs/IPSs, and DNS and DHCP devices, to name a few.

DNS will need regular configuration updates as hosts and devices are added to, and removed from, the network. "A" records that map the domain name to the IP address need to be changed every time a device's name has been modified, deleted, or added. While many cloud providers offer DNS services, it is usually your responsibility to actually mange the day-to-day operations of DNS.

Troubleshooting will consist of verifying that the current configuration of the DNS records matches the addressing in each server. If there is a mismatch, devices trying to reach a host in your cloud fleet by its domain name may be offered an incorrect IP address that causes the requesting device to contact the incorrect server. Use the nslookup or dig utility to query the DNS server and verify that it is returning accurate information for the record you are troubleshooting. Also, to make sure that the DNS servers are reachable on the network, run a standard ping test. If the ping test fails, a traceroute to the server will show where along the path the traffic is stopping.

Quality of Service

Many different types of traffic are passing through your cloud data network. Not all of this traffic is created equally. Different types of applications have very different network requirements. Actions such as transferring files or sending an e-mail message are not delay-sensitive and have no issues with being buffered because of congestion as they traverse the network from source to destination. However, other types of traffic are susceptible to latency and jitter across the network. Collaboration applications send voice and video over the same network as all other traffic. However, if voice is delayed or a video conference is losing data and suffering long delays in the network, the quality will suffer and could ultimately cause the session to fail. The concept of quality of service addresses these issues.

Quality of service (QoS) is a general networking term for the ability of the network to provide differentiated services based on information in the Ethernet packet. For example, voice and video traffic are real time and delay-sensitive, storage traffic requires a lossless connection, and mail and file transfers are not sensitive to network delays. Using QoS, the network can be configured to take the various application needs into consideration and determine the optimal ordering of traffic through the network.

TCP/IP headers have fields that tell the networking devices how their QoS values are configured. Routers can also be configured to look at the port numbers or IP addresses to configure QoS in a network. The access layer switches can either honor the QoS settings in a frame or impose their own settings by modifying or stamping QoS values into the frame.

Each device that the frame passes through must be configured to honor the QoS settings inside the frame, so the configuration can become complex. You can control QoS inside the data center but not over the Internet since the Internet backbone is beyond your administrative control. Also, if the network links are not saturated, then there is little need for QoS since there is no contention and ample bandwidth to transmit all traffic. However, when the links become saturated, then the QoS configurations can prioritize certain traffic flows over others.

For example, the long file transfers that take place during a backup can involve a large amount of data moving across the network, but it is not time-sensitive on the delivery. Also, when you send an e-mail, you are not concerned if it is sent in real time. However, if you are talking on a telephone that uses Voice over IP, you will most certainly notice delays of more than 250 milliseconds. If you are meeting over a video conference, jitter or latency in the network can cause the screen to freeze or drop.

If there is sufficient network capacity, there is available bandwidth for all traffic types. However, when the network interconnections reach 100 percent traffic load, then QoS is needed to arbitrate which traffic flows will take priority over the others. In normal operations, traffic is forwarded on a first-come, first-serve basis. QoS may be configured, but there is no current need to prioritize traffic until the network saturates.

You must also consider that the background control of the network, such as the routing protocols and the management applications, must command a high priority because if they are starved for bandwidth, the whole network could very well fail.

QoS can be configured on each step of the network that will define the priority of the traffic being sent across the network. There are many variations to QoS, and it can be a quite complex topic. Understand that each packet has information in its headers that you can use to make QoS decisions, and the network devices can be configured to act on this information and favor one type of traffic over another.

Maximum Transmission Units

The standard Ethernet frame called *Maximum Transmit Unit (MTU)* is 1,518 bytes, which defines the largest Ethernet frame size that can be transmitted into the network. Frames that are larger than the MTU are fragmented, or divided, into multiple frames to support the standard frame size. Any Ethernet frame larger than the standard size is referred to as a *jumbo frame*.

It is often more efficient to use a larger Ethernet frame size than the standard Ethernet MTU inside the data center to reduce networking overhead. Jumbo frames allow for higher network performance by reducing the overhead in each Ethernet frame by using fewer but larger frames. Jumbo frames also reduce the number of times that a CPU will be interrupted to process Ethernet traffic since each jumbo frame can be up to six times as large as a standard frame.

Jumbo frames are now common in the cloud and enterprise data centers and are extensively used for storage over LAN technologies such as Internet Small Computer Systems Interface (iSCSI) and Fibre Channel over Ethernet. Modern data center switches will usually support jumbo frames up to 9,000 bytes. To support jumbo frames in the network, you will need to enable this feature on the switches, Network Interface Cards (NIC), and any other devices in the data path.

To troubleshoot MTU issues, look at the interface statistics to see whether there is fragmentation taking place. If the MTU of a frame is too large, a router interface may fragment it into smaller frames. This is not an optimal situation, and you would need to verify that all devices in the source to destination path are configured for jumbo frames. The most common jumbo setting on network devices is 9,000 bytes, which is the standard frame size for storage traffic over the network.

Available Bandwidth

Bandwidth testing measures the throughput of the network, which directly affects the network response. A network with insufficient bandwidth will experience high latency, which may cause applications to fail or not work as expected. Many tools are available that you can use to measure network throughput. IPerf, for example, will give you a reading of the speed (in megabits per second) of the network from a source to a destination. Testing can also be as simple as downloading a large file and measuring the time the download takes to complete; based on that information, the actual network bandwidth can be calculated. It is important to note that in a cloud data center the core network will be architected with multiple high-speed Ethernet links optimized for the traffic patterns commonly found in a data center. Also, network monitoring and management systems can alert the engineering staff if the links are saturated and additional bandwidth needs to be provisioned.

Validating Firewall and Proxy Configurations

After new firewall rules have been implemented, your change management plan will call for you to validate that the rule is operating as expected. A firewall rule will have a protocol, source and destination IP addresses or domain names, application port numbers, a permit or deny statement, and usually a firewall source and destination zone.

Firewall rules are compared in a top-down operation. When there is a match, the rule is acted upon, and further rule processing is stopped. Be aware that this order of operations can produce unexpected results. For instance, if you add the new rule at the bottom of the configuration that permits all Internet traffic to connect to an File Transfer Protocol (FTP) server on one of your public-facing cloud servers, check to see whether there is not another rule above this preventing FTP access to your site that gets checked before your new rule. In this case, the FTP deny rule would be seen first, and the connection would be blocked. Since there is no more rule processing that would be done, your permit FTP rule will never be seen. The solution would be to place the FTP permit higher in the search sequence than a deny rule. Enabling logging can provide invaluable troubleshooting information when troubleshooting a firewall as the data provided in the logs will specify exactly what the firewall is processing and give details on the rules it referenced.

A proxy is a device that is inserted into the middle of a traffic flow and terminates the connections in both directions and monitors the traffic between the source and the destination. Proxy systems are found in enterprise environments and in load balancers in the cloud. When troubleshooting proxy issues, make sure that the browser or client is not misconfigured for the proxy settings and has a valid IP address, subnet mask, and default gateway. Verify that the URL of the site you are trying to reach is not down and that there are no ongoing network issues that may be the root cause of the problem. Check the log files for the device performing the proxy function that may indicate if the issue is local to the server. Test from another computer on the same subnet and a different subnet that connects through the same proxy server. Verify whether the problems are consistent or intermittent. By gathering the background information of the proxy issue, you can then work to determine where the problem resides and develop a test and resolution plan.

VLAN and VxLAN Issues

VLANs and VxLANs are layer 2 segmentation standards that allow you to take physical switches and logically divide them into many separate or individual logical switches. The IEEE 802.1D, often referred to as Dot1Q, defines VLANs that can have a maximum of 4,094 VLANs per system. This may seem like a large number, but many VLANs are reserved, and often the switches in the data center may not be able to support this maximum number. Dot1Q works by inserting a header in the Ethernet frame that identifies the VLAN that this frame belongs to. Also included in the header is the priority field that is used for QoS calculations.

When hyperscale cloud computing arrived, it was clear that the standard VLAN limit of 4,094 was insufficient. Even if every customer used just one VLAN (hint, they use many), the limit would be only around 4,000 customers! To increase the VLAN count, VxLAN was introduced. Also, traditional VLANs were intended to stay local to the data center and not be "stretched" across to a remote data center.

VxLAN radically changes the way VLANs transit a network. VxLAN is an encapsulation method. It takes an Ethernet frame and encapsulates it in an IP packet using User Datagram Protocol (UDP) as its transport. Another name for this is MAC-in-IP encapsulation (some call it MAC-in-UDP) because the layer 2 frame is untouched and wrapped in a normal IP/UDP packet.

The VxLAN header is 8 bytes, or 64 bits. The VxLAN Network Identifier (VNI) uses 24 bits of that header. The VNI is synonymous with the traditional VLAN identifier discussed. In the VxLAN case, however, the VNI scales to more than 16 million segments. These are private segments too. Show me a cloud provider that doesn't want 16 million segments belonging to millions of customers! The traditional VLAN ID maps to the VxLAN ID. For ease of use, some networks map similar numbers to a higher numerical number in VxLAN. The significance in VxLAN is the unique VxLAN ID. Each switch respects the mapping when encapsulating or removing the encapsulation. This helps cloud providers significantly, as there are more than 16 million VxLAN IDs. This solves the VLAN ID starvation aspect discussed earlier.

Automation, routing, and specialized monitoring systems track VLAN/VxLAN configurations and operations. It is important to know that layer 2 VLANs will traditionally map to a layer 3 IP subnet. When troubleshooting, make sure that these mappings are correct and that the links, or trunks, that interconnect network switches have the VLANs configured on them to enable them to pass traffic on that VLAN from one switch to another.

VxLAN troubleshooting will almost always fall to the cloud provider as this is considered infrastructure. However, by analyzing log files, vendor monitoring applications, and command-line utilities, you can uncover where the issue is originating from and begin troubleshooting.

Network Troubleshooting and Connectivity Tools

A cloud network infrastructure is usually not static; rather, it changes as new services, servers, and storage are added. In this section, you'll learn about the tools commonly used to configure and troubleshoot the cloud network infrastructure.

There are many different command-line tools and utilities that are invaluable for gathering information and for troubleshooting. You will learn about common command-line utilities found in the Windows and Linux operating systems that network engineers can use to learn how the network interfaces are configured, determine the current status of these interfaces, and gather valuable troubleshooting information. You can run commands to test connectivity, resolve domain names, look at routing tables, log into remote devices, and much more. Let's look at the most common and useful utilities for network troubleshooting.

ARP

Have you ever wondered how a workstation can find a device on a network if it does not have complete addressing information needed to reach that device? Well, if it is a TCP/ IP device (as just about everything is nowadays), it will use the *Address Resolution Protocol (ARP)*. ARP is the protocol that determines the mapping of the IP address to the physical MAC address on a local network.

By using ARP, all devices on the LAN build a table of IP to MAC address bindings. For example, a workstation may need to communicate with a server at IP address

192.168.1.123. If it is in the same VLAN, the workstation will need to know the server's physical, or MAC, address to construct an Ethernet frame with accurate source (workstation) and destination (server) MAC addresses.

The workstation will send out an ARP broadcast frame to all devices in the VLAN requesting the MAC address of the 192.168.1.123 server. All devices on the local LAN will process the ARP request, and only the device that matches the 192.168.1.123 IP address will respond with its hardware address.

When each device on the segment receives and looks into the ARP packet, it will ask, "Who has IP address 192.168.1.123?" If the receiving device is configured with that address, it will reply with "That is my IP address, and my Ethernet MAC address is attached." Then communications can proceed because the device that sent the ARP packet now has all the information it needs to communicate with the remote device. Address resolution is constantly running in the background and rarely seen unless you have a packet sniffer attached to the network. To verify that the network or host you are logged into can see the remote device's IP/MAC address, check the ARP tables when troubleshooting.

The arp command-line utility will show information on the local ARP table, as shown in the following output from a Windows server:

```
C:\Users\todd>arp -a
Interface: 192.168.1.90 — 0xa
Internet Address        Physical Address        Type
192.168.1.1             d0-39-b3-4b-a9-83       dynamic
192.168.1.67            d8-25-22-77-cb-c6       dynamic
192.168.1.71            e4-98-d6-89-cc-b0       dynamic
192.168.1.75            f0-4f-7c-f1-92-e4       dynamic
192.168.1.77            00-20-00-72-4a-fa       dynamic
192.168.1.78            a8-86-dd-9a-9d-7a       dynamic
192.168.1.80            84-a4-66-c5-a7-02       dynamic
192.168.1.83            3c-a8-2a-a2-9c-7a       dynamic
192.168.1.89            00-10-75-44-1b-ad       dynamic
192.168.1.91            00-21-70-32-81-55       dynamic
192.168.1.96            fc-db-b3-c5-31-bc       dynamic
192.168.1.249           00-02-b9-f8-cd-c0       dynamic
192.168.1.250           00-24-dc-d1-16-00       dynamic
192.168.1.251           00-0d-65-49-87-00       dynamic
192.168.1.254           d0-39-b3-4b-a9-80       dynamic
192.168.1.255           ff-ff-ff-ff-ff-ff       static
224.0.0.5               01-00-5e-00-00-05       static
224.0.0.22              01-00-5e-00-00-16       static
224.0.0.253             01-00-5e-00-00-fd       static
```

ipconfig/ifconfig

ipconfig on Windows and ifconfig on Linux are command-line utilities used to verify and configure the local network interfaces. In the following example, this workstation is running both IP versions 4 and 6, and the addressing is provided in the command output. These utilities' output can be expanded by using switches to obtain specific and detailed information. These are important troubleshooting tools to run to verify that the network interfaces are configured as expected.

```
C:\Users\todd>ipconfig
Windows IP Configuration
Ethernet adapter Local Area Connection:
Connection-specific DNS Suffix  . : attlocal.net
IPv6 Address. . . . . . . . . . : 2602:306:8b80:2570::40
IPv6 Address. . . . . . . . . . : 2602:306:8b80:2570:2d34:e50:95ef:1dcd Temporary
IPv6 Address. . . . . . . . . . : 2602:306:8b80:2570:c84b:f814:a4ce:cfe1

Link-local IPv6 Address . . . . . . . . . : fe80::2d34:e50:95ef:1dcd%10
IPv4 Address. . . . . . . . . . : 192.168.1.90
Subnet Mask . . . . . . . . . . : 255.255.255.0
Default Gateway . . . . . . . . : 192.168.1.1
```

ifconfig is the Linux utility to view and change network interface configurations.

```
host#ifconfig
eth0
Link encap:Ethernet
HWaddr 0B:55:65:DE:E9:23:F1
inet addr:192.168.28.10
Bcast:192.168.28.255
Mask:255.255.255.0
UP BROADCAST RUNNING MULTICAST  MTU:1500  Metric:1
RX packets:2472694671 errors:1 dropped:0 overruns:0 frame:0
TX packets:44641779 errors:0 dropped:0 overruns:0 carrier:0
collisions:0 txqueuelen:1000
RX bytes:1761467179 (1679.7 Mb)
TX bytes:2870928587 (2737.9 Mb)

Interrupt:28
```

netstat

netstat is a network statistics utility found on both Windows and Linux workstations and servers. You can use netstat when troubleshooting to see which network connections are open to remote applications, to view detailed protocol information, to see addresses used both locally and remotely, and to determine which state the TCP connections are currently in on the device. The basic `netstat` output is illustrated here:

```
C:\Users\todd>netstat
Active Connections
Proto  Local Address          Foreign Address            State
TCP    192.168.1.90:49546     8.18.25.62:https           ESTABLISHED
TCP    192.168.1.90:49550     unknown000d65498700:telnet ESTABLISHED
TCP    192.168.1.90:49573     ec2-107-22-225-24:http     ESTABLISHED
TCP    192.168.1.90:49576     a-0001:https               ESTABLISHED
TCP    192.168.1.90:49577     a-0001:https               ESTABLISHED
TCP    192.168.1.90:49578     a-0001:https               ESTABLISHED
TCP    192.168.1.90:58113     os-in-f188:5228            ESTABLISHED
```

There are many options for the `netstat` utility, including the one shown here where you're asking for TCP network statistics. By combining `netstat` options, you can get granular and detailed output like this:

```
C:\Users\todd>netstat -ps
IPv4 Statistics
Packets Received                     = 559794
Received Header Errors               = 0
Received Address Errors              = 35694
Datagrams Forwarded                  = 0
Unknown Protocols Received           = 0
Received Packets Discarded           = 16057
Received Packets Delivered           = 871906
Output Requests                      = 286165
Routing Discards                     = 0
Discarded Output Packets             = 75730
Output Packet No Route               = 0
Reassembly Required                  = 16241
Reassembly Successful                = 8085
Reassembly Failures                  = 0
Datagrams Successfully Fragmented    = 0
Datagrams Failing Fragmentation      = 0
Fragments Created                    = 0

ICMPv4 Statistics
                       Received     Sent
Messages               63761        31278
Errors                 0            0
Destination Unreachable 63727       31242
```

```
Time Exceeded                        27           0
Parameter Problems                    0           0
Source Quenches                       0           0
Redirects                             0           0
Echo Replies                          7           0
Echos                                 0          36
Timestamps                            0           0
Timestamp Replies                     0           0
Address Masks                         0           0
Address Mask Replies                  0           0
Router Solicitations                  0           0
Router Advertisements                 0           0
Router Renumberings                   0           0

TCP Statistics for IPv4
Active Opens                  = 6293
Passive Opens                 = 88
Failed Connection Attempt     = 50
Reset Connections             = 360
Current Connections           = 1
Segments Received             = 109317
Segments Sent                 = 83586
Segments Retransmitted        = 2593

UDP Statistics for IPv4
Datagrams Received            = 176647
No Ports                      = 234005
Receive Errors                = 1
Datagrams Sent                = 156556
```

nslookup/dig

nslookup and dig are command-line utilities used to resolve hostnames to IP addresses using a DNS server. nslookup is the Windows variant, and its Linux equivalent is called dig. If you need to learn the IP address of a domain, use these applications to resolve the DNS name to the IP address, as shown here:

```
  C:\Users\todd>nslookup
 > 8.8.8.8
Server:  dsldevice.attlocal.net
Address:  192.168.1.254
Name:    google-public-dns-a.google.com
Address: 8.8.8.8
```

dig is a Linux-based utility that serves the same function. It queries a DNS system by giving a domain name and receives the corresponding IP address. While dig has extensive command options, the basic command returns a remarkable amount of information, as shown here:

```
linux# dig www.google.com
; <> DiG 9.3.3rc2 <> www.google.com
; (1 server found)
;; global options: printcmd
;; Got answer:
;; ->>HEADER<<;; flags: qr aa rd ra; QUERY: 1, ANSWER: 1, AUTHORITY: 3, ADDITIONAL: 3
;; QUESTION SECTION:
;www.google.com. IN A
;; ANSWER SECTION:
http://www.google.com/. 43200 IN A 200.99.187.2
;; AUTHORITY SECTION:
http://www.google.com/. 43200 IN NS ns2.google.com.
http://www.google.com/. 43200 IN NS ns3.google.com.
http://www.google.com/. 43200 IN NS ns1.google.com.
;; ADDITIONAL SECTION:
ns1.google.com. 43200 IN A 222.54.11.86
ns2.google.com. 43200 IN A 220.225.37.222
ns3.google.com. 43200 IN A 203.199.147.233
;; Query time: 1 msec
;; SERVER: 222.54.11.86#53(222.54.11.86)
;; WHEN: Wed Nov 18 18:31:12 2009
;; MSG SIZE rcvd: 152
[root@tipofthehat ~]#
```

ping

ping is part of the TCP/IP family of protocols; it is used to verify that a device is available and reachable on the network and also to get a reading of the response time at that moment in time. You can send a ping packet to a remote IP address and have it return, as shown in the following example. This will tell you that the IP stack is configured correctly and that you can reach IP devices on both the local and remote networks. ping is a fundamental and frequently used troubleshooting tool for verifying network connectivity. ping is useful in verifying that the remote device is reachable and finding out if there is any packet loss from the source to the destination and back. Also, ping will show the network delays for that moment in time.

```
C:\Users\todd>ping 8.8.8.8
Pinging 8.8.8.8 with 32 bytes of data:
Reply from 8.8.8.8: bytes=32 time=177ms TTL=53
```

```
Reply from 8.8.8.8: bytes=32 time=9ms TTL=53
Reply from 8.8.8.8: bytes=32 time=9ms TTL=53
Reply from 8.8.8.8: bytes=32 time=9ms TTL=53
Ping statistics for 8.8.8.8:
Packets: Sent = 4, Received = 4, Lost = 0 (0% loss),
Approximate round trip times in milli-seconds:
Minimum = 9ms, Maximum = 177ms, Average = 51ms
```

route

The route command-line utility shown in the following example can assist you in troubleshooting network reachability issues. Use this utility when troubleshooting to look at a local workstation's or server's local routing tables. This is local to the device only and does not give you visibility into the actual network routing table.

```
C:\Users\todd>route print
===========================================================
Interface List 10…00 1e 37 1e c1 60 ......Intel(R) 82566MM Gigabit Network Connection
===========================================================
    IPv4 Route Table
===========================================================
Active Routes:
Network Destination     Netmask           Gateway        Interface       Metric
0.0.0.0                 0.0.0.0           192.168.1.254  192.168.1.90    20
127.0.0.0               255.0.0.0         On-link        127.0.0.1       306
127.0.0.1               255.255.255.255   On-link        127.0.0.1       306
127.255.255.255         255.255.255.255   On-link        127.0.0.1       306
192.168.1.0             255.255.255.0     On-link        192.168.1.90    276
192.168.1.90            255.255.255.255   On-link        192.168.1.90    276
192.168.1.255           255.255.255.255   On-link        192.168.1.90    276
192.168.74.0            255.255.255.0     On-link        192.168.74.1    276
192.168.74.1            255.255.255.255   On-link        192.168.74.1    276
192.168.74.255          255.255.255.255   On-link        192.168.74.1    276
192.168.223.0           255.255.255.0     On-link        192.168.223.1   276
192.168.223.1           255.255.255.255   On-link        192.168.223.1   276
192.168.223.255         255.255.255.255   On-link        192.168.223.1   276
224.0.0.0               240.0.0.0         On-link        127.0.0.1       306
224.0.0.0               240.0.0.0         On-link        192.168.74.1    276
224.0.0.0               240.0.0.0         On-link        192.168.223.1   276
224.0.0.0               240.0.0.0         On-link        192.168.1.90    276
255.255.255.255         255.255.255.255   On-link        127.0.0.1       306
```

```
255.255.255.255        255.255.255.255   On-link    192.168.74.1   276
255.255.255.255        255.255.255.255   On-link    192.168.223.1  276
255.255.255.255        255.255.255.255   On-link    192.168.1.90   276
===========================================================================
Persistent Routes:
None
```

SSH

Secure Shell (SSH) is the encrypted version of the Telnet protocol and is used to access remote devices using a command-line interface.

SSH, Secure Copy Protocol (SCP), and Secure File Transfer Protocol (SFTP) all use port 22 for communications. Notice that having several applications sharing the same port number is acceptable. SSH terminal applications are widely used access remote systems' command interfaces. SSH has replaced the insecure Telnet application because SSH offers an encrypted network connection. It is strongly recommended that you use SSH and avoid using Telnet.

```
$ssh todd@192.168.1.23
```

Telnet

Telnet is a virtual terminal application that allows for command-line logins to a remote device. The Telnet application will allow you to log into remote servers or network gear in the cloud as if you are locally connected to your laptop or server.

Telnet is an industry-standard application, and while still used, it is not secure in that all commands, including your username and password, are sent over the network in the clear, unencrypted. Because of this limitation, the SSH application, which sends and receives encrypted data, has largely replaced Telnet. Here's an example of logging into a remotely located network switch using Telnet:

```
telnet 192.168.1.251
User Access Verification
Username: cloudplus
Password:
Core_rtr_a>
```

tcpdump

tcpdump allows a Linux system to capture live network traffic and is useful in monitoring and troubleshooting. Sometimes called *sniffing*, tcpdump allows you to set up filters to select the traffic you are interested in capturing for troubleshooting. Think of tcpdump as a command-line network analyzer.

```
$tcpdump -v -n
tcpdump: listening on eth0, link-type EN10MB (Ethernet), capture size 65535 bytes
```

```
16:43:13.058660 IP (tos 0x20, ttl 54, id 50249, offset 0, flags [DF], proto TCP (6), length 40)
    64.41.140.209.5222 > 192.168.1.101.35783: Flags [.], cksum 0x6d32 (correct), ack 1617156745,
win 9648, length 0
16:43:13.214621 IP (tos 0x0, ttl 64, id 0, offset 0, flags [DF], proto ICMP (1), length 84)
    192.168.1.101 > 173.194.36.6: ICMP echo request, id 19941, seq 1659, length 64
16:43:13.355334 IP (tos 0x20, ttl 54, id 48656, offset 0, flags [none], proto ICMP (1), length 84)
    173.194.36.6 > 192.168.1.101: ICMP echo reply, id 19941, seq 1659, length 64
16:43:13.355719 IP (tos 0x0, ttl 64, id 0, offset 0, flags [DF], proto UDP (17), length 71)
    192.168.1.101.22181 > 218.248.255.163.53: 28650+ PTR? 6.36.194.173.in-addr.arpa. (43)
16:43:13.362941 IP (tos 0x0, ttl 251, id 63454, offset 0, flags [DF], proto UDP (17), length 223)
    218.248.255.163.53 > 192.168.1.101.22181: 28650 1/4/2 6.36.194.173.in-addr.arpa.
PTR bom04s01-in-f6.1e100.net. (195)
16:43:13.880338 ARP, Ethernet (len 6), IPv4 (len 4), Request who-has 192.168.1.3 tell 192.168.1.101,
length 28
16:43:14.215904 IP (tos 0x0, ttl 64, id 0, offset 0, flags [DF], proto ICMP (1), length 84)
    192.168.1.101 > 173.194.36.6: ICMP echo request, id 19941, seq 1660, length 64
```

tracert/traceroute

The tracert/traceroute utilities are useful for network path troubleshooting. The traceroute utility displays the routed path a packet of data takes from source to destination. You can use it to determine whether routing is working as expected or whether there is a route failure in the path. In the following code snippet, a traceroute command details the path taken out of the local network and across the Internet, along with the latency for each router hop taken to a remote destination. If a DNS name is associated with the IP address, the traceroute utility can resolve the IP address to help you identify the device that the trace utility is taking.

For Microsoft products, the command-line utility is tracert, and the traceroute command is used for Linux operating systems.

```
C:\Users\todd>tracert 8.8.8.8
Tracing route to google-public-dns-a.google.com [8.8.8.8] over a maximum of 30 hops:
1     1 ms      1 ms     1 ms    dsldevice.attlocal.net [192.168.1.254]
2   172 ms     49 ms     7 ms    108-218-244-1.lightspeed.austtx.sbcglobal.net
[108.218.244.1]
3     4 ms      5 ms     3 ms    71.149.77.70
4     5 ms      3 ms     3 ms    75.8.128.140
5     4 ms      5 ms     6 ms    12.81.225.241
6     9 ms      9 ms     9 ms    12.122.85.197
7    61 ms     59 ms    58 ms    206.121.120.66
8     9 ms      9 ms     9 ms    216.239.54.109
```

```
9     12 ms    11 ms    11 ms  72.14.234.145
10    11 ms     9 ms     9 ms  google-public-dns-a.google.com [8.8.8.8]
Trace complete
```

This is an example of traceroute with Linux:

```
$ traceroute google.com
traceroute to google.com (74.125.236.132), 30 hops max, 60 byte packets
1   118.26.54.19 (118.26.54.19)  89.174 ms   89.094 ms   89.054 ms
2   182.56.49.175 ( 182.56.49.175)  109.037 ms  108.994 ms  108.963 ms
3   16.178.22.165 (16.178.22.165)  108.937 ms  121.322 ms  121.300 ms
4   * 119.255.128.45 (119.255.128.45)  113.754 ms  113.692 ms
5   72.14.212.118 (72.14.212.118)  123.585 ms  123.558 ms  123.527 ms
6   72.14.232.202 (72.14.232.202)  123.499 ms  123.475 ms  143.523 ms
7   216.239.48.179 (216.239.48.179)  143.503 ms  95.106 ms  95.026 ms
8   bom03s02-in-f4.1e100.net (74.125.236.132)  94.980 ms  104.989 ms  104.954 ms
```

Remote Access Tools

When troubleshooting networks, it is not common that you will be directly in front of the equipment given that devices tend to be geographically dispersed and housed in secure locations. However, it is a common practice to connect to, log in, and access networks remotely. Common approaches include remotely connecting to a terminal server in the data center and logging into devices or using a standard web browser for HTTP access as most devices now have web-based consoles. Windows-based systems can be managed with the remote desktop utilities. Command-line interfaces are prevalent in most servers, security, and network systems. The secure remote access method to the CLI is to use the SHH server.

Each of these will be investigated in more detail next.

Console Port

Console ports are common in networking environments and are used to configure switches and routers from a command-line interface (CLI). Linux servers also use the console or serial ports for CLI access. In a data center, devices called *terminal servers* are deployed that have several serial ports, each cabled to a console port on a device that is being managed, as shown in Figure 10.2. This allows you to make an SSH or a Telnet connection to the terminal server and then use the serial interfaces to access the console ports on the devices you want to connect to. Also, a VM can use port redirections to connect to a physical serial port on the server for console connections.

FIGURE 10.2 Console port access

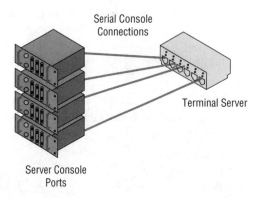

HTTP

Probably the most common and easiest way of managing remote devices is to use a standard web browser and access the remote device's web interface, as illustrated in Figure 10.3. When connected and authenticated, the web-based applications allow for a graphical interface that can be used to monitor and configure a device.

FIGURE 10.3 Console port access

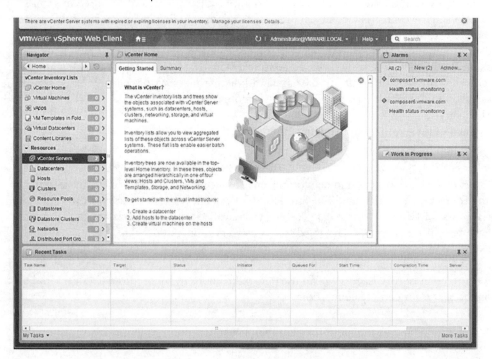

There has been a trend to move away from client applications that need to be installed on the local workstation and move everything to a web interface for ease of use. It is also common to use a web browser to connect to a hypervisor, virtual machine, or network device and then download and install the management application. HTTPS, which uses TCP port 443, is the suggested remote access protocol for web-based access since it is secure. The nonencrypted HTTP port 80 is rarely supported because of its lack of security.

RDP

The Remote Desktop Protocol (RDP) allows remote access to Windows devices. Microsoft calls the application Remote Desktop Service and in the past has called it Terminal Services. RDP is a client-server application, which means RDP has to be installed and running on both the server and the local workstation you are using to access the cloud server. The desktop application comes preinstalled on most versions of Windows.

Figure 10.4 shows a local computer running the RDP application to remotely access a cloud Windows server graphical interface.

FIGURE 10.4   Local computer running the RDP application to remotely access a cloud with a Windows server graphical interface

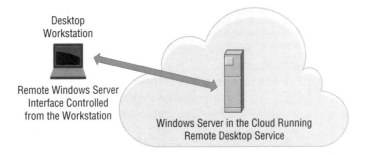

The graphical client will request the name of the remote server in the cloud, and once connected, you will be presented with a standard Windows interface to log into. Then you will see the standard Windows desktop of the remote server on your local workstation.

RDP is invaluable for managing remote Windows virtual machines since it allows you to work remotely as if you were locally connected to the server.

SSH

SSH is commonly used as a remote access utility for command-line access. The ability to support encryption and its widespread use across many different types of products and services makes it a popular application. As you learned above, the Secure Shell protocol has largely replaced Telnet as a remote access method. SSH supports encryption, whereas Telnet does not, making Telnet insecure and largely obsolete. To use SSH, the SSH service must be supported on the server or device in the cloud data center and enabled. This is pretty much standard on any Linux distribution, router, firewall, load balancer, or switch and SSH can also be installed on Windows devices.

Many SSH clients are available on the market, both commercial software and free of charge in the public domain. The SSH client connects over the network using TCP port 22 over an encrypted connection, as shown in Figure 10.5. Once you are connected, you have a command-line interface to manage your cloud services. SSH is a common remote connection method used to configure network devices such as switches and routers.

FIGURE 10.5   Secure Shell–encrypted remote access

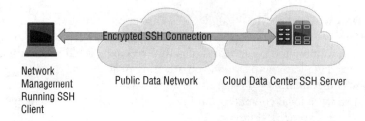

Network Management Running SSH Client   Public Data Network   Cloud Data Center SSH Server

Troubleshooting Security Issues

In this section, you will learn about troubleshooting security-related issues in the cloud. I will discuss the most common problems you will find as a cloud customer and give you insight into how to begin troubleshooting them.

Keep in mind that the cloud provider will be responsible for the security of the underlying infrastructure, and you will take responsibility for the "top of the stack." This will include the security posture of your cloud deployments. You will learn about security maintenance in troubleshooting as it relates to user accounts, sign-on issues, authentication, authorization, device hardening, and digital certificates.

Account Privilege Escalation

Privilege escalation can be defined as a user receiving account privileges that they are not allowed to possess. A storage administrator in your cloud deployment usually would not be granted full control over the firewalls, for example. If they were able to gain firewall configuration attributes, that would be an example of privilege escalation. Privilege escalation can occur because of a bug, a design oversight, or delegating user account management to a person who is willing to change user account settings without gaining necessary approvals. Figure 10.6 illustrates the account privilege escalation pyramid.

Operating systems are designed to support multiple users and support multiple accounts. It is a critical security issue to grant users access privileges to the level required for them to perform their duties but not in addition to what they need. When troubleshooting privilege escalation issues, check for up-to-date antivirus software, that the applications are running with the least privileges required for them to operate, and that, if possible, kernel applications are digitally signed. Also make sure you have configured security for mandatory access controls, as discussed in Chapter 3.

FIGURE 10.6   Account privilege escalation

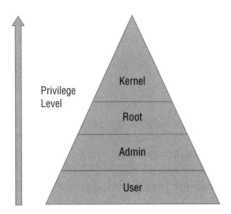

Sign-On Issues

Signing in to remote resources in the cloud has many dependencies. Access control lists and firewalls must be configured to allow you to access a cloud service with its destination IP address and port number. Often, for additional security, the source IP range from your office is added to the security rules, and if you are not connecting from that specific location (range of IP addresses), you will be denied access. Many cloud providers have device-level security groups that block incoming traffic unless it is specifically configured to allow the connection.

Account sign-in management may require two-factor or biometric authentications, which I will discuss next.

Authentication

To review from Chapter 2, *authentication* is the ability to identify who a user is, usually during the login process. Users and devices can be authenticated using a wide variety of methods. However, the most common is the standard method of a username and password. Other methods include Multi-Factor Authentication (MFA) tokens and biometrics such as fingerprint or iris scanners.

When troubleshooting authentication issues, the most valuable source of information will be in the logging files. When authentication fails, a log file will be generated and information included on the reason for the failure. Accounts can be disabled and passwords expired. Also, if the user fails after the defined number of password attempts, most systems will lock the user out, and they will not be allowed to log in.

Authorization

Once a user is authenticated, or logged into a system, they are granted or authorized rights to resources on that system. It is common that when a user is created, they are authorized to access few, if any, services. The systems administrator must grant access to each user by explicitly assigning authorizations to the account or placing that user into a group that has authorization.

When troubleshooting authorization issues, it is best to check the user's account configuration to see whether they are assigned to the required groups or have direct object authorization. Also, logging will generate records for every successful and failed authorization activity.

Confederations

Instead of managing a separate database of cloud users, federations can be used to access your on-premise user accounts such as those in Active Directory. Confederations save a lot of administrative work and serve to consolidate user permissions into a central repository. Most cloud providers offer different options to connect the cloud to these already existing user accounts. While each implementation will be different, you should closely follow the cloud provider's documentation or, if available, wizards. Once the federation connection is made, there should be monitoring and logging data available on the health of the connection. When troubleshooting federation problems, you will most likely need to get your internal directory services team involved to get visibility on both ends of the connection.

Certificate Configuration Issues

As discussed in Chapter 9, it is important to keep security certificates up-to-date and not expired. Keep track of all certificate expiration dates and renew them prior to expiration!

Certificate management can be a complex and wide-ranging topic. In cloud computing, there are many different types of certificates and a variety of services offerings that range from your organization having complete control of the security certificates to mixed offerings to the cloud provider taking responsibility for certificate management.

Troubleshooting will be dependent on your key management plan. As usual, review log files, collect and distill the information you have collected, and plan your approach to troubleshooting certificate issues. Oh, and check the expiration date!

Device-Hardening Settings

To prevent intrusions and hacks, all devices must be hardened from attacks. These processes can be rather extensive and are specific to the device or service. It is suggested that you follow the vendor or cloud provider's best practices on hardening each specific device or service. The best practices are usually published on the support websites or offered as white papers.

Follow the hardening procedures exactly as outlined, and do not hesitate to contact the document publisher should you have any questions. This is not where you want to guess or make assumptions!

After the hardening process has been completed, you must validate the configurations. Here, it is suggested that you consider contracting a third-party security testing company for impartial validation services.

External Attacks

It is common for cloud providers to provide first-level external attack protection since they control the cloud network resources. This will include denial-of-service and scanning attacks, to name a few. However, cloud providers cannot be responsible for preventing all attacks. Your monitoring systems should show anomalies away from your baseline. Many firewall systems also have the intelligence to recognize an attack and take measures to block and mitigate them. As this is occurring, you, or your monitoring systems, have access to the attack log data that should provide invaluable information about troubleshooting the attack.

There are security companies, government agencies, large carriers, and network operators that will publish "Internet health dashboards" that you can check to see the scope of the intrusion.

Identifying Weak or Obsolete Security Technologies

As part of your ongoing operations management practice, your cloud team should regularly evaluate the state of the security market and offerings. It is truly amazing how fast cloud technologies are developed and introduced to the marketplace. As the technologies are continuously being improved, by definition, many existing technologies become obsolete or do not have the critical feature sets the newer offerings have. It is critical that you follow developments offered in white papers, blogs, vendor announcements, conferences, communities of interest, and any other outlet to keep abreast of cloud security offerings and implement those that offer benefits to your organization.

Internal Attacks

Social engineering is the most predominate internal attack where someone is tricked into providing credentials or holding a door open into a secure data center, for example. Training seems to be ongoing to educate the workforce on common tracks to obtain information or access using social engineering. Use common sense and always be a bit suspicious if someone asks you to do something you do not feel comfortable with or seems out of the ordinary.

Servers can be initiated inside the security perimeter and can be configured to capture data, scan the network, or masquerade as another system. Most cloud provider security operations will shut down a device that is doing a port scan of their infrastructure. Cloud systems monitor for intrusion detection and prevention, taking the needed actions to mitigate the threat.

Maintain Sufficient Security Controls and Processes

The cloud provider will most certainly have a dedicated security department that encompasses not only security from a technology standpoint but also physical security.

Security practices are critical to avoid breaches and to keep in front of those who want to damage you or your company's reputation.

As part of an effective and complete cloud operation, your company should develop and document your security posture and controls. This should be part of your regular operations documentation and project updates.

The concept of least privilege is important as it only grants security permissions for what is actually required and nothing additional. Division of duties is common where there is no one single person who has end-to-end access responsibility. With the division of duties, a single individual cannot take control because there is a second person who has access to a critical part of the cloud that the other does not possess but needs to complete the role.

Security processes and controls are large topics that are rapidly evolving. CompTIA offers separate education tracks on security.

Network Access Tunneling and Encryption

When interconnecting networks, especially over a public network such as the Internet, it is mandatory that you encrypt all traffic from the source to the destination.

Encryption can be a complex topic, as you have learned throughout this book. Use the most current encryption types and transforms such as AES-256 to protect your data. Cloud providers commonly offer encrypted VPN connections from your facility to your cloud fleet of services. Use their best practices and follow the guidelines that they publish online. You will need this information when configuring and testing a VPN connection. Sometimes the terminology can be confusing. It is mandatory that you read the manual to make this work!

Physical Access, Infrastructure, and Availability

It is a standard policy that there be no data center access unless there is an explicit need to gain entrance. Cloud providers do not make it a practice to let visitors into their data centers. If there is a need to access the data center for vendor support, an approval process usually takes place, and if approved, access is granted for a time window that usually is during a change window.

When arriving at a cloud facility, you will be asked to provide identification and possibly a trouble or work ticket. You may have to undergo a search of your possessions that you intend to take into the data center. If you are not a regular employee, you will probably need to be escorted when inside the data center.

Data centers have elaborate security measures including locked sections and extensive video monitoring systems. Yes, you are being watched.

Cloud data centers are highly secure and often hidden away in nondescript buildings with no company logos. However, the power substations nearby, security fences, cameras, and security stations are usually a giveaway!

One trade-off is between security and safety. For example, how should security systems default in the event of a power failure? Should locked doors default to an unlocked state if there is no power? This would allow for a quick exit of personnel and avoid the possibility of being trapped in the data center in the event of an emergency. Most times, safety will supersede security in an emergency.

Unencrypted Communications and Data

Data sent across a network unencrypted is susceptible to interception and allows an attacker easy access to your data because all the information will be in clear text. For example, using Telnet for remote command-line access exposes your username and password credentials to anyone with a network sniffer and the ability to connect to your network. If you must conform to regulatory requirements such as HIPPA, SOX, or PCI regulations in the United States or to meet corporate security directives, you will need to replace these older systems with current, more secure applications. Telnet has been replaced with Secure Shell (SSH). FTP has a secure version called SFTP. Web browsers support the unsecure HTTP protocol and the SSL/TLS protocol commonly referred to as HTTPS.

Remote network connections use VPNs that are encrypted with IPsec or other encryption architectures. Secure systems can be difficult to troubleshoot as the data is, by definition, encrypted and offers minimal insight on any issues it may be experiencing. Log files can be useful when troubleshooting encrypted systems as they are readable in plain english and, if consolidated, offer insight on both ends of the link.

Troubleshooting Methodology

Network systems can develop operational problems from many sources including configuration errors, software bugs, hardware failure, human error, traffic patterns (a malicious attack or network saturation), and others.

To effectively resolve technical issues, you should have a solid plan of action and follow a formalized approach to troubleshooting. By following a structured plan to your troubleshooting, you will be much more effective than just searching all over the network looking for the problem. Fortunately, there are multiple standard approaches to choose from.

Troubleshooting is the process of diagnosing the cause of an impairment and resolving the issue. The ideal situation is that the monitoring and reporting systems will trigger an alarm if there is an impairment and, using either automation or the expertise of the cloud support staff, will resolve the issue prior to there being any impact on operations. So, when you are called upon to resolve a problem, it is important that you be prepared with a well-thought-out methodology for troubleshooting.

The troubleshooting process includes collecting and analyzing data, eliminating irrelevant data, creating a hypothesis of what the problem may be, testing that assumption, and, after the issue has been identified, resolving it. To effectively perform troubleshooting, a logical and structured approach is mandatory. Without any structure, much time is wasted searching in a seemingly random fashion that does not allow for a logical collection of facts that can be used to resolve the issue. Using a haphazard approach may resolve the problem but does not lead to an effective explanation as your troubleshooting approach was very confusing! You may not be able to recall what you tested, when, and in what order. Basically, you will lose track of what affected what. This makes it hard to provide feedback and document steps to prevent the issue from recurring in the future. A structured approach allows you to reduce duplicate troubleshooting steps and ensures you do not skip any steps and are able to effectively update others about the potential issues you have eliminated and what still needs to be investigated.

This is not to say that experienced troubleshooters may, to quickly resolve the problem, bypass a structured approach and, using past experience, go directly to the problem. This approach works if the assumptions are correct. If they are in error, then valuable time may have been wasted.

There are many structured troubleshooting methods, with many being variations or combination of others. The most common are top-down, bottom-up, divide-and-conquer, follow the path, configuration comparisons, and device swapping.

Of these, the first three are the most common. The top-down approach references the Open Systems Interconnection (OSI) model, starting at the application layer and working downward until the problem is identified. Using application-level utilities, such as the ones explained earlier in this chapter like ping, traceroute, and others, you can work your way down the stack, as shown in Figure 10.7.

FIGURE 10.7   Top-down troubleshooting approach

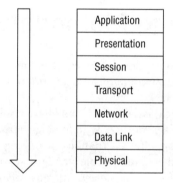

The authors prefer the bottom-up approach shown in Figure 10.8. Since the upper layers of the OSI model are dependent on the lower layers being operational, it is logical to investigate the lower parts of the network and work your way up to the applications.

FIGURE 10.8   Bottom-up troubleshooting approach

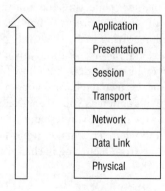

Divide-and-conquer is a variation of top-down and bottom-up where you start in the middle of the OSI model, say at the transport layer, and based on your testing results, either work up the stack or down, as shown in Figure 10.9.

FIGURE 10.9   Divide-and-conquer troubleshooting approach

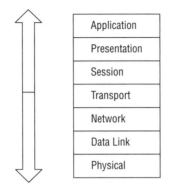

Another effective method to use when troubleshooting network issues is to follow the traffic path until you reach the failure point. Utilities such as ping and traceroute will be helpful when implementing this approach.

Configuration comparisons may be helpful in determining whether a change was made to the network that caused the issue under investigation. Cloud companies offer configuration backup services that allow you to go back and see what the last good configuration was and view change log reports. Also, as a last resort, you may want to swap cables, switch ports, switches, and so forth, to see whether a physical device is the issue without spending time in the console looking at interface statistics.

Corporate Policies, Procedures, and the Impact of Implementing Changes

Chapter 2 covered the subject of change management and corporate policies that are in place to ensure that there is a structure to the change process, with the intent of reducing the risk of implementing changes.

To review, change management is the process of managing all aspects of ongoing upgrades, repairs, and reconfigurations. Change management involves planning and managing changes to minimize any disruptions of service.

Change management outlines policies and procedures and provides a standardized process to follow, including the following:

- Recording the change
- Planning for the change
- Testing documentation
- Getting approvals
- Evaluating

- Validating
- Compiling instructions for backing out the change
- Doing a post-change review if desired

The process of managing technical configuration and customization changes can be detailed in large data center or cloud operations. A change management procedure usually includes the name of the requester, what the change is going to be, and the reason or justification for making the change. Other areas include a description of the expected result of making the change and what risks are involved. You must also outline what resources will be needed and coordinate the activities of the various groups involved in the change. A list of individuals responsible for the various aspects of the change including the design, configuration, deployment, and validation steps must be prepared. There also needs to be an investigation into other changes that are taking place to make sure no conflicts exist between those changes and yours. Also, if one change requires another change to take place before it can be implemented, the change sequences will have to be coordinated.

Steps to Identify the Problem

When a problem arises, the logging system's data and user descriptions can vary widely and not always provide an accurate description of the problem (usually just the symptoms). However, the information can act as a pointer to where the real issue may reside. Your responsibility is to clearly define the problem based on your initial investigation and outside information provided.

Gather Information

Trouble reports may not always be informative and are reflections of what is known at that point in time. It is the responsibility of the troubleshooter to gather as much information as possible to get the big picture and look for clues of the problem. Impacted users and monitoring tools are prime data sources. Also, the cloud provider's health dashboard offers insight into their internal operations. Many Internet support boards give affected groups a collaboration point, such as chat rooms or forums to discuss and collect data.

Companies may implement a war room where all groups can gather and work together on a problem. There are many instances where the information that needs to be gathered falls under multiple areas of responsibility (or as they are sometimes called, *silos*). The war room allows the different groups to interact with each other to gather the required data and consolidate the information into one area.

Distill the Issue

After gathering information on the issue, the next step is to analyze the information for clues as to what may be causing the problem. Keep an open mind and look for patterns in the data or values that do not appear to be in the benchmark ranges. If you identify an anomaly, ask yourself if this may be the problem or if it is possibly the result of a problem elsewhere that is affecting this component. You may need to gather additional information as you work to distill the cause of the issue to validate the information you have gathered.

During this process, look for symptoms or indicators that may point to the underlying cause of the problem. Also, look for evidence that eliminates areas that could have been part of the issue. The troubleshooting process should include comparing what should be occurring to what is actually occurring. It is important to know this because it will lead you to identify the problem. Compare the data with the baseline to determine the delta between when the device was functioning properly and the current object values.

In this step, you may need to research the suspected issue. This includes eliminating potential causes and forming conclusions from the collected data. It is important to always challenge your conclusions to make sure you are not misinterpreting the data and symptoms reported.

Research

After you have distilled the issue, the next step is to research the data and create a hypothesis of the underlying issue to test against. Look at all available resources to validate that reported issue and the steps available to resolve it.

Create a Plan of Action

After you have collected the information, distilled the data down to identify where the problem resides, and researched the issue, the next step is to create an action plan to resolve the issue. The actions required to test and resolve the issue may be out of your area of control, and working with different internal groups such as the storage, networking, or virtualization teams will be required. Additionally, you may need to contact the cloud vendor's support group and open a troubleshooting ticket for assistance.

Determine what steps to take to resolve the issue. For instance, you may make a setting change, test the results, and, if necessary, remove the change. The process of troubleshooting processes and testing will continue until the issue is resolved.

Test and Verify

After you have a solid plan of action, the next step is to implement the plan and test to verify the results. It is extremely important to document the steps taken and the results observed as you go through this process. This will help you to follow what has been tested and what has not. This data is also valuable for documenting the incident upon resolution.

Continue through the testing and validation process until problem resolution. If you exhaust all possibilities, you may need to open a trouble ticket with the cloud vendor or other third parties that may be of assistance.

Document and Resolve

After the issue has been resolved, it is helpful to document your findings so that, should the issue return, you have historical information on how to troubleshoot and resolve the incident.

As part of the resolution process, it is important to communicate to the user community, or appropriate parties, that the issue has been resolved. This can be accomplished by updating a status dashboard or sending an update to a group e-mail address, for example.

Documentation also includes backing up the configurations if necessary. If you made any changes to a device configuration, add what was changed and why the change was made to resolve the issue in your documentation and then back up the actual configuration to a server as an archive.

Summary

This chapter covered troubleshooting from a networking perspective. You were introduced to many of the common networking issues you will find in the field including IP addressing issues such as subnetting, routing, and gateway configurations. Troubleshooting DNS, QoS, VLAN/VxLAN, firewall configurations, network latency, MTU, and proxies were all introduced and discussed.

There are many utilities offered for both the Windows and Linux operating systems that are invaluable aids in troubleshooting networking problems. The primary tools are ping, tracert/traceroute, telnet, netstat, nslookup/dig, ipconfig/ifconfig, route, arp, ssh, and tcpdump. We gave use cases and showed the text output to help you understand how to use these critical tools when troubleshooting network problems.

Since the cloud is usually at a remote facility, there are different methods to access these resources from your location. The common tools used are SSH, HTTP, RDP, terminal servers, and Telnet.

Troubleshooting account issues is common, so you learned about what to look for when working on sign-on, authentication, authorization, and confederation problems. Privilege escalation and role changes were also included in this section.

Troubleshooting security issues includes dealing with certificates, encrypted communications, security hardening, and physical facility access; keeping your security technologies up-to-date by following new developments; and assessing your security posture to new offerings on the market.

The chapter ended with a general overview of troubleshooting and some of the different troubleshooting models that can be used, such as top-down, bottom-up, and divide-and-conquer. Then you learned about additional troubleshooting processes to follow for effective and timely resolution of the issue.

A troubleshooting methodology includes identifying the problem, establishing a theory of the probable cause, and testing the theory to determine its cause. Then you establish a plan of action to resolve the problem and implement the solution. After these steps, verify full functionality; finally, you should document the findings, actions, and outcomes.

Exam Essentials

Know the various network connectivity issues and how to troubleshoot them.   Common network issues that you can expect to be tested on include IP addressing such as incorrectly defined subnet masks, default gateway configurations, errors in routing, and DNS configurations.

Know at a basic level what QoS is and the symptoms of network saturation. Be able to identify what the actual problem is for the exam. For example, poor network performance would point to a latency or QoS issue, and if the question is about a failure to connect to a remote site using its domain name, it would be a DNS problem.

Know how to identify networking issues.   There may be questions on network traffic not being able to make it to its destination where you need to identify the network issue. This can include using command-line troubleshooting tools, investigating log files, and monitoring systems to gather information on the reported issue. There may be a long scenario where you are given a large amount of detail, and you should be able to discard what does not apply and select from the answers given the core processes to identify the problem.

Differentiate user account issues.   You may see questions on the exam with a description of a user not being able to access the cloud and a brief explanation of the symptoms. You need to be able to distill the problem to common user issues such as account lockouts, authentication and authorization problems, and account federation problems.

Describe the process of identifying certificate problems.   Know that security certificates have expiration dates and that you need to renew them prior to that time. Certificate management can be a fully managed cloud service or handled internally by your organization. You may be asked what steps to take when troubleshooting a certificate problem and be able to identify the correct answer offered given the scenario.

Identify network attacks.   You may be given an example of a network attack, and you should be able to identify whether it is originating internally or externally.

Explain remote access technologies and uses.   Know how to access the cloud remotely. Vendor management utilities—such as the Remote Desktop Protocol, which is commonly used for remote server administration—are available for remote hypervisor access. Remote command-line access uses the Secure Shell protocol because it is encrypted and more secure than Telnet. Console ports are used for command-line serial port access for remote configuration and monitoring. Many devices offer a web-based configuration interface that can be accessed using the HTTP protocol much like accessing websites on the Internet.

Summarize the various approaches to troubleshooting.   Troubleshooting methods include top-down, bottom-up, and divide and conquer.

Know how to use a troubleshooting methodology.   You may be presented with a question where a description is given of a troubleshooting step and then asked to identify which step in the troubleshooting process is being used. Examples are identifying the problem, establishing a theory of the probable cause, testing the theory to determine its cause, establishing a plan of action to resolve the problem, and implementing the solution. The final step is documenting the findings, actions, and outcomes.

Written Lab

Fill in the blanks for the questions provided in the written lab. You can find the answers to the written labs in Appendix B.

1. When a network becomes saturated, _QOS_ can be implemented to define priorities.

2. An Ethernet frame larger than the standard size is a _jumbo frame_ .

3. A _proxy_ is a device that is inserted into the middle of a traffic flow and terminates connections in both directions and monitors traffic between the source and the destination.

4. Hyperscale cloud data centers implement _123_ overlays to extend cloud customer private segments to more than 16 million networks.

5. The _netstat_ network utility is found in both Windows and Linux operating systems and is used to show what network connections are open to remote applications.

6. Both the Linux _dig_ and the Windows _nslookup_ utilities query a DNS system, giving a domain name and receiving the corresponding IP address.

7. When the cloud issue has been resolved, the final step in the troubleshooting process is to provide resolution _documentation_ .

8. After you have distilled the issue, the next step is to _research_ the data and create a hypothesis of the underlying issue to test against. Look at all the available resources to validate the reported issue and the steps available to resolve it.

9. Social engineering is the most predominate _internal_ attack where someone is tricked into providing credentials or holding a door open into a secure data center, for example.

10. _Privilege escalation_ can be defined as a user receiving account privileges that they are not allowed to possess.

Review Questions

The following questions are designed to test your understanding of this chapter's material. You can find the answers to the questions in Appendix A. For more information on how to obtain additional questions, please see this book's Introduction.

1. Carrie is researching various remote access options to access her Linux servers in a public cloud. She has been asked to provide a standardized and secure solution that protects against snooping. As a Cloud+ architect, you have been asked to assist. What protocol would you advise she implement?

   A. RDP

   B. Telnet

   C. IPsec

   D. SSH

   E. Terminal server

2. James is troubleshooting a DNS issue and wants to look at DNS frames being sent and received from his network adapter card on a web server. What utility would he use to collect the traces?

   A. dig

   B. netstat

   C. tcpdump

   D. nslookup

3. An intern at your company is asking about the mappings between the layer 2 MAC address and the gateway router. He wants to verify that the VM has the correct network mapping information. Which utility would you tell him to use to gather this information?

   A. dig

   B. ipconfig

   C. arp

   D. netstat

4. Sharon is unable to reach her Linux-based web server hosted in the Singapore zone of the cloud. She is located in Austin, Texas. What utility can she use to verify the connection path?

   A. traceroute

   B. ipconfig

   C. arp

   D. netstat

   E. ping

   F. tcpdump

   G. route print

5. Connie is documenting different methods that her remote operations center can use to access the Calgary fleet of servers operating in a community cloud. Which of the following are not viable methods? (Choose two.)

   A. RDP

   B. Telnet

   C. IDS/IPS

   D. Terminal server

   E. DNS

   F. HTTP

6. Allison is in the process of migrating graphical vendor management utilities away from locally installed applications on her desktop and to an approach that does not require any local installations and will be easier to implement and use. What approach would meet these requirements?

   A. Java

   B. CSS

   C. Web

   D. RDP

   E. SSH

7. The remote disaster recovery location follows the warm site model. To configure the network switches, routers, and firewalls remotely, Mark will need serial port access from his company's operations center. He has 14 serial ports currently but needs to be prepared for any unplanned expansion requirements during a disaster recover cutover. What device would you recommend he implement at the warm site?

   A. RDP

   B. Telnet

   C. IPsec

   D. SSH

   E. Terminal server

8. Sarah manages user accounts for her company's cloud presence. She has a trouble ticket open with Jill to assist her in accessing an SSD storage volume in the San Paulo region of the public cloud. What kind of user issue is she investigating?

   A. Authentication

   B. Authorization

   C. Federation

   D. SSO

9. Harold is getting alarms from the public cloud's application load balancer about security failures. Harold reviews his problem resolution documentation to investigate, and there have been no troubles reported in the past year. The load balancer has been configured to offload port 443 web traffic from the backend fleet of web servers. As a Cloud+ consultant brought in to assist, what should be the focus of the investigation?

    A. HTTPS

    B. Certificates

    C. IPsec

    D. RDP

    E. ssldump

    F. netstat

10. Multiple users are complaining that they cannot access a cloud-based collaboration system. The operations center has been investigating and has, so far, verified that the MFA applications are operational. What user system are they troubleshooting?

    A. Authentication

    B. Authorization

    C. Federation

    D. SSO

11. The backend fleet of web servers is intermittently failing load balancer health checks and dropping out of the pool. You are involved in troubleshooting and begin your investigation by making sure the web application is operational. What approach are you undertaking?

    A. Top down

    B. Bottom up

    C. Divide and conquer

    D. Evaluation

    E. Validation

12. Your web servers have lost communications to the SQL backend database on your e-commerce public website. You have been brought in to assist in resolving the problem. After reviewing the log files and the monitoring system, you suspect it may be a network-related issue. You devise a series of tests that starts with checking the server's connection to the database. What troubleshooting approach are you implementing?

    A. Top down

    B. Bottom up

    C. Divide and conquer

    D. Evaluation

    E. Validation

13. A middleware application running in the cloud is reporting session drops in its log files. You need to quickly resolve the issue and get the server back online. You decide to run `ping` and `traceroute` tests on the server as your first line of troubleshooting. What approach are you using?

   A. Top down

   B. Bottom up

   C. Divide and conquer

   D. Evaluation

   E. Validation

14. What are common troubleshooting steps? (Choose all that apply.)

   A. Gather information

   B. Distill the issue

   C. Research

   D. Create a plan of action

   E. Test and verify

15. Your cloud provider's data center is in an industrial park with no company signage, extensive video cameras in the parking lot, and biometrics at the guard shack. What type of security is the provider implementing?

   A. Building

   B. Device

   C. Infrastructure

   D. Tunneling

16. Kelly has picked up a trouble ticket that shows the connection between the Toledo field office and the Detroit cloud edge location has dropped. She confirms it is a secure Internet-based access solution. What type of connection is this?

   A. Direct peering

   B. IDS

   C. VPN

   D. AES-256

   E. RDP

17. Nick is setting up a new fleet of IIS web servers in his IaaS e-commerce site. The company has elected to use a hybrid approach and desires graphical connections to the Windows bastion hosts. What traffic must he permit through the external-facing firewall to the host?

   A. SSH

   B. RDP

   C. DNS

   D. IPS

18. Jill logs into her NoSQL database server residing in a private subnet on a public cloud. She needs to verify network connectivity with the application tier. What utility can she use as a quick connectivity test?

   A. arproute

   B. netstat

   C. tcpdump

   D. ping

19. After deploying a new public website, your validation steps ask you to check the domain name to IP address mappings. What utility can you use for validation? (Choose two.)

   A. RDP

   B. dig

   C. SSH

   D. nslookup

   E. IPsec

   F. IPS

20. Donna logged into her cloud bastion host by making an SSH connection from her operations center desktop. She uses the Linux host to connect to other systems in the private cloud. She needs to add an access control list rule to allow the bastion server to access a new subnet. She needs the source IP address of her host. What command can she run on the server to collect this information?

   A. curl /localhost/metadata/global/interface

   B. ipconfig

   C. ifconfig

   D. netstat

Appendix A

Answers to Review Questions

Chapter 1: An Introduction to Cloud Computing Configurations and Deployments

1. A. Infrastructure as a Service offers computing hardware, storage, and networking but not the operating systems or applications.

2. C. Resource pooling is the allocation of compute resources into a group, or pool, and then these pools are made available to a multitenant cloud environment.

3. A, C, D. Elements and objects are examples of devices and systems in the cloud. In this question, the elements are CPU, memory, and storage.

4. C. Pooled virtual resources include memory, storage, networking, and CPU. Security is a general technology area and not a physical resource that can be pooled.

5. B, D. One of the prime advantages of cloud-based computing and the automation and virtualization it offers in the background is the ability to leverage the rapid provisioning of virtual resources to allow for on-demand computing.

6. A, B, E. Elasticity, on-demand-computing, and pay-as-you-grow are all examples of being able to expand cloud compute resources as your needs require.

7. B. The interconnection of multiple cloud models is referred to as a hybrid cloud.

8. C. A virtual switch is a software extraction of a physical Ethernet LAN switch that runs on a hypervisor and interconnects a VM's virtual network interface card to the outside, physical data network.

9. B. The pay-as-you-grow cloud characteristic allows billing for only the services used.

10. A, C, G. It is common practice and strongly encouraged to split operations into different and isolated sections of the cloud to prevent interference between development, operations, and quality assurance networks.

11. D. On-demand cloud computing allows the consumer to dynamically add and change resources with the use of an online portal.

12. C. Software as a Service offers cloud-managed applications as well as the underlying platform and infrastructure support.

13. A, E, G, I. Network delays, storage input/output performance, swap file usage, and the ability to scale are all examples of cloud performance components. Firewalls and encryption are security components, IaaS is a service model, and memory pooling is not relevant to the question.

14. A. Cloud operators segment their operations into regions for customer proximity, regulatory compliance, resiliency, and survivability.

15. A, B, D. Prior to performing a cloud migration, baseline measurements, a determination of capacity requirements, and complete documentation are all requirements for success.

16. C. The shared responsibility model outlines what services and portions of the cloud operations the cloud consumer and provider are responsible for.

17. C. Penetration testing is the process of testing your cloud access to determine whether there is any vulnerability that an attacker could exploit.

18. C. Community clouds are offered for a specific community of interest and shared by companies with similar requirements for regulatory compliance, security, or policy.

19. B. Orchestration platforms automate the provisioning of cloud services and often include a self-service dashboard that allows the consumer to manage and deploy cloud services with a web browser. The automation used by cloud providers allows for fast deployment of new services and applications.

20. B. Platform as a Service offers computing hardware, storage, networking, and the operating systems but not the application software.

Chapter 2: Cloud Deployments

1. C. A private cloud is used exclusively by a single organization.

2. D. A community cloud is used by companies with similar needs such as medical or financial services.

3. D. Multifactor authentication systems use a token generator as something that you have and a PIN/password as something you know.

4. B. With asynchronous replication, there will be a delay as the data is copied to the backup site and provides eventual consistency as it uses a store-and-forward design. The backup storage array is normally several transactions behind the primary.

5. C, D. When migrating stored data to the cloud, the two available options are online and offline.

6. B. When migrating a server that is running on bare metal to a hypervisor-based system, you would be performing a physical-to-virtual migration.

7. C, E, G. Hypertext Transport Protocol Secure, Secure Shell, and File Transfer Protocol Secure all provide encrypted transmission of data.

8. B. Obfuscation is a means to complicate or confuse the ability to decipher storage information.

9. D. A storage area network (SAN) is a high-speed network dedicated to storage transfers across a shared network. Block access is not a networking technology. Zoning is for restricting LUNs in a SAN, and VMFS is a VMware filesystem.

10. C. Authentication is the term used to describe the process of determining the identity of a user or device.

11. A, C, E. Application programmable interfaces, command-line interfaces, and GUI-based interfaces are all commonly used tools to migrate, monitor, manage, and troubleshoot cloud-based resources.

12. B, D, F. A virtual machine will consume virtualized resources including virtual RAM, virtual CPUs, and memory pools.

13. C. Tiering is the process of defining the storage needs of the cloud customer and aligning them with the cloud provider's offerings. RAID is a hardware storage family of redundancy types. Multipathing is a redundant SAN technique, and policies are not related to the question.

14. B. RAID combines physical disks for redundancy and performance. Multipathing is a redundancy SAN design, masking is a LUN access process, and tiering is a storage hierarchy technique.

15. D. RAID 5 has parity information that is striped across multiple drives that allows the drive array to be rebuilt if a single drive in the array fails. The other options do not have parity data.

16. B. The service level agreement outlines specific metrics and the minimum performance provided by the cloud provider.

17. C. Storage area networks support block-based storage.

18. B. Identity systems using federations allow multiple organizations to use the same data for identification when accessing the networks or resources of everyone in the group.

19. B, D. Both migration WAN bandwidth and compatible VM file formats are critical to a successful migration.

20. D. Intrusion detection systems monitor network traffic for malicious activity and generate reports and alerts. Intrusion prevention takes this a step further and actively attempts to shut down the intrusion as it is happening.

Chapter 3: Security in the Cloud

1. B. The Platform as a Service model offers operating system security provided by the service provider.

2. B, C. Logging into a system is referred to as authentication, and the use of a token to log in describes two-factor authentication.

3. C. The question outlines the function of a role-based access control approach.

4. C. Service Organization Controls 3 reports are for public disclosure of financial controls and security reporting.

5. B. The National Institute of Standards and Technology (NIST) FIPS 140-2 publication coordinates the requirements and standards for cryptography modules.

6. B. The Department of Defense Information Assurance Certification and Accreditation Process (DIACAP) is the process for computer systems IT security. DIACAP compliance is required to be certified to meet the U.S. Department of Defense security requirements for contractors.

7. B. The Health Insurance Portability and Accountability Act defines the standards for protecting medical data and is mandatory for Mary's requirements.

8. A, B, E. Firewalls, load balancers, and DHCP servers are all considered cloud-based services.

9. A. The mandatory access control approach is often found in high-security environments where access to sensitive data needs to be highly controlled. Using the mandatory access control approach, a user will authenticate, or log into, a system. Based on the user's identity and security levels of the individual, access rights will be determined by comparing that data against the security properties of the system being accessed.

10. B. The Federal Risk and Authorization Management Program is a U.S. federal government program that outlines the standards for a security assessment, authorization, and continuous monitoring for cloud products and services.

11. B. The company's security policy outlines all aspects of your cloud security posture.

12. B. Two-factor authentication includes something that you have and something that you know.

13. C. Advanced Encryption Standard is a symmetrical block cipher that has options to use three lengths, including 128, 192, and 256 bits. AES 256 is a very secure standard, and it would take an extremely long time and a lot of processing power to even come close to breaking the code. AES has been approved and adopted by many governments, including the United States and Canada, to encrypt sensitive data. AES has also been adopted as a standard by the National Institute of Standards and Technology.

14. B, C. Lightweight Directory Access Protocol and Active Directory are two technologies that enable SSO access to cloud resources.

15. B, D. Virtual storage area networks are implemented at the SAN level, and LUN masking is configured on storage controllers, and they are both low-level storage access methods.

16. A. Multifactor uses temporarily issued numerical tokens that must be entered at the time of user authentication.

17. C. Secure Sockets Layer (SSL) makes up a protocol group that operates on top of TCP to provide an encrypted session between the client and the server. It is commonly seen on websites implemented as the Hypertext Transport Protocol Secure (HTTPS) protocol.

18. C. Many IPSec implementations are found in routers and firewalls within VPNs, application security, and network security to provide a secure connection over an insecure network such as the Internet.

19. A, B, D, F. Securing user accounts and policies include installing antivirus software, disabling unused servers, implementing host-based firewall services, and shutting down all default user accounts.

20. B. Single sign-on allows a user to log in one time and be granted access to multiple systems without having to authenticate to each one individually.

Chapter 4: Implementing Cloud Security

1. A, C, D. Cloud segmentation is the process of dividing up your cloud deployment into sections that allow for granular security. Common segments include compute, network, and storage. APIs, JSON, and XML are software constructs to enable automation.

2. B, D. One-time numerical tokens are generated on keyfob hardware devices and smartphone soft-token applications.

3. C. Applying security applications on a virtual server will cause an increase in CPU usage.

4. C. Automation of cloud deployments was instrumental in the growth of cloud-based services.

5. B, D. Storage systems and database applications are both examples of data at rest or being processed in the cloud. While VPNs and client encryption are valid security systems, they are not associated with your internal cloud security posture.

6. C. A dashboard is a graphical portal that provides updates and an overview of operations.

7. C. Ultimately the responsibility for data in the cloud belongs to the organization that owns the data.

8. C. Orchestration systems are software packages or services that automate cloud operations.

9. A, B, C, D, E. All of these cloud services have APIs that can be accessed for configuration and monitoring using standard RESTful XML and/or JSON interfaces.

10. E. A host-based authentication detection systems will allow Jim to apply intrusion protection to a specific virtual machine.

11. D. Multifactor authentication services use a token that is generated on a schedule and can be a numerical value. The other answers offered are not valid to the question.

12. C. An application programming interface (API) offers programmatic access, control, and configuration of a device between different and discrete software components.

13. B, C, E, F. All compliance requirements should be integrated into the complete life cycle of a project including the design, planning, implementation, and validation phases of the project.

14. A, B. Extensible Markup Language (XML) and JavaScript Object Notation (JSON) provide a flexible way to describe data and create information formats and electronically share structured data between computing systems. Both are lightweight data-interchange formats that are easily readable for computing systems to parse and to generate.

15. C. Intrusion prevention systems will monitor for malicious activity and actively take countermeasures to eliminate or reduce the effects of the intrusion.

16. B. SSL/TLS security is the most common remote access encryption technology and is commonly used in browsers and smartphone applications. MD5 is a hash algorithm, and IPSec is a security framework; they do not apply to the question. VPNs are not as common as SSL/TLS for the scenario given.

17. C, D. Temporary storage volumes that are only in existence when the VM is deployed are referred to as ephemeral or nondurable storage.

18. B. It is considered a best practice to group compute resources into like segments and apply security to the segment.

19. B. The command-line interface is a text-based interface to most network services that allows for remote and local configurations.

20. C. Based on the information given, the description is for a vendor-based management application.

Chapter 5: Maintaining Cloud Operations

1. A. Full backups offer the advantage of a complete and up-to-date copy of your data in one operation. They have the disadvantage of taking a long time to perform because all the data in a storage system must be copied instead of just the modified data from the last backup.

2. C, D. Cloud configuration front ends as well as automation systems using scripting or API calls can shut down and restart virtual machines as required. Both restarts and shutdowns may be performed because of a code upgrade, troubleshooting, or other needs. The shutdown and restart processes can be monitored through the management systems and dashboards that are offered by the cloud provider. If they do not respond, these systems can be configured to generate an alarm.

3. A, C, E. Common patch management offerings are Chef, Puppet, and Ansible.

4. B. A patch is a piece of software that is intended to update an application, operating system, or any other software-based system to fix or improve its operations. Generally, patches are synonymous with fixes for security vulnerabilities or any other type of operational bug.

5. C. Cloning takes the master image and clones it to be used as another separate and independent VM. Important components of a server are changed to prevent address conflicts; these include the UUID and MAC addresses of the cloned server.

6. B. A snapshot is a file-based image of the current state of a VM including the complete operating systems and all applications that are stored on it. The snapshot will record the data on the disk, its current state, and the VM's configuration at that instant in time. Snapshots can be created while the VM is in operation and are used as a record of that VM's state. They can be saved to roll back to at a later time.

7. A. Many corporate and most regulatory requirements will specify that the backup data must be located at a separate data center from the origin data center and must be geographically away from each other. Many cloud providers interconnect their data centers into regions and availability zones using very high-speed, directly connect, fiber networks that allow large backup sets to traverse the data network between the data centers and that make remote backups feasible.

8. C. A version update is the process of replacing a software product with a newer version of the same product. Version updates can add new features, bring the system up-to-date, provide a rollup of all previous patches, and improve the product.

9. B. Workflow automation defines a structured process for a series of actions that should be taken to complete a process. With cloud-based workflow services, special workflow applications are offered as a managed service that creates a defined sequence of events, or workflow, with each procedure tracked and passed to the next process in the workflow.

10. C. The main function of orchestration systems is to combine and execute the multiple tasks that must be completed to accomplish an operation. These tasks are combined into a workflow that defines the order of events and steps needed to complete the operation. The orchestration system uses software systems and processes to carry out the workflow.

11. A, D. By placing a system into maintenance mode and disabling system alerts, the management systems will not alert on false positives when a system undergoing regular maintenance does not respond when polled by management systems, and it will not send out unsolicited alarms because of the maintenance being performed.

12. A. A hotfix is a software update type that is intended to fix an immediate and specific problem with a quick release procedure.

13. C. Online backup storage is a system that can be accessed at any time without the requirement for a network administrator to mount the media into a storage system. Online is the most common storage design, and backups offer an always-available method to store and retrieve the data.

14. C. A cluster is a group of tightly coupled systems designed for high availability and that still operate if one or more nodes is offline.

15. B, C, E. Infrastructure that is part of the IaaS service provider's area of responsibility includes load balancers, hypervisors, and routers. A virtual machine, database, or e-mail server would be the responsibility of the customer.

16. B. A rolling configuration will sequentially upgrade the web servers without causing a complete outage and would meet the requirements outlined in the question.

17. D. The manager is requesting data on the results of the quality assurance testing on the release. Rollout is a patch deployment process, and both automation and orchestration systems are used to install the patch.

18. C. Blue-green is a software deployment methodology that uses two configurations for production that are identical to each other. These deployments can alternate between each other, with one being active and the other being inactive.

19. C. Incremental backups are operations based on the change of the source data since the last incremental backup was performed. Incremental backups can be run, for example, on a nightly basis and capture the changes that were made since the previous backup was run the night before. This allows for an efficient backup operation since only the changes in the past 24 hours are stored on the backup media. Incremental backups are much less time- and resource-consuming than a full backup and are used to complement them.

20. D. Offline storage requires the administrator to make the data available by inserting a tape or other media into a storage system for retrieval. Offline storage can be transported to remote storage facilities or stored in vaults for protection.

Chapter 6: Disaster Recovery, Business Continuity, and Ongoing Maintenance

1. B. Asynchronous replication is when data is written to the primary first, and then later a copy is written to the remote site on a scheduled arrangement or in nearly real time.

2. A. The hot site model is the most viable option given the requirements. A hot site is a fully functional backup site that can assume operations immediately should the primary location fail or go offline.

3. B, C. The restore point and restore time objectives are the measurements for the amount of data lost and the time needed to get back online after an outage.

4. B. Edge locations are not complete cloud data centers. They are cloud connection points located in major cities and offer the benefits outlined in the question.

5. B. Access control systems are used to grant users object access in an operating system. For ongoing maintenance and best security practices, it is important to delete old and unused access control policies.

6. B. The restore point objective is the point in time that data can be recovered; James had to update the RPO metric.

7. B. Moving inactive data or data that is no longer being used to a separate storage facility for long-term storage is referred to as *archiving*. It can be more cost effective to store archived data in less expensive storage systems and still allow the cloud consumer access to that data for backup and retrieval as needed.

8. B, F. The backup site's network connections must be engineered to accept the expected traffic load and prevent bandwidth starvation.

9. B. Automation systems are backend processes for frontend systems such as dashboards or catalogs.

10. C. Firewalls contain a list of policies, or rules, that either permit or deny traffic. Over time as the environment changes, it is a best practice to review the firewall rules and remove or modify any rules that are obsolete or unused.

11. D. Stale or out-of-date domain name entries may point to servers that are no longer in use. Also, certain domain names may have never been removed from DNS, causing replies from unexpected devices.

12. H. It is important to review all of your network services to address any changes required when implementing a disaster recovery plan.

13. C. The recovery time objective is the amount of time a system can be offline during a disaster; it is the amount of time it takes to get a service online and available after a failure.

14. E. A cold site is a backup data center provisioned to take over operations in the event of a primary data center failure, but the servers and infrastructure are not deployed or operational until needed.

15. A. Synchronous replication offerings write data to both the primary storage system and the replica simultaneously to ensure that the remote data is current with local replicas.

16. D. Cloud edge locations are often used for proximity services at remote locations that provide data caching locally and offloads the need for calls to the web server fleet.

17. C. File transfers occur in the background from the primary data center to a backup site. Synchronous and asynchronous replication are ongoing file synchronization processes.

18. C. Orphaned resources are cloud-based services that are left over when a service terminates and they are no longer needed or used.

19. B. A warm site approach to recovering from a primary data center outage is when the remote backup of the site is offline except for critical data storage, which is usually a database. The warm site will host an operational database server that is in sync with the database server at the primary data center and is sometimes referred to as the *candlelight design*.

20. C. DNS records can be modified by external operations and can map domain names to IP addresses. There you will find occurrences of DNS entries not being deleted and becoming stale over time.

Chapter 7: Cloud Management

1. G. All of the options given are valid metrics for establishing a baseline.

2. C. The establishment of average usage over time is the data that gets collected for a baseline report.

3. C. Password complexity defines password length, if it is a nondictionary word and if upper/lowercase or special characters are required.

4. D. A lockout policy can be applied to an account that defines the parameters that create a lockup event. It is most common to apply a lockout policy to failed login attempts. For example, you can define a policy where four failed login attempts in five minutes will disable an account for thirty minutes. A lockout policy will most likely be defined by your information security group, and you may be asked to create and apply the policy as part of your duties.

5. A. Access control systems are user configurations that grant roles and duties to users or groups of users and also systems such as VMs, applications, and storage volumes. For example, database administrators can be given full access to manage a database application but be restricted from performing VM or storage operations.

6. B. With the PaaS model, the cloud provider will maintain the operating system and all supporting infrastructure.

7. C. The process of taking a large amount of event data and comparing the logs to determine the sequence of events is referred to as event correlation.

8. C. The ability to disable an account can be helpful in situations where the account will need to be re-activated at a future date and does not need to be deleted. Account disablement can be managed in the same manner as other account operations with a web front end or with the use of APIs for scripted and automated processes.

9. B. Resource access definitions allow access to approved resources, and these permissions contain any number of rights, such as read-write permissions for a storage volume and access to run certain applications. Not only access permissions can be defined, but detail on what functions the user is allowed to perform can be defined.

10. A. Once the collection policy has been created, it can be reused and applied to other objects as they are created or migrated. Event collection policies reduce the amount of management overhead and enforce consistency in your deployments.

11. A, B, D. Cloud computing operates with a utility business model that charges you only for the resources you consume. This model enables you to scale your cloud fleet to meet its current workload and be able to add and remove capacity as needed. There are many options to use elasticity to scale cloud operations including vertical and horizontal scaling and bursting.

12. F. All of the answers offered are valid event notification service receivers.

13. B. The measurement of the difference between a current reading and the baseline value is referred to as the variance.

14. B. Scaling up, or vertical scaling, will add resources such as CPU instances or more RAM. When you scale up, you are basically increasing your compute, network, or storage capabilities.

15. C. Cloud automation systems offer the ability to dynamically add and remove resources as needed; this is referred to as elasticity.

16. B. Cloud bursting allows for adding capacity from another cloud service during times when additional compute resources are needed.

17. A, B. Mergers and acquisitions may necessitate combining two cloud operations into one single system. You should be prepared to work with new groups and departments to look at how the other company's cloud deployment is architected and what options are available to integrate them. Applications may be duplicated, and there could be efficiencies gained by integrating them.

18. C. Change management includes recording the change, planning for the change, testing the documentation, getting approvals, evaluating and validating, writing instructions for backing out the change if needed, and doing post-change review if desired.

19. F. Managing the life cycle of an application will include deployments, upgrades, migrations, feature additions and deletions, replacements, and retirements.

20. C. The higher up the services stack you go, from IaaS to SaaS, the more difficult it will be to migrate. With IaaS, most of the cloud operations are under your direct control, which gives you the most flexibility to migrate. However, if the cloud provider controls the application, you may not have many options to migrate.

Chapter 8: Cloud Management Baselines, Performance, and SLAs

1. B. If a server is using all of its network bandwidth, then the most logical solution is to add more. You can do this by installing a second network adapter and connecting it to a different subnet. The other solutions could conceivably address the problem, but the success is less likely.

2. D. Performance baselines characterize hardware performance, so the OS update history would be of little or no use for future comparisons. A server baseline typically consists of CPU, memory, disk, and network performance statistics.

3. E. Vertical scaling is the process of upgrading or replacing a server with one that has greater capabilities.

4. A, D, E. Incident reports include events such as opening trouble tickets and contacting customer support and outages. Scaling and service level agreements are not considered impairments.

5. A. Most databases are designed to scale vertically.

6. C, D. Service level agreements outline performance and availability commitments and not configurations.

7. A, B, D, E. Cloud reporting is intended for internal corporate groups such as marketing, management, accounting, and operations.

8. D. Objects are queried to gather metric data.

9. D. Cloud reports are formatted collections of data contained in the management or monitoring applications.

10. C. A dashboard is a configurable graphical representation of current operational data.

11. C. After performing a major system upgrade, you should collect new baseline data as the overall system performance has changed.

12. A, D, E. CPU, RAM, and network utilization are all important object to manage for capacity and utilization tracking. Storage volume tiers and OS versions do not apply to this scenario.

13. A, B, D, E. Autoscaling allows for adding and removing cloud compute capacity, providing capacity changes based on the time of day, and maintaining a minimum number of VMs. Report generation and SLA object tracking are not autoscaling functions.

14. B, E. Both Excel and PDF are the most common reporting formats. The other database, programming, and scripting options are not applicable to report generation.

15. A. Horizontal scaling is the process of adding additional servers for increased capacity. Round robin is a load-balancing metric and does not apply. Elasticity is the ability to add and remove resources, autoscaling is the automated process of adding and removing capacity, and vertical scaling is expanding a server.

16. A, C, D. Databases return data from read operations and are a critical performance metric. CPU saturation could cause a slowdown as well as network issues such as packet loss.

17. B, E, F. Trends, usage, and deficiencies are all management report outputs that can be identified using object tracking.

18. A, C, D. Server performance can be increased by adding additional CPU processing, memory, and network capacity. SLA, ACL, and DNS are not related to increasing server capacity.

19. B. Tracking object performance data should match with the guaranteed levels outlined in the service level agreement.

20. A, C, D. High-performance computing relies on the servers being in close proximity to reduce network and storage latency. Being in the same availability zone, in the same group, and on the same hypervisor accomplishes this. There is no such thing as a group cache.

Chapter 9: Troubleshooting

1. A, C, D. Resources such as the amount of RAM needed, CPU cycles, and storage capacity are common systems that may become saturated as your cloud compute requirements grow.

2. C. Database read and write requests utilize storage I/O and should be the focus for troubleshooting.

3. A, C, D. When troubleshooting, it is helpful to have access to configurations, documentation, and diagrams to provide information on your cloud deployment.

4. D. Cloud autoscaling can dynamically add server capacity based on loading.

5. B. A large number of users downloading a new application would cause an increase in network bandwidth usage.

6. E. Any of these answers would be correct depending on his licensing agreement with the database provider.

7. B, C, D. In addition to the web servers, IP addresses may be required for the NTP and DNS services and the default gateway.

8. C. Elasticity allows for cloud services to expand and contract based on actual usage and would be applicable to increasing storage capacity.

9. B. When troubleshooting cloud performance issues, the current number of users on the system can be an important indicator of load. When there are high user counts, you can track what parts of your deployment are most heavily used and track the load on all the devices to see where the congestion points are.

10. D. A baseline measurement is used as a reference to determine cloud capacity increases and decreases.

11. B. The cloud service provider owns its automation and orchestration systems, and they cannot be directly accessed by the customer.

12. C. The change management process would need to be modified to prevent one change from affecting another that is taking place simultaneously.

13. C. The domain name system records need to be changed to reflect the new IP address mapped to the domain name.

14. B. Templates are software definitions of a cloud network and are used for automated deployments.

15. C. Workflow applications track a process from start to finish and sequence the applications that are required to complete the process.

16. A, B, D. Symptoms of reaching the capacity boundary of a service include the application failing, increased delays, and latency and requests to drop.

17. B. The common measurement for an API request is total connections performed each second.

18. C. It is common for batch processing to be performed on database applications.

19. B, C. The total number of CPU cores and clock speed are common parameters to define when configuring a machine image.

20. D. The subnet mask determines the size of a IP network.

Chapter 10: Troubleshooting Networking and Security Issues and Understanding Methodologies

1. D. SSH is the encrypted version of the Telnet protocol and is used to access remote devices using a command-line interface. RDP is a Windows graphical interface. Telnet does not offer encryption, and terminal servers offer serial port access but may or may not support encrypted network access.

2. C. tcpdump allows a Linux system to capture live network traffic and is useful in monitoring and troubleshooting. Sometimes called sniffing, tcpdump allows you to set up filters to select the traffic you are interested in capturing for troubleshooting. Think of tcpdump as a command-line network analyzer. dig and nslookup show DNS resolution but do not display the actual packets going across the wire. netstat shows connection information and is not DNS related.

3. C. ARP is the protocol that determines the mapping of an IP address to the physical MAC address on a local network. The mappings can be seen with the arp command-line utility. dig is used for DNS resolution, ipconfig shows the network adapter parameters, and netstat shows connections.

4. A. The tracert and traceroute utilities are useful for network path troubleshooting. This utility shows the routed path a packet of data takes from source to destination. You can use it to determine whether routing is working as expected or whether there is a route failure in the path. The other answers were all incorrect as they do not provide network path data.

5. C, E. Common remote access tools include RDP, SSH, and terminal servers. IDSs/IPSs are for intrusion detection, and DNS is for domain name to IP address mappings and is not a utility for remote access.

6. C. Of the options given, the web approach does not require any local application installations and offers a graphical systems management interface.

7. E. In a data center, terminal servers are deployed and have several serial ports, each cabled to a console port on a device that is being managed. This allows you to make an SSH or a Telnet connection to the terminal server and then use the serial interfaces to access the console ports on the devices you want to connect to. The other options given do not provide serial port connections.

8. B. The question is asking about being able to access a specific cloud service. This would concern Jill having authorization to access the storage volume. Authentication and SSO are login systems and not rights to services. A federation links user databases.

9. B. The question shows that the load balancer is terminating SSL/TLS traffic from the web. SSL certificates have expiration dates and so, as part of the troubleshooting approach, security certificate expirations need to be investigated. The other options do not accomplish this requirement.

10. A. Logging into systems is referred to as *authentication*. Also, the question references multifactor authentication (MFA) as part of the system. Authorization is the access of services after the authentication process, federations interconnect external user accounts to the cloud, and single sign-on (SSO) allows a user to authenticate one time to access all resources in the cloud.

11. A. The top-down approach references the OSI model; it starts at the application layer and works downward until the problem is identified. The application is checked first, and if that is operational, you continue to work down the network stack until you identify the problem.

12. B. The bottom-up approach starts at the lowest level of the ISO model with the physical network connections, such as cabling, and works upward by investigating VLANs, IP addressing, and so on, until the issue is located.

13. C. The divide-and-conquer troubleshooting approach starts in the middle of the OSI networking stack and, depending on the results, directs future tests. In this case, the troubleshooter began at the network layer, which is in the middle of the OSI model. This is the divide-and-conquer approach.

14. A, B, C, D, E. All of the answers given are common troubleshooting steps.

15. C. Infrastructure security is the hardening of the facility and includes the steps outlined in the question including nondescript facilities, video surveillance, and biometric access.

16. C. A secure Internet-based connection would be a VPN.

17. B. The Windows Remote Desktop Protocol allows for remote connections to a Windows graphical user desktop.

18. D. The ping utility verifies end-to-end network connectivity and is the correct answer. The other options offered either do not apply such as tcpdump and netstat or are not valid utilities such as arproute.

19. B, D. nslookup is a Windows command-line utility for resolving domain names to IP addressing. The Linux equivalent is the dig utility. The other answers offered are not valid for the solution required in the question.

20. C. The Linux command ifconfig will display all network-related configuration information for that computer and is the correct answer. ipconfig is the Windows equivalent and is not relevant to this question. netstat and the query string are not applicable to the question.

Appendix

B

Answers to Written Labs

Chapter 1: An Introduction to Cloud Computing Configurations and Deployments

1. Software
2. Infrastructure
3. Platform
4. Ubiquitous access
5. Virtualization
6. Direct connection, VPN
7. Replication
8. Load balancers
9. SSH, RDP
10. Baselines

Chapter 2: Cloud Deployments

1. Memory ballooning
2. Storage area network
3. Fault tolerance
4. Synchronous replication
5. Virtual-to-virtual
6. Application portability
7. Federations
8. Load balancer
9. Benchmark
10. Intrusion prevention system

Chapter 3: Security in the Cloud

1. Know, have
2. Security policy
3. Discretionary access

4. Single sign-on
5. Cipher
6. Automation
7. Object
8. Shared
9. Public key infrastructure
10. Software as a Service

Chapter 4: Implementing Cloud Security

1. Data classification
2. Segmentation
3. At rest
4. Know, have
5. Automation
6. API
7. Graphical user interface
8. Intrusion prevention systems
9. CPU
10. Automation

Chapter 5: Maintaining Cloud Operations

1. Blue-green
2. Rolling update
3. Rollback
4. Snapshots cloning
5. Backup target
6. Replicas
7. Hotfix
8. Differential backup
9. System alerts
10. Backup window

Chapter 6: Disaster Recovery, Business Continuity, and Ongoing Maintenance

1. Archiving
2. Disaster recovery
3. Business continuity
4. Disaster recovery
5. Inactive
6. Replication
7. RPO, RTO
8. Logs
9. Orphaned resources
10. Synchronous

Chapter 7: Cloud Management

1. Metric
2. Orchestration
3. Anomaly
4. Trigger
5. Infrastructure, SLA
6. Change management
7. Lifecycle management
8. Permissions
9. Complexity
10. Back out

Chapter 8: Cloud Management Baselines, Performance, and SLAs

1. Baseline
2. Metric
3. Objects
4. Horizontal
5. Memory
6. Latency
7. Resiliency
8. Service level agreement
9. Vertical scaling
10. Auditing

Chapter 9: Troubleshooting

1. Templates
2. Network Time Protocol
3. Capacity
4. Reduce load, add capacity
5. Mergers, acquisitions
6. Domain name, IP address
7. Validate
8. Log files
9. Configuration
10. Diagrams

Chapter 10: Troubleshooting Networking and Security Issues and Understanding Methodologies

1. QoS
2. Jumbo frame
3. Proxy
4. 123
5. `netstat`
6. `dig nslookup`
7. Documentation
8. Research
9. Internal
10. Privilege escalation

Index

A

access. *See also* connections
    RBAC (role-based access control), 88–89
    Remote Hypervisor access, 28–29
    ubiquitous access, 14
access control
    authentication, multifactor, 120–122
    cloud deployment models, 119–120
    cloud service models
        IaaS, 118
        PaaS, 119
        SaaS, 119
    cloud-based objects
        authentication, 116
        authorization, 116
        compute systems, 117
        network-based control, 117
        SAN, 118
        securing services, 118
        storage access, 117–118
        user accounts, 117
        user groups, 117
        VSAN, 118
    discretionary access, 121
    MAC (mandatory access control), 120–121
    maintenance automation, 202
    nondiscretionary access, 121
    RBAC (role-based access control), 120
    SSO (single-sign on), 122
accounting, 255
accounts
    automation, 233–234
    creating, 233
    disabling, 234
    life cycle, 232
    mismatched, 277
    orchestration, 233–234
    permission settings, 234
    removing, 234
    resource access, 234
addresses, troubleshooting, 274–275

AH (authentication header), 109
alert methods, deployment and, 218
alert triggers, deployment and, 218–219
anomalies, deployment and, 217–218
antivirus software, 115, 142
APIs (application programming interfaces)
    capacity, troubleshooting, 273
    security automation and, 138
applications, 13
    life cycle, 228
        deployments, 229
        features, 229
        migrations, 229
        replacements, 229
        retirements, 229
        upgrades, 229
    migration, portability, 86
    patching and, 157
archiving data, disaster recovery, 191
ARP (Address Resolution Protocol), 298–299
asynchronous replication, 23–24
audits, object tracking and, 247
authentication, 88–89
    multifactor, 88, 120–122
        hardware keyfob, 135
        login screen, 135
        smartphone-based token, 136
    resources and, 231
    SSO (single sign-on) systems, 90
    storage security, 81
    troubleshooting, 311
authorization
    cloud services, 89
    resources and, 232
    troubleshooting, 311–312
automation, 13, 25, 32
    accounts, 233–234
    elasticity, 256
    maintenance
        ACLs, 202
        DNS entries, stale, 199–200
        firewalls, 200–201
        inactive account removal, 199

log files archive, 198
orphaned resources, 200
resource reclamation, 201
rules, outdated, 200–201
storage compression, 199
security, 114
APIs, 138
CLI, 138
dashboards, 139
GUIs, 138–139
portals, 139
tools, 137
vendor-based solutions, 138
setup, 52
tool incompatibility, 278
troubleshooting, 267–268, 276–280
workflow
orchestration, 163–164
runbooks, 163
availability, 215
regions and, 27
zones, 28
AZs (availability zones), 28

B

backups
backup window, 171
block change tracking, 169
block-level backups, 167
business continuity and, 194
cloning, 167, 168
configurations, 171–172
delta change tracking, 169
dependencies, 172
differential, 169
disaster backups, 167
file backups, 167
full backup, 168
ghosting, 167
image backups, 167
incremental, 169
objects, 172
offline storage, 172
online storage, 172
recovery sites, 194–195
scheduling, 171
SLAs (service level agreements), 171
snapshots, 168
targets, 169

local backups, 170
remote backups, 170–171
replicas, 170
bandwidth, troubleshooting, 273–274, 296
bare-metal server, 14–15
baselines, 33, 245
compute tuning, 251–252
deployment and, 217
exceeding, 275–276
network changes, 252
object tracking and, 246
application versions, 247
audit process, 247
CPU usage, 247
network usage, 248
patch versions, 248–249
RAM usage, 249
storage usage, 249
tool compliance, 247–248
performance trending and, 250
SaaS solutions, 253
SLAs (service level agreements) and, 251
storage tuning, 252–253
troubleshooting, 275–276
validation, 250–251
benchmarks, 62, 66
block changes, 169
blue-green model of patching, 159–160
bottom-up approach to troubleshooting, 316
BPaaS (Business Process as a Service), 7,
10–11
business continuity, 183, 192
alternate sites, 193
availability zones, 193
backups, 194
continuity of operations, 193
corporate policies, 184–185
edge sites, 194
network connectivity, 193–194
recovery sites, 194–195
SLAs (service level agreements), 195–196

C

CaaS (Communications as a Service), 7, 10
capacity, troubleshooting, 272–273
API requests, 273
bandwidth, 273–274
baselines, exceeding, 275–276
batch job scheduling, 274

boundaries, 273
compute resources, 274
expansions, unplanned, 276
network addressing, 274–275
storage, 275
users, numbers, 275
certificate services, 91
troubleshooting, 312
change management
action plan documentation, 223–224
back-out plans, 223–224
breakdown troubleshooting, 277
change advisory board, 223
change approvals, 223
corporate changes, 229–230
troubleshooting and, 317–318
chargebacks, 255
ciphers
3DES (Triple Data Encryption Standard),
110–111
AES (Advanced Encryption Standard), 110
block ciphers, 110
DSA (Digital Signature Algorithm), 111
RC4 (Rivest Cipher 4), 111
RC5 (Rivest Cipher 5), 111
RSA, 111
stream ciphers, 110
ciphertext, 108
CLI (command-line interface), security
automation and, 138
client-server computing, 6
cloning, 168
cloud
community cloud, 55
off-premise hosting, 12
on-premise hosting, 12
development networks, 19
hybrid, 13, 55
moving to, preparation, 15
organizational uses, 19–20
private cloud, 11, 55
production networks, 20
public cloud, 54
quality assurance networks, 20
service provider, 3
cloud bursting, 224, 225
cloud computing, 3, 7
advantages, 4
architecture, 15–16
energy savings, 66

in-house computing comparison, 4–5
NIST description, 3
on-demand, 20
resources, 14–15
cloud deployment models, security and,
119–120
cloud management, 214
deployment monitoring, 216–217
network topology, 214
cloud service models
access control
IaaS, 118
PaaS, 119
SaaS, 119
BPaaS (Business Process as a Service), 7,
10–11
CaaS (Communications as a Service), 7, 10
DaaS (Desktop as a Service), 7, 10
IaaS (Infrastructure as a Service), 7, 8–9
PaaS (Platform as a Service), 7
SaaS (Software as a Service), 7, 8
UCaas (Unified Communications as a
Service), 10
XaaS (Anything as a Service), 7, 10
cloud services
authorization, 89
consumers, 3
cloud systems, scaling, 20–21
cloud-based objects, access control
authentication, 116
authorization, 116
compute systems, 117
network-based control, 117
SAN, 118
securing services, 118
storage access, 117–118
user accounts, 117
user groups, 117
VSAN, 118
clusters, patching and, 157
co-location, 6
community cloud, 55–56
off-premise hosting, 12
on-premise hosting, 12
community scaling, 227
compliance
audits, 107–108
security implementation and, 136–137
compute pools, 17–18
computing, 13

configuration management, 222–223
    change management
        action plan documentation, 223–224
        back-out plans, 223–224
        change advisory board, 223
        change approvals, 223
connections. *See also* access
    console ports, 31
    direct, 28–32
    HTTP, 31–32
    RDP (Remote Desktop Protocol), 29
    Remote Hypervisor Access, 28–29
    SSH (Secure Shell), 30–31
    virtual, 28–32
connectivity
    reporting and, 256
    tools
        ARP, 298–299
        dig, 302–303
        ipconfig/ifconfig, 300
        netstat, 300–302
        nslookup, 302–303
        ping, 303–304
        route, 304–305
        SSH (Secure Shell), 305
        tcpdump, 305–306
        Telnct, 305
        traceroute, 306–307
        tracert, 306–307
console ports, 31
continuous delivery, rolling updates
        and, 159
copy-on-write snapshots, 168
corporate changes, 229–230
CPU
    hyper-threading, 64
    hypervisor optimization, 64
    object tracking and, 247
    overcommitment ratios, 65
    wait time, 65
CPU affinity, 18
CRCs (Cyclic Redundancy Checks), 293

D

DaaS (Desktop as a Service), 7, 10
    VDI (virtual desktop infrastructure), 10
dashboards
    reporting and, 256
    security automation and, 139

data at rest, 134
    encryption, 71
data centers, 3
    connecting to, 22
    hardware resources, 67
data classification, 131–132
    metadata, 131
data in-flight, 134
data integrity, 32
    automation and, 32
    baselines and, 33
    documentation and, 33
database utilization, 215
delivery models, 11
delta changes, 169
dependencies, backups, 172
deployment
    application life cycle, 228
    change management and, 48–49
    maintenance window, 50
    migration, 50
    models
        community, 55–56
        hybrid, 55
        private, 55
        public, 54
        security, 119–120
    monitoring, 216–217
        alert methods, 218
        alert triggers, 218–219
        anomalies, 217–218
        baselines, 217
        event collection, 220–221
        event correlation, 219–220
        event dissemination, 221
        event information, 219
        log information, 219
    multi-availability zone architecture, 133
    network
        addressing, 61
        configurations, 58
        DMZ, 60
        IDSs, 59
        IPSs, 59
        multiple on block, 61–62
        ports, 57–58
        protocols, 56–57
        VPNs, 58
        VxLAN, 60–61
    network management and, 53

resource pooling, 16–17
    compute pools, 17–18
    CPU affinity, 18
    memory pools, 18
    network pools, 18
    storage pools, 19
    virtual CPUs, 17
    segmentation, 132–134
    service level agreements, 62
    stakeholders and, 49
development networks, 19
    patching and, 159
DHCP (Dynamic Host Configuration
    Protocol), 57, 91
    disaster recovery and, 186
DIACAP (Department of Defense
    Information Assurance Certification
    and Accreditation Process), 106
diagonal scaling, 227
differential backups, 169
dig, 302–303
direct connections, 28–32
divide-and-conquer approach to
    troubleshooting, 317
DMZ (demilitarized zone), 60
DNS (Domain Name System), 57, 91
    changes, 277–278
    disaster recovery and, 186
    services, 16
    stale entries, 199–200
    troubleshooting, 291, 294
documentation, 33
    benchmarks, 62
    initial, 14
    migration and, 50–51
        services, 51
downtime reports, 257
DR (disaster recovery), 65, 183
    archiving, 191
    availability zones, 186
    DHCP (Dynamic Host Configuration
        Protocol) and, 186
    DNS (Domain Name Service) and, 186
    file transfers, 191
    FTP (File Transfer Protocol) and, 186
    ISP limitations, 186
    network capacity and, 185–186
    planning, 185
    RADIUS (Remote Authentication Dial-In
        User Service) and, 186

replication, 189
    asynchronous, 190–191
    synchronous, 190–191
    RPOs (recovery point objectives), 184
    RTOs (recovery time objectives), 184
    service providers and, 183
    site mirroring, 186–187
        candlelight design, 187
        cold sites, 188–189
        hot sites, 187
        warm sites, 187, 188
    TACACS (Terminal Access Controller
        Access-Control System) and, 186
    third-party vendors, 191–192, 195

E

edge facilities, 194
elasticity, 26
    automation and, 256
    scaling and, 228
elements, 16
    security, 155
    updates, 161
        automation, 165
        hotfixes, 162
        maintenance mode, 166
        patches, 162
        rollbacks, 162–163
        snapshots, 164–165
        system alerts, 166
        system restart, 166
        system shutdown, 166
        version updates, 162
        virtual devices, 165
        workflow automation, 163–164
encryption
    ciphers
        3DES, 110–111
        AES, 110
        block ciphers, 110
        DSA, 111
        RC4, 111
        RC5, 111
        RSA, 111
        stream ciphers, 110
    data at rest, 71, 134
    IPsec (IP Security)
        AH (authentication header), 109
        ciphertext, 108

ESP (encapsulating security payload), 109
MACs (message authentication codes), 109
transport mode, 108
tunnel mode, 108
SSL (Secure Sockets Layer)
    HTTPS, 109
    PKI, 110
    TLS, 109
troubleshooting, 314
ephemeral volumes, 133
ESP (encapsulating security payload), 109
events, deployment and
    collection, 220–221
    correlation, 219–220
    dissemination, deployment and, 221
    information, 219
expansions, unplanned, 276
extending scope, 228

F

FabricPath, 51
failover, patching and, 160–161
FCAPS (Fault, Configuration, Accounting, Performance, Security), 53
federations, 89–90
FedRAMP (Federal Risk and Authorization Management Program), 106
file transfers, disaster recovery, 191
files, swap files, 18
FIPS 140-2, 106
firewalls, 141–142
    host-based, 115
    maintenance automation, 200–201
    troubleshooting, 296–297
FISMA (Federal Information Security Management), 106
FTP (File Transfer Protocol), 56
    disaster recovery and, 186
FTPS (File Transfer Protocol Secure), 57
full backups, 168

G

gateways, default, 292–293
GRE (Generic Routing Encapsulation), 113
GUI (graphical user interface), security automation and, 138–139

H

hardening a system, 114–115
    troubleshooting, 312
hardware
    multifactor authentication token, 135
    virtualization, 6
health reports, 257
high-availability operations, 21–22
HIPAA (Health Insurance Portability and Accountability Act), 107
horizontal scaling, 226, 254–255
horizontal server scalability, 215
hotfixes, 162
HTTP (Hypertext Transfer Protocol), 31–32, 56
HTTPS (Hypertext Transfer Protocol Secure), 56, 109
hybrid cloud, 13, 55
hybrid-based cloud, scaling and, 227
hypervisors, patching and, 156

I

IaaS (Infrastructure as a Service), 7, 8–9
    access control and, 118
identity
    applications, 89
    federations, 89–90
IDSs (intrusion detection systems), 59
inactive accounts, 199
incident reports, 257
incremental backups, 169
in-flight data, 134
in-house computing
    client-server computing, 6
    cloud computing comparison, 4–5
    mainframe computers, 5, 6
instance initialization time, 215
interconnection, troubleshooting and, 269
interoperability, troubleshooting and, 268–269
intrusion detection, 142–143
IP addressing, 292
ipconfig/ifconfig, 300
IPsec (IP Security)
    AH (authentication header), 109
    ciphertext, 108
    ESP (encapsulating security payload), 109

MACs (message authentication codes), 109
transport mode, 108
tunnel mode, 108
IPSs (intrusion prevention systems), 59
iSCSI (Internet Small Computer Systems Interface), 296
ISO (International Organization for Standardization) standards, 106
ISPs, DR (disaster recovery) and, 186
ITAR (International Traffic in Arms Regulations), 106

J

JSON (JavaScript Object Notation), security automation and, 138
jumbo frames, 296
jump servers, 140

L

L2TP (layer 2 tunneling protocol), 113
language, troubleshooting and, 269
latency, 248, 256–257
CRCs (Cyclic Redundancy Checks), 293
troubleshooting, 293–294
licensing, troubleshooting and, 269–270
load balancing, 24–25, 90–91
load testing, 25
logs
deployment and, 219
files, maintenance automation, 198
security and, 103–104

M

MAC (mandatory access control), 120–121
MACs (message authentication codes), 109
mainframe computers, 5, 6
maintenance, 196
automation, 197
ACLs, 202
DNS entries, stale, 199–200
firewalls, 200–201
inactive account removal, 199
log files archive, 198

orphaned resources, 200
resource reclamation, 201
rules, outdated, 200–201
storage compression, 199
operation interruptions, 197
windows, 196–197
malware prevention software, 142
management systems, 52–54
management tools, object tracking and, 247
memory pools, 18
metrics, 215–216, 245
MFA (Multi-Factor Authentication), 314
migration, 82–83
applications
life cycle, 228
portability, 86
authentication, SSO (single sign-on) systems, 90
certificate services, 91
cloud services, authorization, 89
data, 84–85
DHCP (Dynamic Host Configuration Protocol), 91
DNS (domain name service), 91
documentation, 50–51
firewall security, 92–93
identity applications, 89
identity federations, 89–90
infrastructure
downtime, 87
network capacity, 86–87
timing, 87
legal issues, 87
load balancing, 90–91
maintenance window, 50
multilayer user authentication services, 92
offline, 85
online, 85
P2V (physical-to-virtual), 83
procedures, 50–51
RBAC (role-based access control), 88–89
timeline, 50
V2P (virtual-to-physical), 84
V2V (virtual-to-virtual), 83
virtualization formats, 85
workload, 86
MPAA (Motion Picture Society of America), 107
MSaaS (Managed Security as a Service), 140
MTBF (mean time between failure), 215

MTSO (mean time to switchover), 215
MTSR (mean time system recovery), 215
MTTR (mean time to repair), 215
MTUs (Maximum Transmission Units),
 269, 296
multi-availability zone architecture, 133
multifactor authentication, 88, 120–122
  hardware keyfob, 135
  login screen, 135
  smartphone-based token, 136

N

NAT (network address translation), 16
netstat, 300–302
network management, 53
network pools, 18
network systems, patching and, 156–157
networking, 13
  bandwidth, 296
  DNS (Domain Name System), 294
  firewall configuration, 296–297
  gateways, default, 292–293
  infrastructure, 293
  IP addressing, 292
  latency, 293–294
  MTUs (Maximum Transmit Units), 296
  proxy configuration, 296–297
  QoS (quality of service), 294–295
  routers, 292–293
  subnet issues, 291
  troubleshooting, 270, 290–291
    ARP, 298–299
    bandwidth, 296
    default gateways, 292–293
    dig, 302–303
    DNS, 294
    firewall configuration, 296–297
    infrastructure, 293
    IP addressing, 292
    ipconfig/ifconfig, 300
    latency, 293–294
    MTUs, 296
    netstat, 300–302
    nslookup, 302–303
    ping, 303–304
    proxy configuration, 296–297
    QoS (quality of service), 294–295
    remote access tools, 307–310

    route, 304–305
    routing, 292–293
    SSH, 305
    subnet issues, 291
    tcpdump, 305–306
    Telnet, 305
    traceroute, 306–307
    tracert, 306–307
    VLANs, 297–298
    VxLANs, 297–298
networks
  addressing, 61
  capacity, 215, 248
  configurations, 58
  development, 20
  DMZ (demilitarized zone), 60
  IDSs (intrusion detection systems), 59
  IPSs (intrusion prevention systems), 59
  jitter, 248
  latency, 248, 256–257
  multiple on block, 61–62
  object tracking and, 248
  packet loss, 248
  ports, 57–58
  protocols
    DHCP, 57
    DNS, 57
    FTP, 56
    FTPS, 57
    HTTP, 56
    HTTPS, 56
    SFTP, 57
    SMTP, 57
    SSH, 57
  QOS (quality of service), 248
  quality assurance, 20
  topology, 214
  VPNs (virtual private networks), 58
  VxLAN (virtual extensible LAN), 60–61
NIST (National Institute of Standards), 3
nslookup, 302–303
NTP (Network Time Protocol), 272

O

object tracking, baselines, 246
  application versions, 247
  audit process, 247
  CPU usage, 247

network usage, 248
patch versions, 248–249
RAM usage, 249
storage usage, 249
tool compliance, 247–248
objects, 16, 245
offline migration, 85
offline storage, 172
off-premise hosting, 12
on-demand cloud services, 26
on-demand computing, 20
online migration, 85
online storage, 172
on-premise hosting, 12
orchestration
    platforms, 25
        security implementation, 140
    troubleshooting, 276–280
    workflow automation and, 163
orphaned resources, 200
outage time, 216

P

PaaS (Platform as a Service), 7
    access control and, 119
passwords, 114
patch management, 158
patching
    applications and, 157
    automation, 165
    blue-green and, 159–160
    clusters and, 157
    continuous delivery, 159
    dependencies and, 161
    development systems and, 159
    hypervisors and, 156
    maintenance mode, 166
    methodologies, 157–161
    network systems and, 156–157
    object tracking and, 248–249
    order of operations, 161
    production systems, 158
    QA tests, 159
    rolling updates, 159
    snapshots and, 164–165
    storage and, 157
    system alerts
        disabling, 166
        enabling, 166

system restart, 166
system shutdown, 166
virtual appliances and, 156
virtual devices, cloning, 165
VMs and, 156
PAYG (pay as you grow), 26
PCI-DSS (Payment Card Industry Data
    Security Standard), 106
penetration testing, 25
performance, 21
    horizontal scaling and, 254–255
    metrics, 34
    vertical scaling and, 253–254
physical resources, 62
    benchmarks, 66
    cloud data centers, 67
    CPU, 64–65
    high availability, 65
    memory, 64
    processors, 63
physical security, 143–144
ping, 303–304
PKI (Public Key Infrastructure), 110, 111
    framework components, 112
    PKIaaS (PKI as a Service), 113
PKIaaS (PKI as a Service), 113
points of preference, 194
policies
    reporting, 255
    security, 104–105
portals, security automation and, 139
PPTP (Point-to-Point Tunneling Protocol), 113
private cloud, 11, 55
    scaling, 227
privilege escalation, 310–311
procedures, migration and, 50–51
production networks, 20
    patching and, 158
protocols
    DHCP (Dynamic Host Configuration
        Protocol), 57
    DNS (Domain Name System), 57
    FTP (File Transfer Protocol), 56
    FTPS (File Transfer Protocol Secure), 57
    HTTP (Hypertext Transfer Protocol), 56
    HTTPS (Hypertext Transfer Protocol
        Secure), 56
    SFTP (Secure File Transfer Protocol), 57
    SMTP (Simple Mail Transfer Protocol), 57
    SSH (Secure Shell), 57

proxies, configuration, 296–297
public cloud, 54
    scaling, 227–228
push services, 218

Q

QoS (quality of service), 294–295
quality assurance networks, 20

R

RADIUS (Remote Authentication Dial-In
    User Service), disaster recovery
    and, 186
RAM usage, object tracking and, 249
RBAC (role-based access control), 88–89, 120
RDP (Remote Desktop Protocol), 29
redirect-on-write snapshots, 168
reference designs, 11
regions, availability and, 27
regulatory requirements
    DIACAP (Department of Defense
        Information Assurance Certification
        and Accreditation Process), 106
    FedRAMP (Federal Risk and
        Authorization Management
        Program), 106
    FIPS 140-2, 106
    FISMA (Federal Information Security
        Management), 106
    HIPAA (Health Insurance Portability and
        Accountability Act), 107
    ISO (International Organization for
        Standardization) standards, 106
    ITAR (International Traffic in Arms
        Regulations), 106
    MPAA (Motion Picture Society of
        America), 107
    PCI-DSS (Payment Card Industry Data
        Security Standard), 106
    security implementation and,
        136–137
    SOC (Service Organization Controls),
        105–106
reliability, 216
remote access

security
    GRE, 113
    L2TP, 113
    PPTP, 113
    tools, 307
        console ports, 307–308
        HTTP, 308–309
        RDP (Remote Desktop
            Protocol), 309
        SSH (Secure Shell), 309–310
Remote Hypervisor Access, 28–29
remote management
    replication and, 22–24
    VPNs (virtual private networks)
        and, 22
replication, 22
    asynchronous, 23–24
    disaster recovery and, 189
        asynchronous, 190–191
        synchronous, 190–191
    site-to-site, 22
    synchronous, 23
reporting
    capacity, 257
    company policies, 255
    connectivity and, 256
    dashboards, 256
    downtime, 257
    health reports, 257
    incident reports, 257
    latency, 256–257
    SLAs and, 255
    uptime, 257
    utilization, 257
resource pooling, 16–17
    compute pools, 17–18
    CPU affinity, 18
    memory pools, 18
    network pools, 18
    storage pools, 19
    virtual CPUs, 17
resources, 14–15
    account automation, 233–234
    account identification, 231
    account life cycle, 232
    account orchestration,
        233–234
    account provisioning, 230–231

application life cycle, 228
  deployments, 229
  features, 229
  migrations, 229
  replacements, 229
  retirements, 229
  upgrades, 229
authentication, 231
authorization and
    ACLs, 232
    permission-based, 232
cloud bursting, 224
contention, 271
corporate changes, 229–230
physical, 62
  benchmarks, 66
  cloud data centers, 67
  CPU, 64–65
  high availability, 65
  memory, 63–64
  processors, 63
providers, migration between, 224–225
reclamation, 201
scaling, 225
  capacity reduction, 227
  cloud bursting, 225
  community scaling, 227
  diagonal scaling, 227
  elasticity and, 228
  horizontal scaling, 226
  hybrid-based cloud and, 227
  private cloud, 228
  public cloud, 227–228
  vertical scaling, 225–226
scope, extending, 228
starvation, 271
usage patterns, 224
virtual, 63
  CPU, 64–65
  high availability, 65
  memory, 63–64
  processors, 63
response time, 216
REST (Representational State Transfer),
    security automation and, 138
rollbacks, 162–163
rolling updates, 159
route, 304–305

routers, 292–293
RPOs (recovery point objectives),
    168, 184
RTOs (recovery time objectives), 168, 184
rules, outdated, 200–201
runbooks, 163

S

SaaS (Software as a Service), 7, 8
  access control and, 119
scalability, server
  horizontal, 215
  vertical, 216
scaling, 20–21
  capacity reduction, 227
  cloud bursting, 224
  community scaling, 227
  diagonal scaling, 227
  elasticity and, 228
  horizontal scaling, 226, 254–255
  hybrid-based cloud and, 227
  private cloud, 228
  public cloud, 227–228
  resources and, 225
  system requirements, 26
  vertical scaling, 225–226, 254–255
scope, extending, 228
SCP (Secure Copy Protocol), 305
script-based services, security
    implementation, 140
security, 14
  access control
    applications, 120–122
    cloud deployment models, 119–120
    cloud service models, 118–119
    cloud-based objects, 116–118
  account shutdown, 116
  antivirus software, 115, 142
  automation, 114
    APIs, 138
    CLI, 138
    critical systems and, 144
    dashboards, 139
    GUIs, 138–139
    portals, 139
    tools, 137
    vendor-based solutions, 138

certificates, 111
compliance audits, 107–108
data classification, 131–132
data protection, 107
elements, 155
encryption
    ciphers, 110–111
    IPsec, 108–109
    SSL, 109–110
firewalls, 141–142
    host-based, 115
implementation
    compliance and, 136–137
    customized approaches, 140–141
    orchestration systems, 140
    script-based services, 140
implementation, regulatory issues,
        136–137
intrusion detection and prevention,
        142–143
    host-based, 143
logging and, 103–104
malware prevention software, 142
passwords, 114
patches, 155
physical security, 143–144
PKI (public key infrastructure),
        111–113
policies, 104–105
regulatory requirements, 105–107
remote access
    GRE, 113
    L2TP, 113
    PPTP, 113
segmentation
    computing, 133–134
    storage, 133
server patches, 115
services, disabling, 114–115
system hardening, 114–115
troubleshooting
    authentication, 311
    authorization, 311–312
    availability, 314
    certificate configuration, 312
    confederations, 312
    controls maintenance, 313–314

device hardening, 312
encryption, 314
external attacks, 313
infrastructure, 314
internal attacks, 313
physical access, 314
privilege escalation, 310–311
processes maintenance, 313–314
sign-on issues, 311
technologies, 313
tunneling, 314
unencrypted data, 315
user accounts, 114
segmentation, 132–133
    computing, 133–134
    multi-availability zone architecture, 133
    storage, 133
        durable, 133
        ephemeral volumes, 133
        nondurable, 133
    three-tier architecture, 133
servers
    bare-metal, 14–15
    capacity, 216
    name changes, 277–278
    scalability
        horizontal, 215
        vertical, 216
    security patches, 115
service level agreements, 62
service outages, troubleshooting, 271
service providers
    disaster recovery and, 183
    guidelines, 185
    migration between, 224–225
    policies, 185
    responsibilities, 33–34
services, security, disabling, 114–115
SFTP (Secure File Transfer Protocol), 57, 305
sign-on issues, 311
site mirroring, disaster recovery and,
        186–187
    candlelight design, 187
    cold sites, 188–189
    hot sites, 187
    warm sites, 187, 188
site-to-site replication, 22

SLAs (service level agreements)
   backups and, 171
   maintenance responsibilities, 222
   reporting and, 255
smartphone-based multifactor authentication
   token, 136
SMTP (Simple Mail Transfer Protocol), 57
snapshots
   copy-on-write, 168
   redirect-on-write, 168
   RPOs (recovery point objectives), 168
   RTOs (recovery time objectives), 168
SNMP (Simple Network Management
   Protocol), 116
SOC (Service Organization Controls),
   105–106
Spanning Tree, 51
SSH (Secure Shell), 30–31, 57, 305
SSL (Secure Sockets Layer)
   HTTPS (Hypertext Transport Protocol
     Secure), 109
   PKI (Public Key Infrastructure), 110
   TLS (Transport Layer Security), 109
SSO (single sign-on), 90, 122
stakeholders, deployment and, 49
storage, 14, 166
   access, 81
   backups
     block change tracking, 169
     block-level backups, 167
     cloning, 167, 168
     delta change tracking, 169
     differential, 169
     disaster backups, 167
     file backups, 167
     full backup, 168
     ghosting, 167
     image backups, 167
     incremental, 169
     snapshots, 168
   cloning, 74
   compression, automation, 199
   configurations, 67
     DAS, 68
     NAS, 68
     object-based storage, 69–70
     SANs, 69

data migration, 84–85
data replication, 73
   asynchronous replication, 74
   synchronous replication,
     74
   durable, 133
   ephemeral volumes, 133
   fault tolerance and, 73
   high availability and, 73
   mirrors, 74
   nondurable, 133
   object tracking and, 249
   offline, 172
   online, 172
   patching and, 157
   provisioning
     data at rest, encryption, 71
     thick, 70
     thin, 70–71
     token models, 72
   RAID controllers, 75
   RAID levels, 75
     RAID 0, 75
     RAID 0+1, 77
     RAID 1, 76
     RAID 1+0, 76
     RAID 5, 77
     RAID 6, 78
   scalability, 216
   security
     access, 81
     ACL, 79
     authentication, 81
     authorization, 81
     LUN masking, 79–81
     obfuscation, 79
     SAN, 79–81
     zoning, 79–81
   tiers, 72–73
   total capacity, 216
   troubleshooting, 275
storage pools, 19
subnet masks, 291
support agreements, 221
swap files, 18
synchronous replication, 23
system requirements, scaling, 26

T

TACACS (Terminal Access Controller
  Access-Control System), disaster
  recovery and, 186
task runtime, 216
tcpdump, 305–306
Telnet, 305
templates, troubleshooting, 272
terminal services, 31
testing
  load testing, 25
  penetration testing, 25
  QA tests, patching and, 159
  vulnerability scanning, 25
thick provisioning, 70
thin provisioning, 70–71
three-tier architecture, 133
time synchronization, 272
timeline, migration, 50
TLS (Transport Layer Security), 109
token models, 72
top-down approach to troubleshooting, 316
traceroute, 306–307
tracert, 306–307
transport mode, IPsec, 108
TRILL, 51
troubleshooting
  accounts, mismatched, 277
  automation, 267–268, 276–280
    tool incompatibility, 278
  capacity, 272–273
    API requests, 273
    bandwidth, 273–274
    baselines, exceeding, 275–276
    batch job scheduling, 274
    boundaries, 273
    compute resources, 274
    expansions, unplanned, 276
    network addressing, 274–275
    storage, 275
    users, numbers, 275
  change management breakdowns, 277
  DNS changes, 277–278
  feature mismatches, 279
  interconnection, 269
  IP addresses, 278

language support and, 269
licensing issues, 269–270
location changes, 279
methodology, 315
  bottom-up, 316
  change management, 317–318
  distillation of issue, 318–319
  divide-and-conquer, 317
  documentation, 319–320
  information gathering, 318
  planning, 319
  research, 319
  resolution, 319–320
  testing, 319
  top-down, 316
  verification, 319
networking, 270, 290–291
  ARP, 298–299
  bandwidth, 296
  default gateways, 292–293
  dig, 302–303
  DNS, 294
  firewall configuration, 296–297
  infrastructure, 293
  IP addressing, 292
  ipconfig/ifconfig, 300
  latency, 293–294
  MTUs, 296
  netstat, 300–302
  nslookup, 302–303
  ping, 303–304
  proxy configuration, 296–297
  QoS (quality of service), 294–295
  remote access tools, 307–310
  route, 304–305
  routing, 292–293
  SSH, 305
  subnet issues, 291
  tcpdump, 305–306
  Telnet, 305
  traceroute, 306–307
  tracert, 306–307
  VLANs, 297–298
  VxLANs, 297–298
orchestration, 276–280
process issues, 276–277
resource contention, 271

resource starvation, 271
security
    authentication, 311
    authorization, 311–312
    availability, 314
    certificate configuration, 312
    confederations, 312
    controls maintenance, 313–314
    device hardening, 312
    encryption, 314
    external attacks, 313
    infrastructure, 314
    internal attacks, 313
    physical access, 314
    privilege escalation, 310–311
    processes maintenance, 313–314
    sign-on issues, 311
    technologies, 313
    tunneling, 314
    unencrypted data, 315
server name changes, 277–278
service outages, 271
templates, 272
time synchronization, 272
version mismatches, 279
work validation, 279–280
workflow issues, 276–277
workflow services, 272
tunnel mode, 314
    IPsec, 108

U

ubiquitous access, 14
UCaas (Unified Communications as a
    Service), 10
uptime reports, 257
usage patterns, resources and, 224
user accounts
    securing, 114
    troubleshooting, 275
users
    identity applications, 89
    RBAC (role-based access control), 88–89

V

VDI (virtual desktop infrastructure), 10
vertical scaling, 225–226, 254–255
vertical server scalability, 216
virtual appliances, patching
    and, 156
virtual connections, 28–32
virtual CPUs, 17
virtual switches, 18
virtualization, 6, 7, 14
    formats, migration, 85
VLANs (virtual LANs), 51, 291
    troubleshooting, 297–298
VMs (virtual machines), 14
    patching and, 156
VNI (VxLAN Network Identifier), 298
vNIC (virtual network interface
    card), 18
VPNs (virtual private networks),
    22, 58
    troubleshooting and, 269
vulnerability scanning, 25
VxLANs (Virtual Extensible LANs), 51,
    60–61, 291
    troubleshooting, 297–298

W

web server utilization, 216
workflow, 52
    automation, 163
        orchestration, 163–164
        runbooks, 163
    services, troubleshooting, 272
    troubleshooting, 276–277
workload migration, 86

X-Y-Z

XaaS (Anything as a Service), 7, 10
XML (Extensible Markup Language),
    security automation and, 138

Comprehensive Online Learning Environment

Register to gain one year of FREE access to the online interactive learning environment and test bank to help you study for your CompTIA Cloud+ certification exam—included with your purchase of this book!

The online test bank includes the following:

- **Assessment Test** to help you focus your study to specific objectives
- **Chapter Tests** to reinforce what you've learned
- **Practice Exams** to test your knowledge of the material
- **Digital Flashcards** to reinforce your learning and provide last-minute test prep before the exam
- **Searchable Glossary** to define the key terms you'll need to know for the exam

Register and Access the Online Test Bank

To register your book and get access to the online test bank, follow these steps:

1. Go to `bit.ly/SybexTest`.
2. Select your book from the list.
3. Complete the required registration information including answering the security verification proving book ownership. You will be emailed a pin code.
4. Go to `http://www.wiley.com/go/sybextestprep` and find your book on that page and click the "Register or Login" link under your book.
5. If you already have an account at `testbanks.wiley.com`, login and then click the "Redeem Access Code" button to add your new book with the pin code you received. If you don't have an account already, create a new account and use the PIN code you received.